A Brief History of Western Civilisation

西 方 文 明 简 史

主　　编　常晓梅
副 主 编　王　玥　赵玉珊　李玉梅　李晓丽
编　　者　王　蕾　李　蕊　林晓冰　赵　鹍
　　　　　咸慧慧　徐高楠　韩　玲
语言顾问　Deborah Murray
　　　　　Finnie Murray
　　　　　Eeckman Karen

山东大学出版社

图书在版编目(CIP)数据

西方文明简史/常晓梅主编.
—济南:山东大学出版社,2013.1
ISBN 978-7-5607-4748-4

Ⅰ.①西…
Ⅱ.①常…
Ⅲ.①西方文化—文化史
Ⅳ.①K500.3

中国版本图书馆 CIP 数据核字(2013)第 035641 号

责任编辑:王潇
封面设计:张荔

出版发行:山东大学出版社
社　址　山东省济南市山大南路 20 号
邮　编　250100
电　话　市场部(0531)88364466
经　销:山东省新华书店
印　刷:济南景升印业有限公司印刷
规　格:787 毫米×1092 毫米　1/16
23 印张　531 千字
版　次:2013 年 1 月第 1 版
印　次:2013 年 1 月第 1 次印刷
定　价:48.00 元

前 言

中国有句古话:“读史早知今日事。”英国哲学家 Francis Bacon 在他的 Of Studies 一文中也提到:“Histories make men wise.”在东、西方文明日渐碰撞、交融的当代社会,学习者在积累并完善对本族文化认识的同时,了解并掌握西方文明和社会文化知识,不仅能够在跨文化交际的过程中更理性、更深刻地理解中国文化,对待世界文明,培养对异族文化的包容性,去除民族中心主义思想,从而达到世界之和谐。同时,在更广阔的背景下透过历史,反思得失,认识文明发展的规律,便可“更知今日事”。

在长期的英语教学中我们发现,许多中国学生在跨文化交际过程中,由于不了解目的语社会文化背景、价值取向、思维方式等,常常把母语文化的观念套用到目的语文化上,从而形成了“外语语法+外语词汇+中国文化背景”的畸形图示。他们把外语镶嵌到自己母语的文化背景之中,割裂了语言与文化的关系,造出了许多中式英语。对于外语学习者来说,若要掌握地道的外语,提高学习效率和实际交际能力,必须最大限度地在目的语文化的浸入中提高语言的运用能力。

与此同时,我们发现本科学生对英语国家文明史的了解通常只限于英、美两国。对英、美之外的其它西方国家的相关知识,还基本停留在对中学课本《世界历史》所掌握的程度。然而,英、美两国家并非西方文明的源头,充其量只是西方文明的洪流在一定时段所涌现的两个关系紧密的峰值,即便如此,它们的发生、发展也脱离不了整个西方文明的渊源。

汉语版的《世界历史》固然可以为我们提供以历史事件为主线的世界文明,但是,在英语阅读和交流中,语言的切换,势必伴随着信息对应的问题。英语语言是西方文明重要的载体和结晶,英语中难以计数的典故、格言、成语是出自古希腊和古罗马的经典著作;希伯来的圣经几乎成为英语文学一个永不枯竭的源头:文艺复兴、宗教改革、启蒙运动、现代思潮等,每一个时期的思想、科技、政治、经济、社会方面的重大事件和重要人物,无不在当今社会各领域有相应的沉淀和展现;即使英语语言本身的演变,也是文明发展、变迁的见证。

由此可见,用英语讲授西方文明是一举两得的事情,更是在当今世界多元文化的大背景下,提高学习者文化生存和适应能力的迫切要求。《大学英语课程教学要求》(教育部高等教育司,2007)在教学性质和目标中明确提出,大学英语是以“英语语言知识与应用技能、跨文化交际”为主要内容,其教学目标是“培养学生的英语综合应用能力”,提高其“综合文化素养,以适应我国社会主义发展和国际交流的需要”。不仅如此,课程设置中也指出:“大学英语不仅是一门语言基础课程,也是拓宽知识、了解世界文化的素质教育课程,兼有工具性和人文性。”为此，我们开设了大学英语拓展课程——西方文明简史。

在选定教材的过程中，教师发现现有的国外原版教材及国内出版的相关教材均不适合。国外大部头的教材信息量大，但很繁杂，缺少针对性和学习效果检测，对国内学生来说阅读难度较大，而国内相关的教材，汉语版偏多，又多以掌握历史为目的，主要介绍英语国家的历史和文化。为此，我们根据实际需要，试着综合这两方面的优势，边教学实践边总结编写，完成了这部 A Brief History of Western Civilisation 教材。

考虑到学生的知识结构以及课时安排，我们将西方文明凝缩在十个章节中：近东文明、古希腊文明、古罗马文明、中世纪文明、文艺复兴、宗教改革、早期现代文明、政治革命与工业革命、欧洲现代主义、战争与西方社会新布局。每一章节都力求以历史为纲，以文化信息点为目；从面上总览一个时代，从点上洞悉其文化精髓。

为了拉近学习者与古代和近代文明的距离，帮助其领略每一时期的文明精华，我们设计了相关的名人名言，明确了学习目标，提供了中文导读、专家评论、专有名词索引和图文并茂的文化链接等栏目，并在脚注和专有名词部分注重文化知识的补充。期待学习者通过阅读，有所感悟。

另外，本教材在介绍西方文化的同时，注重对学习者语言实践能力的培养，针对每一章内容设计了相关的练习题，既有考查对重要知识点的认知和熟记的练习题（第一、二题），也有锻炼学习者简单应用和综合应用语言、独立思考和分析问题能力的练习题（第三、四题），并附有答案，还有开阔视野，提高英语思辨能力的中西文化对比讨论题（第五题），便于课堂使用及课后自主学习和检测效果。

衷心感谢翻译学院副院长张彩波副教授、李杰、李楠、陈怀凯、谷秀春老师们所做的大量前期工作，衷心感谢英国国家图书馆专家 Julian Harrison 先生对部分章节的语言进行的审定。由于编者能力有限，在教材的内容和语言上难免会有疏漏之处，希望读者及时提出宝贵的意见和建议，在此真诚地表示感谢。

编　者

2012 年 12 月 18 日

Contents

Chapter One The Ancient Near East: The Cradle of Civilisation (c. 4000 B. C. —70 A. D.)

The ancient Near East is, or should be, the province not only of historian of the Near East but also of the historian of humanity in general.[①]

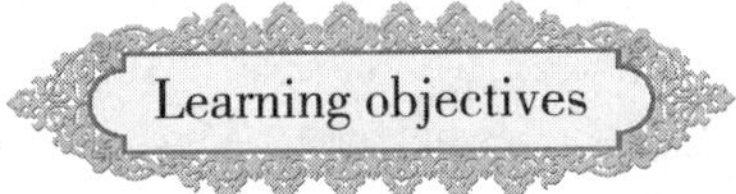

After reading this chapter, you will be able to:

1. *Understand better the two foundation stones for the building of Western civilisation—Mesopotamia and Egypt;*
2. *Be familiar with the developments on the fringes of Mesopotamian and Egyptian civilisations;*
3. *Understand one of the small nations—Hebrew nation, and its contribution to the religious developments;*
4. *Be familiar with the Assyrian Empire and its achievements in architecture, sculpture, literature and religion;*
5. *Know more about the great power—the Persian Empire and its innovation in political and military affairs.*

---

① William H. Hallo & William Kelly Simpson, *The Ancient Near East A History*, 2nd ed., Harcourt Brace & Company, 1998, p. 5.

近东文明——西方文明的起源。

美索不达米亚文明，又称“两河流域文明”，孕育了第一种文字、第一座城市、第一部法典，和第一个“世界和大洪水”的神话。埃及的金字塔和神庙，象征着王权与神权的紧密结合，以及人类寻求和谐与实践永恒的理想和对不朽来世的期望。公元前12世纪初达到极盛时期的腓尼基人，是古老文明的杰出传播者。曾掌控地中海地区的海洋贸易长达三千年之久；所完善的字母文字可以称为“欧洲国家字母文字的始祖”。古老的希伯来民族，是犹太人的祖先。《旧约》的历史书卷记录了这个民族的起源和历史发展；《新约》时期后，改称为“犹太人”，与犹太教的历史继续发展到现代巴勒斯坦、以色列的建立。位于古代西亚的亚述帝国，是世界史上第一个可以称得上“军事帝国”的国家，历代诸王几乎都是在不断扩张征伐中度过，其军事发展的完备堪称是古代世界最发达的。波斯帝国，兴起于伊朗高原，是世界上第一个地跨亚、非、欧三大洲的帝国，其文化多受两河流域文化影响，其宗教琐罗亚斯德教对宗教发展影响深远。

Section One　Mesopotamian Civilisation (c. 4000—539 B. C.)

One of the foundation stones for the building of Western civilisation was laid by the Mesopotamians.

Mesopotamia　The valley of the Tigris-Euphrates, referred to as Mesopotamia, was the site of one of the earliest high civilisations. But the natural resources and the climatic conditions of the region were, in fact, not conducive to agriculture. There was little rainfall, but the soil of the plain in this valley in southern Mesopotamia was enlarged and enriched over the years by layers of silt deposited by the two rivers. Every year in mid-March when snows in the upland mountains, where the rivers began, melted, the two rivers overflowed their banks and deposited their fertile silt. However, the flooding was irregular and sometimes disastrous. Under such conditions, the region required massive and sophisticated human effort in the form of irrigation and drainage ditches to control the flow of the rivers and to produce abundant food and to develop agriculture for which it later became famous. No doubt such efforts and accomplishments had much to do with the emergence of high civilisation in the region.

Characteristics of Civilisation　With the development of human societies, civilisation came into existence. "A civilisation is a complex culture in which large numbers of human beings share a number of common elements."① Civilisations have been characterised by the means of subsistence of the people, types of livelihood, settlement patterns, forms of government, social hierarchy, economic system, literacy and other cultural systems. The development of a civilisation typically follows a progression of steps:

① Jackson J. Spielvogel, *Western Civilisation: A Brief History*, Volume I: To 1715, Belmont: Wadsworth, 1999, p. 6.

1. Intensive agricultural techniques bring about a surplus of food that results in labour division and a more diverse range of human activity.
2. As communities evolve from subsistence—hunting, gathering, and farming activities, cities become the centre of political, economic, social, cultural, and religious development; most non-farmers move into cities to work and trade.
3. More complex political structure arises with the formation of the state: There are complex social hierarchies and central government planning. The ruling class controls much of the surplus and exercises its will through the actions of an organised government bureaucracy.
4. People accumulate more personal possessions and acquire landed property. They trade goods, services or extra food for other necessities in a market system. Money is developed as a medium of increasingly complex transactions.
5. Writing, a system of record-keeping, is regarded as a symbol of civilisation. It is used for recording history, trade and business as well as communication.
6. Other diverse cultural traits include organised religion, formal system of education, e. g. apprenticeship and schooling systems, development in art, architecture, and new advances in science and technology.

Sumerian City-States The people who established the beginnings of true civilisation were the Sumerians①(a people who already resided in southern Mesopotamia as early as 4000 B. C.) whose origins remain unknown. By 3000 B. C., they had established a number of independent cities in southern Mesopotamia, such as Ur, Umma and Lagash. As cities expanded in size, they came to exercise political and economic control over the surrounding countryside, forming city-states②, the basic units of Sumerian civilisation.

The economy of the Sumerian city-states was primarily irrigated farming. Animal husbandry, commerce and industry were also important. The people of Mesopotamia produced woollen textiles, pottery, and the metalwork for which they were especially well-known. Foreign trade mainly involved dried fish, wool, barley, and the metal goods produced by Mesopotamian craftsmen in exchange for copper and tin, aromatic woods, and fruit trees by land or by sea. The invention of the wheel around 3000 B. C. led to carts with wheels that made the transport of goods easier.

In a Sumerian city, Lagash, temples took the most prominent position in its economy and society. They owned much of the city land and livestock, and served not only as the physical centre of the city, but also the economic and political centre. The Sumerians believed that gods and goddess owned the cities, and they used much wealth to build temples and houses for the priests, who supervised the temples and their

---

① Sumerian:苏美尔人。

② city-state:城邦或称城市国家,是在一定历史条件下由原始公社演化而来的一种公民集体。

property and had great power in ruling in this period. However, the power to rule passed eventually into the hands of kings.

Sumerian city-states consisted of three major social groups, nobles, commoners, and slaves. Nobles included royal and priestly officials and their families. Commoners included the nobles' clients and other free citizens, such as farmers, merchants, fishermen, and craftspeople. Slaves belonged to palace officials, temple officials and rich landowners as well.

Empires in Ancient Mesopotamia With the development of Sumerian city-states, conflicts and wars among them arose and continued for control of land and water. These conflicts led to the burning and sacking of cities and the rise and fall of city-states over the centuries.

Located on the flat land of Mesopotamia, the Sumerian city-states were also open to invasion. Around 2340 B. C. , the Akkadians, a Semitic people (Table 1. 1) due to the type of language they spoke, came from the north under the leadership of Sargon. He conquered the Sumerian city-states and built a strong empire that, at its height, dominated all of the Euphrates basin and much of the land lying beyond its great bend as far as the Mediterranean Sea. The Akkadian empire lasted for about two and a half centuries, but it eventually collapsed and was divided between such petty states as Lagash, Umma, and a much reduced Akkad. Around 2060 B. C. , Ur-Nammu of Ur reunified most of Mesopotamia and established Ur Ⅲ, another powerful empire in the Near East. But this final flowering of Sumerian culture declined with the rise of the Amorites, or Old Babylonians, a large group of Semitic-speaking semi-nomads. Under Hammurabi, a new empire was created.

Table 1. 1 **Some Semitic Languages**①

Assyrian②	Akkadian③	Aramaic④	Arabic⑤	Babylonian⑥
Canaanitic⑦	Hebrew⑧	Phoenician⑨	Syriac⑩	

① Semitic language:闪米特语,语言学家分辨出的与雅利安诸语不同的另一语系。西伯来语、阿拉伯语、古亚述语、腓尼基语和若干有联系的语言都源于这种原始语言。

② Assyrian:亚述语,属闪米特语。

③ Akkadian:阿卡德语,古代在美索不达米亚使用的闪语族的东方语支。

④ Aramaic:阿拉姆语,属闪米特语族,公元前 9 世纪通用于古叙利亚,后来一度成为亚洲西南部的通用语,犹太人文献及早期基督教文学多以此语写成。

⑤ Arabic:阿拉伯语,源于闪米特语,现为北非、中东一带许多国家使用。

⑥ Babylonian:巴比伦语,属闪米特语。

⑦ Canaanitic:迦南语,属闪米特语。

⑧ Hebrew:希伯来语,属闪米特语。

⑨ Phoenician:腓尼基语,是叙利亚和小亚细亚的通用语言。

⑩ Syriac:古叙利亚语,属闪米特语。

Hammurabi (1792—1750 B. C.), the sixth in a line of Old Babylonian kings, was one of the commanding figures of Mesopotamian history. He established a strong and powerful centralised empire with his personal genius and by an adroit alternation of warfare and diplomacy. He was best remembered and today is still famous for his "law code"① as well as for his political achievement, the reunification of Mesopotamia. He was a man of war and peace. His schools maintained the old traditions of Sumerian learning and meanwhile promoted the flowering of a native literature in Akkadian. Any survey of Mesopotamian law and society, religion and literature, learning and daily life reveals a picture of Hammurabi's Babylonia. After his death, however, a series of weak kings were unable to keep Hammurabi's empire united, and it finally fell to new invaders.

Hammurabi's law code is the most complete, though not the earliest, in Mesopotamian history. It is a collection of 282 laws, which provides considerable insight into almost every aspect of everyday life there and provides valuable material for the understanding and study of Old Babylonian society. It was inscribed on a stone stele. The upper part of it is a bas-relief picturing Hammurabi receiving the order to record the law from the seated sun god Shamash, also the god of justice. The lower part of it contains the actual code. The code recognised three social classes in Babylonia (nobles, freemen, and slaves) and emphasised the principle of retaliation ("an eye for an eye, a tooth for a tooth") and punishments for crimes that were severe and varied, according to the social status of the victim. It also included laws dealing with job performance, marriage and family affairs, and even sexual relations. It reveals a society with a strict system of justice.

Mesopotamian Culture Writing was important because it enabled a society to keep records and maintain knowledge of previous practices and events. "History begins when writing begins and where writing begins"②, and "writing began in the ancient Near East, specially Sumer, ..."③. The oldest Mesopotamian texts date back to around 3000 B. C., and were written by the Sumerians. Like that of ancient Egypt, Sumerian writing developed from pictographic signs of concrete objects to simplified and stylised signs, and eventually to a phonetic system freeing writing from its dependence on representational depiction and enabling it to render not only the separate words but also the individual sounds to make possible the written expression of abstract ideas. The

---

① law code：古巴比伦王国的《汉穆拉比法典》是迄今楔形文字法中最完善的一部法律文献，也是两河流域城邦国家法律的集大成者，其本文以楔形文字刻在高 2.25 米的黑色玄武岩石碑上。

② William H. Hallo & William Kelly Simpson, *The Ancient Near East A History*, 2nd ed., Harcourt Brace & Company, 1998, p. 4.

③ William H. Hallo & William Kelly Simpson, The Ancient Near East A History, 2nd ed., Harcourt Brace & Company, 1998, p. 4.

Sumerians made wedge-shaped impressions, a cuneiform[①] system of writing, on clay tablets with a reed stylus, which were then baked in the sun. Once dried, these tablets were virtually indestructible.

Writing was primarily used by Mesopotamian peoples for record-keeping, transactions of daily life, monumental texts, and the texts for teaching purposes. The cuneiform system of writing was later adopted by other countries in the ancient Near East, such as Babylon, Assyria and Hittite.

Writing also made it possible for people to express ideas, which is evident in Mesopotamian literature. Most of the early Sumerian and Babylonian literary works were religious myths and legends. The master piece was *The Epic of Gilgamesh*[②], an epic poem that recounts the fruitless struggle of a legendary hero, Gilgamesh, king of Uruk, to find immortality, a venture leading him through numerous encounters with angry divine spirits and challenges him with the forces they create to destroy him. The epic includes a story told to Gilgamesh by Utnapishtim about how the god, Ea, advised him to build a boat, and how he survived the flood unleashed by the gods to destroy humankind, a Mesopotamian version of the later biblical Noah, and came to land his boat at the end of the flood.

Mesopotamian religion was closely bound up with its culture as a whole. It was polytheistic[③] in nature. The temples dominated individual and commercial life. Mesopotamians also believed that humans were insecure because they could never be sure of the gods' actions and the world was controlled by supernatural forces. Humans bore a terrible burden in trying to keep the unpredictable divine rulers happy. Humans also developed predictive techniques, such as killing animals and observing their entrails, interpreting dreams or patterns of smoke from burning incense, and reading stars (astrology) with a desire to discover the planning of the gods and predict events.

The Mesopotamians were skilled and creative artists. Their major architectural works were the temple complexes built in every city to honour its patron god or goddess, the typical one being the temple tower, ziggurat[④]. They were also skilled in sculpture. Most three-dimensional statues are portrayals of deities and kings. Their work, strongly influenced by geometrical forms, cylinders and cones, is solid, stiff,

---

① cuneiform：楔形文字，来源于拉丁语，由 cuneus(楔子)和 forma(形状)两个词构成，也叫“钉头文字”或“箭头字”，笔画成楔状，颇像钉头或箭头，为古代西亚所用，多刻写在石头或泥板(泥砖)上。

② *The Epic of Gilgamesh*：《吉尔伽美什》，美索不达米亚文学，人类历史上第一部史诗。

③ polytheism：多神教，相信有众多神灵存在，但各神的地位、神通、威力不尽相同，所受的崇拜亦不相等。多神教崇拜的神灵，有的是自然体、自然力的人格化，如埃及宗教中的太阳神；或是拟人的动、植物；或是将社会现象和力量人格化。而佛教则被认为是全球三大宗教中唯一的多神教。

④ ziggurat：(古代亚述和巴比伦的)金字塔神殿，一座神庙的塔楼，其外形酷似金字塔，是苏美尔人留下的最重要的建筑。

motionless, but gives a distinctive character to the faces of the subjects. The most exquisite carving was done by seal makers on stones that could be used to press an identifying mark into clay.

Particularly in mathematics and astronomy, the Mesopotamians made outstanding achievements. By a combination of accurate observation and astute calculation, both based on their unmatched arithmetic notation, they devised a system of time reckoning based on a seven-day week, on months tied to the moon's cycles, and on a year derived from the sun's movements. They developed a standard of weights and measures. The counting system of the Sumerians combined a decimal system and the sexagesimal system①. They were able to add, subtract, multiple, and divide and to perform geometrical functions, such as measuring fields, erecting buildings, and finding the volume of a cylinder. Inspired by an urge to foretell the future, they gathered accurate information about the movements of the stars and charted the heavenly constellations. In addition, the Mesopotamians compiled a considerable store of geographical knowledge based chiefly on their travels as conquerors and traders.

Section Two Egyptian Civilisation (c. 3100—c. 332 B.C.)

The other foundation stone for the building of Western civilisation was laid by the Egyptians.

Geographical Conditions Egypt, like Mesopotamia, was a river valley civilisation. It is geographically divided into two big areas, Upper (or southern) Egypt, the area in historical times that extended northward from the first cataract in the Nile at Aswan, to the apex of the Delta just south of Memphis, near modern Cairo, and Lower Egypt in the northland or Delta area.

Ancient Egypt was protected for a long time from invasion by natural barriers that isolated it from her neighbours: the deserts to the east and west of the Nile, the barren lands to the south and the cataracts on the southern part of the Nile, and the Mediterranean Sea to the north.

The land played a dominant role in the development of Egyptian civilisation. Egypt was formed by a belt of fertile soil deposited annually by the flooding of the Nile, which rose in the summer from rains in central Africa and crested in Egypt in September and October, leaving rich cultivation along the river and in the Delta in the north. The Egyptians called their fertile belt the "black land", and the deserts beyond it the "red land". In ancient Egypt, and even today, most of Egypt's people were crowded along the banks of the Nile River and Egypt's important cities developed at the tip of the Delta.

The regularity of the Nile and the relative isolation of the Egyptians brought about

---

① sexagesimal system:六十进位计数法。

a sense of security. With the Egyptian kings' basic and unchanging principles of justice at the beginning of each reign, the society achieved a remarkable degree of continuity over thousands of years that featured the Egyptian civilisation.

The Old, Middle and New Kingdoms The study of ancient Egypt history covers a period from the beginning of Egyptian history, about 3100 B. C., to the conquest of Egypt by Alexander the Great of Macedon in 332 B. C. The original division of its long span is the work of Manetho, an Egyptian priest in the early 3rd century B. C. A more general and meaningful pattern, according to Hallo and Simpson, is that of major eras and intermediate periods including the Early Dynastic Period (Dynasty 1 and Dynasty 2), the Old Kingdom or Pyramid Age (Dynasty 3 to Dynasty 8), the First Intermediate Period (Dynasty 9 to preconquest Dynasty 11), the Middle Kingdom (postconquest Dynasty 11 to Dynasty 13), the Second Intermediate Period (Dynasty 14 to Dynasty 17), the New Kingdom or Empire Period (Dynasty 18 to Dynasty 20, of which the last two are named the Ramesside Period), the Third Intermediate Period (Dynasty 21 to Dynasty 25), the Saite Period (Dynasty 26), and the Late Dynasty Period (Dynasty 27 to Dynasty 31). The major periods saw long-term stability characterised by a strong, centralised monarchy ruling the entire land, a stable bureaucracy with effective means for taxation, firm control of the borders, the exploitation of quarries and mines, construction of temples, royal and private funerary structures, typically pyramids, and a high level of achievement in the arts of architecture, sculpture, and painting. But the intermediate periods were characterised by weak political structures, interference from invasion, a decline in monumental public building, a divided kingship in the land with rival and contemporary dynasties, and a restructuring of society.

In Predynastic Egypt the land was divided into Upper Egypt and Lower Egypt, the kings of each wore, respectively, the headdresses of a tall white crown with a bulbous terminal at the top, and a red wickerwork crown with a tall element at the back and a curious, thin piece with a fiddle-head curve in front, implying a predynastic union of north and south. Besides, they had their own protective goddess, vulture goddess of Nekhen and cobra goddess Wadjet. There was no term for king, and later the title "pharaoh"① was given.

The Early Dynastic Period begins at the end of the Predynastic Period with the establishment of the double kingship in the first dynasty. According to the records, the founder of the double kingship was named Menes, a ruler arising from the south, reunifying the land after a period of weakness and dominating the north from Memphis.

---

① pharaoh:法老,音译自埃及语的希伯来文,意为"大房屋",在古王国时代仅指王宫,新王国第十八王朝图特摩斯三世起,开始用于国王自身,并逐渐演变成对国王的一种尊称。第二十二王朝以后,成为国王的正式头衔。习惯上把古埃及的国王通称为法老。作为奴隶制专制君主,掌握全国的军政、司法、宗教大权,其意志就是法律,是古埃及的最高统治者,是神的代理人和化身。

He was called "King of Upper and King of Lower Egypt", and the royal crown was a double diadem, symbolising the unification of all Egypt. The length of time the first two dynasties cover is about 400 years.

The Old Kingdom (c. 2700—2200 B. C.) with its capital at Memphis is also named the Pyramid Age because the surviving monuments are pyramidal royal tombs with their associated funerary buildings. The most glorious was the 3rd and 4th dynasties when Egypt became the major civilisation of the world, rivaled only by Sargon's kingdom of Akkad on the Tigris and Euphrates. It was an age of prosperity and splendour when the greatest and largest pyramids in Egyptian history were constructed. The pyramid is an ever-present reminder of the majesty and might of the absolute monarch. It symbolises a staircase to heaven for the king's spirit. It reflects the immense wealth of a society unified in exploiting the Nile and the great power of the rulers.

The key to the success of the Third Dynasty was the political system that took shape. Its central feature was the absolute power of the pharaoh, a special kind of ruler, a god. He is the son of the sun god Re as well as the incarnation of Horus, the son of Osiris. He ruled on his own behalf, but according to set principles. The overall principle is maat[①], the concept of order, justice, and harmony that should prevail throughout the universe. Pharaohs maintained maat and were themselves subject to it. The following text summarises the role of king: to judge humankind; to please the gods through worship; to make Maat effective; to crush chaos and evil; offer gifts to the gods, and carry out the cult needs of the dead.

Re has installed king N
upon the earth of the living
for ever and eternity,
judging men, satisfying the gods,
realizing Maat, annilating Isfet (evil).
He gives offerings to the gods
and mortuary offerings to the dead.[②]

The god-kings of the Old Kingdom ruled with the loyal and able aid of a host of high officials, such as a chief minister, a treasurer, a chief of irrigation, record keeper, and high priests and priestesses, each assisted by numerous state servants of lesser rank. Besides, each nome[③], altogether twenty-two nomes in the Upper and twenty in

---

① maat：古代埃及人认为，世界在创建之初，创世之神就创建了神圣的宇宙秩序——玛特，它是自然界和人类社会的运行法则。

② William H. Hallo & William Kelly Simpson, *The Ancient Near East A History*, 2nd ed., Harcourt Brace & Company, 1998, p. 191.

③ nome：（古代埃及）州。

Lower Egypt, was governed by a nomarch, the Egyptian title for governor, and by royal officials who were held closely accountable in Memphis. Every nome was divided into villages, where the mass of people lived and the officials appeared regularly to enforce the pharaoh's commands and collect taxes.

The short-lived dynasties 7 and 8 brought the Old Kingdom to an end and sent Egypt into a period of chaos, the First Intermediate Period. These times were hard. There were famines, and skirmishes among nomes. Dynasty 10 in the north at Herakleopolis and Dynasty 11 in the south at Thebes were contemporary. The causes for the disintegration of the Old Kingdom are complex, mainly through internal weakness. Pharaohs became ineffectual figures. Instead innumerable local rulers held power, whose pursuit of their own interests resulted in internal wars, economic depression, lawlessness, and injustice. One factor contributing to the demoralisation and impoverishment was the cumulative expenditure of human and land resources on the building and maintenance of the royal pyramids. Besides, the nomes that the king was increasingly dependent on became more and more independent until eventually a power vacuum developed in Memphis, and the autocratic Egyptian state with its administrative and technical skills mirrored in the pyramids collapsed.

Toward the end of Dynasty 11, the princes of Thebes conquered Herakleopolis, and the reunification of the country under Nebhepetre Mentuhotpe of Thebes ushered in the Middle Kingdom (2050—1652 B. C.). The kingship of Upper and Lower Egypt was assumed by Amunemhet Ⅰ, the founder of Dynasty 12 when the kingdom reached its peak.

Amunemhet Ⅰ was an extraordinary innovator and administrator. First, he established a new residence just south of Memphis, from which the land could be more effectively controlled than from Thebes. Second, the nome structure was reorganised. The nomarchs' territory was precisely surveyed and marked, and their obligations to the state were defined. The nomarchs were confirmed as hereditary officeholders but with the understanding that their duties must be performed faithfully, such as the collection of taxes and dues for the state and the supply of labour forces for royal projects and military expeditions.

In this dynasty the nature of the kingship itself was changed. The inaccessible god-king of the Old Kingdom became the good shepherd of his people. The concept of maat was interpreted in a way that emphasised the pharaoh's responsibility for providing justice, protection, and respect for the lower classes of society. This gave the government of the Middle Kingdom a humane quality rarely seen in the history of the ancient Near East. A major reflection of it was the effort of the pharaohs of the 12th

Dynasty to decrease the power of the old nobility by giving greater authority to scribes[1] to carry out the multitude of functions connected with directing a centralised state.

Furthermore, Egypt witnessed changes in its relations with the neighbours. She exploited the trade to the south for African products, and Nubia itself for gold, copper, semiprecious stones, and quarries. The dynasty's effective administrative system resulted in its success in establishing a strong government at home and considerable influence abroad.

The prosperity was in decline in Dynasty 13. Its end was hastened by the outside invasion into the eastern Delta by the Hyksos, a Semitic-speaking people from Asia, whose presence sank Egypt into division, lawlessness, and violence. At this point Egypt entered the Second Intermediate Period with a divided kingship. The Hyksos ruled the country for over a century (Dynasty 15 and Dynasty 16) and prospered, extending their influence through much of Egypt. They introduced to Egypt Bronze Age technology by teaching the Egyptians how to make and use bronze tools in agriculture and bronze weapons (the latter, unknown to Egyptians, being the partial reason for the Hyksos' ability to seize the control of part of Egypt) as well as horse-drawn chariots, heavier swords, and compound bows.

In Dynasty 17 established by the Theban rulers, the Theban brothers Kamose and Ahmose initiated campaigns against the Hyksos using the new weapons they learned from them. Eventually the northern Hyksos were driven out of Egypt and the country was reunited. With the accession of Ahmose and the founding of Dynasty 18 began a radically new era in Egypt's history, the New Kingdom (1567—1085 B. C.).

During the period of the New Kingdom, Egypt was at its best in military, political, economic and cultural aspects. It became the most powerful state in the Middle East. The period was also referred to as the imperial period. Under Thutmose Ⅲ, in particular, the Egyptians gained the control of Syria and Palestine and some city-states along the Phoenician coast, gathered tribute from such countries as the Middle Euphrates state of Mitanni, Hittite of Asia Minor, and Assyria and Babylon. He also moved westward to Libya and Nubia to the south.

The subsequent stage of the dynasty under Thutmose Ⅳ and, especially, Amunhotpe Ⅲ witnessed extreme luxury in the royal court, unmatched building programmes for palaces and temples. Examples of well-known temples are those Luxor and Karnak which were dedicated to Amun-Re. Another well-known building project from this period is the great statue of the Colossus of Memnon.

The reign of Amunhotpe Ⅳ (Akhenaten) (1364 — 1347 B. C.), Tutankhamen (1347—1338 B. C.), and others marks another stage in the dynasty. More has been

① scribe：书吏。

written of Amunhotpe Ⅳ than of any other pharaoh due to his introduction to the worship of Aten, god of the sun disk, as the chief god and his pursuit of it with zest. This stage in the dynasty parallels the Reformation[①] in Europe in the 16th century in terms of changes in the dominant religion. The god that Amunhotpe Ⅳ introduced to his people was a more specific aspect of the sun, the Aten. In its crucial elements Atenism represented a return to the religion of the sun god Re, and open rebellion against the establishment of Amun, the state religion of Amun-Re. By changing his name from Amunhotpe to Akhenaten (the effective spirit of the Aten) and the capital at Thebes to a new city north of Thebes, named Akhetaten, the modern Amarna, closing the temples of other gods, and dedicating the town and all its lands and people to the Aten, the king endeavoured to lessen the power of Amun-Re and his priesthood at Thebes, check or eliminate their great influence, and reassert the primacy and power of his kingship.

However, the Akhenaten reformation met with strong royal defiance. At the same time, the Hittites rose to a level of power that was enough to challenge Egypt's overall domination. The military campaigns became relatively unimportant to the king while he was preoccupied with the religious issue at home, which caused him to ignore foreign affairs and even led to the loss of both Syria and Palestine. After his death, the boy-pharaoh, Tutankhamen came to the throne. He changed his name from Tutankhaten to Tutankhamen and soon abandoned Amarna for the traditional capital at Thebes. He also restored the old gods and the old order in art and politics as well. A strong storm of protest eventually doomed the Akhenaten reformation.

Dynasty 19 managed to restore Egyptian power one more time. In the reign of Ramses Ⅱ (1279—1213 B. C.), the Egyptians regained control of Palestine but were unable to re-establish the borders of their earlier empire. New invasions by the "Sea Peoples", so called by Egyptians, destroyed Egyptian power in Palestine and forced the Egyptians back into their old boundaries. The empire period ended, with which the New Kingdom also ended at the end of Dynasty 20.

The Third Intermediate Period embraced diverse dynasties between the Ramesside and Saite periods in more than four hundred years, and Egypt developed along very different lines. The flourishing Delta cities took the place of Upper Egypt and became dominant in terms of politics and traditions. Cities in the modern sense first developed. The Libyan incursions, frequent in the Ramesside period, snowballed into massive settlements. Events in Asia and Africa boiled over into confrontation of Sudanese and Assyrian armies in Egypt, and Egypt was conquered by the Sudanese Piankhy of Dynasty 25, a force that finally brought the Third Intermediate Period to an end and the Delta dynasty of the Saites was founded in Dynasty 26.

---

① the Reformation：16 世纪发生在欧洲的宗教改革运动，详见第六章。

The Saite Period, so called after its capital city of Sais in the western Delta, lasted for 139 years. It witnessed a return to a single pharaoh over the land and an end of foreign rulers. Its rulers were native Egyptians. And once again Egypt became independent and briefly enjoyed internal order, prosperity and international prestige, but the Egyptians were unable to meet the needs of the new era. The pharaohs had to rely on foreign mercenaries, chiefly Greeks, to provide troops, which caused internal trouble. Old age had gripped Egyptian society, making it incapable of resisting Persian armies, which resulted in its fall with almost no struggle in 525 B. C.

In the Late Dynasty Period, Egypt was dominated by Persians, and finally Macedonians after conquest by Alexander the Great, which marked a turning point in Egyptian history. Then, in the 1st century B. C. , Egypt became a province in the mighty Roman Empire.

Social and Economic Life in Ancient Egypt The social structure of ancient Egypt was organised in a hierarchical system①. At its top stood the pharaoh, the god-king who enjoyed command over all elements of society and control over the total wealth of the state. The upper class consisted of the royal families, priests and nobles whom the pharaoh chose to help run the government and reward with wealth. They conducted the elaborate round of rituals of life that surrounded the pharaoh.

Royal officials and local landowners played a prime role in organising the labour of the merchants and artisans to tame the Nile, which produced full range of benefits to the aristocracy. The merchants engaged in active trade along the Nile and in town and village markets as well. They also engaged in international trade, bringing wood and other products from Crete and Syria, ivory from Nubia, and incense and spices from Punt on the Red Sea. The artisans made a variety of items: stone dishes, beautifully painted clay boxes, wooden furniture, linen clothes, and gold, silver and copper tools, all of which reflected their high standards of craftsmanship and physical beauty. Merchants went forth to trade these goods for needed raw materials.

The achievements of the Old and Middle Kingdoms were mainly due to a carefully controlled agriculture system that made full use of the rich soil and the bountiful waters of the Nile. The backbone of the economy was the peasant population. Most of the lower classes were serfs②, who devoted their lives to an endless round of labour on the land to keep the irrigation system working, and to plant and harvest crops, vegetables and fruits. To this was added the extra labour on the immense building projects of the

---

① hierarchical system：等级制度。等级是一定的社会集团。等级制度的实质是法律规定了的人与人之间的不平等；上下等级之间一般是统治与隶属关系，它起着稳定统治秩序和保证统治集团利益的作用。

② serf：农奴，不同于奴隶，一般不能被农奴主杀戮，但能随意处罚或连同土地买卖、抵押和转让。有少量劳动工具和牲畜，以奴役性的条件从农奴主领得小块份地从事耕作，或缴纳代役租，并承担其他无偿劳役和贡赋。

pharaohs, the religious leaders, the royal officials, and the landowners. They paid taxes and lived in small villages in mud huts. In the imperial period, another class was added, called mercenaries, who were below nobles. At the bottom of the hierarchy were slaves who played a minor role during the Old and Middle Kingdoms and mainly provided military service later.

Women appeared to have felt no special social disability. The queens of the great pharaohs were extended high respect by their god-husbands. Highborn women shared most of aspects of aristocratic life materially in the form of splendid clothing, jewels, and cosmetics. Noble women had the right of owning property and inheritance. They could function as priestesses, and some queens even became pharaohs in their own right, the most famous being Hatshepsut in the New Kingdom who was addressed as "His Majesty" though she was clothed and bearded like a king. The husband was master in the house, but the wife was respected and responsible for the household and education of the children. Lower-class women worked with their husbands in the fields, indicating that they played an integral part in the economy.

Ancient Egyptians had a positive attitude toward daily life. Monogamy was the general rule, even for the pharaoh, though it was socially accepted that a husband could keep additional wives, especially if the first wife was childless. Marriages were arranged by parents. The major reason for a marriage was to produce children, particularly sons, who were the only persons that could carry on the family name. Besides, divorce was allowed, usually with compensation for the wife. But adultery was strictly prohibited with severe punishments, especially for women.

The Culture of Egypt Success in unifying ancient Egypt and conquering the Nile was accompanied by a brilliant and sustained flowering of intellectual and artistic achievements that impress the world as one of the great accomplishments of humankind.

Egyptian culture was rooted in powerful religious beliefs that inspired and shaped every aspect of thought and expression. Religion was part of Egyptian civilisation. The deities worshiped by the Egyptians numbered in the thousands. They were associated with heavenly bodies and natural forces in a confusing variety of forms, as animals, humans, birds, plants, inanimate forms, and mixtures of any two or three of these forms. Over the centuries, two groups, sun gods and land gods, achieved special prominence and were thought to have unusual powers. The sun was the source of life, and a sun cult developed. The sun god took on different forms and names, depending on his specific function. He was worshiped as Re who had a human body but the head of a falcon. The pharaoh took the title of Sun of Re. Eventually, Re became associated with Amun, an air god of Thebes, as Amun-Re.

River and land gods included Osiris and Isis, his wife, and Horus, their child, who was related to the Nile and the sun as well. The worship of Osiris had advanced to a

central place in religious life by the Middle Kingdom and was embodied in an Egyptian myth. Osiris, who brought civilisation to Egypt, was killed by his wicked brother, Seth, who cut his body into fourteen parts and scattered them over the face of the earth. Osiris' wife, Isis, patiently gathered them up and restored him to life. Thereafter, he became the symbol of resurrection and the judge of the dead.

The Egyptians were convinced that the abundant harvests, peace, and security proved that the gods were happy with their earthly subjects. They made efforts to please the gods and goddesses and win their favours. An elaborate set of ritual practices was established early in Egyptian history and changed little over the centuries. The pharaoh's prime responsibility was to bring the favour of his fellow gods and goddesses upon his land and people.

Concern with immortality was a unique aspect of Egyptian religion from early times. The Egyptians believed that everybody had two bodies, a physical one and a spiritual one known as the ka① that lived on after death. The physical body was properly preserved by mummification so that the ka could continue to dwell in it, and an everlasting tomb, furnished with all the objects of regular life, was built to shelter the ka.

Tomb building reached its peak in the Old Kingdom in the construction of pyramids, one of the greatest achievements of Egyptian civilisation. Surrounding a large pyramid for the pharaoh's burial was a complex of smaller pyramids for his family and mastabas② for his noble officials. The largest and most magnificent of all the pyramids, the Great Pyramid, was built for Khufu, or Cheops, in Dynasty 4. Its most noticeable quality is its single, massive geometric form, but its internal ascending corridor and grand gallery represent a majestic architectural feat of all time. The pyramid, towering 481.4 feet high and measuring 756 feet on each side at the base, covers 13.1 acres. Its four sides are almost precisely oriented to the four points of the compass.

Gradually the expectation of gaining immortality was democratised and universalised when the gates of heaven were open to all Egyptians. The worship of Osiris expressed the new concept of immortality, the moral worth attached to each person. Osiris was concerned with goodness in evaluating people's eligibility for eternal life rather than their wealth and social status. Although Egyptians continued to provide for the material welfare of the dead, since the Middle Kingdom the emphasis was less on the grandeur of the tomb and more on its decoration with a record in pictures and writing to convince Osiris that the occupant had lived a "good" life. Osiris worship heightened moral awareness in a way that was unknown in Mesopotamia.

---

① ka:(古埃及人或偶像的)灵魂,鬼魂,阴灵,通常译为"灵魂"或"精神"。

② mastaba:古埃及墓室。

The constant effort to understand, please and thank the deities inspired impressive literary and artistic achievements for their high level of technique, unity and coherence. The literature includes poems and narratives, the most appealing being the marvellous tales of fancy and romance about adventures. Other literature of this period includes collections of maxims and wise sayings, and a large body of religious texts, mainly pyramid texts including carved hymns, prayers, magical incantations, and bits of mythology. On the whole, Egyptian literature, though less profound, is more varied and versatile than Mesopotamian literature. The latter never developed lyric poetry, romances, and tales of fancy; the former created nothing comparable to the *Epic of Gilgamesh*.

Egyptian art mirrors the ability of the creative genius to work with set forms and subjects without losing freshness and vitality. It was largely functional. Wall paintings and statues of gods and kings in temples served a specifically spiritual purpose. They were an integral part of the ritual practice.

Architecture was the queen of all the arts in Egypt. The most monumental work was in stone, typically the pyramids. The basic temple form was the hypostyle hall, consisting of a roof on columns which were modelled by the architects after plants, like the palm tree, the lotus plant, etc., to achieve splendid artistic effects.

Egypt's sculptors matched the architects in skill. Sculpture was the supporter of religion. The chief subjects of three-dimensional statues intended for tombs and temples were the deities, the pharaohs, etc. Human forms were usually massive, stiff, unemotional portrayals, and the sculpture's purpose was to show power, majesty, and devotion. Egyptian sculptors were also skilled at relief work. Inside the tombs and on the pillars and walls of temples, endless series of scenes depict more about Egyptians' daily life than all Egyptian writing does. Again, they let the space available determine the size and the shape of their figures, and they often used conventional designs to represent objects. Especially characteristic was the convention of combining the profile, semi-profile, and frontal views of the human body in relief work and painting to represent each part of the body accurately. Although the sculptors worked within highly conventionalised canons, each face is different—a display of the dynamic quality of the Egyptian achievement in art.

The language of the ancient Egyptians is written with a system of writing, hieroglyphic, Greek for "sacred writings". Like cuneiform writing, it began as pictographs. Gradually symbols were developed to represent sounds and these were combined to form words. Hieroglyphic, the formal script, was used for inscriptions on stone and carved or painted on walls. The cursive version of the same script was usually written with a reed on papyrus①.

The Egyptians' advances in technology and practical science rivaled the work of the Mesopotamians. They recorded information about the movement of the stars, from which they developed an accurate time reckoning system based on the annual appearance of the star, Sirius, and a calendar of twelve thirty-day months plus five days added at the end of each year. They developed a system of numbers to perform basic arithmetic functions and to calculate areas and volumes. In medicine, they developed surgical techniques and learned to use a wide range of drugs. Their observations made in the process of mummifying the dead resulted in their extensive understanding of anatomy.

Section Three Other Early Civilisations (c. 3000—c. 147 B. C.)

In late Neolithic② Europe, megalithic③ structures were built. Of these the most famous is Stonehenge, a prehistoric monument in England erected in about 3000 B. C. The alignment of the stones leaves little doubt that the circle is connected with the sun and the passing of the seasons, and that its builders possessed a sophisticated understanding of both arithmetic and astronomy.

During the period of 2000—800 B. C., the institutions, techniques, and ideas that had been shaped in Mesopotamia and Egypt and were the basis of higher civilisation began to spread outward from the river valleys. In this complex process of cultural diffusion④, traders, travellers, soldiers, and diplomats were chiefly the carriers of ideas and techniques. The peoples imitated the superior ways of the river valley civilisations. Especially important was the impact of new peoples who came to share and even match the glories of Mesopotamia and Egypt.

These new peoples included two groups. One was the Semitic-speaking inhabitants of the Arabian Desert, who came to Mesopotamia prior to 2000 B. C. as intruders. After 1800 B. C., these semi-nomadic desert dwellers continued to play a major role in the history of northern Mesopotamia, Syria, Palestine, and Egypt. The other people were the Indo-Europeans⑤, who spoke a language new to the Near East from which later

---

① papyrus：(古埃及人等用纸莎草造的)纸莎草纸。

② Neolithic：新石器时代(的)，在考古学上是石器时代的最后一个阶段，以使用磨制石器为标志的人类物质文化发展阶段。为英国考古学家卢伯克于1865年首先提出。在地质年代上已进入全新世。大约从1万年前开始，结束时间从距今5000多年至2000多年不等。

③ megalith：希腊语"巨石"。

④ cultural diffusion：文化传播。一种文化中的文化集丛或文化元素从其发祥地扩散到不同地方而被模仿、采借和接受的社会现象和过程。文化传播的媒介主要是人的迁移和流动：移民、战争、入侵、占领、通商、旅游等。在当代，由于交通通信技术手段的发达，世界范围内的文化传播正通过各种途径，以前所未有的规模和速度进行着，由此必然导致世界文化的同质性日益增强。文化传播是引起社会变迁的重要原因之一，有批判地采借和吸入外来文化是实行社会改革、推动社会进步的必要条件。

⑤ Indo-Europeans：讲印欧语系语言的人。

evolved Sanskrit①, Persian, Greek, Latin, and most modern European languages. (Table 1.2) Their general cultural level was more primitive except that in one area they had the upper hand: a superior military system, based on horse-drawn chariots and a skilled warrior class.

Table 1.2　　Some Indo-European Languages②

Subfamily③	Languages
Indo-Iranian④	Sanskrit *, Persian
Balto-Slavic⑤	Russian, Serbo-Croatian⑥, Czech, Polish, Lithuanian⑦
Hellenic⑧	Greek
Italic⑨	Latin *, Romance languages⑩ (French, Italian, Spanish, Portuguese, Romanian)
Celtic	Irish, Gaelic
Ger manic⑪	Swedish, Danish, Norwegian, German, Dutch, English

Note: Languages with * are no longer spoken.

Hittite Empire　From about 2000 B.C. the Indo-Europeans began to move from their ancient homeland, probably north of the Black Sea or in south-western Asia, in modern Iran or Afghanistan, into Central Europe, Italy, Greece and the Aegean Islands, Iran, and India. The newcomers established a series of small principalities led by petty war lords. Gradually these principalities coalesced and expanded by conquering native peoples to create large kingdoms, such as Mitanni and Hittites.

---

① Sanskrit:梵语。

② 印欧语系(Indo-European family)是世界上分布区域最广的语系。18 世纪后期,英国学者提出这些语言有共同的来源。19 世纪初,学者们开始称之为印欧语系,因该语系分布于印度和欧洲。德国学者曾依据分布地两端的语言将其易名为“印度—日耳曼语系”。此外,还有少数学者称之为“雅(利安)—欧语系”。

③ subfamily: 亚语系。

④ Indo-Iranian:(印欧语系中)印度伊朗语族。

⑤ Balto-Slavic:(印欧语系中)波罗的—斯拉夫语族。

⑥ Serbo-Croatian:塞尔维亚—克罗地亚语,南斯拉夫通用语言,属印欧语系斯拉夫语族。

⑦ Lithuanian: 立陶宛语。

⑧ Hellenic:(印欧语系中)希腊语族。

⑨ Italic: 意大利语族。

⑩ Romance languages: 罗曼诸语言,罗曼语(属印欧语系语族,自拉丁语衍生,主要有法语、意大利语、西班牙语、葡萄牙语、罗马尼亚语等)。

⑪ Germanic:(印欧语系中)日耳曼语族。

Of all the new peoples the Hittites enjoyed the most success. Their history began in central and eastern Asia Minor from about 1800 B. C. By about 1600 B. C., they created their own empire in western Asia with its capital at Hattusas (near modern Ankara in Turkey). The unified kingdom developed an advanced culture, a cultural outpost of an older civilisation and a prime example of cultural diffusion. The Hittites added native elements to what they borrowed, including a way to smelt iron.

The Hittites were able to expand their influence to the south and the east. By 1400 B. C., they were actively engaged in encouraging and supporting rebellion among Egypt's subject states throughout Syria and Palestine. Their presence threatened the Egyptian Empire. However, around 1200 B. C., the Hittite Empire was completely destroyed by new waves of Indo-European invaders known as the Sea Peoples.

The Phoenicians In the period of 1200—800 B. C. after the collapse of the Hittite and Egyptian empires that left the Near East without a dominant power centre for about four centuries, several small groups seized the opportunity to establish their independence. As they struggled to establish and maintain themselves, they borrowed from Mesopotamian and Egyptian cultures. The cultural diffusion remained the basic characteristic of the era.

Among the small nations the Phoenicians stood out as borrowers and disseminators of the older civilisations. A Semitic-speaking people, the Phoenicians were located in the narrow band of territory lying between the Mediterranean Sea and the mountains of Lebanon. By 1200 B. C., they were already highly civilised due to the conquest of and strong influence by Mesopotamians, Egyptians, and Hittites. They built a number of independent cities. But they eventually fell subject to the Assyrians, Chaldeans, and Persians.

The Phoenicians derived most of their wealth from trading ventures. They took to the seas and established a virtual monopoly on trade in the Mediterranean. Their merchants carried manufactured goods, such as glass, wine and lumber, from the whole Near East to the less developed peoples of Greece, Italy, North Africa, Spain, and southern France and brought raw materials of these areas back. From these merchants many barbarian peoples also got their first taste of higher civilisation. The Phoenicians, in addition, established colonies abroad, notably the North African city of Carthage①, which became one of the leading centres of civilisation in the western Mediterranean after 800 B. C. Culturally significant was the fact that the Phoenicians did an perfect alphabet that was later passed on to the Greeks. From the Greek alphabet was derived

① Carthage：迦太基，古国名，位于今北非突尼斯北部。公元前 9 世纪末，来自提尔(Tyre)的腓尼基人(Phoenicians)横渡地中海，在此建立殖民城邦。公元前 7 世纪，迦太基发展成为强大的奴隶制国家，垄断西地中海海上贸易。

the Roman alphabet that we still use today.

Section Four　The Hebrew Civilization (c. 2000 B.C. —c. 70 A.D.)

The most significant civilisation of the small nations was that of the Hebrews who also settled in the area of Palestine. The Hebrews originated as Semitic nomads and had a tradition that was eventually written down in the literary record they created, the Hebrew Bible known to Christians as *The Old Testament*①.

Very early in their wanderings they left the Arabian Desert to settle in Mesopotamia. In about 1800 B.C., roughly in the time of Hammurabi, some of the nomads, led by the patriarch Abraham, left Mesopotamia to search for a new homeland in the Syria-Palestine area, where they encountered the well-established and highly civilised Canaanites. Most Hebrews were forced to live a hard life in the semi-arid parts of the area in small tribes under patriarchal leaders such as Isaac and Jacob. Eventually some of them made their way to Egypt, perhaps as part of the Hyksos invasion or as prisoners captured during Egyptian raids on the Syria-Palestine area. Given lands in the Delta region (the Biblical land of Goshen), they prospered until a pharaoh of probably Dynasty 18 enslaved them. This mistreatment led to a turning point in Hebrew history, the Exodus out of Egypt led by Moses shortly before 1200 B.C.

The Hebrews then began to search for their Promised Land. Loosely organised into twelve tribes, they wandered for many years in the desert until they entered Palestine, where they were involved in struggles with the Canaanites first and then the Philistines, a warlike people settling in southern Palestine. The kings, Saul, David and Solomon (c. 1020—930 B.C.), smashed Philistine power and subdued many small principalities in Palestine and Syria, making the Hebrew nation the leading power in that area. A centralised government developed at Jerusalem, replacing the independent ways of the twelve Hebrew tribes, and the formerly nomadic Hebrews became a settled community based on farming and urban life. Diplomatic relations were established with most other nations of the Near East. Solomon expanded the political and military establishments to strengthen royal power, and he was especially active in extending trade activities that brought the Hebrews into contact with peoples throughout the Near East, provided new sources of wealth, and acquainted the Hebrews with many aspects of other cultures. For a time, the kings were able to maintain a unified kingdom enjoying power and prestige.

---

① *The Old Testament*：基督教的《旧约全书》。据犹太教的说法，旧约全书本是犹太人所写，而被基督教抢夺的犹太教义。是基督宗教的启示性经典文献，内容和希伯来圣经一致，但编排不同。主要包括摩西五经、历史书、诗歌智慧书、大先知书、小先知书，共 39 卷(希伯来古本为 24 卷)，分四类：律法书、历史书、智慧书、先知书。从公元前 12 世纪至公元前 2 世纪，陆续用希伯来语写成。

However, even while Solomon reigned in all his glory, deep-seated discontents threatened political unity due to autocratic methods of the kings, the emergence of economic and social inequality, and foreign religious usages that slipped into the rituals at the great temple in Jerusalem. Immediately after Solomon's death these discontents ended the unity of the Hebrew nation. The ten northern tribes refused to recognise his son as king, and formed a new kingdom, Israel, with its centre at Samaria, while the southern two tribes formed a kingdom, Judah, under kings descended from David, with its capital at Jerusalem. In 722 B. C. , the Assyrians conquered Israel and deported many Hebrews to other parts of the Assyrian empire. These people gradually lost their identity and were thus referred to as the Ten Lost Tribes. Judah survived until 586 B. C. , when the Chaldeans captured Jerusalem, and took large numbers of Hebrews to Babylon as captives after having destroyed Assyria.

Although the Hebrews achieved modest success in the long history of ancient Near East, they had written one of the great chapters in the spiritual and moral history of humanity. Early Hebrews probably worshiped many gods, including nature spirits dwelling in trees and rocks. The Exodus set the stage for a religious experience among the Hebrews wandering in the Sinai Peninsula from Egypt led by Moses in that during the hardship-filled years God entered into a covenant, or contract, with the tribes of Israel who believed that Yahweh, a powerful and somewhat terrible natured god, had spoken to them through Moses. Yahweh promised to care for his people under any circumstance. In return, the Hebrews promised to obey Yahweh and follow his law, enshrined in the Bible as the Ten Commandments, that was to govern the way each behaved. With the acceptance of these ideas, Moses' "mixed multitude"① became a "nation", the Israelites, bound together by the worship of one god. The gradual refinement of these concepts and their adjustment to new historical situations led ultimately to the great contribution of the Hebrews to the history of the world, Judaism. ②

Amidst the successes enjoyed by the Hebrews between about 1200 and 930 B. C. , Judaism continued to develop. The daily lives of the Hebrews were related to the religious principles rooted in the covenant by a system of law. A shared set of religious practices shaped by an emerging priesthood took on increasing importance as a part of Hebrew life. In the time of David and Solomon, Jerusalem became the cult centre of the Hebrew nation, especially after Solomon built the splendid Temple, viewed as the symbolic centre of their religion by the Hebrews. The Temple was built to house the Ark of the Covenant, the holy chest containing the sacred relics of the Hebrew faith,

---

① mixed multitude：出自《圣经·旧约》尼希米记(Nehemiah)13：3。

② Judaism：犹太教。

the commandments Yahweh had given his people in the time of Moses. These religious developments produced a body of writings much of which was later incorporated in the final form of the Bible.

After 900 B. C. , Hebrew religious life took on new depth. In the period of the divided kingdoms and foreign conquests, religion became the sole force that sustained a sense of nationhood and uniqueness. The basic concepts of Hebrew religion were reformulated by powerful religious leaders or "holy men", called prophets[①]. Several of these ranks among the world's greatest spiritual spokesmen: Elijah, Amos, Isaiah, Jeremiah, Ezekiel, and Haggai. They went forth as individuals of humble origins who raised their voices of personal conviction and spiritual insight. They all proclaimed a common message that the Hebrews were abandoning their covenant with Yahweh. Their reformulation of a set of religious ideas, that became the essence of Judaism, put into writing in the prophetic books of the Bible, established a set of key religious concepts that not only sustained Judaism but also became the basis for major religious systems in the future, especially Christianity and Islam.

First, the prophets proclaimed a true monotheism. They made Yahweh the only god in the universe and denied that any other deities existed. To give any sign of recognition of any deity except Yahweh was sure to bring disaster.

Second, the prophets proclaimed a new concept of Yahweh's nature. Yahweh was the creator of all things, existing outside time and space. He was a god outside nature. Therefore, he could not be portrayed in any natural form. He was a god of justice, acting according to a definite law. He was omnipotent, controlling the whole universe and causing everything in the past, present, and future to happen. He was a god with a plan for the world and for humanity. He was a god of righteousness, pleased by those who did good, vengeful toward those who did evil. He was a caring god, merciful and gracious, long-suffering, and abundant in goodness and truth, always watchful over his entire creation.

Third, the prophets proclaimed a new vision of the essence of human nature. As Yahweh's special creatures, human beings were created to become godlike. This could be achieved only by moral perfections, involving a choice between good and evil. Human beings were not Yahweh's slaves; but rather, each was his child who could earn divine mercy and love and favour by righteousness. Created to be righteous, individuals had the ability to choose how their natures would evolve and to determine what kind of humans they wished to be. Such moral freedom imposed a burden, but it also opened

---

① prophet：(宗教)先知。先知对未来的描述来自于神，这点和算命不同。犹太先知的思想大都反映在《希伯来圣经》的"十二先知书"中。他们认为，信仰上帝并不是要求子民们对其狂热崇拜，而是要有良好的个人道德，社会上有更多品质高尚的人。

avenues of human aspiration and action not offered by the other religious systems that had developed in the ancient Near East.

Fourth, the prophets proclaimed a new basis for defining the conduct of one individual toward others and of a community toward its members. Just as Yahweh treated men and women with righteousness and justice, so must individuals treat all others according to these same principles. And the community of Yahweh's followers must arrange its collective activities to promote righteousness and justice. The principles of social righteousness and justice were handed down by Yahweh in a code of law, called the Torah, that all were obliged to observe if they were to be counted among those faithful to Yahweh. God's laws of morality applied to all areas of life. These laws made no class distinctions and emphasised the protection of the poor, widows, orphans, and slaves. It was the ethical emphasis the Hebrew religion had that made it unique.

Finally, the prophets proclaimed that the Hebrews were the people chosen to carry out Yahweh's will on earth. No matter when and what disasters might befall them, they would ultimately emerge victorious over the other peoples of the earth, and through them the one god would be worshipped by all eventually. Yahweh would aid in this venture, since it was his plan for the world that was destined to be worked out in history. He would send a Messiah to lead the Hebrews to victory. While awaiting that final victory, the Hebrews must retain their ties with one another. If they could not all live in an independent kingdom, they could rely on their common religious beliefs as a binding tie to sustain the Hebrew "nation" as a community.

These ideas had been seriously considered by relatively few people by the 4th century B. C., when the ancient Near East was conquered by Alexander the Great and its civilisation submitted to heavy Greek influences. However, the ideas would have tremendous impact on later civilisations, serving as the basis upon which Christianity and Islam would be built.

Section Five The Assyrian Empire (c. 1000—612 B. C.)

A people of Semitic origin, the Assyrians lived in the land between the Tigris and the Euphrates rivers, due to which the Assyrians received powerful influence from the Mesopotamian civilisation.

The Assyrians came to rule powerful empires a number of times through history. In the Old Assyrian period (c. 2500—1500 B. C.), under the leadership of Shamshi-Adad, the Assyrians succeeded in creating their own empire, but they were then under the Babylonian and Mitanni-Hurrian domination respectively that were, in turn, overcome by the growing Hittite Empire. In about mid-14th century B. C., the great king, Ashur-uballit I established the powerful empire, known as the Middle Assyrian Empire (c. 1400 — 1078 B. C.). During this period, Assyria overthrew the Mitanni and the

Hittite Empire.

Being assaulted by surrounding nations at times, the Assyrians met the challenge by developing one of the best military forces in the Near East. Assyria again became a great power over the next three centuries, the Neo-Assyrian Empire (c. 1000—612 B. C.). Under a series of able rulers, the Assyrian domain gradually expanded. At the height of its power, the empire extended to the Mediterranean Sea from West Asia and southward to the Nile delta. What had begun as defensive raids eventually became wars aimed at conquest and the establishment of permanent control over Assyria's enemies.

The founder of the Assyrian Empire was Tiglath-pileser Ⅲ (745—727 B. C.). He and Sargon Ⅱ (721—705 B. C.) shaped the heartland of the empire by leading the Assyrian armies to destroy the chief political powers from southern Mesopotamia into Syria and Palestine. Assyrian governors were sent to rule the conquered lands and ensure the delivery of tribute. The central administration in Assyria was enlarged to supervise the conduct of imperial affairs, and effective means of communication were devised to keep the royal court informed of affairs in the empire. The army continued its brutal practices of terrorism to crush resistance. Other successors dealt with outsiders who insisted on interfering with Assyrian rule successfully. During this period, the Neo-Assyrian Empire assumed a position as the most powerful state on earth.

However, the Assyrian terrorism aroused an irreconcilable hatred among subject peoples, such as the Babylonians. Besides, some of the later Assyrian rulers were more inclined to enjoy the fruits of victory than to exercise the active leadership to hold the great empire together. Worst of all, Assyria encountered the plague of all empire builders, enemies beyond the frontiers aroused by the threat of absorption. After the death of Ashurbanipal, the Medes[①] and Chaldeans destroyed the Assyrian capital at Nineveh. The powerful empire was dissolved in the end.

The Hebrew prophet Nahum said, "All who hear the news of you clap their hands at your downfall." However, the Assyrians' bad reputation should not conceal their contribution to history. Their effort to create a single state out of many different peoples was a great breakthrough. They protected a beneficial peace on the Near East for nearly three centuries against barbarians who might have destroyed its civilisation had they succeeded in seizing control.

Economically, the Assyrians encouraged internal and foreign trade and assisted it by breaking down barriers for the free flow of goods across the Near East and wide spread of technical skills among peoples of technologically backward.

Though the Assyrians were not creative in cultural activity, they made a notable contribution through imitations, which can be seen best in architecture and sculpture.

---

① Medes:米提亚人。

Great cities of Assur and Nineveh were built as monuments of the power and glory of Assyrian kings by following closely the earlier Mesopotamian architectural styles, and temples and palaces were decorated with massive sculptured pieces and excellent stone reliefs. The Assyrian artists gave a unique quality to the tradition they honoured. The carved friezes to decorate the royal palaces were very impressive in that a succession of carved panels narrate in realistic detail battle or hunting scenes.

In literature the Assyrians devoted a great deal of effort to collecting older works in Sumerian and Akkadian. One of Assyria's kings built a huge library at Nineveh for thousands of copies of cuneiform tables. Though most of the writing in Assyrian included the religion epics and creation stories so dear to Mesopotamians, the Assyrians did show some originality in compiling annals about the military campaigns of the kings.

Assyrian religion also borrowed from Mesopotamia. The great state god of Assyria, Assur, resembled the Amorite Marduk. Their rituals, prayers, and priesthoods are almost indistinguishable from those of the earlier Mesopotamians.

In all these ways the Assyrians kept alive some of the most precious cultural traditions in the Near East.

Section Six The Persian Empire (550—330 B.C.)

Assyria's sudden collapse led to spirited competition for power. Of all Assyria's successors, the most spectacular was the empire of the Chaldeans, a Semitic people who established a kingdom based in Mesopotamia and from there spread out to create an extensive realm. Under the one great Chaldean ruler, Nebuchadnezzar Ⅱ (605—562 B.C.), all of Syria-Palestine was joined with the Tigris-Euphrates Valley in a single empire.

Nebuchadnezzar Ⅱ was well-known as a conqueror and a champion of culture as well. He rebuilt Babylon as his capital. Its massive walls, beautiful temples and palaces, impressive sculpture and painting, and, most famous of all, fabulous Hanging Gardens made it one of the most splendid of ancient cities. Besides, a religious revival in this period brought all the ancient Mesopotamian deities again to the centre of the stage.

Nevertheless, the Neo-Babylonian Empire was not strong due to its worshiping the past, its limited military resources, and Nebuchadnezzar's weak heirs who had little interest in political problems. When the Persians captured Babylon in 539 B.C., it collapsed immediately.

The Persians were an Indo-European-speaking people who originally settled in the barren plateau of Iran as simple farmers and herders. Over the years, they were influenced by Mesopotamian civilisation, but meanwhile they maintained the significant aspects of their old Indo-European pattern of life, especially in religion and language. In the late 7th century B.C. they were forced to accept the overlordship of the Medes, who were closely akin to them in language and culture. But the Persian king, Cyrus (559—530 B. C.) overthrew the Median ruler and created a powerful Persian state that rearranged the political map of the ancient Near East.

Cyrus and his successors, Cambyses (530—522 B. C.) and Darius I "the Great" (522—486 B. C.) extended the Persian Empire from the Aegean and Mediterranean seas to India and from the mountains bounding the Near East on the north to far south in the Nile Valley. It was one of the largest empires ever created.

These rulers were not only successful conquerors but also wise statesmen, and they laid the basis for sound government of their huge territory. Cyrus practised a policy of tolerance toward defeated people, which is illustrated by his willingness in permitting the Hebrews, who had been brought to Babylon, to return to Jerusalem to rebuild the temple of Yahweh. For this he won their loyalty.

Darius laid the basis for one of the great political systems of all history by borrowing and adapting old ideas and practices in government. He established himself as absolute ruler, claiming full authority to make laws, to judge, and to command the services of his subjects. He created a magnificent court etiquette to impress upon everyone that he was "The Great King". For ruling widely scattered possessions inhabited by many different peoples, he divided his empire into twenty districts, satrapies. Over each he appointed a governor, usually a Persian and often a member of the royal family. For communication, an excellent road system was developed, the Royal Road, linking the satrapies to the capital allowing constant correspondence to be kept with the court. Royal armies under trusted commanders were stationed in strategic spots. Careful tax records were kept at the capital as a means of accounting for each governor's administration.

Apart from his greatest political innovation, the armed forces were the key to Darius' power. A standing army was created of professional soldiers of various peoples from the subject population of the empire, truly international in character. Its main force consisted of a cavalry force of 10,000 and an elite infantry force of 10,000 Medes and Persians, who were known as the Immortals because they were never reduced below 10,000 in number. When one was killed, he was immediately replaced. The Persians also commanded excellent naval forces, composed largely of hired Phoenician, Egyptian, and Greek ships and crews.

In spite of their talents for administration and military affairs, the Persians' contributions to cultural development were not as spectacular. In general, like the Assyrians, they synthesised their borrowings from the existing cultural treasure in a way that created a culture meaningful to a variety of different peoples. Their tolerant attitude toward the many different cultural elements in their empire is of great importance in the history of Western civilisation because it was from the Persians that the Greeks derived and transmitted westward knowledge of many ancient Near Eastern ideas.

One outstanding contribution they made was in religion. They created a new religion, Zoroastrianism①, and helped spread some of its ideas. Early Persian religion focused on the worship of the powers of nature, including the sun, moon, fire, and winds. Zoroaster (Zarathustra in the Persian language), a great religious reformer, was a semi-legendary figure who, according to Persian tradition, lived in the 7th century B. C., He spent the early part of his life in contemplation in the desert, finally receiving a revelation of the true way from Ahura, the god of the sky.

Zoroaster made the basic obligation of human beings clear. Only good conduct would win favour in the eyes of Ahura Mazda. Certainly none of the religions in the world that the Persians were soon to rule, except Judaism, gave such emphasis to ethical issues, and not even Judaism placed the burden so squarely on each individual. Zoroaster's message was aimed at all humankind rather than a particular chosen people.

The spread of Zoroastrianism was due to its acceptance by the Great Kings of Persia. The inscriptions of Darius made it clear that he believed Ahura Mazda was the only god. But dramatic changes occurred, and polytheism crept back into religious life. The struggle between good and evil was taken beyond the abstractions of Zoroaster into a strong ethical dualism: good associated with purely spiritual things, and evil with material things. The new changes drew Zoroastrianism back toward the patterns of ancient Near Eastern religions.

The general policy of tolerance in the empire had meant that other faiths had maintained their hold, and thus Zoroastrianism did not have a very large base. Despite this setback, Zoroastrianism has survived till today; its modern adherents, Parsees②, are located chiefly in Iran and India. It has also powerfully impacted other religions including Judaism, Christianity, and Islam.

By the middle of the 4th century B. C., Persian power encountered a strong attack from outside led by a Macedonian king, Alexander the Great, who was able to take possession of the whole Persian Empire before his death in 323 B. C., However, the Persian spirit which permitted local elements to persist while providing the means for all people at many levels of civilisation to exchange ideas and culture leading to a universal community was always there in a long chapter in history.

Chapter Review

This chapter focused on the two foundation stones for the building of Western

---

① Zoroastianism: 琐罗亚斯德教,是在基督教诞生之前中东最有影响的宗教,是古代波斯帝国的国教,俗称"拜火教"。

② Parsees:帕西人,琐罗亚斯德教的信徒。

civilisation in Mesopotamia and in Egypt. The inventors of true civilisation, the Sumerians formed city-states, the basic units of Sumerian civilisation. The Egyptians made great innovations in political systems, of which the central feature was the absolute power of the pharaoh. Cultural diffusion played a significant role in the development of small nations. Among these the most significant was that of the Hebrews who made great contributions to major religious systems, Judaism, Christianity and Islam. Besides, the Assyrian Empire and its successor, the Persian Empire made contributions to the temporary unification of the whole civilised Near East. In a word, the ancient Near East was a period full of wars and struggles, but its achievements in western civilisation should not be ignored.

Exercise

Ⅰ. *According to the information provided in this chapter, choose the correct alternative among A, B, C, and D that can complete each of the following statements.*

1. One of the greatest Sumerian achievements (of Mesopotamia) was the development of a writing system, ________.

   A. alphabet B. Semitics C. cuneiform D. hieroglyphic

2. In Mesopotamian history one of the most well-known kings, Hammurabi established ________.

   A. Old Babylonia B. Hittite Empire
   C. Assyrian Empire D. Sumerian city-states

3. In Egyptian history, the greatest and largest pyramids were mainly constructed in the ________, and symbolised glory and prosperity of the major ancient civilisation of the world.

   A. New Kingdom B. 12th dynasty
   C. third and fourth dynasties D. Second Intermediate Period

4. Of the following peoples, ________ were not of Semitic origin.

   A. the Hebrews B. the Persians
   C. the Assyrians D. the Phoenicians

5. The Persians made their outstanding contribution to the world civilisation in the area of ________.

   A. literature B. writing
   C. architecture D. administration

Ⅱ. *Fill in the blanks with what you have learned in this chapter.*

1. The people who established ________ of true civilisation were the Sumerians, who formed ______, the basic units of Sumerian civilisation.
2. Ancient Egypt was geographically divided into ________ Egypt, extending

northward from the first cataract at Aswan to the south of Memphis, and ________ Egypt, the Delta area. The Egyptians call their rich belt the "________", and the deserts beyond it the "________".

3. The Hebrew Bible is known to Christians as ________. It provides a historical ________ far superior to that produced by any other ancient Near Eastern people.
4. The Assyrians had a bad reputation of ________ and ________, but in contrast, the ________ policy of tolerance won the loyalty of the conquered.
5. The empire of the Chaldeans was created after the fall of the Assyrian Empire. It was also known as the ________, when Babylon was rebuilt as the capital of the empire, and ________, known as one of the Seven Wonders of the ancient world, made the city one of the most splendid of ancient cities.

Ⅲ. *According to what you have learned, answer the following questions briefly in your own words.*

1. Why is the Old Kingdom also named the Pyramid Age in Egyptian history? What is the significance of the pyramid?
2. Who were David and Solomon? What do you know about them?
3. What was the greatest contribution of the Hebrews to the history of the world? And what was its significance?
4. What breakthrough did the Assyrians make in the world history by establishing the Assyrian Empire? Please comment on it.
5. Why was the Persians' tolerant attitude of great importance in the history of Western civilisation?

Ⅳ. *With critical analysis, answer the following essay questions in your own words.*

1. What are the similarities and differences between the two river valley civilisations, Mesopotamia and Egypt, in the aspects of natural environment and political, economic, social, and cultural life?
2. What is the significance of Hammurabi's law code? Please make comments on it.

Ⅴ. *Work in small groups and make comparisons based on the following topic.*

Please compare and contrast the slave society of China and that of Egypt in terms of political system, economic development and culture.

Voices on Key Points

Egyptian Civilisation

By 3000 B. C. the art of Egypt was so ripe and so far advanced that it is surprising to find any student of early culture proposing that the crude contemporary art of the early Babylonians is the product of a civilisation earlier than that of the Nile.

——James H. Breasted

Egypt, the Egypt of antiquity, at a later time, exercised a mysterious fascination over me. I recognised a picture of it immediately, without hesitation and astonishment, in an illustrated magazine.

——Pierre Loti

The Hebrew Civilisation

Had the Hebrews not been disturbed in their progress a thousand and more years ago, they would have solved all the great problems of civilisation which are being solved now under all the difficulties imposed by the spirit of the Middle Ages.

——Isaac Mayer Wise

The Hebrews have done more to civilise men than any other nation. If I were an atheist, and believed blind eternal fate, I should still believe that fate had ordained the Jews to be the most essential instrument for civilizing the nations.

——John Adams

Suggested Reading

1. Hallo, William W. & Simpson, William Kelly. *The Ancient Near East: A History* (2nd Ed.). Belmont: Wadsworth Publishing Company, 1997.
2. Marc Van De Mieroop. *A History of the Ancient Near East: ca. 3000 — 323 BC*. New York: Wiley-Blackwell, 2003.
3. Marc Van De Mieroop. *A History of Ancient Egypt*. New York: Wiley-Blackwell, 2010.
4. Sasson, Jack. *The Civilisations of the Ancient Near East*. New York: Scribner,1995.
5. (法)J.博太罗等著,余中先译:《美索不达米亚:追溯近东文明的起点》,上海书店出版社2004年版。
6. (美)戴尔·布朗主编,王淑芳译:《苏美尔:伊甸园的城市》,华夏出版社2002年版。
7. (美)亨利·富兰克弗特,子林译:《近东文明的起源》,格致出版社2009年版。
8. (挪)托利弗·伯曼,吴勇立译:《希伯来与希腊思想比较》,上海书店出版社2007年版。
9. 许朝华编著:《埃及文明》,北京出版社2008年版。
10. 中华世纪坛世界艺术馆编:《美索不达米亚文明》,文物出版社2007年版。
11. 朱维之主编:《希伯来文化》,上海社会科学院出版社2004年版。

Chapter Two　Greek Civilisation (c. 2000—30 B. C.)

We are all Greeks.

——*Shelley*

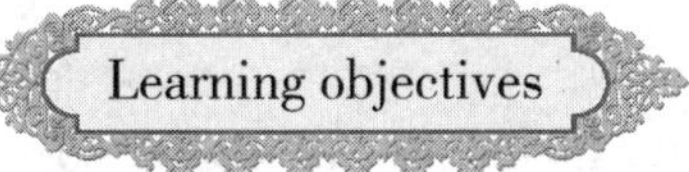

After reading this chapter, you will be able to:

1. *Get to know the historical context of ancient Greece;*
2. *Get to know the social and political structure of ancient Greece;*
3. *Be familiar with literature, philosophy, science, architecture and sculpture in ancient Greece;*
4. *Understand the historical meaning of the Conquests of Alexander;*
5. *Understand the significance and impact of Greek culture.*

古代希腊包括希腊、爱琴海和爱奥尼亚海上的诸多岛屿、小亚细亚和黑海沿岸地区。爱琴海是古希腊文明的摇篮。早在古希腊文明兴起之前，爱琴海地区就孕育了灿烂的克里特文明和迈锡尼文明。大约在公元前1200年，野蛮的多利亚人毁灭了迈锡尼文明，希腊从此进入"黑暗时代"。自公元前8世纪起，希腊社会结构发生变革，众多的城邦逐渐形成，其中最著名的是斯巴达城邦和雅典城邦。公元前5世纪，波斯与希腊为扩张各自版图而进行的波希战争以雅典的胜利而告终，希腊文明达到鼎盛时期。然而随之而来的斯巴达与雅典之间争夺霸主地位的伯罗奔尼撒战争却宣告了希腊文明鼎盛期的结束。这场战争后，希腊各城邦陷入混战，希腊北部的马其顿在此时崛起。公元前336年，亚历山大即位成为马其顿国王，拉开了他征服世界的序幕。亚历山大率军东征西讨，先是确立了在希腊的统治地位，后又灭亡了波斯帝国，在横跨欧亚非大陆的辽阔疆域内创下了辉煌业绩，促进了东西方文化的交流和经济的发展。公元前323年，亚历山大病死，他的庞大帝国也随之分裂，古希腊时代结束，希腊化时代开始。古代希腊在哲学、戏剧、建筑、雕塑、科技、数学等方面做出了杰出贡献，成为后世欧洲文明发展的源头。

In the history of human civilisation, no one can deny the legacy of Greek civilisation, the fountainhead of western culture. All southern and western Europe and the new lands including Americas and Australia share a common cultural heritage which originated in Greece. The culture, as expressed in poetry, philosophy, music, architecture, sculpture, government, and the outlook this shaped had its roots in Greek civilisation and laid the foundation of western civilisation.

Section One The Emergence of Greece (c. 2000—1100 B.C.)

The discoveries of archaeologists have traced the beginning of Greek civilisation to Aegean civilisation① centreing on Crete and Mycenae②, hence Crete-Mycenane civilisation③(c. 2000—1100 B.C.). Unlike the river-valley civilisation of Mesopotamia and Egypt, the Aegean Sea is the cradle of Greek civilisation. The mountains and the sea played significant roles in the development of Greek history, and it is the mountains that helped determine the major territories into which Greece was ultimately divided until 338 B.C., when the Greeks were conquered by the Macedonian king Philip Ⅱ.

Minoan Crete is the largest island in the east Mediterranean. It was inhabited by groups of Indo-Europeans in the early times. Later it became the residence of migrants from Asia Minor or Syria. The Minoans were a Bronze Age people living in Crete, and they created the first known civilisation in Europe between 3000 and 1400 B.C. The

① Aegean civilisation：爱琴文明，希腊及爱琴地区史前文明的总称。

② Mycenae：迈锡尼城，位于伯罗奔尼撒半岛。迈锡尼文明由此得名。

③ 因克里特岛和迈锡尼先后成为爱琴文明的两大中心，历史上称史里特—迈锡尼文明。

civilisation of Minoan[①] Crete was first discovered by the English archaeologist Arthur Evans. Evans divided the Minoan civilisation into three eras on the basis of the stylistic changes of the pottery. His comparative chronology included an Early (3000—2100 B. C.), a Middle (2100—1500 B. C.), and a Late Minoan period (1500—1100 B. C.).

The Minoan civilisation reached its height between 2000 and 1450 B. C. The excavated temple ruins and paintings brought to light by the archaeologists demonstrated how prosperous and powerful this Minoan civilisation was. The sudden termination of the Minoan Crete civilisation remains uncertain. The catastrophic collapse might have resulted from a tsunami triggered by a powerful volcanic eruption or from the attacks of the mainland Greeks known as the Mycenaeans.

Minoan Palaces Several prehistoric Minoan palaces are found on the island of Crete. In the development of the Minoan civilisation, they began to build palaces around 1900 B. C., and these palaces had important cultural, religious, commercial, and administrative functions.

The Minoan palaces were used for gatherings and celebrations. They were also used to store harvested crops and as workshops for artists. The palaces were located in low hills at several locations of strategic importance around the island. The structure of the buildings was so sophisticated that they seemed to be mazes to visitors. In addition, the designers of these palaces applied advanced technology in the creation of their water systems. Drainage and irrigation systems, aqueducts, and deep wells that were very advanced for the time were found in association with the palaces. Thematic-storied palace buildings were graced with impressive interior and exterior staircases, light wells, massive columns, storage magazines and outdoor gathering places—the precursor to ancient theatres.

Rough stones and ceramic bricks used as building materials were connected by mortar in the interior walls, and the corners of the buildings were shaped with large rectangular blocks. None of the Minoan palaces unearthed was surrounded by defensive walls, which proved the Minoan supremacy at sea.

Knossos was undeniably the capital of Minoan Crete. It was grander, more complex, and more flamboyant than any of the other palaces known to us, and it is now located about 5 km from the south of the modern port town of Iraklio.

Religion played an important role in Minoan Crete and many activities, and many artistic products revolved around religious cult. As evidenced in the art of the period, the Minoans deified the natural world and found in it a logical order that allowed man to live in harmony with the natural environment.

Holy caves, hilltops, sanctuaries, and palaces were used to hold ritual

① Minoan Civilisation：米诺斯文明，源自古希腊神话中克里特贤王米诺斯，是欧洲最早的古代文明，是希腊古典文明的前驱，以精美的王宫建筑、壁画、陶器和工艺品等著称于世。该文明的发展主要在克里特岛。

celebrations. Worship of the great female nature goddess involved parades, as well as animal and bloodless sacrifices. People believed they could communicate with the supernatural through music, dance and prayer during these ceremonies.

In the Minoan religious ceremonies, bull sacrifice and games about the animal were of particular importance. They symbolised man's interaction with powerful natural elements. The bull mask, the double axe, and the bull horns are some of the ritual objects that have been unearthed during excavations around Crete[①].

Technology Civilisations of the Middle East provided the Minoans the art of metalworking. Minoans' delicate jewellery decorated the collections of noble palace residents and admired around the Mediterranean.

Archaeological excavations in Crete found many gold artefacts and a variety of copper instruments dating back to 2300 B. C. Although Crete did not have abundant copper, research shows the Minoans imported copper from Cyprus in trade.

The Minoan metal craftsmen enjoyed such a high reputation in the ancient world that many of them worked on mainland Greece and on island in the Aegean Sea. It was from the Minoan artisans that the Mycenaeans learned the art of insetting bronze with gold.

Language The first written scripts of the Minoans resemble Egyptian hieroglyphs[②]. The Phaistos Disk[③], dating to 1700 B. C. , is an example of such script. Later a syllable based script, Linear A emerged on the island. Since Linear A still remains undecipherable[④], its content or origin is a mystery, but archaeological excavations have found large numbers of Linear A tablets on Crete.

Linear B, used by the Mycenaeans, was deciphered in 1953. According to the translations of the tablets, most of them are detailed lists of stored goods. The life of a booming society was revealed to some extent by these inventories in Linear B. Linguists believed that Linear B is an original form of Greek.

The Mycenaeans[⑤] With the decline of Crete civilisation, Mycenaean became the centre of Greek civilisation. They were an Indo-European family of peoples who migrated into southern and Western Europe, India, and Iran. The civilisation that took root on the mainland is called Mycenaean. The Mycenaeans were the first speakers of the Greek language. They did not form themselves into a united kingdom, but rather

---

① 克里特人一种流行的表演就是人与凶猛的公牛相斗，斗牛者手握牛角，在牛背上翻筋斗，然后双足落地，投入一女伴怀中。克里特出土的工艺品上有很多猎牛和斗牛的场面；在神堂上，都有牛的“圣角”造型。学者们由此推断，克里特人是一个牛图腾民族。

② hieroglyphs：象形文字，见第一章。

③ Phaistos Disk：希腊菲斯特斯圆盘，上面记载着至今无法破译的象形文字。

④ undecipherable：无法破译的。

⑤ 被学者们誉为“现代化”的克里特文明衰落后，代之而起的是线性文字 B 的创造者——阿卡亚人的迈锡尼文明。西方文明的历史舞台第一次更换了主角，文明的中心开始从海岛向大陆北移。

independent states. There seems to be two groups of free men in Mycenaean society: the king's entourage[①], who conducted administrative duties at the palace, and the people, da-mo (demos), who lived at the commune level. The demos performed duties and paid taxes under the supervision of royal officials. Unlike the open palaces of the Minoan, Mycenaean palaces were strong forts with high walls. Members of different social strata lived within the palace. Wealthy officials lived in the spacious quarters. Palace workers were confined to the range due to their duties, and their living conditions were as undesirable as craftsmen, farmers and merchants who also lived in the palace. Male and female slaves (c. f. δoλo /doúlos) occupied the very bottom of the social ladder.

Mycenaean Bronze Age civilisation was centred on the Peloponnesian peninsula and reached its high point between 1400 and 1200 B. C. , The reasons of the collapse are different. Some theories hold that the Dorian invasion is the main reason, while other theories insist that natural disasters and climate changing is the reason of the collapse. The major Mycenaean cites were Mycenae and Tiryns in Argolis, Pylos in Messenia, Athens in Attica, Thebes and Orchomenus in Boeotia, and Lolkos in Thessaly.

The Mycenaeans were a warrior people who prided themselves on their heroic deeds in battle.[②] Victory in the Troy War did not advance but ruined Mycenaean civilisation whose glorious past can still be touched today at the Lion Gate of Agamemnon castle.[③] Thanks to the amazing excavations made by the amateur German archaeologist Heinrich Schliemann, we are able to identify the indispensable page of Greek history that would otherwise only make up an episode of Homer's works.

The economic organisation of the Mycenaean kingdoms seemed to have been bipartite[④]: a first group worked within palace, while another was self-employed. Often persons working for the palace also ran their own businesses on the side. Scribes supervised the economic operation. They were in charge of recording incoming and outgoing goods, assigning work, and distributing rations. It seems that an official, known as a du-ma-te, was a kind of supervising quartermaster.

---

① entourage：国王的随从，也称"王的扈从"。扮演着行政长官的角色。根据泥板文书、出土文物等可以认为，迈锡尼是当时希腊大陆的霸主，其政治制度应该是专制君主，君主下面有将军、王的扈从，以及各种官吏和祭司等，政治机构有贵族会议和民众大会。社会的基层组织是公社，由长老领导。

② 从地理上说，尚武精神的迈锡尼文明是希腊人创造的本土文明。他们大约从公元前1650年开始，从巴尔干半岛北部入侵希腊半岛中部和南部。约公元前1600年左右，阿卡亚人部落进入南希腊，成为当地统治者。据考古学所知，此时的生产力发展比较迅速，金银工艺品和陶器制品远销埃及、腓尼基、塞浦路斯和特洛伊等地。此时出现迈锡尼人使用的线性文字B，这种文字与克里特的线性文字A有继承关系，显然，这是迈锡尼人依照克里特人的文字创造的。

③ 迈锡尼文明的最后一幕是特洛伊战争，《伊利亚特》对此有生动的描述。传说战争打了10年，虽然被智多星奥德赛用木马计攻破，但作为胜利者的迈锡尼文明也开始走下坡路。10年的战争使其元气大伤，相对的统一局面被破坏了，这就给野蛮的多利安人的入侵创造了有利的客观条件。公元前12世纪，居住在希腊北部的多利安人大规模南下，他们消灭了阿卡亚人各城邦，毁灭了迈锡尼文明。

④ bipartite：两分的。当时社会的经济组织状况主要由两部分组成，一部分是为宫殿工作的人，另一部分是自主经营者，但是二者的分工又不是绝对的，有的为宫殿工作的人同时也会从事自主经营。

Language The Mycenaeans spoke an early form of Greek. Archaeologists have concluded that the Mycenaean rulers adopted the Linear A script of the Minoans and transformed it to write their own language. This written language is called Linear B. Linear B was undecipherable until the code was cracked in 1952.

Art and Craftwork The Minoan culture of Crete had great influence on Mycenaean arts and crafts. Mycenaeans made great deal of pottery. There were various kinds of pottery products, including stirrup jars, pitchers, kraters, and chalices for example. Although pottery production developed quickly and large numbers of ceramic items were exported, these vessels' shapes remained almost unchanged during the whole Mycenaean period. The export products were luxurious, and they were designed with delicate decorations that incorporated myth, warrior, or animal themes. At Mycenaean sites, there was also another type of vessels made of metal. These metal objects were generally tripods, basins, or lamps.

Excavations at the Mycenaean site revealed that the statues of this period were mostly made of clay. Despite exquisite handicraft, the statues were small. The majority of these statuettes are anthropomorphic figurines, both male and female. They are painted, monochrome or polychrome. Although the purpose of these statues still remains vague, some researchers suggest they might be used in prayer because they were found in the places which appeared to be worship sites. Painting of the Mycenaean age was much influenced by the Minoan. Some mural paintings found in Mycenaean palaces represented different themes, such as tauromachy, battles, parades, and mythological stories. Other paintings are made up of geometric motifs. Some pottery was also painted (see above) with identical themes.

Section Two Dark Age and Homer's World (1100—750 B. C.)

The Greeks in a Dark Age[①] **(1100—750 B. C.)** The turmoil during 1200—1000 B. C. weakened many city-states in Greece. Many of the people who survived suffered from grinding poverty. Few written records are available for research or reference regarding this period of destruction and rehabilitation. Historians call this period a Dark Age for two reasons. On the one hand, people appeared to have led an extremely difficult life. On the other hand, lack of reliable information makes it impossible to fully appreciate the real situation in which they lived. The Greeks did not fully regain their strength until about 750 B. C. (In contrast, the Near East recovered much sooner, ending its Dark Age around 900 B. C.)

---

① 公元前12世纪,居住在希腊北部的多利安人大规模南下,这些处在原始社会的好战的野蛮人,消灭了阿卡亚人的各个城邦,把迈锡尼文明,连同克里特文明一扫而光,遍布希腊大陆的几乎都是多利安人的原始社会的景象,总体看来社会进入大倒退时代,因而学者们把这一时期成为黑暗时代或荷马时代。

The Poverty of the Early Greek Dark Age The depressed economic conditions in Greece after the fall of Mycenaean civilisation typify the desperately reduced circumstances during the worst years of the Dark Age. It appears that the Greeks lost their knowledge of writing along with the decline of the Mycenaean civilisation early in the Dark Age. Linear B script was mastered only by a few scribes in order to record palace affairs. They wrote only to track the flow of goods in and out of the palaces. Oral transmission kept Greek cultural traditions alive.

Archaeological excavations have shown that developed political states no longer existed in Greece, and the people eked out their existence as herders, shepherds, and subsistence farmers lived in tiny settlements. The Greek population decreased in the early Dark Age. As the population shrank, less land was cultivated, leading to a decline in food production. The diminished food supply, in turn, prompted further drop in population.

Even though many types of farming disappeared, the Greek agricultural economy was still complex. More Greeks than ever before made their living by herding animals. This change in life style made people more mobile. Consequently, people had to build simple huts with minimal necessities to adapt to this nomadic life. Unlike their Bronze Age forebears, Greeks in the Dark Age had no monumental architecture, and they had neither the energy nor time to create artistic designs on pottery.

Not until 850 B. C. was farming revived. At the same time some new developments provide the basis for a revived Greece. Kings ruled throughout this period until eventually they were replaced with an aristocracy. In the military, the infantry became more important than cavalry in battles. Due to its low production costs and local availability, iron replaced bronze as the metal of choice in the manufacturing of tools and weapons. People from different classes pursued equality and this brought about the decline of kings and the ascent of families. Families tried to trace their origins back to heroes of the Trojan War in the attempt to establish a glorious family history.

With the recovery of town life around 800 B. C. , Greek civilisation revived. From then on, the Greek world generally extended from the Black Sea to Spain.

The Rise of a New Writing System A new alphabet system from the Semitic Phoenicians by degrees replaced the syllabary system of the Minoans. It was used to write not only the Greek language, but also other languages in the Eastern Mediterranean at the time. Before this turbulent time, Mycenaeans wrote their Greek language in Linear B, but after the 8th century B. C. , the Greeks adopted the Phoenician alphabet to give themselves a new system of writing. Near the very end of this so-called Dark Age appeared the work of Homer who definitely wrote in Greek. The history was being recorded once again in what we find the more familiar alpha-beta-gamma. From the 8th century B. C. , the renewal of the language benefited the

Etruscans in the form of Italic variants. However, the former linear scripts did not entirely disappear. The Cypriot syllabary, developed from Linear A, was used on Cyprus for Greek and Eteocypriot inscriptions until the rise of Hellenism.

Homer and His Epics The oldest of the Greek works of literature were the epic poems ascribed to Homer written in about 750 B. C. : the *Iliad* and the *Odyssey*. The two epic poems became the treasured heritage from a legendary Heroic Age. These works were epic in that they illustrated in heroic proportions the ethical ideals of the Greeks. The *Iliad*, epic of the Trojan War, tells of a Greek siege of the ancient city of Troy. According to the legend, the Trojan War began with the famous judgment of Paris as to which of the three goddesses—Hera, Athena, and Aphrodite—was the most beautiful. The *Iliad* opens in the last year of conflict with the quarrel between Achilles and Agamemnon. For Homer, says British classicist H. D. F. Kitto, "actions must have their consequences; ill-judged actions must have uncomfortable results. "①

The Trojan War spanning about ten years has a grand spectacle, including the battle for Helen of Troy, the Greek siege of Troy, Trojan counterblow, and the tactics of the Trojan Horse. Actually, all these events were vividly and stately represented in Homer's *Iliad*. Homer touches on the capricious conduct of the strong gods who are incalculable in contrast to the tragic experience of man whose violence and recklessness often lead to disaster. Homer also brings together the gods and men in close association. Herodotus found that the *Iliad* was a chief source of information about the gods.

The *Odyssey* is an epic romance that describes the wanderings of Odysseus and his ultimate return to his wife. Odysseus is one of the Greek heroes after the fall of Troy. With the guidance of Athena, the wise hero evades an irritated Poseidon and overcomes numerous difficulties, including a fantastic cast of adversaries—Cyclops the one-eyed giant, the enchantress Circe, cannibals, sirens, and many other monstrous creatures. Homer delivers the moral principle in the *Odyssey*, "that virtue is a better policy than vice. "②

There is far less history in the *Odyssey* than in the *Iliad*, and the accounts of the far wandering Odysseus, the sea adventurer, are for the most part a myth. Homer's world reflects the values of aristocratic heroes of courage and honour.

Although the *Iliad* and the *Odyssey* supposedly deal with the heroes of the Mycenaean age of the 13th century B. C. , many scholars believe that they really describe the social conditions of the Dark Age. According to the Homeric view, Greece was a society based on agriculture in which a landed warrior-aristocracy controlled much wealth and exercised considerable power. Homer's world shows the values of

① H. D. F. Kitto, *The Greeks*, Baltimore: Penguin Books, 1957, p. 60.

② Homer, *Odyssey*, trans. E. V. Rieu, Harmondsworth, 1946. p. 337.

aristocratic heroes.

The Homeric poems give us our first glimpse of the Greek's view of divinity—vain, vengeful, and volatile. In Homer's writing, which idealised the warrior spirit, excellence was interpreted as courage and skill in battle. Homer's portrayal of excellence was one that combines thought with action. Thus, the wise Phoenix told the stubborn Achilles that a man of true worth is both "a speaker of words and a doer of deeds"①. We can find the earliest statement of the Greek educational ideal: the moulding of a man who, says classicist Werner Jaeger, "united nobility of action with nobility of mind"②, and who realised "the whole of human potentialities"③.

Homer's masterpieces greatly contributed to the shaping of the Greek spirit. Homer's heroes who pursued honour and confronted hardship with bravery were always admired by the Greeks.

Greek Mythology Since its emergence, myth retained everlasting popularity in the development of human society. Greek mythology, because of its systematic integrity and literary value, is known throughout the whole world. Greek mythology has had a profound influence on religion, philosophy, literature and art of the West. Contact with western culture is bound to involve allusions from Greek mythology. Without exaggeration almost every western classic literary work involves Greek mythological characters or plots. Therefore a general acquaintance with Greek mythology is essential for educated people today.

Greek mythology includes stories of gods and legends of heroes. The stories of gods involve the origins of the universe and of human beings, the emergence of gods, and the gods' lineage.

According to Greek mythology about creation, Chaos was the foundation of all things. From Chaos came Gaia (the goddess of earth). Gaia bore and married Uranus who was the god of heaven. Gaia and Uranus gave birth to the Titans, gigantic and powerful gods, and the Cyclopes, one-eyed giants who made thunderbolts. Among the Titans, the youngest and the most important one was Cronus. He castrated and overthrew his father, Uranus. However, the same fate awaited Cronus after the birth of his youngest son, Zeus. With help of other brothers and sisters, Zeus made war on Cronus and the Titans and defeated them. He established a new regime, based on Mount Olympus in northern Greece.

---

① Werner Jaeger, *Paideia: The Ideals of Greek Culture*, Vol. Ⅰ, trans. Gilbert Highet, Oxford University Press, 1986, p. 8.

② Werner Jaeger, *Paideia: The Ideals of Greek Culture*, Vol. Ⅰ, trans. Gilbert Highet, Oxford University Press, 1939, p. 8.

③ Werner Jaeger, *Paideia: The Ideals of Greek Culture*, Vol. Ⅰ, trans. Gilbert Highet, Oxford University Press, 1939, p. 8.

The gods and goddesses living on Mount Olympus were known as the Olympians[①]. The Olympian gods and goddesses shared the same appearance and characteristics of human beings. They had both the human form and human passion. The only difference between gods and men was the former enjoyed immortality but the latter suffered from sickness and death. The Greeks endowed their gods with distinguishable personalities, but elements such as asceticism and mysticism are rarely found in Greek mythology. To a very real extent, the Greek gods and goddesses "were thoroughly humans, sharing in an exaggerated manner not only human strengths and virtues but also weaknesses and vices"[②].

The legends of heroes originated from the worship of ancestors. These heroes were mostly the descendants of gods and men-demigods. Their extraordinary physical strength and remarkable courage reflected the heroic spirit and mighty will shown by human beings in the process of conquering nature. These heroes were the personification of the ancient people's collective strength and wisdom. Jason taking the Golden Fleece, Achilles in the Trojan War and Odysseus' returning home were the most famous and everlasting legends.

Greek mythology's unique appeal to people is mainly due to two reasons, "first, because it expresses the nature of a people gifted with a peculiarly fine and artistic soul; secondly, because our own thought and art are, in great part, a heritage from the civilisation of Greece."[③]

Section Three Sparta and Athens: Greek City-States (750—500 B. C.)

During the period between 800 and 500 B. C., the Greek world experienced dramatic changes. The first evidence of these changes was a sharp increase in population in the 8th century B. C. The rising population brought about three main consequences. First of all, more population implied a more stable life style. People generally abandoned nomadism and built villages and towns. Second, the increase in population put higher demands on agricultural production. Thereupon land shortage shunted some people to commerce. Third, with the development of trade, labour division became more definite, which led to a more complex structure of society. These changes

---

① 希腊神话中有奥林匹斯十二大主神，分别为：天神宙斯（Zeus）、天后赫拉（Hera）、海洋之神波塞冬（Poseidon）、地狱之神哈迪斯（Hades）、智慧女神雅典娜（Athena）、太阳神阿波罗（Apollo）、月亮女神阿尔忒弥斯（Artemis）、美神阿佛洛狄忒（Aphrodite）、战神阿瑞斯（Ares）、火与工匠之神赫菲斯托斯（Hephaestus）、神使赫尔墨斯（Hermes）和酒神狄俄尼索斯（Dionysus）。

② Mark Kishlansky, *A Brief History of Western Civilisation*, Beijing: China Remin University Press, 2008, p. 34.

③ Jessie M. Tatlock, *Greek and Roman Mythology*, Beijing: Central Compilation & Translation Press, 2008, p. 1.

produced a corresponding transformation in the political system. The old tribes and chieftains were no longer adequate to handle societal affairs.

In response to this social development, different tribes began to recombine by annexation and fusion. Hence developed the Greek socio-political institution known as the polis, or city-state which is the centre of classical Greek civilisation. The Greek polis (plural poleis) developed slowly during the Dark Age and by the 8th century B. C. had emerged as a truly unique and fundamental institution in Greek society. Ancient Greece was divided into hundreds of poleis, each being a tiny unit politically independent and culturally unique, consisting of a town or village and the surrounding territory.

The polis, a politically autonomous community, was the base on which the Greeks developed their social, political and cultural life. The citizens enjoyed rights to participate in the decision-making process. However, on the other hand, slaves and aliens had none of these rights at all. In the following centuries, the polis laid a solid foundation for the most outstanding Greek characteristic: democracy.

The polis was governed by the assembly consisting of all male citizens that had final authority in the passing of laws after free and open debate. Every male citizen (over eighteen years of age) was a member of the Assembly, the sole legislative body of the city-state. From the Assembly a Council of Five Hundred was chosen annually to supervise the administrative affairs of the polis; from the Council, an executive committee of fifty was chosen to execute the daily business of administration for a term lasting one-tenth of a year; one member of this committee was chosen as chairman for one-day periods. The English historian, Kitto, regarded the polis as, "the only framework within which man could realise his spiritual, moral, and intellectual capacities."①

During the later Archaic and Classical periods, Athens and Sparta, two typical representatives of the Greek polis, developed into the most important and influential city-states. All the other city-states eventually sided with one of these two principal powers.

Sparta② was an agrarian economy, resting on the fertile lands of Laconia and Messenia (the south-eastern and south-western part of the Peloponnesus, respectively).

---

① H. D. F. Kitto, *The Greeks*, Baltimore: Penguin Books, 1957, p. 78.

② Sparta：在为数众多的城邦中，斯巴达和雅典是两个逐渐强大起来的城邦。不同于希腊的海外扩张，斯巴达走的是陆上扩张的道路，他征服了兄弟邻邦美塞尼亚，并把自己的兄弟变为农业奴隶，即“希洛人”。斯巴达的政治制度是希腊城邦中贵族寡头政治的典型。国家机构由两个国王、长老会议、公民大会、检察官委员会组成。二王是世袭制，地位和权力平等，战时一个留守，一个统军打仗。长老会议是实权机构，由 30 人组成，除了两个国王外，其余 28 个由年逾 60 的贵族相任，终身制。公民大会由男性公民组成，每月召开一次，形式上是最高权力机关，实际上是权力装饰品。检察官由 5 人组成，一年一任，初始的职责只是监督公民“刮净胡须、遵守法律”，但后来权力越来越大，拥有指挥国家一切政治生活的实权。检察官委员会实际上就是斯巴达的政府。

These lands were cultivated by public serfs, the helots, who had to contribute a certain amount of their product to their Spartan masters. The helots, who vastly outnumbered their Spartan masters, were continually seeking an opportunity to revolt. Consequently, the Spartans all the more strengthened their power to surpass the helots. The Spartans were forced to organise their state like a military camp in order to keep down the large subject population. Everything was subordinated to military needs. Since the Spartans did not have to earn a living, they devoted their whole life from the age of seven onwards to military training. At birth, each child was examined by state officials who decided whether it was fit to live. Those judged unfit were abandoned to die. Boys were taken from their mothers at the age of seven and put under control of the state for military training. The long and intensive training made the Spartans the best soldiers of the world, and the state, the most militarily dominated. The strategies and policies of Sparta accounted for the power of conquest.

At the head of Spartan government were two kings who led the Spartan army on its campaigns. Additionally, five men, known as ephor①, were elected each year and were responsible for the education of youth and the conduct of all citizens. A council of elders, composed of the two kings and twenty-eight citizens over the age of sixty decided on the issues that would be presented to an assembly. This assembly of all male citizens did not debate, but only voted on the issues by the council of elders.

The Spartans isolated themselves from the outside world in order to protect the military safety of the polis. They banned foreigners from visiting Sparta out of the fear of new things and ideas. Moreover, subjects like philosophy, literature and the arts were prohibited from being studied by Spartan citizens. The rulers spared no effort to shape their people into fearless warriors. Consequently, the Spartans contributed little to the Greek humanities; however, they are remembered for their art of war.

In the 6th century B. C. , Sparta gained greater control of Peloponnesus② by organizing an alliance of almost all the Peloponnesian states. By 500 B. C. , Sparta had become a powerful military city-state and took charge of order and stability in Peloponnesus.

Athenians had been developing a different type of society from Sparta. By 700 B. C. , Athens had established a unified polis on the peninsula of Attica. The polis had fallen under the control of its aristocrats. The polis was originally by no means a harmonious community since it possessed few powers. Near the end of the 7th century

---

① ephor：古代斯巴达民选的五长官之一。

② Peloponnesus：斯巴达几十年如一日，保守、反对改革，缺乏社会进步，但是斯巴达凭借优良军队，对内镇压，对外扩张，但鉴于邻邦誓死抵抗，斯巴达的扩张受到限制。于是斯巴达改兼并政策为同盟政策，即各盟邦不向其纳贡，只承认其盟主地位，这个同盟就是古希腊历史上有名的“伯罗奔尼撒同盟”，斯巴达就是依靠自己的军事实力在这个同盟中称霸的。

B. C. , Athens faced political turmoil because of serious economic problems. Many farmers became slaves when they were unable to repay the loans they had borrowed from their aristocratic neighbours. Pleas to cancel debts and to give land to the poor could be heard everywhere. Athens seemed on the edge of civil war.

In 594 B. C. , all parties agreed upon the appointment of Solon as chief magistrate with full powers for reform. He restored to the debtors full title to their land, freed all citizens who had been enslaved for unpaid debts and made such enslavement illegal in the future. But many problems remained unsolved. In short, Solon's contribution was to create the constitutional base upon which the Athenian democracy of later times was to be built. Pisistratus, an aristocrat, seized power in 560 B. C. He made Athens wealthy, powerful and a centre of culture. He preserved the Solonian constitution, but made sure that he and his family held all the offices of state. He was succeeded by his sons who proved incapable. In about 506 B. C. , Cleisthenes gained control. He abolished the old tribes, setting up ten new ones that were based on territorial divisions rather than kinship. This innovation contributed much to weakening the political power of the aristocrats. He established a new Council of 500 for which all male citizens over thirty were eligible. With these reforms of Cleisthenes, by 500 B. C. Athens had emerged as a democracy, while Sparta remained a militarised and regimented society.

Athenian democracy reached its summit during the Age of Pericles (461—429 B. C.). Although an aristocrat by birth, Pericles was an earnest democrat who completed the transference of power to the Assembly, of which all adult male citizens were members. He also introduced "pay for service" in most public offices so that the poor could afford to assume such offices. A large body of city magistrates, usually chosen by lot, without regard to class, handled routine administrative tasks. That means citizen of the polis might have an opportunity to serve as the chief administrative officer of Athens for one day. Athenians had also devised the practice of ostracism to protect themselves from overly ambitious politicians. When the decision at hand was to banish or exile a person they disliked or considered most harmful to the polis, citizen peers would cast their vote by writing the name of the person on the piece of pottery; the vote was counted and if unfavourable, the person was put out of the city.

By far the most important form, with regard to later Western history, was the Athenian democracy, particularly as it appeared in the Age of Pericles during the 5th century B. C.

Section Four Greece in Classical Period[①] (c. 500—330 B.C.)

In 480 B.C., the alliance of the southern Greek city-states succeeded in repulsing the Persian invasion. This crucial victory is viewed as the transition from the Archaic period to Classical period of Greece.

According to historians, Classical Greece mainly refers to Greek culture from around 500 B.C. to the conquest of Greece by the Macedonian king Philip Ⅱ in 338 B.C. This period saw the flowering of democracy in Athens under the leadership of Pericles (495—429 B.C.) and witnessed the mighty confrontation at the end of the 5th century B.C. between Greek states and the mammoth Persian Empire—the Persian Wars. It was a period of great achievements deriving from democracy in Athens under Pericles' leadership. Many of the lasting contributions of the Greeks occurred during this period.

The Persian Wars[②] The growth and expansion into the Mediterranean of Greek civilisation would inevitably bring itself into contact with the big power to the east—the Persian Empire. As early as the mid-sixth century B.C., the Persian Empire had already conquered the Ionian Greek cities in western Asia Minor.

The Persian Wars were a series of wars between Greek states and Persia, in particular two invasions of Greece by Persia (490 B.C., 480—479 B.C.). When Darius Ⅰ came to power in Persia in 522 B.C., the Ionian Greek city-states in Anatolia were under Persian control. They rose up unsuccessfully in the Ionian revolt (499—494 B.C.). Athens supported Ionia, which irritated Darius Ⅰ and stimulated him to invade Greece in 492 B.C.; however, his fleet was destroyed in a storm, this invasion came to nothing. In 490 B.C. Darius Ⅰ massed huge troops on a plain near Athens. The Greek general Miltiades led his ten-thousand infantrymen and annihilated the Persians in the Battle of Marathon[③]. In 480 B.C. the Persians under Xerxes Ⅰ invaded Greece again. The whole of Greece was forced to unite together, with Sparta in charge of the army and Athens of the navy. Spartans were defeated at the Battle of Thermopylae, leaving the way clear for the Persian army to attack Athens where Persians burned, killed and

---

① 古典时代是古希腊文明由盛到衰的时代。具体地说，公元前5世纪是古希腊文明的繁荣时期，公元前5世纪末到前4世纪中叶，是古典文明的衰落时期。

② The Persian Wars：希波战争从公元前500年开始到前449年结束，前后约半个世纪，这次战争主要集中在前492到479年期间，波斯先后向希腊本土发动大规模的进攻。

③ Battle of Marathon：马拉松战役，发生在第二次希波战争时期。波斯大军在马拉松平原登陆，直指雅典。在万分紧急的情况下，一位名叫米太雅德的将军，率1万步兵大胜波斯大军，这就是著名的以少胜多的马拉松战役。这次战役中波斯10万大军阵亡6400人，而雅典1万人只阵亡192人。战役结束后，米太雅德将军派一名叫斐力庇第斯的战士回雅典报捷，他在三小时内跑完了从马拉松到雅典的路程，共42公里，当他回到雅典时，只喊了一句："高兴吧，我们胜利了！"就倒地而死。为了纪念这位英雄，决定从1896年开始，即近代第一届奥林匹克运动会期间，定期举行马拉松赛跑。

looted (480 B. C.) the city. This war ended with the defeat of the Persian navy at the Battle of Salamis, compelling Xerxes to withdraw to Persia. Afterward, the Persian army was defeated again at the Battle of Plataea in 479 B. C. and their navy met a similar fate at Mycale on the Anatolian coast. Sporadic fighting went on for 30 more years, during which Athens formed the Delian League[①] to free the Ionians. Finally *The Peace of Callias*[②](449 B. C.) ended the hostilities.

The Great Peloponnesian War After the defeat of the Persians, the Greeks were divided into two major camps: Sparta and Athens. The two rivals, different from each other in a wide range from social structure to ideologies, were unable to tolerate the other's system. The divergence evolved into a radical conflict—the Peloponnesian War that broke out in 431 B. C.

At the beginning of the war, both sides were confident of their winning strategies. The Athenians planned to shelter themselves behind the solid walls while the overseas empire and navy kept them supplied. The Spartans kept attacking Athens hoping to fight them beyond the walls. The Athenians fought on for another twenty-seven years before Athens was besieged and surrendered in 404 B. C. The Athenian Empire was destroyed.

The Great Peloponnesian War weakened the Greek states and certainly destroyed any possibility of cooperation among the Greek states. The next seventy years of Greek history saw the continuous conflicts among Sparta, Athens and Thebes, a New Greek power, but the Greeks didn't notice that Macedonia to their north had grown more powerful and threatening.

The Culture of Classical Greece In the 4th century the great city-states fell prey to the invading Macedonians from the north. However, many scholars are convinced that the high point of Western civilisation is represented by Athens in the 5th century B. C. and to them, it remains the most civilised society that has yet existed. Over two thousand years later, the world still marvels at the accomplishments of the Athenians—in art and architecture, literature, history, political theories, science, mathematics, philosophy, and religion.

History is essentially story-telling, the story of what has happened in the past. Accounts of these events can be verified by records and evidence from the past, and we take them to be true precisely because history claims an authority based on facts. The

---

① Delian League：提洛同盟。公元前 478 年，雅典组织中希腊、爱琴诸岛和小亚细亚的一些城邦形成新的同盟，同盟金库设在提洛岛，故名"提洛同盟"。其目的原是为继续对付波斯联合作战，后成为雅典称霸工具，又称"雅典海上同盟"。公元前 454 年同盟金库迁到雅典。公元前 404 年，由于在伯罗奔尼撒战争中战败，雅典被迫解散提洛同盟。

② *The Peace of Callias*：在以雅典为首的希腊城邦联盟的有力抗击下，公元前 449 年，希腊和波斯双方缔《结卡里亚斯和约》。波斯放弃对爱琴海的霸权，承认小亚细亚海岸希腊城市的独立。持续半个世纪之久的波希战争以希腊人的胜利而告终。

first historian Herodotus (484 — 424 B. C.) was a citizen of the Greek city-state of Halicarnassus in Asia Minor. He undertook to record the history of the wars between the city-states of Greece and the great Persian Empire, entitled *The History of the Persian Wars*. He skilfully unfolded his tale in nine books, each being named for one of the nine muses of Greek mythology.

Herodotus went beyond simply story-telling. He examined sources critically, covered subjects systematically, analysed the events and provided explanations in rational rather than mythical terms. For this reason, he earned the title "the father of history" and his deeds justified the term of history—the Greek word historia (history) means "research" or "investigation".

Thucydides (460—400 B. C.) was the greatest historian of the ancient world and might even be ranked as the greatest historian in Western civilisation. Thucydides' primary concern was to present the true history of the Peloponnesian war in the 5th century B. C. between Athens and Sparta. He was a general in the Athenian army and was later sent into exile for twenty years for his failure to prevent a Spartan force from capturing an important military stronghold. He spent much of his time travelling around and observing the course of the struggle. As an active participant of the war, he witnessed the war; as a keen observer, he tried to be completely objective. He was so critical that he never told any story that could not be verified by documentary evidence or eye-witness accounts, or that failed to stand the test of a logical analysis. Thucydides often put speeches into the mouths of historical personages to flash back historical scenes, such as Pericles' Funeral oration delivered in 431 B. C. and the Melian Dialogue①. He wrote to preserve the memory of the great events. He wrote to enlighten and to teach people of future generations to avoid the mistakes the Greeks had made.

As we know, drama was created by the Greeks. Greek Dramas were part of the religious festivals aimed more to educate than entertain. They were used to educate citizens and were supported by the state for that reason. The form remained stable with a cast of three male actors. Action was very limited, because the emphasis was on the story and its meaning. Content was generally based on myths or legends that the audience already knew. The most important heritage of Greek drama is its tragedies.

---

① Melian Dialogue：米洛斯人的对话。古希腊历史学家修昔底德的著作《伯罗奔尼撒战争史》第五册 85～113 中的章节。是一个经典的关于国际关系上自由与现实的冲撞的例证，经常在被称为"现实主义思考"的讨论中用来解释说明。历史背景是公元前 461 年伯罗奔尼撒战争期间雅典人侵米洛斯这段历史的一部分。米洛斯人一直拒绝提洛同盟所施加的影响，并且同样反抗着这场入侵。雅典人让米洛斯人作出选择：米洛斯岛可以向雅典进贡来幸免于难，或者和雅典作战，从而被摧毁。米洛斯人同样提供了几个观点：向米洛斯人展现仁慈将会给雅典赢得更多的盟友。斯巴达人会帮助他们，以及神会保护他们。由于米洛斯人拒绝臣服，雅典立刻开始了对米洛斯的包围。一支从雅典赶来的增援部队，和预料中没有赶来增援的斯巴达人，以及米洛斯人内部的背叛行为确保了雅典人的胜利。米洛斯人的对话最终说明：强者做他们想做的，而弱者承受他们必须承受的苦难。

Tragedies were often the suffering of a hero, usually ending in disaster. Aeschylus was the first tragedian.

Aeschylus (525－456 B. C.) was said to have fought brilliantly at the Battle of Marathon (490 B. C.). His works were written during the flourishing period of early Athenian hegemony in Greece. His *Suppliants* (490 B. C) is known as the earliest of surviving Greek tragedies. *The Persians* (472 B. C.) is embedded with the developing Greek conception of civilised law and order. *Prometheus Bound*① presents the basic conflict between reason and tyranny; force represented by Zeus and justice by Prometheus. His latest tragedies were the *Oresteia* tetralogy② (458 B. C.), which consists of *Agamemnon*, *The Libation Bearers*, *The Furies* (the fourth, a satyr play, *Proteus*, is lost). *Agamemnon* remains the greatest of the tragedies of Aeschylus.

Sophocles (496－406 B. C.) was born into a noble Athenian family and was said to have lived a very contented, happy life, communing daily with his friends or companions, the great minds of the Periclean Age—Herodotus, Socrates, Thucydides, Aeschylus, and Euripides, etc. He witnessed the prosperity of the splendid Age of Pericles and died just before the fall of Athens (404 B. C.). Sophocles established himself as a talented poet and more than 120 plays are attributed to him, of which *Oedipus the King*③ is especially popular with modern readers. According to Delphic oracle, Oedipus (the king of Thebes) was to slay his father Laius and marry his mother.

Euripides (485－406 B. C.) tried to create more realistic characters. *The Medea*④ is generally agreed to be the most powerful of the surviving plays. The greatest of all his plays was *The Bacchae*, which dealt with the introduction of the hysterical rites associated with Dionysus, god of wine.

Greek tragedies dealt with universal themes still relevant to our day. They probed such problems as the nature of good and evil, the conflict between spiritual values and the demands of the individuals. The tragedy was that humans were free but could only operate within limitations imposed by the gods.

Greek comedy developed later than tragedy. We see comedies first at the festival of Dionysus in Athens in 488/487 B. C. Aristophanes⑤ (450 － 385 B. C.) used both grotesque and obscene jokes to entertain the audience which are examples of Old

---

① *Prometheus Bound*：埃斯库罗斯的代表作《被束缚的普罗米修斯》，塑造了一个为人类谋福利而不屈不挠的高大斗士的形象。

② tetralogy：古代希腊四联剧。

③ *Oedipus the King*：索福克里斯的代表作《俄狄浦斯王》歌颂了主人公对命运的积极反抗的精神。索福克里斯是“戏剧艺术的荷马”。

④ *The Medea*：《美狄亚》，是有“舞台上的哲学家”之称的尤利披底斯的代表作，谴责了那些喜新厌旧的男子，赞扬了一位痴情和受骗女子的反抗精神。

⑤ 阿里斯托芬，有“喜剧之父”之称，其作品以反映社会现实为主。

Comedy. *The Clouds* (423 B. C.) contributed to his ill repute among Athenians. Although the execution of Socrates demonstrated the limits of free speech in Athens, the liberty with which Aristophanes challenged public policy and social convention suggests a very open society.

Philosophy is a Greek word that originally meant "love of wisdom". The Greeks believed that the universe is a rational order, operating according to fixed laws. Early Greek philosophers were concerned with the development of rational thought about the nature of the universe and the place of divine forces in it.

"Love of wisdom" was interpreted in a different light in the fifth-century Athens by the Sophists, a group of philosophical teachers, who contended that the universe was beyond the reach of the human mind. Individuals should give priority to self-improving; thus the study of human behaviour was the sole worthwhile object. The Sophists focused on developing their skill in public speaking. They were experts in opening debates and stirring audiences. Under the influence of the Sophists, much importance was attached to rhetoric in democratic Athens. According to the Sophists, true wisdom consisted of being able to perceive and pursue one's own good. Therefore, in this philosophy, neither absolute right nor absolute wrong existed. This was considered harmful to society and especially dangerous to the values of young people.

Socrates (469 — 399 B. C.) left no writings; we know about him only from his pupils, especially his most famous one, Plato. Socrates was a stonemason with a true love for philosophy and great fondness for teaching his pupils in the unique question-and-answer or dialectical method known as "Socratic method". His teachings emphasised a new conception of individual morality as the foundation of the Athenian state. According to Socrates, all real knowledge is within each person; only critical examination was needed to call it forth. This was the real task of philosophy since "the unexamined life is not worth living". Because Socrates boldly opposed authority and ruthlessly revealed public ignorance, he was brought to trial in 399 B. C. for corrupting the Athenian youth and sentenced to death. He refused the opportunity to escape due to his respect for Athenian law. He died by drinking hemlock juice. He was remembered by his friends and followers as a martyr for the cause of the freedom for the spirit, and as a teacher of incomparable intellectual and spiritual power.

Plato (429 — 347 B. C.) was one of Socrates' disciples and was considered as the greatest philosopher of Western civilisation. His real name was Aristocles, but he soon acquired the nickname Plato ("the broad-shouldered one"). To follow his teacher, Plato adopted the oral teaching method and attached much importance to educating the young. He established his famous Academy about 385 B. C., the first university in the west, with the chief purpose of preparing his pupils for political service through the study of science and philosophy. Unlike his teacher Socrates, Plato wrote a lot. His writings are in the form of dialogues, with Socrates as the principal philosophical debater.

The Allegory presents most of Plato's major philosophical theories: his belief that the world revealed by our senses is not the real world but only a poor copy of it, and that the real world can be understood only intellectually; his idea that knowledge cannot be transferred from teacher to student, but rather that education consists of directing the student's mind toward what is real and important and allowing him to apprehend it for himself; his faith that the universe ultimately is good and his conviction that enlightened men have an obligation to the rest of society, and that a good society must be one in which truly wise men are the rulers.

The Republic, the earliest Utopian literature and Plato's best known work, touches on the nature of justice and an ideal state ruled by philosophers. It was also his criticism of Athenian democracy. According to Plato, intoxicated by liberty, the citizens of a democracy could lose all sense of balance, self-discipline, and respect for law: "The citizens becomes so sensitive that they resent the slightest application of control as intolerable tyranny, and in their resolve to have no master they end up by disregarding even the law, written or unwritten."① To retain his hold over the state, the tyrant "begins by stirring up one war after another, in order that the people may feel their need of a leader"②. His *The Apology of Socrates* is the idealised dramatisation of Socrates' last plea and reveals a new concept of spiritual freedom in Greece.

Aristotle (384—322 B. C.) was a native of Macedonia. At the age of seventeen or eighteen he enrolled as a student in the Academy and stayed there for twenty years until the death of Plato (348 B. C.). He later became a tutor to Alexander the Great in 335 B. C. When Alexander was out to conquer the world, Aristotle returned to Athens and established a school, the Lyceum or Peripatetic School. At the death of Alexander in 323 B. C., Aristotle found himself unpopular with Athens for his association with Alexander, so he left Athens and died the following year in exile.

Aristotle is Plato's chief rival for philosophical pre-eminence in the world of antiquity. Like Plato, Aristotle believed in universal principles or forms, but he believed that form and matter were inseparable. Aristotle began a shift in his scientific research from Platonic Idealism③ to the examination and classification of material phenomena.

Aristotle's interests were wide ranging and his contributions to knowledge were immense, covering nearly every field of higher learning: ethics, logic, politics, poetry, astronomy, geology, biology, and physics. Under his direction various scientific studies

① Plato, *The Rupublic*, trans. F. M. Cornford, New York: Oxford University Press, 1945, p. 289.

② Plato, *The Rupublic*, trans. F. M. Cornford, New York: Oxford University Press, 1945, p. 293.

③ Idealism：理想主义，这里是指柏拉图所倡导的乌托邦式的社会模型。

flourished, especially in the research of Theophrastus into botany and of Aristoxenus into musical theory. Aristotle wrote a great deal, but much was lost. His scientific works such as *Physics* and *On the Heavens* were considered authority, and, therefore, a serious hindrance to progress. More important works by Aristotle are *Poetics*, *Ethics*, and *Politics*. *Poetics*, concerning epic, tragedy, and comedy, is one of the most illuminating works of literary criticism. The section on tragedy was most satisfactory and famous. The *Nicomachean Ethics* is the best exposition of Greek ideas of conduct. It represents Aristotle's agreement with Plato on the point that the public and private conduct was the proper political ethic in the administration of a state. In *Politics*, Aristotle examined the constitutions of 158 states and came up with general categories for organizing governments. He thought there were three good forms of government: monarchy, aristocracy, and constitutional government, and the last one was his favourite.

The Arts and Architecture Classical Greek arts also centred in Athens, but it had begun long before. Art expressed civic life and reflected predominant Athenian aesthetic, social, and spiritual aspirations. The well known pieces of sculpture are the Discus Thrower, Venus de Milo, Laocoon group, etc.

The best example of Greek art is presented by the architecture, mainly the building of temples. The greatest example is the Parthenon, built between 447 and 432 B. C., and located on the Acropolis. The Parthenon was dedicated to Athena, the patron goddess of the city. It exemplifies the search for calmness, clarity, and freedom from superfluous detail. Greek architecture can be classified into three styles: the Doric Style (masculine), the Ionic style (the feminine style) and the Corinthian style (which is known for its ornamental luxury).

The architecture reveals much about the Greek view of life as it had developed through the earlier times to the classical period. The portion of the temple in which the tension between human aspiration and the limits of space was most evident is the pediment; developing a sculptural scene for the gentle slope below the roof required considerable ingenuity. The efforts of Greek artists to express themselves in this confining space are symbolic of the human struggle to achieve greatness despite the shortness of life and the inevitability of death. The essential elements of the Greek view of life—restraint, dignity, and proportion as well as violence, passion, and competitiveness—are all present in classical Greek art.

In Greek religion from the beginning, there was never any insistence upon a rigid and unquestioning conformance to dogmatic belief that would prevent the Greek from seeing things as they really are, and no dependence upon a consecrated priesthood for the regulation of a spiritual or civic life. This freedom was sustained by the nature of the Greek religion. The Olympian religion of the Greeks was a state institution and it was

intricately connected to every aspect of daily life. Religion was a civic cult necessary for the well-being of the state.

The works of Homer and Hesiod[①] explained how the roles of the gods gave Greek religion a definite structure. The Greeks maintained, along with the feeling of humanistic intimacy with the gods, a reverence for their religious belief as a reality, a fact that was well illustrated in Greek mythology. Festivals were also a way to honour the gods and goddesses. For example, the Olympic Festival was first held in 776 B. C. and every four years thereafter to honour Zeus.

The Greeks had a great desire to know the will of the gods. To do so, they made use of the oracle, a sacred shrine dedicated to a god or goddess who revealed the future. Delphi, the site of the shrine of Apollo, was highly regarded because of its status as a deeply trusted oracle. Before making any important decision, Greeks as early as the 8th century B. C. would travel to Delphi for Apollo's advice which was delivered by a priestess in a state of ecstasy.

Composition of Greek Society Classical Athens was a male dominant community. Only adult male citizens took part in public life. The family was an important institution in ancient Athens. It was composed of husband, wife, and children. A family's main function is to produce new citizens for the society. There were slaves in the ancient world. But slavery in most instances was a substitute for wage labour. Women were citizens, but could not own property aside from personal items, and they were expected to remain at home. They were barred from any political activity and always had a male guardian. They were kept under strict control. Most of them were cut off from any formal education. Male homosexuality was socially acceptable. It occurred between a mature man and a young male. It was an aristocratic ideal and not one practiced by the common people. The relationship was physical and educational. The Greeks had a high tolerance for the coexistence of homosexual and heterosexual. In their eyes, the two sexual orientations were natural and not viewed as social or individual problems.

The civilisation of the ancient Greeks was the fountain head of Western culture. The philosophies of Socrates, Plato, and Aristotle established the foundations of Western philosophy. The works of Herodotus and Thucydides created the discipline of history. Our literary forms nowadays are largely derived from Greek poetry and drama, especially the tragedy which contributed immensely to modern drama. A rational method of inquiry was conceived in ancient Greece.

---

① Hesiod：赫西奥德，古希腊诗人，生活在大约公元前8世纪，其作品《工作与时日》包括生产技术的指导和伦理道德的训诫；《神谱》把纷繁复杂的希腊诸神系统化为一个单一的世系，从而把希腊神话纳入了一个统一体，是希腊奥林巴斯教发展的重要里程碑。

Section Five The Hellenistic Era (330—30 B.C.)

The word Hellenistic is derived from a Greek word meaning "to imitate Greeks". It is an appropriate way, then, to describe an age that saw the extension of the Greek language and ideas to the non-Greek world of the Near East.

The Conquests of Alexander① While the Greek city-states were being hampered by continual wars, Macedonia②, a new and powerful kingdom, arose to the north. Macedonians were a Greek-speaking people, and claimed themselves Greeks; however, they were contemptuously called barbarians by the southern Greeks. Macedonians were organised into tribes, not city-states. King Philip Ⅱ (359 — 336 B. C.) turned Macedonia into the chief power of the Greek world. He was soon drawn into the interstate conflicts of the Greeks; his Macedonian army crushed the Greeks in 338 B. C. The independent Greek polis came to an end as Philip formed a league of the Greek states. Before he could invade the Persian Empire, Philip was assassinated in 336 B. C., leaving the task to his son Alexander, who became the king in 334 B. C. at the age of twenty with the consensus of the courtiers.

Young as he was, Alexander was prepared for kingship by his father, who had taken Alexander along on military campaigns and even had given him control of the cavalry at the important battle of Chaeronea. Alexander soon established his authority in securing the Macedonian frontiers and controlling the rebellious Greece. He then turned to invade the Persian Empire, which was his father's dream.

In the spring of 334 B. C., Alexander entered Asia Minor from the west with an army made up of Macedonians, Greeks and other allies. The Persian Empire, although weakened in some respects, was a strong state. Neither Alexander's fleet nor his wealth was the match of the Persians.

Alexander's first confrontation with the Persians, at the battle at the Granicus River in 334 B. C., almost cost him his life, but resulted in a major victory. Within one year the entire western half of Asia Minor was under his control. Meanwhile, the Persian king Darius Ⅲ mobilised his forces to stop Alexander's army. Before it was even clear who would be victorious, Darius deserted the army and fled for his life. He was captured with his family by Alexander. After his victory at Issus in 333 B. C., Alexander turned south and by the winter of 332 B. C., he had taken Syria, Palestine,

---

① Alexander (356—323 B. C.)：亚历山大，世界古代史上有名的帝王。

② Macedonia：马其顿，位于古希腊北部，相当于今天的阿尔巴尼亚和塞黑南部地区。当古希腊进入黄金时代时，马其顿才出现国家，腓力二世统治时期，马其顿开始强大，后来腓力于公元前336年死于宫廷阴谋，其子亚历山大继位，并开始了他的征服霸业。公元前323年，他制定了出征阿拉伯的计划，先头部队已经出发，但据说他本人在大军出发前一天暴病而死。他死后，部将立即展开争夺权利的斗争，大战的结果是帝国分裂为托勒密王国、塞琉古王国、马其顿王国。

and Egypt under his control. He took the title of pharaoh of Egypt and founded Alexandria, naming the city after himself, as the Greek administrative capital of Egypt. It became a centre of western civilisation.

In 331 B. C. , Alexander moved into the ancient Mesopotamian kingdoms, and fought the decisive battle with the Persians at Gaugamela, near Babylon. Alexander's men were clearly outnumbered by the Persian forces, but Alexander was victorious and Darius had to withdraw to spare his life.

Alexander entered Babylon and then proceeded to the Persian capitals at Susa and Persepolis and took the title and office of the Great King of the Persians, but this was not the entirety of his plan. He moved further and his vision for conquering a large area was exceedingly lofty. By summer 327 B. C. , he had entered India. He spent a long time of fighting in exotic and difficult terrain. This fact enormously dampened the morale of his troops, who complained and refused to go on. Alexander had to give in. They returned to Babylon, having suffered heavy losses on the way back. In June 323 B. C. , weakened from wounds, fever, and probably excessive alcohol, Alexander died at the young age of thirty-two.

Alexander is one of the most puzzling great figures in history. He is both a great military leader and a brave and even reckless fighter. He admired godlike hero Achilles, the warrior-hero of Homer's *Iliad*, claimed to be descended from a god Heracles (the Greek hero who came to be worshiped as a god).

Although Alexander's reign lasted only 13 years, he truly created a new age, the Hellenistic era. His destruction of the Persian monarchy had extended Greco-Macedonian rule over an enormous area. His conquests also started the spreading of Greek language, art, architecture, and literature throughout the Near East. The Greeks provided a sense of unity as a result of the diffusion of Greek culture throughout the Hellenistic world. While they spread their culture in the East, the Greeks were also inevitably influenced by eastern ways. Thus, Alexander's legacy created one of the basic characteristics of the Hellenistic world: the collision and the conflation of diverse cultures.

Culture in the Hellenistic World The Hellenistic era was a period of considerable cultural accomplishment in many areas—literature, art, science, and philosophy. The great Hellenistic cities of Alexandria and Pergamum stood out as two leading cultural centres. In both cities, cultural developments were encouraged by the rulers themselves. Rich Hellenistic kings had sufficient resources to patronise culture.

The Hellenistic era witnessed a more conscious separation of science from philosophy. In the Hellenistic age, the sciences tended to be studied in their own right. The 3rd century B. C. was marked by extraordinary advances in science, mathematics, engineering, and navigation. Nothing like it would be seen again until the scientific revolution of the 16th and 17th centuries.

Some of the work done at Alexandria was scholarship—the compilation and transmission of earlier ideas. There were few new ideas in Euclid's *Elements of Geometry*, but it became the authority for instruction in modern geometry. Aristarchus of Samos (310—230 B.C.) disputed Aristotle's theory that the Earth was the centre of the universe. Eratosthenes of Cyrene (276—194 B.C.) was a mathematician. He spent most of his life as head of the Library at Alexandria and founded mathematical geography.

The most famous scientist of the Hellenistic period was Archimedes (287—212 B.C.) of Syracuse in the western Mediterranean region. Archimedes was especially renowned for his work on the geometry of spheres and cylinders. He is said to have emphasised the importance of levers by proclaiming to the King of Syracuse: "Give me a lever and a place to stand on and I will move the earth."

Hellenistic drama favoured comedies rather than tragedies. Poets abandoned the heroic tradition even when they attempted to write epics. The *Argonautica* by Apollonius of Rhodes was probably the most popular poem of the age. Its version of Iason and Medea and the search for the Golden Fleece is romantic in its thematic approach and in its phraseology.

Painting and sculpture flourished as never before. Painting reached unprecedented excellence, but because the fragility of paintings on the media of those times, none have survived. As for sculpture, we can appreciate part of its essence in Roman copies. The Greek sculpturers designed exaggerated facial expressions and muscular tension on figures to bring forth their emotion.

The stream of Greek philosophy continued and Athens remained the prime centre of philosophy even in the Hellenistic world. This centre, the home of Socrates, Plato, and Aristotle, continued to attract the most illustrious philosophers from the Greek world. New schools of philosophical thought reinforced Athens's reputation as a philosophical centre. Hellenistic philosophy reflected the shift in values, abandoning political theory in favour of individualistic prescriptions for the good life. They argued that the best life was a life close to nature, and that wisdom lay in abandoning worldly goods and ambition.

Zeno (335—263 B.C.), a native of Phoenician Cyprus, established a school at Athens named the Stoa. Followers of this school, the Stoic, believed that living in harmony with nature was essential—the rule of nature was the divine principle of the universe. Each human being and each object had the logos within it and acted according to a divine, predetermined plan. Sickness, death, and misfortune were all part of a

providential order that could not be escaped but endured. Stoicism[①] was a philosophy that gave great importance to the exercise of self-control and to overcoming destructive emotions to improve one's moral and ethical well-being; that virtue leads to happiness. To them, happiness, the supreme good, could be found only in virtue, which meant essentially living in harmony with the will of God. One achieved happiness by choosing to follow the will of God through the free exercise of one's own will. Stoicism was rooted in physical and epistemological principles derived at some distance from Aristotle. Subsequently, stoicism was a philosophy embraced by many intellectuals. It became the dominant belief among the Roman upper classes and strongly influenced the development of Christianity.

Stoicism's chief rival was Epicureanism[②]. Epicurus (341—270 B. C.), the founder of Epicureanism, established a school in Athens near the end of the 4th century B. C. Epicurus' famous belief in a doctrine of "pleasure" began with his view of the world. Though he did not deny the existence of the gods, he did not believe they played any active role in the world. The universe ran on its own. This left human beings free to follow self-interest as a basic motivating force. Happiness was the goal of life, and the means to achieve it was the pursuit of pleasure, the only true good. Pleasure came from both body and spirit. Epicurus distinguished active pleasure from passive pleasure and gave priority to the latter. Happiness of body was imposed on the human; however, the human could control happiness of spirit. On the other hand, one should refrain from desires to maintain peace of mind. Epicurus thoroughly rejected the assumption that the greatest good for a human being was virtuous activity. He maintained that the greatest good for a human being was the tranquillity that virtuous activity always and contemplative activity sometimes, brings about.

Epicureanism and especially Stoicism appealed to large numbers of people in the Hellenistic world. They both attached great importance to human happiness, but their doctrines were a radical change in the thought of the Greeks. To the classical Greeks, individual pleasure was closely related to the polis and everyone pursued happiness in the community. In the Hellenistic kingdoms, in contrast, with the clash and fusion of different cultures, collective consciousness generally weakened and individuals began to turn to new philosophies to fulfil personal pleasure. A new openness to thoughts of universality could also emerge. For some people, Stoicism embodied this larger sense of

---

① Stoicism：斯多葛学派，是塞浦路斯岛人芝诺(约前 336～约前 264)于公元前 300 年左右在雅典创立的学派，是希腊化时代一个有极大影响的思想派别，被认为是自然法理论的真正奠基者。斯多葛学派认为世界理性即神性决定事物的发展变化，因此人应协调自身，与宇宙的大方向保持一致。斯葛多学派是唯心主义的。

② Epicureanism：伊壁鸠鲁学说，是古希腊最完整的快乐主义道德理论，主要宗旨是要人达到不受干扰的快乐状态。伊壁鸠鲁学派认为快乐是生活的目的，是天生的最高的善。但是应当区分不同的快乐，解除对神灵和死亡的恐惧，达到身体健康和心灵平静。

community. The appeal of new philosophies in the Hellenistic era can also be explained by the apparent decline in certain aspects of traditional religion, which we can see by examining the status of Hellenistic religion.

When the Greeks spread throughout the Hellenistic kingdoms, their gods no longer seemed sufficient to satisfy peoples' emotional needs. They began to seek the answer from the numerous religious cults of the eastern world. Hence in the Hellenistic cities of the Near East, the traditional civic cults of their own gods and foreign cults existed side by side, and the strongest appeal of eastern religions to Greeks came from the mystery religions, such as the Egyptian deities. There are the same fundamental premises in all of the mystery religions: individuals could pursue a path to salvation and achieve eternal life by worshiping with a savior god or goddess who had died and risen again.

The artistic and intellectual achievements of the Greeks within a relatively brief period were remarkable. Greek sculpture established aesthetic standards that guided subsequent artists for centuries, and the influence of Hellenistic architecture is still powerful in the West today. The tragedies of the 5th-century B. C. Athens and the myths with which they dealt have formed the basis of a long and continuing literary tradition and the influence of Plato and Aristotle on Western thought has been incalculable. The Hellenistic Age witnessed the culmination of centuries of scientific speculation in which Greeks drew on the accumulated wisdom of Egypt and Western Asia. Western political thought also owes much to the Greeks in general and to the articulation of democratic ideals in Athens, in particular. The Greeks' difficulty in envisioning a state larger than the polis, however, undermined the endurance of their civilisation. Under the great influence of the Greeks, the Romans built a complex empire.

Chapter Review

This chapter mainly depicted the social development of Greece and the unique achievements in the intellectuals' and artists' new vision of humankind shown in their representative works in different historical periods. The political consciousness that flowered in the Hellenic world bequeathed an enduring legacy to humankind. The great struggle of the 5th century B. C. may be regarded as the high-water mark of classical Greek civilisation. The Greek legacy to Western society was their habits of thought together with a mass of learning and speculation drawn from the most diverse sources. The Greeks borrowed the ideas and beliefs of others at the very beginning. In doing so, they formed a kind of intellectual unity which was passed on intact to the Romans and from the Romans to the modern Western society. However, Greek thought has its limitations. The Peloponnesian Wars revealed the flaw at the heart of the Greek society. Be it good or bad, the ancient world is viewed through Greek eyes.

Exercise

Ⅰ. *According to the information provided in this chapter, choose the correct alternative among A, B, C, and D that can complete each of the following statements.*

1. Thucydides' primary concern was to present the true history of ________ in the 5th century B. C. between Athens and Sparta.

   A. the Persian war　　B. Sparta

   C. the Peloponnesian war　　D. Athens

2. Greek dramas were part of ________ aimed more to educate than entertain.

   A. ceremonies　　B. politics

   C. education　　D. religious festivals

3. ________ was the founder of Epicureanism.

   A. Zeno　　B. Epicurus　　C. Archimedes　　D. Socrates

4. The Hellenistic era witnessed a more conscious separation of science from ________.

   A. art　　B. history　　C. literature　　D. philosophy

5. *The Republic*, the earliest ________ literature, Plato's best known work touches on the nature of justice and an ideal state ruled by philosophers.

   A. Utopian　　B. classic　　C. romantic　　D. modern

Ⅱ. *Fill in the blanks with what you have learned in this chapter.*

1. The English archaeologist Arthur Evans proved to have found the palace at Knossos and named it Minoan after ________, the legendary king of Crete who reigned in the mid 2000 B. C.
2. Homer's epic poetry the *Iliad* deals with the alliance of the states of the southern mainland of Greece, led by Agamemnon, the king of ________, in their ten-year war against the city of Troy.
3. Homer's world reflects the values of aristocratic of ________ and ________.
4. The centre of classical Greek civilisation was the ________ of city-state.
5. Classic Greece mainly refers to Athens in from around 500 B. C. to the conquest of Greece by ________ in 338 B. C.

Ⅲ. *According to what you have learned, answer the following questions briefly in your own words.*

1. What role did Homer's epics play in the Greek culture?
2. What is meant by the Greeks in a Dark Age? Who is the most remarkable poet in this period?
3. What were the main Greek city-states? What were the major conflicts between them?
4. Why was the civilisation of the ancient Greeks the fountainhead of Western

culture?

5. What is meant by the Hellenistic world?

Ⅳ. *With critical analysis, answer the following essay questions in your own words.*

1. What's the origin of Democracy? Please make some comments on Greek Polis.

2. What caused the decline of Greek states?

Ⅴ. *Work in small groups and make comparisons based on the following topic.*

Ancient Greece was an enlightened period in Western civilisation in terms of ideological trends or "rule of law" thoughts. Meanwhile, these thoughts got well developed in China's Spring-Autumn and Warring States Period. Please compare and contrast the thoughts in Ancient Greece and that of China's Spring-Autumn and Warring States Period.

Voices on Key Points

Dark Age

Everybody thinks that this civilisation has lasted a very long time but it really does take very few grandfathers' granddaughters to take us back to the dark ages.

——Gertrude Stein

We have relegated the saints to a pink and blue and gold world of plaster statuary that belongs to the past; it is a hangover, a relic, of the Dark Ages when men were the children of fantasy's magic.

——C. Kilmer Myers

Homer's World

Homer has taught all other poets the art of telling lies skilfully.

——Aristotle

Homer's whole language, the language in which he lived, the language that he breathed, because he never saw it, or certainly those who formed his tradition never saw it, in characters on the pages. It was all on the tongue and in the ear.

——Robert Fitzgerald

Athens

A great city, whose image dwells in the memory of man, is the type of some great idea. Rome represents conquest; Faith hovers over the towers of Jerusalem; and Athens embodies the pre-eminent quality of the antique world, Art.

——Benjamin Disraeli

How great are the dangers I face to win a good name in Athens.

——Alexander the Great

Suggested reading

1. Boardman, John, et al. *The Oxford History of the Classical World*. Oxford:

Oxford University Press, 1986.

2. Kitto, H. D. F. *The Greek*. Baltimore: Penguin Books, 1957.
3. (美)保罗·麦克金德里克,晏绍祥译:《会说话的希腊石头》,浙江人民出版社 2000 年版。
4. (美)戴尔·布朗主编,李旭影译:《爱琴海沿岸的奇异王国》,华夏出版社 2002 年版。
5. (英)列昂纳德·柯特勒尔著,卢剑波译:《爱琴文明探源》,四川人民出版社 1985 年版。
6. (英)吉尔伯特·默雷著,孙席珍等译:《古希腊文学史》,上海译文出版社 1988 年版。
7. (俄)俄尼·库恩编著,朱志顺译:《希腊神话》,上海译文出版社 2006 年版。
8. 吴于廑:《古代的希腊和罗马》,三联书店 2008 年版。

Chapter Three Roman Civilisation (753 B.C. —476 A.D.)

Rome is not built in a day.
Every road leads to Rome.
When in Rome do as Romans do.

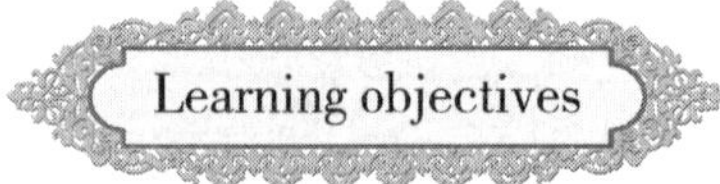

After reading this chapter, you will be able to:

1. *Know the historical context of ancient Rome and be familiar with Roman history;*
2. *Know Roman Law and its influence on western civilisation;*
3. *Understand the origin and development of Christianity;*
4. *Be acquainted with ancient Romans' achievements in such fields as literature and philosophy;*
5. *Be clear about Roman social life, public life and morality.*

古代罗马兴起于意大利半岛台伯河畔，经过几个世纪的对外扩张，罗马由一个小城邦发展成为地跨欧亚非三洲的世界帝国。罗马政体发展先后经历了王政时代(约前753～前509)、共和时代(前509～前27)和帝国时代(前27-395)。公元395年，罗马帝国分裂为东西两部分。西罗马帝国亡于476年。东罗马帝国(即拜占庭帝国)变为封建国家，1453年为奥斯曼帝国所灭。

罗马文化是对希腊文化的继承和发展，它在宗教、哲学、文学和艺术等方面明显受到希腊文明的影响，但在政治与法律方面，罗马远远超越了希腊。古罗马对西方文明的重要贡献之一就是其完备的法律体系，罗马人的法律精神对后世影响深远。罗马帝国的特定历史环境孕育了基督教，并为其传播提供了有利条件。公元2～3世纪，基督教在罗马的广泛传播深刻影响了罗马的政治、经济和文化。古罗马的公共建筑体现了罗马艺术的最高成就，罗马人修筑了畅通的道路、宏大的广场、壮观的竞技场、奢华的公共浴池和复杂的城市水道。罗马人广泛吸收四邻各族的文化成果，创造了罗马文明，为世界文化增添了新的财富。

In the years when Greek civilisation was at its height, Rome was still a modest settlement in central Italy. Poor and surrounded by powerful enemies, it survived by developing a superb army and a political system that was based upon the active participation of its citizens and the rule of law. By the middle of the 3rd century B. C. Rome controlled the Italian peninsula. By 133 B. C. it had defeated both Carthage and Macedon and acquired an empire that stretched from Spain to Greece.

The Romans were a practical people. Unlike the Greeks, who reserved their citizenship for small, select groups, the Romans often offered their citizenship to the peoples they conquered, thus laying the groundwork for a strong, integrated empire. The Romans also did not hesitate to borrow ideas and culture from the Greeks. Roman strength lay in government, law and engineering. The Romans knew how to govern people, establish legal structures, and construct the roads that took them to the ends of the known world. They applied systematic laws, political organisations, advanced engineering and the Latin language throughout their empire. Even after the Romans were gone, those same gifts continued to play an important role in the civilisations that came after them. The Romans made the right decisions at the right time, which is to say, the Romans were a people distinguished by a high degree of political wisdom.

Section One The Rise of Rome (753－509 B. C.)

The Origins of Rome We know little about primitive Rome①. The Latin, one of the main branches of Indo-European people, moved into Italy and settled in the plain of

① 罗马城的起源一直是模糊不清且争议颇多的问题，甚至在罗马时期对它的起源和发展进行解释的神话和传说就有很多种。早在公元前两千纪年后期的青铜时代，该地区已经出现了某种形式的聚落。

Latium between the Apennines and the Tyrrhenian Sea. Rome was probably developed from a small village on the plain where the geographical position was fairly favourable. Located at the Tiber fords, Rome benefited from the fertile flood plain and had access to the sea. Built within the hills, Rome was easy to defend. In a word, Rome had a very good central location in Italy from which to expand.

Ancient Italy was the home to several groups of people besides the Latin who later founded Rome. The development of Rome was greatly influenced by the Etruscans[①] in the north and Greeks in the south.

The origin of the Etruscans is not clear. Etruscans settled north of Rome in Etruria. The word "Rome" is derived from the Etruscan word "rumon" (river). In the 7th century B. C., they expanded and became dominant in culture and economy in much of the area known now as Italy. Rome was believed by historians to have been under Etruscans' control. In the next century Etruscans were at the height of their power. In the 5th century B. C., Etruscan power began to decline. The true nature of the relationship between Rome and the Etruscans is unclear. According to Livy (Titus Liviue, 59 B. C. —17 A. D.), who wrote about Rome's early history, Etruscan rule may reflect nothing more than the cultural dominance of a more advanced culture over its neighbour. Etruscan influence contributed greatly to Roman civilisation. The Romans adopted the Etruscan alphabet, learned Etruscan metalworking, civic planning, and architecture, and adopted many Etruscan religious customs and political institutions. Etruscans had a great impact on Rome in the way of urbanisation. By the beginning of the 6th century B. C., Rome had changed from a pastoral community to a city.[②] Etruscans were capable of an outstanding building programme, which may have led later to the Romans' construction legacy to the world.

The Greeks had also considerable influence on Rome. The Greeks reached southern Italy during the age of Greek colonisation (750—550 B. C.) and brought with them their alphabetic writing system and their advanced art and literature, etc. With more intimate contact with the Greeks, the Etruscans became more and more mature. They created an alphabet according to the Greek letters, and they had their own style of sculpture and painting. They developed their religion which was based on the Greek gods, all of which was inherited by Romans. No wonder many historians consider Roman culture the continuation of Greek culture.

Early Romans Romans traced their history to legendary stories that tell of the heroes who made Rome great. According to one Roman legend, Trojan Aeneas, whose mother was Venus, the goddess of love and beauty in Roman mythology, founded the

---

① the Etruscans：伊特拉斯坎人，古代意大利西北部伊特鲁里亚地区（今意大利半岛及科西嘉岛）古老的民族。

② 伊特鲁利亚人对罗马的城市建设有很大影响，对罗马从乡村到城市的改变起了重大作用。

city of Rome after the fall of Troy. Another legend traced the origin of Rome to Romulus and Remus[①], twin sons of the god of war Mars. In the legend, the twins were saved and raised by a she-wolf after having been thrown into the Tiber River. The brothers established Rome, named for Romulus. Romulus was the first of the legendary seven kings. Whatever is the origin of Rome, humble or celebrated, Rome has written itself into history with its undoubted glory and grandeur.

The majority of early Romans were small farmers. They planted grain between rows of vines or olive trees and replaced the grain with beans or other legumes in alternate years. The Romans practiced crop rotation[②] and were careful to enrich the soil through composing and animal fertilizers. Because grazing land was scarce, there was never enough manure. Sheep were raised for their wool and for milk, while cattle were used as draft animals. Heroic efforts produced a balanced but simple diet: wheat or barley gruel supplemented by olives, cabbage, and beans. Milk, cheese, fruit, and baked bread, and meat, usually pork, was reserved for special occasions. Sheep, goats, and cattle were too valuable to be slaughtered for their meat but sometimes found their way to the table after serving as a burnt offering to the gods. Hogs provided not only hams and sausages, but also the greatest of all Romans delicacies: roast suckling pig.

Roman farms were usually worked by the owner and his familia[③]. It meant the nuclear family as well as the entire household including dependent relatives and slaves. Many families found that owning a few extra workers was a good investment. Some slaves were war captives, but most were Romans subjugated for debt. Under the early republic, slavery was not as harsh[④] as it would later become. But slaves were still property and could be sold, beaten, or killed without recourse to law. Theoretically and legally, the father, or paterfamilias, had absolute power of life and death over his children and slaves. His wife was subject to his will too, but he could neither kill nor sell her. For Rome, like ancient Greece, was a "shame" society. Reputation was vitally important, and the mistreatment of women and children was regarded as shameful. Women guarded their reputations and were generally respected. They managed the day-to-day life of the household just as their Greek counterparts.

---

① Romulus and Remus：战神马尔斯之子罗穆卢斯和雷穆斯。根据罗马人自己流行的一个神话传说，他们是特洛伊人的后代，也是战神马尔斯的后代，罗马城的建立者和罗马人的第一个王是母狼养大的罗穆卢斯。根据罗马历史学家瓦罗的推算，罗马城应在公元前753年建立。

② crop rotation：作物轮作制。

③ familia：家，包括其"核心"成员：一对配偶、子女和奴隶，以及所有品。"家长"是家中在世最年长的男性，是家族的法定主人，对其所有的子女，无论是否已结婚生子，拥有绝对的权威。其权力甚至延伸到生杀予夺之权，他有权遗弃或处死新生儿，抛弃儿童或出卖儿童为奴。只有在其死后，其子女才能独立。

④ harsh：罗马早期虽然产生了奴隶，但是奴隶的生活并不像后期那样悲惨。

Section Two The Roman Republic (509—30 B. C.)

Roman monarchy is said to have been from 753 B. C. to 509 B. C. , reigned in turn by seven kings, of whom three were Etruscans. The once powerful Etruscans made a powerful city-state of Rome. With the decline of Etruscans, Rome had conquered her Latin neighbours and incorporated them into the Roman state. The transition from a monarchy to a republican government was not an easy one. Facing threats in all directions, Rome protected itself by expanding its military power. The military expansion also enabled the Roman conquest of the Italian peninsula. During this period, early monarchical Roman government was overthrown in 509 B. C. and Rome became a Republic and shaped its practical political institutions in accord with its needs for self-defence and expansion.

The chief executive officers of the Roman Republic were the consuls[①] and praetors[②]. The two annually chosen consuls possessed the right to administer the government and lead the army. In 366 B. C. a new office, the praetor, was created. The praetor had the power to govern Rome and lead the army when the consuls were away from the city. The praetor's primary function was the execution of justice. He was in charge of the civil law as it applied to all Roman citizens. With Rome's expansion, another praetor was added in 242 B. C. to judge cases where one or both parties were non-citizens. The consuls and praetors and other elected officials served as magistrates who ran the state.

The magistrates were expected to administer the state aided by the advice of the senate. The Roman senate or council of elders held special position in the Roman Republic. The senate was a select group of about three hundred members of large landowners who served for life and whose function was to advise magistrates. Their power, influencing the entire republic and the empire that followed, derived from their legislative advisory role to the king, financial management of state funds, and supervision of provincial administration. The senate to some degree even had the force of law.

The assembly was also an element of the Roman political institution. Decisions which were not made by the Senate or by individual magistrates might be made by assemblies. The Roman Republic had a number of assemblies. The most important was

① consul：执政官，早期罗马共和国的主要行政长官。

② praetor：在 consul 之后产生的主要长官。主要职责是司法，掌管罗马城内的法律。他们在 consul 不在城内时执掌罗马政府及军队。

the Centuriate Assembly[①] which was established in the 5th century B. C. and was organised by classes based on wealth and was responsible for the election of magistrates and other officials. The Centuriate Assembly elected major magistrates, ratified treaties, and could declare war.

The Struggle of the Orders Early Roman society was divided into groups; the two largest groups were the patricians, and the plebeians[②]. The patricians who possessed wealth and power constituted an aristocratic governing class. Consuls, senators, and other magistrates were all from this class. The plebeians were the inferior class who were independent, poorer and unprivileged. The plebeians enjoyed the seemingly equal rights of voting as the patricians did, but they could not be elected government officials. Intermarriages between patricians and plebeians were forbidden. Thus, the plebeian kept on struggling for both political and social equality with the patricians. Gradually, plebeians won more ground and patricians had to compromise. In 494 B. C. , plebeians were able to vote for their spokesmen—new officials known as Tribunes[③] of the plebeians were instituted to protect the benefit of plebeians. In 445 B. C. , intermarriages between the two groups were legalised. In 336 B. C. , all citizens could strive for political offices. But at that time, officials did not earn a salary, so the equality did not really apply to the poor. The long struggle between patricians and plebeians had considerably influenced the evolution of the Roman constitution. By 287 B. C. all Roman citizens were theoretically equal under the law.

The Roman Conquest One historian of the classical civilisation stated flatly, "Far and away the most important and frequent events in ancient history are wars."[④] This statement perfectly summed up the history of Rome—the history of conquest.

Roman conquest began with that of its neighbours. At the beginning of the Republic was the prey of the neighbouring enemies: the Etruscans to the north and the Sabines[⑤], Volscians[⑥], and Aequi[⑦] to the east and south. The Latin communities on the plain of Latium felt very uneasy with the newly established power of Rome and sought

---

① Centuriate Assembly：公元前 5 世纪创立的森都里亚大会。塞尔维乌斯改革中按百人队设立森都里亚大会（百人队大会），凡是服兵役的都可参加。这个以财产原则建立的新机构，取代了以氏族血缘关系为基础的库里亚大会。库里亚大会的一些重要职权，如宣布战争、选举官吏、重大案件的审判等都转归了森都里亚大会。从此，库里亚大会逐渐地丧失其政治上的重要性。在森都里亚会议进行表决时，每个百人队只有一票，所以第一级的富有者还可操纵绝对多数，平民的胜利还是初步的。

② the patricians and the plebeians：贵族和贫民，是罗马两个主要的组成部分。贵族拥有财富和权利，执行官、议员及其他官员均从这个阶级中产生。平民虽享受同样的选举权，但不能成为政府官员。贵族和贫民不通婚。

③ Tribune：罗马护民官，是罗马平民与贵族政治斗争的产物。护民官被授权保护平民的权利，并对元老院法案和执政官法令具有否决权。

④ Michael Grant, *Ancient History*, London: Methuen & Co., Ltd., 1952, p. 128.

⑤ Sabine：萨宾人，古意大利部落，以其特殊宗教信仰和习俗著称。

⑥ Volscian：沃尔西人，古意大利民族。

⑦ Aequi：埃魁人，古意大利民族，曾长期与罗马为敌。

opportunities to overthrow it. This difficult situation might have helped to mould the character of Romans, which made Rome great. In 396 B. C. Rome defeated the offensive Etruscans. Soon Rome was confronted with the invasion of Celts, known as Gauls. Rome was once defeated. But after a series of fierce struggles, Rome was again victorious and then controlled a large part of Italy. Rome's southward expansion brought itself into direct conflict with the Greeks in southern Italy. During the first two and a half centuries of the republic's history, the Romans brought the entire Italian peninsula under their power. The cities that belonged to the alliance were known as the Latin League. By 264 B. C. Rome had conquered the whole of Italy, except the far north.

The Romans treated defeated people in a way which was totally different from that practiced by the Greeks. They knew clearly that it was in their best interest to extend citizenship to their Italian neighbours. The offer of the Roman citizenship gradually brought forth a steady and longstanding alliance with the people conquered by the Romans. Conquered towns were awarded Roman citizenship to different degrees. Some enjoyed full citizenship and discharge of military duties because their communities played the role of garrisons, while others possessed autonomy in addition to the privilege of Roman citizenship.

The Romans were not satisfied to limit themselves to the Italian peninsula and soon set their eyes on the formidable Mediterranean power—Carthage①. In north Africa, Carthage was founded by Phoenicians from Tyre around the 9th century B. C. It was located in a favourable position in the Mediterranean as it dominated the Mediterranean trade routes. Carthage was extremely wealthy. By the 3rd century B. C., the Carthaginian territory extended from the coast of northern Africa to southern Spain with Sardinia, Corsica, and western Sicily also included. Economically and militarily, Carthage and Rome matched each other in strength. Both of them wanted to dominate western Mediterranean, so in 264 B. C. they decided to fight it out.

The First Punic War② (264 – 241 B. C.) (punicus was the Latin word for Phoenician) was triggered by Rome's interference in a conflict between two Sicily cities which resulted in Rome's victory. Carthage gave up all rights to Sicily and had to pay a large sum of indemnity. Sicily became an overseas province of Rome.

Carthage people were strong-minded and would not accept this position of inferiority. After the war, Carthage made a great effort to recover its strength by extending its domains in Spain and prepared for a second war. When the Romans encouraged one of Carthage's Spanish allies to revolt against Carthage, the Second Punic

① Carthage：迦太基，位于今北非突尼斯北部。见第一章。

② The First Punic War：布匿战争，是罗马人征服西地中海，与迦太基争夺霸权的战争，因罗马人称腓尼基人为布匿人而得名。罗马与迦太基的战争共进行了三次。

War (218—201 B. C.) began with an attack of the greatest of the Carthaginian generals, Hannibal①. Leading a great army, Hannibal started from Spain, moved east, and crossed the Alps, bringing the war home to the Romans. In the history of the Roman Empire, Hannibal's attack and seizure of the Italian peninsula (218—203 B. C.) was the most severe military blow Rome ever experienced. At the Cannae battle in 216 B. C. , Rome suffered a dramatic loss and at once seemed on the brink of disaster. However, Romans held their morale and raised another army and gradually recovered. Romans used a strategy of pushing the Carthaginians out of Spain by 206 B. C. , and then they took the war directly to Carthage. A Roman army led by Scipio Africanus② decisively defeated Hannibal's army in Zama of North Africa and brought the Second Punic War to the end. Spain was made a Roman province. The western Mediterranean was totally under Roman's dominion.

The Romans wanted more: the thorough destruction of Carthage. They soon found an excuse and declared war, the third and last war with Carthage (149 — 146 B. C.). Carthage was no longer Rome's match and was made a Roman province called Africa.

The victories in the Punic Wars brought Romans more confidence and energy in dealing in the Eastern Mediterranean—the Hellenistic world. In about fifty years Rome rearranged the Hellenistic world through the strategy of diplomatic negotiation and military violence. Rome freed the Greek states and made a Roman province of Macedonia in 148 B. C. As to the Greek states, when they attempted to revolt against Rome, the destruction of the leading city Corinth was almost immediate. The inevitable result was to be Rome's subject. The king of Pergamum even presented his kingdom in his will to Rome in 133 B. C. Rome then had a province in Asia and was now the master of the Mediterranean.

Roman conquest consists of three stages: the conquest of Italy, the conquest of the West Mediterranean through the destruction of Carthage and the conquest of the Eastern Mediterranean with the domination of the Hellenistic world in that area. The long road to an Empire was engineered and paved by the Roman army who were highly trained, well equipped and strictly disciplined. Rome enjoyed the most sustained series of military triumphs the world had ever seen. The enormous wealth grabbed from the defeated opponents all financed the expansion of the Romans. The evolution of Roman political and legal institution had in some way provided elites for political or military offices. The strong and powerful Rome made her citizenship appealing to many aliens.

From humble beginnings, Rome had first conquered Italy and then an entire empire. In the mid-second century B. C. the Mediterranean world was politically united

---

① Hannibal：汉尼拔(前 247～前 183)，迦太基著名统帅。

② Scipio Africanus：大西庇阿，古罗马统帅和政治家，第二次布匿战争中罗马方面的主要将领之一。

for the first time. Roman provinces stretched from the Atlantic to Asia Minor, and those peoples who were not under Roman rule were Roman allies or dependents. The Romans understood that security depended on controlling the activities of their neighbours. They achieved this at first through alliances and grants of citizenship. Gradually, "fear of the enemy" gave way to larger ambitions. Rome's elite apparently adopted the goal of imposing order upon the world as they knew it. The Second Punic War was the turning point. After the narrow brush with catastrophe, a combination of greed and impatience led the Romans onward. The military success was a glory of the Roman Republic, but meanwhile it put Rome in the shadow of instability. Roman governors, officials and businessmen found the provinces a source of quick wealth; they were unrestrained by the Senate which was responsible for administering the overseas territories. There were soon exploitation, corruption, looting and extortion. "No administration in history has ever devoted itself so whole-heartedly to fleecing its subjects for the private benefit of its ruling class as Rome of the last age of the Republic," concluded E. Badian.① The Republic Rome was incapable of going on without violent internal change. The complaining, worn out peasant-soldiers, the demanding military leaders, and the wealth gap between the landowners and the land-losers all lead to the disappearance of Roman Republic.

Section Three The Eclipse of the Roman Republic (133—30 B.C.)

Social Conflict and the Failed Reform of the Gracchi② At the early stage of the republic of Rome, a minority of patrician and plebeian families controlled political power. As for the poor, they were primarily obedient to the ruling class although they occasionally protested for their political rights.

Social conditions changed due to the wars abroad. The peasants were exhausted by the heavy burdens of providing war materials for the countless wars. Soldiers accumulated large amounts of wealth in campaigns. And a new social class of businessmen emerged due to the development of overseas markets. There was a special class called the equites③, or equestrians, which stood between the senatorial aristocracy and the ordinary citizens. More senators also developed commercial aspirations than had been the case in earlier centuries. Eventually, commercialism and cosmopolitanism conflicted with the Roman traditional values of urban morality and rural purity. Roman society was full of conflicts between the landowners and land-losers, the rich and the

① E. Badian, *Roman Imperialism in the Late Republic*, Ithaca, N. Y.: Cornell University Press, 1971, p. 87.

② Reform of the Gracchi：格拉古兄弟改革。提比略·格拉古(Tiberius Gracchus,前 168～前 133)和盖乌斯·格拉古(Gaius Gracchus,前 154～前 121)两兄弟是罗马共和国时期著名的政治家、平民派领袖。他们在担任护民官的个自任期内领导了以土地问题为核心的改革,由于改革触犯了保守势力的利益而先后在任上被杀害。

③ equites：罗马骑士阶级,是古罗马时期上层阶级中较低等的一个阶级,位列元老阶级之下。

poor, the upper class and the lower class. The most extensive social change in Rome was the renewal of the peasantry. Slaves from the conquered regions toiled on the latifundia①. Roman soldiers found themselves landless and jobless after they came back from the battlefield.

Tiberius Gracchus (168—133 B. C.) suggested that the government take back the public domain which was illegally occupied by the squirearchy (landed gentry) and distribute the land among the poor. The Senate rejected his proposal and Tiberius sent his bill to the Plebeian Assembly which passed his bill. But on the Election Day the Senate-backed mobs murdered Tiberius and about 300 of his followers. His brother, Gaius, had the same fate for he resolved to carry on Tiberius' policies.

The Rise of Pompey, Caesar, and the First Triumvirate The social conflicts between 130—120 B. C. divided Rome into two classes, the Optimates②, composed of the senatorial aristocracy, and the Populares③, containing the plebeians and some aristocrats. Both classes competed for the backing of the equestrians.

During the war against Jugurtha④, Rome suffered from repeated defeats until Marius⑤ won the seat of consul in 107 B. C. Marius reversed this unfavourable situation using strategic military reformations under the leadership of his general, Sulla. In 105 B. C., Jugurtha was captured by Roman troops and the war ended.

Marius' military reform had a far-reaching influence on Rome. Marius cancelled the regulation of soldiers' property qualification; thus men without property were recruited into the army and became career soldiers. This reform enabled Rome to maintain a highly trained, well equipped army at all times, resulting in continuous success on the battlefield. Following these measures, soldiers gradually shifted their loyalty to the commanders instead of the state. Thus, republican armies became personal ones and the military power was in hands of individuals.

During the following years, there were constant wars. From 99 to 88 B. C., Roman's Italian allies revolted demanding a fuller share of citizenship. There was great loss of life in this Socinual War as some Italians continued to fight even after the Romans had yielded to their demands. Rome, also, was at war with King Mithridates of Pontus in Asia Minor in 88 B. C. Then in 73 B. C., a charismatic slave organised the revolt in Italy itself and struck terror in Rome. Marius, Sulla, and Pompey were the

---

① latifundia：大农场，其中劳动者大部分都是由罗马统治者从各地带回的战俘奴隶。

② Optimates：这里指上等人，包括议员和贵族。

③ Populares：社会公众，罗马的民众。

④ Jugurtha：朱古达，努米底亚（今属阿尔及利亚）国王。

⑤ Marius：马略（约前157～前86），古罗马统帅、政治家。公元前107年任执政官，针对当时罗马军队兵源匮乏等问题，实行军事改革，取消兵役财产资格的规定，军队的给养和武器装备由国家供给，加强军队训练。公元前106年，偕部将苏拉（Sulla）进军努米比亚，翌年俘获朱古达，凯旋罗马，结束了朱古达战争。

famous leaders at that time.

Following Sulla's death, Pompey, Sulla's young protégé[①], gained a great reputation. In the 1st century, three supreme military leaders Crassus, Pompey, and Julius Caesar were prominent in Roman state affairs. Crassus, the richest man in Rome, had put down the major slave rebellion led by Spartacus (73—71 B. C.). Pompey had successfully suppressed the revolt of Spain in 71 B. C. and earned himself a great fame. Julius Caesar had been a spokesman for the populares. In 60 B. C. Caesar joined with Crassus and Pompey to form a coalition that historians call the First Triumvirate.[②] The First Triumvirate, supported by Crassus' economic power, Pompey's military force and Caesar's political influence dominated Rome and benefited them.

When Crassus was killed in a battle in 53 B. C., the relatively balanced Triumvirate was reduced to two opponents. Pompey, supported by the senators, was elected the sole consul in 51 B. C. The senators voted for Caesar to lay down his command in Gaul (modern France) and to come back to Rome as a private citizen. Caesar had completely controlled Gaul and established himself as a great leader, strong in economy, army and politics. Crassus had a mass army who had followed him through thick and thin. Caesar refused to surrender and chose to lead his army, by crossing the Rubicon[③] back to Rome to fight it out. The Rubicon is the river that formed the southern boundary of Gaul, the province of Rome under the control of Caesar. In 49 B. C. Caesar marched on Rome and started the civil war with Pompey's army. Outmatched by Caesar, Pompey fled and died in Alexandria in Egypt. Caesar chased Pompey to Egypt, and successfully interfered in the administration of Egypt by deposing the young king Tuolemi and making Tuolemi's sister Cleopatra the queen of Egypt.

The defeat of Pompey's forces left Caesar in complete control of Roman government. He had been made dictator to re-establish the order of Rome. In 44 B. C., he was made dictator for life. Possessing the supreme power over politics, economy and military, he was virtually a king although he denied the suggested crown. Caesar's power was based on control of a professional army whose ties to the political order had been broken by the Marian reforms. He aimed at building up a great empire to follow the example of Alexander in the 4th century B. C.; however, he was assassinated at the foot of Pompey's statue, in 44 B. C. His dream remained a dream, and Rome's stability was again at stake.

Caesar's death left Rome in the hands of two men who had divided Rome between

---

① protégé：受有权势人物提携或扶掖的人，被保护人。

② the First Triumvirate：前三头同盟，公元前 60 年克拉苏、庞培与恺撒结成秘密的政治同盟，共同反对元老院，史称“前三头”。

③ Rubicon：卢比肯河，意大利北部河流。

them—Octavian, Caesar's heir and adopted son, taking the west, and Antony, Caesar's assistant and ally, taking the east. Antony fell in love, as Caesar had, with Cleopatra, the queen of Egypt, and even gave her a gift of some territory in the east province of Rome. Octavian began a propaganda campaign, accusing Antony of catering to Cleopatra and giving away Roman territory to this "whore of the east". The public was irritated by Antony's relationship with Cleopatra. Octavian took the opportunity to rid himself of his rival. In 31 B. C., at the battle of Actium in Greece[①], Octavian's forces smashed the army and navy of Antony and Cleopatra. Both fled to Egypt. In 30 B. C., Octavian led his army to Alexandria, in despair Antony committed suicide and Cleopatra followed suit.

Now, Octavian, at the age of thirty-two, stood supreme ruler over the Roman world. He became the undisputed ruler of the western world. The civil wars were ended, and so was the Republic, never to be revived.

The Age of Augustus (31 B. C. —14 A. D.) In the process of rebuilding the Roman state and strengthening his own power, Octavian abandoned the former patterns of monarchy and republic. He preferred a new, deceptive system that combined traditional elements with essential, dictatorial control. He enjoyed an almost absolute power over Rome and its armies.

Peace finally rested on the Roman world. The concept of empire and of emperor took several generations to fully emerge. Octavian's first challenge was to establish his personal authority. He slowly gathered into his hands the various powers without directly proclaiming himself an autocrat. He proclaimed the "restoration of the Republic" to satisfy the senatorial aristocracy. Simultaneously many Romans were persuaded that the republic had been restored. In 27 B. C., the senate awarded him the title of Augustus—"the revered one". Carefully avoiding the unpopular title Rex[②], he preferred the title Princeps[③], and adopted the title Imperator[④]. This word came into English as emperor. Under his lengthy domination of forty-five years, Rome experienced a golden age in the western world.

Religious authority was added to Augustus's political power. Casting himself as the champion of the traditional Roman religion, he assumed the office of pontifex maximus[⑤] when Lepidus[⑥] died. He rebuilt more than 80 temples and encouraged the erection of temples, monuments, and statues throughout the empire dedicated to himself and his

---

① the battle of Actium in Greece：阿克兴海战，罗马内战期间，安东尼和屋大维在希腊西部沿海阿克兴海角进行的一场海战。

② Rex：拉丁语，意为国王。

③ Princeps：头等公民。

④ Imperator：绝对统治者。

⑤ pontifex maximus：古罗马宗教中的祭司长。

⑥ Lepidus：雷必达(约前 89～12)，古罗马政治家。

wife, Livia.

Knowing that the peace of Rome and the security of the princeps depended on the army, Augustus stabilised the military and the administrative structures of the Roman Empire. He maintained a standing army of 350,000—400,000 to guard the frontier and maintain the domestic peace within the provinces. He also established the Praetorian Guard[①]—nine cohorts of elite troops, about 9,000 men, to guard the Princeps.

Augustus was the Princeps, the official title of the Roman emperor, and held the supreme power in all important issues; the senate was totally under the control of Augustus in spite of its formal election. To maintain the appearance of the republic, Augustus held regular elections for most of the traditional magistracies. In order to effectively control the enormous Empire, Augustus made an effort to get on good terms with the senate and started a new policy of governing the provinces. He inaugurated the new constitutional order of the Princeps and the aristocratic senate. Elites were constantly put into the senate and assigned important offices. Governors were selected from the senate to administer the provinces. Some provinces were under the name of the senate, for which the senate was responsible to designate the governors; other provinces were allotted to the princes, which the Princeps assigned legates[②] to govern as long as the Princeps chose. The authority of Augustus allowed him to overrule the senatorial governors and establish a uniform imperial policy.

Augustan Society In Augustus' age, the society remained in a system of social stratification[③] in which Roman citizens were divided into three classes: the senatorial, equestrian, and lower classes. The senatorial class, the few with wealth, was the ruling class that held the most important posts in the army and governed the provinces. The equestrian class could also hold less important military posts and government offices. The rest of the citizens, the vast majority, belonged to the lower class. By the way, Roman society possessed a great number of slaves unprecedented in history.

Augustan legislation simulated industry and commerce in the provinces, Egypt became a centre for glass manufacture with its fine sand and Alexandria retained its importance as an international port for the buying and selling of raw materials. Roman traders found themselves exploring even more distant markets with the demand for luxury goods, such as silk, rare fruits, and fine wine. The Indian connection also gave the Roman world better access to China, with its production of high-quality silk.

Augustus led Rome into an era of economic boom. Nevertheless, he realised that the extravagance had corrupted Roman virtues. In addition to accelerating the renewal of

---

① the Praetorian Guard：古罗马执政官禁卫队。

② legate：罗马教皇的使节；使者。

③ stratification：层次化。

traditional religion, Augustus initiated measures to rebuild Roman families. His societal reforms mainly focused on remedying the moral indulgency which was prevalent in the later period of the republic. He attempted to promote the family as a social unit and he was concerned with the falling population of the native Roman citizens. To reverse the declining birth-rate, Augustus even revised tax law which was unfavourable to bachelors, widowers, and married persons who had fewer than three children. He lived simply and unostentatiously, and legislated against adultery and excessive expense on feast. His own daughter Julia was exiled for adultery.

Rome was virtually a patriarchal society. Although fathers enjoyed the absolute superiority over other family members, in most Roman families wives were respected, daughters and sons were equal, and girls had access to education.

Regarding the status of women in Rome, married women kept close connections with their original families. These women's parents had the right to ask for divorce for their daughters. No particular reason or stigma was needed to sanction a divorce. Roman women enjoyed basic human rights such as assembling and holding political office.

Augustus made full use of the arts to reinforce the impression of peace and prosperity. Much of the art produced in Rome during his reign was official, commissioned by the state to serve government purposes. Determined to evoke the glories of the Athenian empire, Augustus encouraged a revival of the classical style. He boasted that he found Rome a city of brick and left it a city of marble. Many of the best specimens of the architecture of his age are found in the provinces. Mrison Carree (Square House) demonstrated Rome's considerable achievements in the field of engineering. From 312 B. C., commencing with the construction of the Appian Way[①], a road leading southeast from Rome, to the 2nd century A. D., Roman engineers built thousands of miles of roads throughout southern Europe, England, the Eastern Mediterranean, and North Africa. The highway network greatly contributed to the prosperity of the Augustan Age[②] and facilitated communication throughout the empire.

Section Four The Roman Empire (30 B. C. —476 A. D.)

The Early Empire (14—180 A. D.) and the Five "Good Emperors" (96—180 A. D.)

Augustus passed on his title of Princeps to his stepson Tiberius thus establishing the so-

① Appian Way：阿庇安大道，古代罗马人修建的第一条军事大道。这条道路从罗马向东南方向延伸121千米到达卡普阿，连接了罗马和其早期征服的一些地区。公元240年，道路又延长了377千米，到达意大利的东海岸。阿庇安大道现在仍在使用。

② the Augustan Age：奥古斯都时代。渥大维统治罗马达44年之久，这一时期被称为"奥古斯都时代"，是罗马帝国最辉煌的时期。

called Julio-Claudian dynasty[①] (14—68 A. D.). Unlike Augustus, his successors were unable to balance the three powers: the senate, the powerful Praetorian Guard and the commanders of the legions. The Empire was no longer in peace. The last successor, Nero (54—68 A. D.), eliminated people at will, including his own mother, whom he had murdered. Nero's extravagance provoked a military revolt and he was forced to commit suicide at last.

Nero's death ended the reign of the Julio-Claudian dynasty and pushed the Roman Empire into new civil wars involving the three major powers' contending for leadership. In 69 A. D. , the strife resulted in the victory of the east legion of Roman Empire thus turning a new page where the emperor might not be from the aristocratic order. In the following decade, the Empire was slow to change. All Spaniards were offered Roman citizenship—consequently the senate was open to them and the constitution of the senate might have been changed accordingly.

From the end of the 1st century (96 A. D.), Rome realised a century of peace and prosperity created by a series of five so-called good emperors[②] (96—180 A. D.).

Trajan (98—117 A. D.), the first Roman emperor born in the province (Spain) was far-sighted. He treated the senate with respect, established a series of building programmes and assisted poor parents in raising and educating their children. As a great commander, he extended the territory of Roman Empire to its largest from Britain to Spain, from Africa to Syria, east or west, thousands upon thousands of people were under the uniform law of Rome, which had been a long cherished vision of Caesar and Augustus. Under Trajan the empire achieved its largest geographical extent.

By adopting capable men as their successors, these good emperors reduced the chances of succession problems. Trajan's successor Hadrian (117—138 A. D.), was also Spanish. Like his predecessor, Hadrian was keen on culture, especially architecture, for which he was known as "architect-emperor". Trajan and Hadrian were especially active in constructing public works—bridges, roads, and harbour facilities throughout the whole Empire. He rebuilt many of the buildings in Athens, e. g. Hadrian's Pantheon. A temple of "all the gods" is one of the grandest ancient buildings surviving in Rome. In Rome Hadrian built a new forum to place his celebrated column of victory over Dacia (modern Romania). In his life Hadrian had visited all the provinces in

① Julio-Claudian dynasty：儒略—克劳迪王朝。儒略和克劳迪是古罗马两个重要的家族，他们通过婚姻和收养关系联系在一起。公元前27年至公元68年，先后有五位统治罗马的皇帝来自这两个家族，分别为：屋大维、提比略、卡里古拉、克劳狄和尼禄，史称“儒略—克劳迪王朝”。

② five good emperors：五贤帝，是在公元96～180年期间统治罗马帝国的五位皇帝，分别为：涅尔瓦(Nerva，96—98A. D.)、图拉真(Trajan，98—117A. D.)、哈德良(Hadrian，117—138A. D.)、安托尼乌斯·皮乌斯(Antoninus Pius，138—161A. D.)和马可·奥里略(Marcus Aurelius，161—180A. D.)。这五位皇帝宽厚谦虚，实行仁政，深受臣民爱戴。在他们统治期间，罗马帝国政治清明，社会安定，经济繁荣，被称为罗马帝国的黄金时代。

the empire, hunting talents for the administrative offices, and admiring the cultural heritage of Greeks and Jews.

Unlike Trajan, Hadrian treated the concept of "conquest" in a more reasonable way. Considering the thorny problems on the frontiers, he was willing to give up some areas than engage in military aggression. To defend the frontiers, he reinforced the fortifications along a line connecting the Rhine and Danube rivers and built a defensive wall 80 miles long across northern Britain to keep the Scots out of Roman Britain. The Hadrian defence wall constructed between 122 A. D. and 188 A. D. in Britain marked the northern boundary and has remained one of the most famous ruins of ancient Roman Britain.

At its height in the 2nd century, the Roman Empire was the greatest state in the west covering about 3. 5 million square miles with a population of about 50 million. While in the east, the Han dynasty of the Chinese Empire (206 B. C. —220 A. D.) flourished almost at the same time. The Roman Empire was then called by Han Chinese Daqin. Both of the two empires lasted for centuries and created a period of prosperity.

Early Rome enjoyed a period of considerable prosperity with its agrarian economy, its commerce and trade benefited from the internal peace, the extensive system of Roman roads, and the advantageous Mediterranean routes. These Mediterranean routes had reached unprecedented levels and had even extended Roman boundaries. Silk goods were imported from China. Large quantities of grain were imported to feed the people of Rome and a great deal of luxury items was traded to satisfy the needs of the wealthy upper class. Increased trade naturally stimulated manufacturing. The first two centuries of the empire also saw the high point of industry development. Additionally, the wealth of the empire was recorded to prove the age of prosperity. Unfortunately, there remained a huge gap between the rich and the poor.

The Decline of the Roman Empire In the 3rd century, the Roman Empire collapsed. After a series of civil wars, Septimius Severus①(193—211 A. D.), who was born in North Africa and spoke Latin with an accent, used his legions to seize power. After his death, the Severan rulers (193 — 235 A. D.) began to create a military monarchy.

Military monarchy was followed by military anarchy. For a period of almost 50 years, from 235 to 284 A. D., the Roman Empire was mired in the chaos of continual civil wars. In these almost fifty years, there were twenty-two emperors, only two of whom did not meet a violent death. Invasions of foreign armies also plagued the empire. In the east, the Sassanid② Persians made inroads into Roman territory. A fitting symbol

---

① Septimius Severus：谢普提米乌斯·塞维鲁(146～211)，罗马皇帝。

② Sassanid：公元226～651年间波斯的萨珊王朝。萨珊王朝对罗马的入侵，加速了罗马帝国的衰落。

of Rome's decline was the capture of the Roman emperor Valerian① (253—260 A. D.) by the Persians and his death in captivity, an event previously unheard of in Roman history. Germanic tribes also poured into the empire. The Goths occupied the Balkans. The Franks advanced into Gaul and Spain. It was not until the reign of Aurelian② (270—275 A. D.) that most of the boundaries were restored. Invasions and civil wars led to an economic collapse of the Roman Empire in the 3rd century. Historians call this period in Rome as Crisis of the Third Century.

The Reforms of Diocletian and Constantine At the end of the 3rd and the beginning of the 4th centuries, the Roman Empire gained a new lease on life through the efforts of two strong emperors, Diocletian and Constantine who restored order and stability. The Roman Empire was virtually transformed into a new state. In politics, Tetrarchs③ was invented to rule the empire; in economy and society, the main structure was rigorous. Besides these changes, Roman religion underwent a dramatic transformation. Christianity was granted the legal status. Believing that the empire had grown too large for a single ruler, Diocletian (284—305 A. D.) divided it into four administrative units. Constantine (306—337 A. D.) continued to develop this political system. Both rulers greatly strengthened and enlarged the administrative bureaucracies of the Roman Empire. From then on, the Roman bureaucracy was distinctly divided into a civil group and a military group. The emperor presided over both hierarchies of officials and served as the only link between them.

In military reforms, flexible units were set up in order to ensure the timely reinforcement to any threatened frontier. Although larger, the army was less competent, being made up of Germans and Yugoslavs④ with less training than the traditional legions.

Constantine was especially interested in building programmes despite the strain they placed on the budget. His biggest project was the construction of a new capital city in the east on the site of the Greek city. Constantine moved the capital to a strategic point for strategic military reasons. The new capital was named after its founder, Constantinople (modern Istanbul). In the eyes of Constantine, the new capital was his "New Rome" in which he constructed many marvellous buildings, including grand palaces and an enormous amphitheatre.

The series of political and military reforms carried out by Diocletian and Constantine advanced the development of civil and army services. These measures

① Valerian：瓦勒良，罗马帝国皇帝。

② Aurelian：奥勒良(214～275)，罗马帝国皇帝，公元270～275年间在位。

③ Tetrarchs：四帝共治。

④ Yugoslav：南斯拉夫人。

consumed large financial resources. In spite of the emperors' efforts to relieve the economic burden, those efforts were always at the cost of individual liberty.

The restored empire of Diocletian and Constantine limped along for more than a century. After Constantine, the empire continued to divide into western and eastern parts. The major breakthrough into the Roman Empire came in the second half of the 4th century. In 395 A. D., Theodosius[①] broke up the united empire to distribute them to his two sons. Hence the Roman Empire split into Western Roman Empire and Eastern Roman Empire. The west came under increasing pressure from invading barbarian[②] forces. Ferocious warriors from Asia, known as Huns, moved into Eastern Europe and put pressure on the Germanic Visigoths[③] who in turn moved south and west. They crossed the Danube into Roman territory, and settled down as Roman allies. However, the Visigoths rebelled against Rome, and in 378 A. D. they defeated the Roman troops at Adrianople, a city near modern Edirne in European Turkey.

Increasing numbers of barbarians then crossed the frontiers. In 410, the Visigoths under Alaric[④] sacked Rome. Vandals[⑤] poured into southern Spain and Africa, Visigoths into Spain and Gaul. The Vandals crossed into Italy from North Africa and sacked Rome in 455 A. D. Twenty-one years later, the western emperor Romulus Augustulus[⑥] (475—476 A. D.) was deposed, and a series of German kingdoms replaced the Roman Empire in the west while the Eastern Roman Empire continued with its centre at Constantinople.

The Fall of the Roman Empire The end of the Roman Empire has given rise to numerous theories that purport to explain the "decline and fall of the Roman Empire". These include the following: Roman military strength and patriotism were replaced by Christianity's spiritual conviction; non-Italians who held predominant positions in Rome did not uphold Roman virtues; lead poisoning through leaden water pipes and cups caused a mental decline; plague decimated the population; Rome failed to advance technologically because of slavery; and Rome was unable to achieve a workable political system. There may be an element of truth in each of these theories, but each of them has also been challenged. History is an intricate web of relationships. There is no explanation which will suffice to explain historical events. One thing is clear. Weakened by a shortage of soldiers, the Roman army in the west was simply not able to fend off

---

① Theodosius：狄奥多西(约 346～395)，罗马皇帝。

② barbarian：野蛮人，蛮夷。在君士坦丁时期，罗马分为两个部分，西部经常受到高地外族的侵略，包括西哥特人，从亚洲过去的匈奴人等。

③ Visigoth：西哥特人。

④ Alaric：阿拉里克，西哥特人首领。

⑤ Vandal：汪达尔人，为古代日耳曼部落的一支。公元 455 年，汪达尔人洗劫了罗马，此后他们的名字就成了肆意破坏和亵渎圣物的同义词。英语中 vandal 一词意为"野蛮人"。

⑥ Romulus Augustulus：罗慕路·奥古斯都路斯，西罗马帝国的最后一位皇帝。

the hordes of people invading Italy and Gaul. In contrast, the Eastern Roman Empire, which would survive for another 1,000 years, remained largely free of invasion.

Edward Gibbon offered two explanations of Rome's fall in his first Volume of *History of the Decline and Fall of the Roman Empire*. One was philosophical: having grown too heavy, the fabric of Roman culture collapsed of its own weight. Another was more concrete: Christianity had diverted vital energy and attention from pressing civil problems.

Some recent historians are focused on other aspects, such as social, economic, political and demographic factors they believe led to the fall. Some of them hold that the lack of violent revolution is mainly responsible; others have insisted the low level of technology and its connection to slavery is the primary reason. The decline has also been associated with a labour shortage. It was suggested that the invasions of the Germans and the Huns were too much for an empire whose economy was exhausted.

The structural weaknesses of Roman society should be taken into consideration. Rome never resolved the tension that had destroyed the republic. Augustus reconstituted the state on the basis of an equilibrium founded on social exhaustion. There were no regular methods of succession and revolution. Assassination was prevalent in the place of legislation and election.

But what we should remember is not the reason of its decline but that Rome survived so long, encompassing the cultures of three continents within a single system of law and government. The dissolution of Rome was in reality a process rather than an event. If the empire's political centre of gravity was the city of Rome, its economic and cultural base had always been in the eastern Mediterranean. In a sense, half of the empire survived there, and its history and culture continued into the Turkish conquest of 1453.

Section Five Christianity in Rome (c. 50 B.C. —313 A.D.)

Constantine's adoption of Christianity in the 4th century heralded a new era of this religion. From then on, Christianity has closely been associated with the West.

Religion in the Roman World Roman religion seemed to be often influenced by other religions as Romans always adapted to their surroundings. When Romans came into contact with Greeks, they adopted Greeks' deities. Therefore, the Greek Zeus became the Roman Jupiter. By the end of the 3rd century B.C., a fairly blended Greek-Roman religion occurred.

The Roman state religion centred on a group of gods and goddesses who were originally from the Greek mythology, such as Jupiter, Mars and Mercury. Practical Romans worshipped many gods in every aspect of their lives. Romans' piety for religion derived from their reverence for order and authority. Roman priests were from the elite who held other official positions so they didn't form a religious status in Rome. "Religion was less a matter of personal relationships with the gods than a public, civic activity that bound society together. "[①]

Romans' Contact with Christianity Romans' religious tolerance set the stage for the development of Christianity in the Roman Empire. Judaea[②] was made a province by 6 A. D. In the midst of the confusion and conflict in Judaea, Jesus of Nazareth (6 B. C. —29 A. D.) began his public preaching. According to Jesus, the importance consisted in the transformation of the inner person: "So in everything, do to others what you would have them do to you, for this sums up the Law and the Prophets. "[③] Jesus presented the ethical concepts—humility, charity, and brotherly love—that would form the pillar of medieval Western civilisation. Jesus was betrayed by one of his disciples and, upon the order of the Roman magistrate Pontius Pilate[④], was crucified. Three days after Jesus' crucifixion, his tomb was found empty so his followers believed that he had been deified. Jesus' disciples spread the story that Jesus had overcome death and had been resurrected.

Jesus' disciple Peter[⑤], "second founder of Christianity" founded the Christian church at Rome, and was honoured to be the first Pope (the representative of Jesus on earth within the Catholic Church). Peter provided a universal foundation for the spread of Christ's ideas. Christian missionaries travelled on the Roman roads to spread their "good news". A Latin translation of the Greek *New Testament* that appeared soon after 200 A. D. helped the spreading of Christianity in the Roman world. It was in the 4th century that Christianity spread due to Constantine's conversion to Christianity and later Theodosius's announcement that Christianity was the state religion in Rome.

Why was Christianity readily accepted in the Roman Empire? It is true that Roman's tolerance of other religions and its underestimation of Christianity's strength contributed to the spread and growth of Christianity. But above all is that Christianity itself was attractive to so many followers. The Christian message offered to the believers' immortality at the sacrificial death of Jesus. Unlike the Roman state religions Christianity gave new meaning to life, offered a personal relationship with God, brotherly love among the believers, and consequently fulfilled the human need to belong.

Among Christians, vulnerable groups such as the poor and women were particularly pious because they were assured by Christian teachings that an afterlife would make up for their present miserable lives. Christian organisers also helped to spread their religion by establishing a network of congregations throughout the cities of the empire.

---

① Mark Kishlansky, *A Brief History of Western Civilisation*, Beijing: China Remin University Press, 2008, p. 78.

② Judaea：犹地亚，古代罗马统治的一个城市。

③ Matthew 7:12，《圣经》马太福音篇。

④ Pontius Pilate：本丟·彼拉多，罗马帝国朱迪亚行省的执政官。根据《新约圣经》所述，彼拉多审判并处死了耶稣。

⑤ Peter：彼得，也被称为西蒙彼得。

Population density in urban areas also caused ideas to spread faster.

However, the spread of Christianity in Rome was not smooth. Since its emergence in Canaan[①], Christianity had been under persecution by the Roman government. It was Pontius Pilate, a Roman magistrate, who crucified Jesus. In the second and third centuries, Christianity was cruelly suppressed. Many bishops and disciples were burned. In 303, the Roman Emperor Diocletian launched the biggest campaign to eliminate Christianity in the Roman history. Firstly, the Christian soldiers were forced to leave the legion. Then the property of the Christian churches was confiscated and all books about the religion were destroyed. At the later stage of the persecution, Christians were forced to abandon their belief, or be executed. These destructive actions lasted till the year of 313 when Constantine issued the Edict of Milan[②].

In the reign of Theodosius, Christianity became the Roman state religion. Theodosius equated paganism with treason and he ruled that those who believed in other religions should be punished as traitors. The absolute singularity of Christianity in Rome laid the foundation for its exclusivity in the Middle Ages.

Section Six The Roman Culture (753 B. C. —476 A. D.)

Latin Literature The brilliant success of Rome against Carthage in the First Punic War stimulated the creation of a Roman literature. The high point of Latin literature was reached in the Augustan Age, so this age has been thought of as the golden age of Latin literature. Litigators and artists who were sponsored by Roman authorities and aristocrats were expected to eulogize the rulers' virtues and achievements. Pride in military glory provided the subject matter for literary works, which revealed the Roman spirit of greatness.

Virgil (70—19 B. C.) was the most distinguished poet of the Augustan Age. He was from a well-off family in northern Italy. His masterpiece, the *Aeneid*, an epic poem composed during the last ten years of his life, was clearly meant to be the rival of Homer's works. It is the story of Aeneas, the son of Anchises[③] of Troy who survived the destruction of the city, and after some years' wandering settled in Latium. The epic consisted of 12 books which were divided into two parts—the first six books were the description of Aeneid's wanderings (like the *Odyssey*), and the latter six books were similar to the *Iliad* and recorded the fight between Aeneid and other Italian groups. The portrait of Aeneid embodied the ideal Roman virtues of duty, piety, and faithfulness.

---

① Canaan：迦南，古地名。见第一章。

② Edict of Milan：米兰敕令，是罗马皇帝君士坦丁一世于公元313年在意大利米兰颁布的一个宽容基督教的敕令。此敕令宣布罗马帝国境内有信仰基督教的自由，并且发还了被没收的教会财产，承认了基督教的合法地位。米兰敕令是基督教历史上的转折点，标志着罗马帝国的统治者对基督教从镇压转为保护和利用。

③ Anchises：安喀塞斯，与女神阿佛洛狄忒生下埃涅阿斯。

The poet expressed the consciousness of the divine destiny of Rome and the profound mission of the Augustan empire by associating Rome's foundation with Greek history. Like Homer's work, the Aeneid has been widely known and regarded as a model of classic works.

Another outstanding Augustan poet was Horace[①](65—8 B. C.), who was born in Apulia. Horace's father took him to Rome where he was well educated and where he associated with sons of Roman senators and patricians. He then went to Athens for advanced study. Virgil was attracted to Horace's verses and introduced him to Octavian and enabled Horace to devote himself to writing poetry.

Ovid[②](43 B. C. —17 A. D.) was the spokesman and interpreter of his age. *The Art of Love* brought him the poetic fame he desired, but also brought the resentment of Augustus, which probably caused the poet's banishment. He died in exile. *Metamorphoses*, the myth of miraculous transformation from chaos to the change of Julius Caesar into a star, was Ovid's most ambitious work. As his masterpiece, *Metamorphoses* is popular in world literature.

The most famous Latin prose work of the golden age was written by the historian Livy[③](59 B. C. —17 A. D.). His masterpiece was his *History of Rome* covering from the foundation of the city to 9 B. C., which celebrated Rome's greatness.

In the history of Latin literature, the century and a half after the Augustus Age is often called the "silver age" to indicate that the literary efforts of the period were not as excellent as that of the golden age.

Lucretius[④](94 — 55 B. C.) was a philosopher-poet, and his poem *De Rerum Natura*[⑤] was devoted to an explanation and defence of the philosophical theory of materialism. Lucretius did not originate the materialistic philosophy which had been developed over a long period of time by various Greek thinkers, including Leucippus[⑥] (5th century B. C.), who originated the theory; and by his pupil Democritus[⑦](460—370 B. C.), who developed it into a complete explanation of the universe.

Almost nothing is known of the life of Lucreteius beyond the traditional. It was said that he was driven mad by a love-potion, wrote his poetry between fits of insanity,

---

① Horace：贺拉斯，古罗马诗人，批评家，奥古斯都时期的宫廷诗人。

② Ovid：奥维德，古罗马诗人。

③ Livy：李维，古罗马历史学家，其代表作《罗马自建城以来的历史》(*History of Rome*) 充满了爱国思想、道德说教和复古主张。

④ Lucretius：卢克莱修，古罗马哲学家。他继承古代原子学说，特别是阐述并发展了伊壁鸠鲁的哲学观点，认为物质的存在是永恒的，反对神创论；认为宇宙是无限的，有其自然发展的过程；承认世界的可知性，驳斥了怀疑论。著有哲学长诗《物性论》。

⑤ *De Rerum Natura*：*On the Nature of Things*《物性论》。

⑥ Leucippus：留基伯(约前 500～前 440)，古希腊唯物主义哲学家。

⑦ Democritus：德谟克利特(约前 460～前 370)，古希腊伟大的唯物主义哲学家。

and finally committed suicide. In his *De Rerum Natura*, Lucretius discusses the theory of materialism and its denial of personal immortality. Because the soul is mortal, death means oblivion; therefore, it is not to be feared. The wise man, rather than thinking of death, will live life to the fullest.

Tacitus[①](56—120 A. D.) was the greatest historian of the silver age. His main works included the *Annals* and *Histories*, which recorded the history of Rome from the reign of Tiberius through the assassination of Domitian (14—96 A. D.). Tacitus used a dense and objective writing style in recording history.

Philosophy The philosophy of Stoicism, although it had been originated by Greeks, was carried to its full development by Romans. Indeed, it might well be called the "official" philosophy of classical Rome, for it numbered among its outstanding spokesmen such political leaders as the emperor Marcus Aurelius[②] and the statesmen, Seneca[③] and Cicero[④]. One might wonder that such men, engaged as they were in practical politics, should find time for philosophizing; nevertheless, they must be credited with two contributions, both of great historical significance, to Stoic political and moral theory. The first of these is the doctrine of Natural Law: nature (or the Universe) is governed by rational Laws because it is the embodiment of an indwelling Reason; men are capable of discovering these Laws of Nature and ought to live in accord with them. Stoicism has persisted as the dominant tradition in Western political theory, underlying the social structure of the Middle Ages and receiving its classic modern affirmation in the preamble of the American *Declaration of Independence*.

The second Roman contribution to Stoicism is the notion of "cosmopolitanism[⑤]". The Law of Nature stands above the edicts of any nation; hence, men are bound equally by this Law. As a rational being, every man is "a citizen of the whole universe, considered as a single Commonwealth". Here the Roman philosophers made a complete break in theory from the political provincialism embodied in the traditional distinction between "Greek" and "barbarian". This break paralleled Rome's break from the political isolationism of the Greek city-state.

Roman Law Of the contributions made by the Romans in government, Roman law is one of the most significant. Roman law is at the root of legal systems for many

---

① Tacitus：塔西佗，古罗马最伟大的历史学家。他提出了客观主义的治史原则，其代表作为《编年史》(*Annals*)、《历史》(*Histories*) 和《日耳曼尼亚志》。

② Marcus Aurelius：马克斯·奥里留斯，古罗马皇帝，公元 161～180 年间在位。奥里留斯是一位具有哲学家风格的统治者，他把斯多葛学派的哲学主张用于政治统治。

③ Seneca：塞内加(约前 4～65)，古罗马时代著名的斯多葛学派哲学家，曾任尼禄皇帝的导师和顾问。

④ Cicero：西塞罗(前 106～前 43)，古罗马著名政治家、演说家、法学家和哲学家。

⑤ cosmopolitanism：世界大同主义。这是一种社会理想，认为全人类都属于同一精神共同体，是与爱国主义和民族主义相对立的思想。世界主义不见得推崇某种形式的世界政府，仅仅是指国家间和民族间更具有包容性的道德、经济和政治关系。

modern western countries, such as Italy, France, Scotland, and the Latin American countries.

Throughout the history of Rome, both at the stage of the Republic and in the era of the Empire, Rome was characterised by making laws, implementing laws and reforming laws. In 450 B. C. , the first code of law in words, the *Law of the Twelve Tables*①, was engraved on bronze tablets. It was a collection of existent Roman laws. This code was the fruit of the plebeians' struggle against the patricians. It was the first time in the Roman history that social orders were protected by a written code of law. *Law of the Twelve Tables* prevented the patricians from misinterpreting laws and marked the outset of the statute law in Rome. Subsequently, a series of laws were issued and a complete legal system came into being.

*Lex Canuleius*②, a law passed in 445 B. C. , was named after the tribune Gaius Canuleius. It allowed the intermarriage between the plebeians and the patricians which had been forbidden in the *Law of the Twelve Tables*. This bill was a milestone for the plebeians' struggle for equal social rights. Another law, *Lex Poetetia Papiria*③ passed in 326 B. C. , abolished the debt slavery and prohibited turning Roman citizens who couldn't pay off the debts into slaves. In 287 B. C. , another law was passed, *Lex Hortensia*④ that exonerated the Plebeian Assembly from its requirement to gain ratification from the senate.

At the later stage of the republic, Rome set up the chancellor system in which chancellors had the right to interpret and maintain the procedural law and could give their judgment indications to the jury. This greatly influenced modern Western law.

The study and codification of the law reached their summits in Rome in the 2nd and 3rd centuries. Several legal scholars⑤ during this period produced research which is now recognised as the greatest achievement in Roman law.

Social Life In Rome, the Forum⑥ functioned as the social, political and religious centre for Roman citizens. It was located in the central part of a city and was shaped in

---

① *Law of the Twelve Tables*：古罗马《十二铜表法》。公元前450年，在平民的强烈要求下，罗马贵族被迫同意制定了罗马历史上第一部成文法典《十二铜表法》，这部法典音铭刻于十二块铜牌上而得名。《十二铜表法》包括继承法、债务法、婚姻法等各个方面，是罗马人传统习惯法的汇编。

② *Lex Canuleius*：《坎努里阿法案》，废除了平民不得与贵族通婚的限制。

③ *Lex Poetetia Papiria*：《波提利阿法案》，规定禁止把负债的罗马公民变为奴隶，废除了债务奴隶制，保证了公民的社会安全。

④ *Lex Hortensia*：《霍腾西阿法案》，规定平民会议的决议无需再经过元老院的批准，并且对全体罗马公民具有法律效力。

⑤ 其中以盖尤斯、帕比尼安、乌尔比安、包鲁斯和莫迪斯蒂努斯这五大法学家最著名。公元426年颁布并在东西罗马帝国同样生效的《引证法》正式承认，五大法学家的解答具有法律效力，并规定法律问题未经明文规定的，可依据这五位法学家的著作来解决问题。

⑥ Roman Forum：古罗马广场，是古罗马时代的城市中心，包括一些罗马最古老和最重要的建筑。

the form of rectangle. Larger cities were sites for more magnificent Forums. The Forum was the site of processions and elections, the venue for public speeches and assemblies, and the place for trade. Around the Forum statues and monuments commemorated the city's great men. The Senate House, government offices, tribunals and temples cluttered the area around the Forum. As the heart of ancient Rome, the Forum was called the most famous meeting place in the world, and in all history, the Roman Forum witnessed the vigour and variety of Roman public life.

Bathing played an important role in ancient Roman culture and society and was one of the most common daily activities for Roman people. Different from most contemporary cultures regarding bathing as a private activity at home, bathing in Rome was a communal activity. Bathing occurred in public facilities that were called thermae①. The Romans raised bathing to a level of art as they socialised in these communal baths. In many aspects, baths were the equivalent of community centres. Many Romans used the baths as a place to invite their friends to hold parties, and many politicians went to the baths to discuss issues. The thermae offered many services besides baths. There were various books for reading and delicious food for tasting. To some extent, Roman thermae were the first modern libraries, art galleries, gymnasiums and spas.

Roman civilisation presented a paradox. On the one hand, Roman culture and law reflected high standards of human civilisation. On the other hand, the Romans were addicted to barbaric practices, such as the gladiatorial shows which were the most popular entertainment programme in Rome. Gladiatorial shows took place in amphitheatres seating a few thousand to tens of thousands of people. The most famous amphitheatre, the Colosseum②, was built in the 1st century and could seat fifty thousand spectators. In most cities and towns, the amphitheatres were the biggest buildings. The gladiators, mainly slaves and condemned criminals, were forced to fight against wild animals till death. The civilised Roman people were transformed into a wild mob when they were spectators in the stands.

In the later republic and early empire, the authority of father and husband over women slackened, and Roman women gained more rights and freedom. In this period, women owned possessions and enjoyed educational opportunities. They shifted their concern from domestic affairs to public lives. Some assertive and independent women pursued a hedonistic lifestyle, which resulted in the moral deterioration in Roman society. Although Augustus urged for a renewal of the traditional values of morality and

---

① thermae：源自希腊语，意为“公共浴池”。

② Colosseum：古罗马圆形大剧场，亦译作罗马斗兽场、罗马大角斗场、罗马竞技场、罗马圆形竞技场，建于公元72至82年间，由4万名战俘用8年时间建造而成。位于今天的意大利罗马市中心，是古罗马时期最大的圆形角斗场。现仅存遗迹。

decency, and even passed legislation to prohibit adultery, Roman women still couldn't resist the zest of lovers. The Stoic philosopher Seneca believed that a husband might regard himself lucky if his wife was contented with no more than two lovers.

The Roman Contribution Different from Greek culture, which focused on abstract thoughts, the Roman civilisation didn't bring forth a new system of philosophy, new forms of literature or new discoveries in science. However, the Romans went beyond their Greek ancestors in public administration. They created an effective republic state and set up an integrated legal system to ensure the operation of the whole society. They excelled in the art of government.

Developing from a primitive farming community in Latium to a mighty state that became the master of the Mediterranean world as well as of Gaul, Britain, and parts of Germany, the Romans met one challenge after another with practicality and efficiency. So that today, the remains of roads, walls, baths, basilicas, amphitheatres, and aqueducts survive as symbols of the Roman contribution to Western civilisation.

Chapter Review

This chapter mainly explored the social development of Rome and the decline of the great empire in the history, and introduced the intellectual achievements and great thoughts represented in different works as well. Caesar and the First Triumvirate showed their influence on the social changes. The age of Augustus and the early emperors has been called the peak of Roman civilisation and the achievements were great. The empire that developed during the last centuries of the republic would extend the life of Rome for hundreds of years. As Christian ideas expanded greatly, Rome transferred from the hierarchical class system to the church hierarchy and in time into the feudal order of the Middle Ages. The Romans made great contributions in law and jurisprudence that have shaped Western Civilisation more than any other people of the ancient world. They served Western Civilisation as the transmitters of Greek culture, and they showed ingenuity both in literature and art as well.

Exercise

Ⅰ. *According to the information provided in this chapter, choose the correct alternative among A, B, C, and D that can complete each of the following statements.*

1. The senate awarded Octavian the title of ________ "the revered one". He preferred the title Princeps.

   A. Augustus B. first citizen

   C. emperor D. prime minister

2. Constantine's building project was the construction of a new capital city in the

east on the site of the Greek city of Byzantium. Constantine endowed the city with a forum, large palaces, and a vast ________.

A. theatre B. amphitheatre C. statue D. park

3. Christianity spread widely in Rome in the ________ century.

A. fifth B. second C. third D. fourth

4. Virgil's masterpiece, the Aeneid, the epic poem, clearly meant to be the rival of ________ works.

A. Aristotle's B. Plato's C. Homer's D. Aeschylus'

5. The philosophy of Stoicism, although it had been originated by ________, was carried to its full development by Romans.

A. Greeks B. Egyptians

C. Jews D. Mesopotamians

Ⅱ. *Fill in the blanks with what you have learned in this chapter.*

1. The development of Rome was much influenced by the Etruscans in the north and ________ in the south.
2. The chief executive officers of the Roman Republic were the consuls and ________.
3. The Roman Republic had a number of assemblies. The most important was ________ Assembly which was established in the 5th century B. C.
4. Roman conquest consists of three stages: the conquest of Italy, the conquest of West Mediterranean through the destruction of ________ and the conquest of the Eastern Mediterranean.
5. In 60 B. C. Caesar joined with Crassus and Pompey to form a coalition that historians call ________.

Ⅲ. *According to what you have learned, answer the following questions briefly in your own words.*

1. What is the process of Roman's conquest?
2. What did Octavian do to Rome after the death of Caesar?
3. Were the Gladiatorial shows an integral part of Roman society? Is this heritage shown in any modern sports?
4. How did Christianity rise and grow in Rome?
5. How did the Roman law evolve?

Ⅳ. *With critical analysis, answer the following essay questions in your own words.*

1. Why were the Romans able to build up such a great empire?
2. How were the Romans connected with the Greeks?

Ⅴ. *Work in small groups and make comparisons based on the following topic.*

Please discuss the wine culture both in Roman period and in China's Han Dynasty, and tell the similarities and differences between them.

Voices on Key Points

Roman Civilisation

Roman civilisation had achieved, within the bounds of its technology, relatively as great a mastery of time and space as we have achieved today.

——Arthur Erickson

The various modes of worship which prevailed in the Roman world were all considered by the people as equally true; by the philosopher as equally false; and by the magistrate as equally useful.

——Edward Gibbon

We may be sure that out of the ruins of our capitalist civilisation a new religion will emerge, just as Christianity emerged from the ruins of the Roman civilization.

——Herbert Read

Roman Empire

The Holy Roman Empire is neither Holy, nor Roman, nor an Empire.

——Voltaire

It was luxuries like air conditioning that brought down the Roman Empire. With air conditioning their windows were shut, they couldn't hear the barbarians coming.

——Garrison Keillor

The Rise of Christianity

Christianity emerged from the religion of Israel. Or rather, it has as its background a persistent strain in that religion. To that strain Christians have looked back, and rightly, as the preparation in history for their faith.

——Kenneth Scott Latourette

Christianity is the greatest civilising, moulding, uplifting power on this globe.

——Mark Hopkins

Suggested Reading

1. Guthrie, W. C. K. *A History of Greek Philosophy*, Vol. 4, *Plato: The Man and His Dialogues: Earlier Period*. Cambridge University Press, 1986.
2. Yavetz, Z. *Slave and Slavery in Ancient Rome*. New Brunswick, USA: Transaction Books, 1988.
3. (英)爱德华·吉本著,黄宜思等译:《罗马帝国衰亡史》(上、下),商务印书馆 1997 年版。
4. (德)特奥多尔·蒙森著,李稼年译:《罗马史》第一卷,商务印书馆 1994 年版。
5. (德)奥托·基弗著,姜瑞璋译:《古罗马风化史》,辽宁教育出版社 2000 年版。
6. 朱龙华:《罗马文化与古典传统》,浙江人民出版社 1993 年版。

Chapter Four Medieval Civilisation (476—c. 1500)

In any case, the Middle Ages were neither asleep nor awful, but instead were a time of constant change. ①

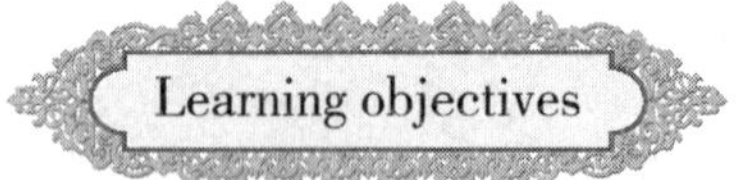

After reading this chapter, you will be able to:

1. *Understand the elements that caused Rome to become Christian and the conditions for the Barbarians to settle in the West of Europe;*
2. *Get acquainted with the early medieval church and the achievements of Pope Gregory the Great;*
3. *Draw a summary of the cultural characteristics in the Middle Ages;*
4. *Understand the reason for the crusades and the role they played in the development of Western civilisation;*
5. *Know the shift of the Middle Ages from boom to depression and the historical conditions behind the change;*
6. *Learn to understand the influence of the Middle Ages on the world from the aspects of economy and politics.*

---

① Judith M. Bennett & C. Warren Hollister, *Medieval Europe: A Short History*, Beijing: Peking University Press, 2007, p. 2.

经历了罗马、希腊文明的辉煌后，西方文明的一个高峰和罗马帝国一起走向了尽头。随着罗马帝国的分裂和外来野蛮民族的入侵，西方文明进入了中世纪时期。中世纪，一度被史学家认为是在愚昧的教士统治之下的“黑暗世纪”、“半梦半醒的一千年”。

在本章中，我们将用近代史学家们的新视角再现中世纪的辉煌与文化融合，让大家领略中世纪的文化活力。从中世纪诞生到其发展的初级阶段，基督教文化以席卷欧洲之势在世界上广泛传播。罗马皈依基督教之后，客观上促进了基督教文化、罗马文化的结合，同时伴随着日耳曼民族对罗马帝国的入侵，日耳曼文化、罗马文化和基督教文化之间相互碰撞、融合，从而给现代欧洲各国打上了独特的文化烙印，促成了现代世界的诞生。在中世纪的鼎盛时期，封建经济腾飞，城市兴起，政治体系完备，文化和宗教也一片繁荣。与此同时，宗教不断膨胀，十字军六次东征，埋下了西方世界和阿拉伯世界相互仇恨的种子。到了中世纪的晚期，宗教势力被不断削弱，教廷的分离使整个欧洲不再有一个统一的精神领袖，战争连绵，加之中世纪文明又经历了人类历史上最严重的疫病——黑死病，整个文明世界呈现出颓败之势。然而，瘟疫过后，她又重现生机，文艺复兴、宗教改革、科技革命开启了近代文明的大门，所有这一切都是建立在中世纪的文化融合和积淀之上。

Section One　The Emergence of the Medieval Civilisation (476—c. 750)

It has been long and generally accepted that the Middle Ages were a disastrous time. Even today, some still believe that the Middle Ages, a thousand years from the 5th century to the 15th century, were a foolish deviation[①] in human progress. One historian once said during those years that human consciousness “lay dreaming or half awake”[②]. At the same time, it was the age of faith, too, a period that witnessed growth and decline of the church.

The history was both chaotic and creative from 400 to 750. Three new entities succeeded to the Roman Empire: the Germanic kingdoms, the Byzantine Empire, and the world of Islam. The Germanic kingdoms and the Byzantine Empire shared a common bond in Christianity, but it proved to be impossible to keep these two great civilisations in harmony politically, and the conflicts between them continued to grow. At the same time, with the rise of Islam, a religious power that was neither Roman nor Christian, the Southern and Eastern Mediterranean worlds of the old Roman Empire were replaced by Rome’s third heir, the world of Islam.

Fall of Roman Civilisation　The reasons of the decline of the Roman Empire are far too complex to be explained by any single theory. But we must keep in mind that the

---

① deviation：背离，偏离。

② Jacob Burckhardt, *The Civilisation of the Renaissance in Italy*, London: Penguin Books, 1995, p. 87.

Roman Empire collapsed only in the West. The Eastern Empire, during this period, was normally called "Byzantine" and not "Roman".

In the Roman Empire, then, the West had always been weaker and less civilised than the East, and its urbanisation was badly destroyed by the political turmoil of the 3rd century. Because of the imperial government and the problem with the turbulent frontiers, the decline of the economy in the West was inevitable.

The fall of the economy was accelerated by the twin evils of population decline and common poverty. Naturally, the first evil turned into a manpower shortage which would soon paralyse the whole society. At the same time, the army continued expanding and the expenses of the government were soaring. Cities were not attractive any more, and the great landowners began to flee away from the city and retired to their estates where they assembled their own armies and often refused to pay the government taxes. The urban nobility began to turn into the rural nobility of the Middle Ages.

This was fatal to the empire and the cities of the West began to decline. It ended the civilisation of Athens, Alexandria and Rome because they could not have enough fighters to continue the wars that had been supporting the whole empire. Because of the growing shortage of manpower and resources, the emperors turned frequently to Germanic peoples for help in order to defend their frontiers and keep their control of the nation. As a consequence, the Roman Army was full of Barbarians, and Germanic military leaders gradually took high positions in the Western Empire.

Invasion from the Germanic Tribes The Germanic peoples had long been intending to invade Rome's Empire. They defeated a Roman army in the reign of Augustus; they had already probed deeply into the Empire in the late 2nd century. But until the late 4th century the invaders were always driven out by the Romans. However, from the beginning of 370 A. D., the exhausted Roman Army was confronted by renewed Barbarian pressures of an unprecedented quantity. Attracted by the wealth, the good soil, and the joyful climate of the Mediterranean world, the Barbarians intended to take the Empire and enjoy the land instead of plundering and destroying it.

The Barbarians' age-long desire for the good soil across the Roman frontier suddenly found a chance to be put into practice when a ferocious tribe known as the Huns conquered one Germanic tribe after another. The two great Gothic tribes, the Ostrogoths[①] and the Visigoths, were on the verge of becoming subject peoples of the Huns. Soon the Ostrogoths fell before the Hun's might. The Visigoths sought to avoid a similar fate by appealing for sanctuary behind the Roman frontier. The Eastern

---

① Ostrogoths：东哥特人，原住在黑海草原西部地区，公元 4 世纪后半期形成部落联盟，为日耳曼民族。Ostro-意为东方的（源于日耳曼语族）。

emperor, Valens, who was a fervent Arian[①], showed sympathy to the Arian Visigoths and allowed the entire tribe to cross peacefully into the Empire.

However, trouble followed that peaceful migration. The Visigoths were cheated and abused by the corrupt Roman officials and the hot-tempered tribesmen went on a rampage[②]. In 378 the Emperor himself was killed at the battle of Adrianople and the Visigoths entered Rome in 410.

The fall of Rome had a great impact on the disintegration of the Western Empire. The Visigoths soon left the city and turned northward into Southern Gaul and Spain where they established a kingdom that lasted until the Muslim conquests of the 8th century.

Around the middle of the 5th century the Huns, led by their brilliant and pitiless leader Attila, moved against the West. In 452, the Western emperor escaped from Rome and left it to Attila's mercy, but the Roman bishop, Pope Leo Ⅰ, travelled from the city to negotiate with the Huns on the slim chance that they might be persuaded to turn back. Oddly enough, Pope Leo succeeded in his mission. The Huns withdrew from Italy, perhaps because the army of the Huns found it really difficult to adapt to the Italian climate. The Hunnish empire collapsed shortly after Attila died and the Huns themselves vanished from history.

Then the Ostrogoths, now free of Hunnish control and led by a brilliant king named Theodoric the Great, advanced into Italy and established a strong state of their own. From 493 — 526, Italy was under the control of Theodoric who showed more appreciation of the Roman culture than any other Barbarian king. In this period, the Arian Ostrogoths and the Orthodox Romans mixed in a relatively harmonious way.

The Visigothic kingdom in Spain had a great number of elements in common with the Ostrogothic kingdom of Italy. They both believed that the Roman and German people could coexist in their community; both practised a warrior system dominating a larger native population; and both kept a lot of the Roman structure of government while excluding Romans from power. However, significant differences could also be found. There were no laws preventing intermarriage, and the Visigothic and Hispano-Roman peoples began to blend. They also developed a new system of law which became common to both peoples.

During the years of Theodoric's rule in Ostrogothic Italy, the only long-lasting German state on the European continent (the kingdom of the Franks) was coming into

---

① Arian：阿里乌斯派信徒。阿里乌斯为当时基督教一大教派，因否定三位一体学说而被斥为异端，并因反对教会占有财产，尤其是占有大量田产遭到正统教会敌视。该教派 4 世纪后在罗马帝国边境地区的哥特人和汪达尔人中广泛传播，6～7 世纪间逐渐消失。

② rampage：撒野，暴乱。对于当时罗马人来说，新迁移来的西哥特异教徒与野兽无异。

being. The Frankish kingdom later proved to be the most enduring of all the Barbarian successor states. The kingdom was created by the famous Barbarian king, Clovis (481—511), who enlisted the backing of the Church of the Occident, due to his conversion to Catholic Christianity. His conversion also smoothed the way for the later conversion to Christianity of the Frankish peoples.

By the year 510, a powerful new Frankish kingdom had been established by Clovis which occupied an area equal to present France and Western part of Germany.

During the following two hundred years, the Frankish and Gallo-Roman[①] cultures and peoples experienced a great time of fusion in the Frankish kingdom. But the Franks were warriors and they encouraged neither urban life nor trade. By 750, Frankish Gaul was still an agricultural society with the old Roman villa system of the late empire in smooth operation. However, in the matter of institutions, Germanic concepts of kingship and customary law had progressively taken the place of the Roman administrative structure.

By the beginning of the 5th century, the Barbarian's threat to the Western Roman Empire had forced the emperors to withdraw the Roman armies and to give up Britain. As a consequence, Anglo-Saxons and Germanic tribes from Denmark and Northern German settled easily in the British Isles. Although these same peoples had made plundering raids for several centuries, the withdrawal of the Roman armies gave them the chance to settle the lands instead of robbing them. However, they met resistance from the Celts, who still controlled the Western regions of Britain at the beginning of the 7th century. The German invaders finally succeeded in building small kingdoms throughout Britain.

The Organisational and Structural Changes of the Early Christian Church After chronic sufferings inflicted on Christians in the 3rd century by Roman rulers, the Roman Empire eventually became Christian in the 4th century. Emperor Constantine (288—337) strongly supported the development of Christianity from every aspect. One reason was that Christianity was spreading widely within the Roman Empire and the number of followers were growing in such rapid speed that they had already become a strong force that could not be ignored. Another reason was that Constantine understood that the Christian belief could meet the ideological foundation in favour of the political steadiness of the empire. Whatever were the purposes of Constantine in upholding the Christian church, Christianity entered a new era from 312, when Constantine united the Roman Empire. Thereafter, the Christian Church was confronted by a new society, and so a new crisis arose.

With the fast spreading and development of Christianity, organisational and

---

① Gallo-Roman：高卢罗马人。高卢人被罗马军队征服后民族融合而成的文化被称为高卢罗马文化。

religious disputes emerged. Throughout the 4th century, the Christian Church had undergone significant changes in its organisation and structure. During the period of Constantine the Great, the Christian Church was organised in accordance with the Roman administration. At that time, the Roman Empire was divided into five administrative regions; the Church government also had five administrative divisions. The Christian community in each city was in the charge of a bishop, whose area of jurisdiction was called a bishopric, or diocese. The bishoprics of each province were all together headed by an archbishop①. The most powerful member in the church was the Roman emperor. The bishops of the four cities in Rome had enjoyed special power in the church government because these four cities asserted that they were founded by the four apostles originally sent by Christ.

One of the reasons why the Christian Church needed a formal organisation was the religious disputes emerging with the fast spreading and development of Christian belief. Contradictory interpretations of the original doctrines came into being and heresies, different teachings from the official beliefs of the Church, divided Christians into various factions. The religious disputes also became political issues, resulting in different political cliques fighting with one another.

Arianism② was one of the major heresies in the 4th century, which involved the Christian Church in the biggest theological debate. Arianism was produced by the followers of Arius (256—336), a priest of Alexandria. He believed that Jesus Christ was actually human and thus not truly God. A bishop of Alexandria, Athanasius strongly opposed this idea and argued that Christ was human but also truly God. The heated disputes disturbed the Emperor Constantine and he decided to hold the first ecumenical council of the Church in 325. to settle the conflicts. The representatives from the entire Christian community assembled in Nicaea and confirmed the belief that Christ was of "the same substance" as God. Arianism was condemned in the council; Orthodox ideas scored the victory and the theory of the Trinity was established.

However, the Council of Nicaea didn't end the controversy and Arianism was still prevailing in some parts of Roman Empire for many years, and many Germanic states in the West converted to Arian Christianity. Due to the chaotic theological disputes in the 4th century, the Christian Church was in an urgent need of a strong leadership.

The Rule of St. Benedict Benedict was born in a good family in the mountains of central Italy and was sent to Rome to study. Not attracted by the city, he fled Rome

---

① archbishop：大主教，总教主。根据天主教及基督教部分教派的制度，数个教区组成一个教省，其教长称为"大主教"。

② Arianism：阿里乌教派，或称"亚流主义学派"等，是由曾任亚历山大主教的阿里乌所领导的基督教派别。根据《圣经》所载，主张耶稣次于天父和反对教会占有大量财富。在不同的大公会议中都斥为异端。

without completing his education; afterwards, he began his life as a hermit living in a cave near the ruins of Nero's country palace. Not long after, his saintly words prevailed and followers gathered around him. Benedict was not only a man of keen psychological insight but also a great organiser knowing how to best live the monastic life. He made significant contributions by collecting ideas from others to the written rule of St. Benedict that had far-reaching historic significance.

The Rule of St. Benedict produced a busy, simple and regulated life, designed for communities of men but also easily adapted to nunneries. While the would-be saints were received by Benedict's monasteries, ordinary people seeking to live pious lives were welcomed too. Even children could join the communities and many children were dedicated to religious life by their parents or guardians. These children were known as oblates①. The everyday arrangement of the monastic community included a series of prescribed activities—communal prayer, devotional reading, and all kinds of work, according to their need and ability. By giving away all personal possessions, the monks and nuns alike were living an unmarried life and obeying the abbot or abbess in order to resist money, sex and ambition, the three great temptations in the secular world. Monasticism was quite necessary in the early development of medieval civilisation. Monks played a heroic role in Christian civilisation. The dedication to God became the highest ideal of Christian life. Monks made copies of Latin works through which the legacy of the ancient world was passed on to Western civilisation. Moreover, the monks played an increasingly significant role in spreading Christianity to the entire European world.

Among all the monasteries founded by Benedict, the one located at Monte Cassino was regarded as the greatest. A generation after Benedict's death, his vision and rule was nearly destroyed. Lombards② plundered Monte Cassino, and its monks were separated in flight. Some sought asylum in Rome, where they met the future pope, Gregory the Great.

The Rise of the Pope's Power Gregory was deeply impressed by the monastic life. On hearing of his election he tried to reject the papal throne with genuine regret and had to be dragged into the basilica③ of St. Peter's to be consecrated. But once he was resigned to his new role, Gregory took full responsibility to extend the papal authority, because he believed that the pope was the rightful ruler of the church. His integrity, wisdom and political ability gave him an almost regal position in Rome and its region.

---

① oblate:(罗马天主教) 修士,修女,主要指献身某些教会,过着隐士般生活的修女和修士。

② Lombard:伦巴族人。公元 6 世纪入侵意大利并在波河河谷建立了一个王国。

③ basilica:有长方形廊柱大厅的基督教堂,此处指圣彼得大教堂。今天也可用来指具有这种建筑风格的巨型建筑。

In the 4th and 5th centuries western Christians accepted the bishop of Rome as head of the church. Under the reign of Gregory the Great, the papacy① and the Roman Catholic Church, the Christian church of the West, were in such a significant position that in the 7th and 8th centuries they played an increasingly prominent role in civilizing the Germans and encouraging the emergence of a distinctly new European civilisation.

Gregory fulfilled his role as pope and built Rome and its surrounding area into an administrative unit, later known as the Papal State. He did what he thought he should do: to prepare Rome for the defence against the Lombards, to establish a government for Rome, and to feed the people. He remained loyal to the empire and continued to recognise the Byzantine emperor as the rightful ruler of Italy.

Gregory also pursued a policy of extending papal authority over the Christian church in the West. He intervened in ecclesiastical conflicts throughout Italy and corresponded with the Frankish rulers, urging them to reform the church in Gaul. Furthermore, he sent missionaries to England to convert it and contributed to the conversion of some Germanic tribes.

St. Augustine and the Conversion of England Gregory sent a group of monks to convert the pagan Anglo-Saxons. The most important agent sent by the Pope was Augustine, a monk from Rome, who arrived in England in 597. The area now known as England was occupied at that time by a number of Germanic kingdoms. Augustine went first to Kent, the most powerful kingdom at that time, where he converted King Ethelbert; then thousands of Ethelbert's subjects were baptised by Augustine. Later Augustine himself became the first archbishop of Canterbury, the chief town of the realm and the headquarters of the new Church at that time.

The northward spreading of Roman Christianity in Britain encountered Irish Christianity moving southward. Eventually Roman Christianity prevailed, but the English church kept some Irish features. However, the most important thing was the concentration on monastic culture with special emphasis on learning and missionary work. By 700, the English church had become the best educated and most learned in Western Europe.

By the 6th century, Irish monasticism had become a flourishing institution with its own unique characteristics. It was strongly austere. Monks performed strenuous self-discipline, prayed and meditated frequently under extreme privations, and confessed their sins on a regular basis to their superiors.

Irish monasticism was also characterised by a great love of learning. Both Latin and Greek culture were favoured by the Irish and education was gradually fostered into a

---

① papacy：罗马教皇之职，在基督教世界中，教皇享有最高的立法权和司法权，能制定或废除教会法规，指定人员组成教廷，创立教区，任命主教，而且"在伦理和信仰上永无谬误"。教皇当选后任职终身，不受罢免，但可自行辞职。

major part of their monastic life. Since spoken Latin was being corrupted on the continent, which was eventually diversified into the Roman languages, such as Italian, French, and Spanish, the Irish monks contributed a lot to preserve classical Latin at the same time.

Encouraged by the Irish example, many English monks travelled to Europe to continue the work of conversion. Among them, the most important figure was Boniface (680—755), who undertook the conversion of pagan Germans. By the year 740, Saint Boniface, the "Apostle① of the Germans", had become the most famous Christian monk in Europe. Unfortunately fourteen years later he was killed while trying to convert the pagan Frisians②. It was the tireless efforts of the numerous Irish and English monks that made Europe the bastion of the Roman Catholic faith.

Christianity and Intellectual Life The Church played a key role in the social and political life especially during the emergence of the Middle Ages. Meanwhile, the churchmen also took the lead in intellectual places, especially the bishops. The culture of this period seems unimpressive and credulous in the eyes of some historians, but it should be remembered that scholars at that time were making the best of very difficult intellectual circumstances. Affected by the long-lasting war between the kingdoms, many scholars had no time for systematical education and they could only write in ungrammatical Latin.

In Ireland, at that time, monastic schools were the best in Western Europe and the monks were able to write perfect Latin. It was even boasted that the Irish monastic schools were the only ones where people could study Greek alongside Latin. The previous mentioned Benedictine monasteries were also important centres of learning, and their schools produced most European readers and writers during the period. Monks there copied as well as studied a vast number of manuscripts, and thus, many works of Latin antiquity were preserved.

Although many Christians in the early period fought the pagan culture of the classical world since they believed the Bible contained all the knowledge they needed, it was impossible to separate Christian theological thought from classical traditions and education. With the development of Christianity in the eastern Roman world, it adopted Greek as its primary language and the New Testament was written in Greek. Christians also got help from Greek thought when they tried to express complicated theological concepts. For this reason, the religion also helped to preserve Greco-Roman culture.

According to many historians, St. Bede the Venerable (673 — 735) could be

① Apostle：使徒，特指耶稣的十二使徒：Peter, Andrew, Jacos, John, Philip, Bartholomew, Thomas, Matthew, James, Thaddaeus, Simon, Judas，也喻指最初的传道者。

② Frisians：弗里西人，指弗里西岛或弗里斯兰省的土著或居民。

regarded as the greatest scholar of that age. Different from most other major scholars of the 500s and 600s, Bede had no connection with the old Roman aristocracy. When he was a child, he entered the monastery at Jarrow and lived his whole life there. *The Ecclesiastical History of England*①, his greatest work, "displays a critical sense far superior to that of his contemporaries"②. After Bede's death, a group of Anglo-Saxon missionaries would take his learning tradition to the Continent during the 8th century.

Jerome (345—420) was another important intellectual of the early church in this period. He pursued literary studies in Rome and became a master of Latin prose. He was a great scholar, and he translated the Old and New Testaments③ into Latin with extensive knowledge of both Hebrew and Greek.

The development of the medieval civilisation was deeply shaped by the church. The political leaders often worked hand in hand with the Churchmen; however, their interactions were accompanied by continuous tension: sometimes conflict, sometimes indifference. Now let us turn to another creative tension and profound influence on the medieval civilisation: its Byzantine and Islamic neighbours. By 700, besides the Eastern and Western halves of the old Roman Empire, a third power in the Mediterranean, Islam, became increasingly influential to the Empire. The lands of the old Roman Empire had been surrounded by three influences. To the west was the growing medieval west, an emerging social synthesis of Roman and Germanic traditions. To the east was the successor of Rome, the Eastern Roman Empire, out of which the Byzantine Empire was taking shape. To the south, the power of a new religion, Islam, had emerged. Historians sometimes take these three civilisations as the "three heirs" of Rome.

The Byzantine Empire During the 4th century, an obvious separation between the western and eastern parts of the Roman Empire gradually appeared. In the course of the 5th century, the Germanic tribes migrated into the western part of the empire and established many Germanic states while the Roman Empire in the east, centred on Constantinople, continued to exist.

While the Western Empire was collapsing, the East was enjoying prosperity. The able Eastern emperors carefully harboured their resources and strengthened their frontiers. The Eastern Empire lost many of its traditions of Latin culture and adopted

---

① *The Ecclesiastical History of England*:《英格兰教会史》，也称 *The Ecclesiastical History of English Race*，用拉丁语写成，是最早一部讲述盎格鲁、撒克逊、朱特人征服英伦诸岛的历史。

② Judith M. Bennett & C. Warren Hollister, *Medieval Europe*: *A Short History*, Boston: McGraw-Hill Education, 2010, p. 65.

③ *Old Testament*：基督教的《旧约全书》。它是基督宗教的启示性经典文献，内容和《希伯来圣经》一致，但编排不同。主要包括摩西五经、历史书、诗歌智慧书、大先知书、小先知书，总共 39 卷，分四类：律法书、历史书、智慧、先知书。从公元前 12 世纪至公元前 2 世纪，陆续用希伯来语写成。*New Testament*：《新约圣经》，又叫《新约全书》，基督教《圣经》的后一部分。

more of the Greek culture. After the fading of the Western Empire, the Eastern emperors still called themselves "Roman" and claimed that they governed the "Roman Empire", but modern historians give them the label—Byzantine Empire. Byzantium became Christian and absorbed Greek culture. It inherited from Roman governmental structure, and emphasised defence and self-preservation. There were some daring emperors in Byzantine history, but the prevailing political attitude was defence instead of conquest.

The Byzantine emperors also drew invaluable strength from the loyalty of their Christian subjects. For Byzantines, Christian faith was a compelling identity that defined their very existence.

In culture, the Byzantine Empire took the inheritance of Greece for most of its cultural traditions. This kind of culture had very little similarity to that of classical Athens. This was the artistic tradition that Byzantium inherited. The artists of the Byzantine Empire were able to produce enduring masterpieces; a classic example is the Hagia Sophia in Constantinople—today's Istanbul. In the picture we can see how the windows that encircle the dome make it appear to float on air.

The Byzantine Empire drew on the governmental traditions it had inherited from the later Roman Empire, on its Eastern Orthodox understanding of Christianity, and on the Greek culture of late antiquity. It saw great emperors and went through periods of greatness.

The Rule of Justinian (527—565) During the reign of Justinian, the Byzantine civilisation saw the first creative surge. When he became emperor of the Eastern Roman Empire, Justinian was driven by the dream of reviving the old Roman Empire by recovering its lost Western lands. Under his direction, his empire included Italy, part of Spain, North Africa, Asia Minor, Palestine, and Syria.

Justinian's most important contribution was his codification of Roman law. It was under his direction that the vast heritage of Roman law was assembled into a single, coherent body of jurisprudence—The Body of Civil Law.

Justinian owed a big part of his achievement to his wife and co-ruler, Empress Theodora, a woman with ambition and resolution. She was connected closely with the Justinian policies; it was sometimes impossible to distinguish her ideas from Justinian's.

The final years of Justinian were unhappy. After the death of Theodora in 548, Justinian became demoralised and irresolute. Devastated by wars and plague, Justinian's empire shrank and ended up bankrupt. Only three years after his death, the Lombards, a Germanic people originally from Northern Europe, conquered much of Italy.

The Rise of Islam In the year 622, an unknown Arab named Muhammad arrived in the town of Medina, the "City of the Prophet". Because his religious belief was not accepted by the local people, he was forced to flee his birth place, Mecca. The journey

to Medina, known as the Hegira[1], was such a momentous turning point in the development of Islam that it marked the beginning of the Muslim calendar. The year of Muhammad's flight to Medina became year one in the official calendar of Islam.

When he was young, Muhammad was hired by a wealthy widow named Khadija and managed the camel caravans for her. Khadija later became Muhammad's wife and his unwavering supporter. Because of his work, he travelled a lot and experienced some of the most prominent religions of his day such as Judaism and Christianity. In his middle years, Muhammad's revelations[2] began during a spiritual retreat in the countryside. In his visions, he got the words from the angel Gabriel that Allah was the single, almighty God, who had created the universe and everything in it. Muhammad held the belief that the final revelations of Allah were now being conveyed to him. Thereafter, the *Quran*[3] (or *Koran*), the written words out of his revelations, came into being, and all the followers of Allah could find the guidelines from it to live by. Muhammad's teachings formed the basis for the religion known as Islam, an Arabic word meaning "submission" or "surrender". Humans must subject themselves to Allah if they wished for an eternal life.

In the town of Medina, Muhammad soon began to win support from local people as well as from members of Bedouin[4] tribes in the surrounding countryside. Supported by these groups, he formed the first Muslim community. To Muslims, religious authority could not be separated from political power, and submission to the will of Allah implied submission to his Prophet, Muhammad. In the light of those guiding ideas, Muhammad became a leader not long after in both religious and political point of view. What's more, with his remarkable political and military skills he was able to build an unfailing military force. Under his guidance, Medina made war on Mecca, and in 630 the city was conquered and converted into the new faith. Henceforward, Muhammad's ideas disseminated across the Arabian Peninsula and united the Arab society both in religion and politics in a short time.

Muhammad's manifestations of divine truth are contained in the Quran with the basic message that there is no God but Allah and Muhammad is his Prophet. The Quran is the bedrock of Islamic faith. Recited to Muhammad by the angel Gabriel, the Quran's divine authority extends not only to its directions but also to its original script (of which there are 323, 621[5]). Strictly speaking, even translation is regarded as an offense

---

① Hegira：回教纪元，公元 622 年穆罕默德从麦加到麦地那的逃亡，标志着伊斯兰教纪元的开始。

② revelation：透露，泄漏，在基督教中指将上帝的指示告知世人，即"启示录"之意。

③ *Quran*：(伊斯兰教)《可兰经》，是穆罕默德在 23 年传教过程中陆续宣布的"安拉启示"。"Quran"一词系阿拉伯语，意为"宣读"、"诵读"或"读物"。

④ Bedouin：贝都因人，一个居无定所的阿拉伯游牧民族。

⑤ Judith M. Bennett & C. Warren Hollister, *Medieval Europe*: *A Short History*, Boston: McGraw-Hill Education, 2010, p. 85.

because it is best understood in Arabic. Therefore, to follow the guidance of Allah one has to learn the Arabic language first.

Islam was a straightforward and simple faith, emphasising the need to obey the will of Allah and assuring the followers eternal salvation. This meant following the five pillars of Islam①: the simple declaration of faith that there was no God but Allah and Muhammad was his messenger; standard prayer five times a day and public prayer on Friday at mid-day to worship Allah; fasting during the daylight hours of the month of Ramadan②(the 9th month in the Muslim calendar); making a pilgrimage (known as the hajj), if possible, to Mecca in one's lifetime; and giving alms to the poor and unfortunate. In addition to the "five pillars", it was not permitted for Muslims to gamble, to eat pork and to drink alcoholic beverages. Dishonest behaviour was prohibited. Sexual practices were also strict. Marriages arranged by parents and contact between unmarried men and women were discouraged. Males were allowed to have more than one wife in Bedouin custom, but Muhammad tried to limit the number of wives to four. The faithful who observed the law were guaranteed a place in an eternal paradise.

The ninth month of the year in the Muslim calendar is called Ramadan, which is the holy month of Islam during which all Muslims must fast from dawn to sunset. Observance of this holy month is regarded as one of the "five pillars" of the faith. Muhammad instituted the self-denial during his stay at Medina.

Islam was not just a set of religious beliefs, but a combination of religion and politics. Since submission to God required submission to his messenger, Muhammad was logically both a religious and political leader. The tension between church and state that troubled medieval Europe was thus weakened in the Muslim world. Muhammad's successors, the caliphs③(Arabic for "successors") were to take the responsibility of guarding both the faith and the faithful, thus a sacred state came into being.

The military prowess of the Arab tribes, now controlled by the teaching of the prophet, became more and more evident to the Mediterranean world. Muhammad and the early caliphs who succeeded him took up the Arabic tribal custom of making raids against one's enemies. The Quran called this activity "striving in the way of Lord", or a

---

① the five pillars of Islam：穆斯林五大教义：1. 信仰真主阿拉并只信阿拉；2. 祷告（每天五次）；3. 乐善好施；4. 守斋月；5. 麦加朝圣（只要身体允许，一年一次）。

② Ramadan：斋月，穆斯林历的第九个月。穆斯林认为这个月是真主阿拉将《可兰经》赐给穆罕默德圣人的月份，并且《可兰经》里明言规定此月符合条件之穆斯林必须守斋戒。在斋月里，每天日出至日落期间，除了患病者、旅行者、乳婴、孕妇、哺乳妇、产妇、正在行经的妇女以及作战的士兵外，成年的穆斯林必须严格守斋，不吃不喝、不抽烟、不饮酒、不行房事等。

③ caliph：哈里发，阿拉伯语意为"代理人"或"继位人"。《可兰经》中有"我必定在大地上设置一个代理人"的经文。穆罕默德及其以前的众先知被认为是阿拉在大地上的代理人。后该词被用于指穆罕默德逝世后继任伊斯兰教国家政教合一的领袖，今天也用来尊称某些伊斯兰国家官员。

jihad[①]. Though it was named "Holy War", the jihad has its origins from traditional Arabic tribal raids taken as a diversion to the warlike energies of the Bedouin tribes. Since conversion to Islam was purely voluntary, the jihad, sometimes regarded as a kind of aggressive activity, was not conducted to convert others to Islam; instead, its purpose was to require those who did not convert only to obey Muslim rule and pay taxes.

Thanks to the youthful vigour of Islam and the weakness of their enemies, the Persian and Byzantine Empires, exhausted in a long, desperate conflict, the Arab armies pushed into Byzantium and Persia quickly. In 636, the Arabs annihilated a huge army and captured Damascus and Jerusalem in Syria (an area much larger than the modern-day state of the same name). In 637, they crushed the army of the Persian Empire and captured Ctesiphon, the capital of Persia. In less than ten years, they had conquered all Persia. Amazingly enough, most Persians accepted the new faith while nevertheless retaining much of their native culture and language. Soon after, the Indian subcontinent was probed deeply by Muslim armies, and the religious foundations of modern Muslim states such as Pakistan and Bangladesh were consolidated. In the same time, other Arab armies were pushing westward toward Egypt. In the 640s, Alexandria, the great metropolis that had for centuries been a centre of culture, science and Jewish and Christian theology, was captured by Arab armies. After conquering Egypt and Syria, Arabs captured the island of Cyprus and raided ancient Rhodes; afterwards, in a sea battle in 655, they destroyed the Byzantine navy.

From 655 to 661, the succession to the Prophet became the problem disturbing the Islamic world. Ali, the cousin and son-in-law of Muhammad himself, competed with the Umayyads, a leading family in the old Meccan commercial elite, for the succession to the caliphate. Ali's followers insisted that only a direct descendant of the Prophet was qualified for the leadership of the Islamic community. By 661, Ali was assassinated and the Umayyad dynasty began. The Umayyad caliphs moved the Islamic capital to Damascus and ruled there for nearly a century. Due to the divergence inside the caliphate, a split in Islam took place between the Shiites[②], who considered only the descendants of Ali as their true rulers, and the Sunnites[③], who considered the descendants of the Umayyads as the true caliphs. This division in Islam began in the 7th century and has lasted until now.

---

① jihad：伊斯兰圣战。伊斯兰圣战是伊斯兰教的一个重要组成部分，是伊斯兰精神最有力的体现。伊斯兰圣战规模大、时间持久、影响深。一般认为，伊斯兰圣战分为两种：一种是为主道和信仰而战的小圣战，另一种是同与生俱来的内在邪恶进行不懈斗争的大圣战。

② Shiites：什叶派(伊斯兰教徒的一派)，什叶派认为只有阿里是穆罕默德的合法继承人，伊斯兰社会应该由阿里及其后裔领导，该派约占世界穆斯林总数的 10%。

③ Sunnites：逊尼派(伊斯兰教徒的一派)，逊尼派承认四大哈里发和以后的伍麦叶王朝、阿拔斯王朝以及奥斯曼土耳其帝国哈里发的合法性，约占世界穆斯林总数的 90%。

At the beginning of the 8th century, the Muslims made new attacks at both the western and eastern ends of the Mediterranean world. After sweeping across North Africa, the Muslims crossed the Strait of Gibraltar and moved into Spain around 710. Meanwhile, the Visigothic kingdom came to an end, and most of Spain was turned into a Muslim state by 725 with its centre at Cordoba. The expansion of Muslims in Europe didn't come to a halt until they were defeated at the Battle of Tours in 732.

At the same time, another Muslim army launched a naval attack on Constantinople hoping to destroy the Byzantine Empire. But the Muslim fleet was destroyed by the Byzantines in the spring of 718. The defeat of the Muslims had no doubt saved the Byzantine Empire and indirectly Christian Europe, since the fall of Constantinople would have opened the door to Muslim invasion of Eastern Europe. Then, the Byzantine Empire and Islam established a delicate frontier in southern Asia Minor.

Since the Southern and Eastern Mediterranean parts of the old Roman Empire had been defeated and conquered, the Arab expansion was eventually brought to a conclusion. Islam dominated much of the old Roman Empire. The expansion had brought enormous wealth and new ethnic groups into the world of Islam, and meanwhile it also brought contact with Byzantine and Persian civilisation. By the mid-700s, Islam, Byzantine, and western Christendom① had divided the old Roman Empire. As a result, both Greek culture and the older civilisations of the ancient Near East together moulded the new Arab empire. Being educated in new ways, the conqueror's offspring would be able to establish a brilliant civilisation that would inevitably impinge upon the intellectual development of Western Europe.

Section Two The Development of the Early Middle Ages (c. 750—c. 1000)

In the Early Middle Ages, the European civilisation entered into a new era of development, with old powers fading and new powers emerging. The realignment of powers redefined the nature of the European civilisation and relocated its centre. In 800, Charlemagne became the Roman emperor. His enthronement was a historic event with symbolic meanings. He was the descendant of a Germanic tribe which converted to Christianity. The mixed cultural identity of the new Roman emperor symbolised the integration of the different European powers—the German tribes, the classical power and the Christian power. The three powers began to emerge and integrate with the decline of the Roman Empire and the founding of the Germanic states resulting in a new Western empire with a unique European identity. The centre of the European civilisation also moved from the South to the North, from Italy and the Mediterranean during the Roman Empire to the North of the Alps.

---

① Christendom：基督教徒，(集合称)基督教界，是对整个基督教国家和基督教徒的统称。

In the same period, Europe also experienced a decentralisation of political power. During the Carolingian rule, power was concentrated in the hands of the lords who dominated in the political landscape of Europe, monopolizing legal, administrative, and military power. However, the centralised political system gradually gave way to the feudal system, in which the ownership of power and properties was disseminated. The invasions by the Muslims, the Magyars①, and the Vikings② accelerated this feudalisation process. According to Karl Marx, the economic relationship between people must comply with the productive force, and a suitable economic relationship can stimulate people's productive force. With the introduction of the feudal system, the rural Europe had witnessed an unprecedented development by 1000 despite its previous backwardness. Europe was embarking on a road of greater prosperity and success. Different from the fast rural development in Europe, the Byzantine and Islamic worlds continued to develop their prosperous urban cultures.

Charlemagne and the Carolingian Empire In the 8th century, Francia and other successor states in the West were dwarfed by the powers of Byzantium and Arabia. The great cities then included Constantinople and Damascus, while the Franks, mainly an agrarian people, had no cities worth the name. Yet by the end of the 700s, Francia had united much of the West into a single dominion which was known as the Carolingian Empire.

The name Carolingian was from carolus, Latin for "Charles", which was not taken from its greatest king but instead from Charlemagne's grandfather Charles Martel(714—741). Charles Martel, son of Pepin of Heristal, was a skilful and ruthless military chieftain. At his time, he was called "the hammer". His leadership provided Francia with a united response against the Muslim attack and his victories over Christians and Muslims alike extended the boundaries of the Frankish state. As grandfather of the greatest king, Charles Martel left his son and grandson a special rewarding system. Charles Martel rewarded his soldiers with land and other properties they took over from the Frankish church. Although the church complained loudly, the soldiers were happy and were encouraged to be brave warriors. In 741, Charles Martel died. His kingdom and power were passed on to his two sons, Carloman and Pepin the Short. The Carolingians practiced the divided succession among male heirs. Thanks to its luck, the Carolingian rulers, over several generations, had only one long-surviving heir. In 747, Carloman retired voluntarily to the monastery of Monte Cassino and left his land to his

① Magyar：马札尔人，生活在顿河和第聂伯河之间的列维底亚，是匈牙利一个主要少数民族，在 9～10 世纪劫掠整个欧洲，后被日耳曼民族打败，皈依基督教。

② Vikings：维京人，北欧海盗。在斯堪的纳维亚语中意为"来自峡湾的人"，今天通常指生活在中世纪早期的斯堪的纳维亚人。

brother, Pepin the Short. Now Pepin had undisputed power over Francia and he was anointed① the name of "king" by Pope Zacharius Ⅰ in 751. The anointing armed the new dynasty with the strongest of spiritual sanctions: Carolingians now ruled not only by force but also by God's favour. Pepin's death in 768 brought to the throne of the Frankish kingdom his son, a dynamic and powerful ruler known to history as Charles the Great, or Charlemagne. Charlemagne was a determined and decisive man, a talented military commander, a statesman of rare ability, an ally of the church, and a friend of learning. During his lengthy rule he greatly expanded the territory of the Carolingian empire.

After the great expansion of the empire, Charlemagne was no longer a mere Frankish king but the master of the West. On the Christmas day of 800 Pope Leo Ⅲ formally recognised Charlemagne's accomplishment by placing the imperial crown on his head, which was later called "the Imperial Coronation of 800".

Although Charlemagne made great advances, his realm remained economically underdeveloped. The industry was minimal and towns were small and scattered. In order to encourage economic growth, Charlemagne constructed roads, bridges, and lighthouses; he even contemplated building a canal to link the Rhine and Danube rivers. Although contemporary evidence is frustratingly thin, a folk memory preserved by later generations of Jews shows that Charlemagne might also have tried to jump-start the Frankish economy by encouraging the further settlement of Jews within Francia. The administration of the empire was also advanced by Charlemagne's considerable innovation. He made laws and rules that were followed throughout his ruling territory. He also sent his men to different places to monitor the enforcement of his laws and rules and to collect taxes.

However, the Carolingian Empire was not as powerful as it appeared to be. On the contrary, the empire was afflicted by its widespread local and regional violence: bloody fighting between aristocratic families, private conflicts over disputed lands, and countless robberies. Charlemagne's efforts to monitor and ensure the loyalty of regional administrators were successful only to a limited extent. The fact was that the local administrators followed the laws and regulations only out of respect and loyalty to Charlemagne as an individual person. They did not do it for patriotism or loyalty to the Empire. They had faith in Charlemagne's power in securing their own interests. It was a mutually beneficial relationship. As a result, because later emperors did not have the same power as Charlemagne to enforce their rule, the loyalty level of the local administrators declined.

Charlemagne had a strong desire to revive learning in his kingdom. Reasons for this

---

① anoint:(如奉圣意般地)选定,指定,为使这一指定更加神圣化,通常会为被选定之人举行抹油的仪式。

desire may have been that he needed educated clergy for the church and literate officials for the government, or maybe he had a strong personal intellectual curiosity. Charlemagne raised the intellectual standards by assembling scholars from all over Europe. The scholars that Charlemagne gathered round him included Charlemagne's biographer, Einhard from Eastern Francia; Paul the Deacon, the poet-historian from Monte Cassino; The odulf from Iberia, and the greatest of all, Alcuin from York in England. They all began at the most basic level by providing basic education for children. Like the Roman emperors, Charlemagne also sought aid from the church for the intellectual revival. Because Francia had no professional teachers, Charlemagne ordered the cathedrals and monasteries of his kingdom to operate schools, and most Carolingian monasteries and cathedrals tried all they could to improve the quality and quantity of the schooling they offered. The students they trained pursued careers as teachers or administrators.

More importantly, the Carolingian scholars invented a new written language, which was later called the Caroline script. It was developed on the basis of both the earlier Irish scripts and the Frankish monasteries. The new written system was much clearer than other systems used at that time. It was so clear that it became the basis of the modern script used today.

Great as Charlemagne's empire was, it could not rival those of Byzantium and Islam. Soon after Charlemagne's death, the Carolingian Empire began to disintegrate. The empire was at its verge of collapse when Charlemagne died in 814. Its process of disintegration was accelerated by the internal conflicts and external invasion. Louis the Pious (814 — 840), Charlemagne's son, was unable to control either the Frankish aristocracy or his own four sons who fought continually. When the civil war between the sons was finally resolved in 843, the Treaty of Verdun reconciled not only the differences of the competing brothers but also differences of the competing regions. This pivotal treaty divided the Carolingian Empire into three new states, and the borders created by the Treaty drew the rough outlines of the modern state of France and Germany. Lothar, the eldest brother, kept the prestigious imperial title but retained practical authority over only a third of the old empire including Rome as well as Aachen, stretching from the centre of the Italian peninsula to the North Sea. This realm soon dissolved after Lothar's death in 855. But the kingdom of his two brothers proved to be more enduring. East Francia was taken by Louis the German, which developed into modern Germany; West Francia was taken by Charles the Bald, which was the beginning of today's France.

Although the internal division had weakened the leadership of the Carolingians seriously, a worse threat was from the outside of the Empire. Muslim pirates, Viking raiders, and Magyar horsemen, like the barbarians who had troubled Rome in the 4th and 5th centuries, brought the Carolingians suffering and terror. From the south came the Muslims. Even in the 7th and early 8th centuries, Muslims sought to settle in Europe. But in the 9th and 10th centuries, they came as raiders rather than as settlers. From the northern Italian peninsula came the Magyars, who were descendants of fierce nomadic horsemen from the Asiatic steppes. And from the north of Charlemagne's old empire came the Vikings (or Northmen) of Scandinavia, the most powerful invaders of all.

The Viking raids and settlements also had important political repercussions. They led to significant changes to the political and social customs. In West Francia, the royal authority got weaker and weaker, since it could not cope with the Viking raids, and the aristocratic power grew strong. Elsewhere royal authorities were challenged by the invasions. Under the pressure of the outside invasion, small kingdoms began to unite, such as England. Seeking protection, Europeans were ready to submit to whatever leadership as long as it could provide an effective defence—whether kings, territorial princes① or even bishops as in the northern Italian peninsula.

Before they were invaded by the Vikings, the small kingdoms in Britain had gradually passed under the control of four larger ones: Northumbria in the north, Mercia in the Midlands, East Anglia in the southeast, and Wessex in the south. At the moment of worst crisis, Alfred the Great rose to the Wessex throne. Alfred was a remarkable leader. In the spring of 878, he defeated the Danish army at the battle of Edington. Alfred extended his realm to the north and east, by 886 he had captured London—Britain's chief city even at that time. The work of Alfred was carried on by his able successors in the first half of the 10th century. His two children—Edward, king of Wessex and Ethelfled, lady of the Mercians—worked in close harmony to defend their realms against the Vikings. In the process, an English kingdom was gradually created out of many realms of the Anglo-Saxons. By the 990s almost all of Britain south of the Firth of Forth was in the hands of Alfred's successors, and the king of Wessex became the king of England.

The World of Feudalism A new type of relationship between free individuals gradually appeared because of the renewed invasions and the disintegration of the Carolingian world. When governments lost the ability of defending their subjects, it became important to find some powerful lord who could offer protection in exchange for service. Thus, a new system of rule known as feudalism came into being.

Feudalism is a modern word; in medieval times it was called vassalage②. Karl Marx

---

① prince：指王室的一名男性成员，但在中世纪时期，指某一地区的统治者。

② vassalage：附庸地位，附属或服从的地位。诸侯是国王的附属，骑士是诸侯的附属，这是欧洲封建制度的框架。

used feudalism to describe the economy of the Middle Ages. For him, feudalism was a stage in economic development, located between slavery and capitalism, in which serfs on their manors were forced to labour on behalf of a warrior class. Many other historians use feudalism to describe the political and social structures instead of the economic structures which are called separately as manorialism①. Here, we will use feudalism to mean political and social arrangements and treat the economic system as manorialism.

The key element of feudalism was vassalage. It was rooted in a relationship between mounted warriors—a lord and his vassal②. It can be dated back to Roman and barbarian traditions. The deal between the lord and vassals was in fact quite simple. The lord gave the knights and nobles land. In return, the knights and nobles fought for the lord. The land-oriented relationship was a typical feudalist relationship. The term feudalism was taken from feudum, the Latin word for fief. Fief in Latin refers exactly to the above land-based agreement between the lord and the vassals. By 900, a series of feudal regimes had emerged in France. By the 10th century another essential part of the feudal landscape appeared in Europe: castles. At this time castles were powerful instruments of defence and territorial control.

With the development of sub-infeudation, land-holding also became increasingly complicated. Some vassals had their own sub-vassals and became sub-lords themselves. Similar to the lord-vassal relationship, the sub-lords provided their sub-vassals with land in exchange for their military service. These sub-vassals might again have had their own sub-sub-vassal. The vassals at the bottom of the hierarchy might be simple knights who did not have hand to bequeath. In this way, the lord-vassal relationship became multi-layered, with the upper layers possessing more land and power than the lower layers.

At all levels, the relationship between lord and vassal was always an honourable one concerning only free men and did not imply any sense of servitude. The system of feudalism became ever more widespread.

Feudalism was closely dependent on the economic system of manorialism. The landholding class of nobles and knights comprised a military elite whose ability to function as warriors depended on having the leisure time to pursue the arts of war. Landed estates, located on the fiefs given to a vassal by his lord and worked by a dependent peasant class, provided the economic sustenance that made this way of life possible. A manor was simply an agricultural estate operated by a lord and worked by peasants. The manor became the fundamental unit of

---

① manorialism：庄园制度。中世纪初期，西欧国家生产力低下，封建领主主要依靠自己的地产生活。国王、教会和大封建主都建立庄园，形成了庄园制度。庄园生产者主要是农奴，封建领主对农奴拥有行政和司法权力，庄园领主派管家主持生产，并设置庄园法庭，以加强对农奴的控制。

② vassal：下属，尤指国王所分封的封臣和诸侯，他们又将自己的封地分封给自己的下属，这种层层附属关系构成了中世纪欧洲封建制度的基本框架。

rural organisation in the Middle Ages.

Manorialism can be seen as a result of the unsettled conditions of the Early Middle Ages. Then, small farmers often needed protection or food in the face of poor harvests. Free peasants exchanged their freedom to the lords of large landed estates for protection and use of the lord's land. Although a large class of free peasants continued to exist, more and more free peasants became serfs. ① By the 9th century, about 60% of the population of Western Europe had become serfs.

The serfs, in exchange for security, provided labour service for the lord. They farmed one third to half of the lands on the manor for the lord, and they used the rest for themselves. Serfs usually worked about three days a week for their lord. Besides farming, they were also supposed to provide other labour services, such as building the barns and digging ditches.

The serfs paid the lord part of their produce as rents. They also had to pay the lord for using the manor's common pasturelands, streams, ponds, and surrounding woodlands. For instance, a serf should turn over part of his catch to his lord for fishing the pond or stream on the lord's manor. In addition, it was the peasants' duty to pay a tenth of their produce to the local village church.

Lords possessed a variety of legal rights over their serfs as a result of their low status. Serfs were legally bound to the lord's lands and could not leave without his permission. They could not marry anyone outside the manor without the lord's approval even though marriage was free. Furthermore, lords were entitled to try peasants in their own court since public rights or political authority was sometimes exercised on their lands. Peasants also had to pay for certain services, such as having their grain ground into flour in the lord's mill. A lord, so to speak, had virtual control over both the lives and property of his serfs.

In the Early Middle Ages, whether free or not, a vast majority of men and women, possibly as high as 90%, worked the land. Compared to the Byzantine Empire or Muslim caliphates, Western Europe in the Early Middle Ages was an underdeveloped, predominantly agricultural society.

The World of Islam The Umayyad dynasty of caliphs had established Damascus as the centre of an Islamic empire created by Arab expansion in the 7th and 8th centuries. But Umayyad rule created resentment, and the Umayyads also helped bring about their own end by their corrupt behaviour. In 750, eighteen years after the battle of Tours, the Umayyads were overthrown. Their successors, the Abbasids moved the capital of the caliphate from Damascus to Baghdad on the Tigris River in the old Persian Empire. The Abbasids' government relied on Persian aristocrats.

---

① serf：农奴，详见第一章。

The Abbasid rulers brought much change to the world of Islam. They tried to break down the distinctions between Arab and non-Arab Muslims. Arabs now shared power with Persians, Syrians① and others. Arabic language united these people, and Muslims began to be affected by the new civilisation around them.

The culture of Baghdad reached its height under the Abbasid caliph Harun al-Rashed (786—809), whose reign was often described as the golden age of the Abbasid caliphate. The era of Harun al-Rashid was notable for its vigorous intellectual life. In Baghdad, Harun's son and successor founded the house of Wisdom which acted as a library, an institute of advanced study, and a centre of translation. In the house of wisdom, scholars of various faiths, Muslim, Christian, Jewish, and even pagan, pursued learning together.

Despite the prosperity, all was not quite well in the empire of the Abbasids. By the later century the trend toward disintegration gained force as Egypt, Syria, and eastern Persia enhanced ties with the government in Baghdad. As province after province broke free, the centralised power of the Abbasids became more notional than real.

Section Three Significant Changes of the High Middle Ages (c. 1001—c. 1300)

Along with fewer invaders, more powerful kings, and increasing literacy, the High Middle Ages also witnessed a better climate, especially for the people who lived to the north. In this period, Europe was warmer and less rainy by several degrees than it had been. The summer growing season became longer, and marshes and bogs receded into fields. New agricultural practices that increased the food supply helped give rise to a commercial and urban revival that, accompanied by a rising population, created new dynamic elements in a formerly static society.

We are still struggling to find out the reasons for this improvement, but we are sure about the results. On the one hand, with agricultural technology innovation and substantial growth in food production, the agricultural products market began to take shape, and people's lives tended to become stable. On the other hand, the increased productivity and population growth brought business recovery and revival of urban life. As a result, a large number of new towns came into being across Europe. In short, the High Middle Ages (1000—1300) was a period of recovery and growth for Western civilisation, characterised by a greater sense of security and a burst of energy and enthusiasm. Both the Catholic Church and the feudal states recovered from the invasions and internal dissension of the Early Middle Ages.

---

① Syrian：叙利亚人，其民族来源可以追溯到阿拉米人、亚述人和迦南人，7世纪被阿拉伯人征服并逐渐阿拉伯化。

Social Life Throughout the Middle Ages, the most important aspect of economic development is the expansion of agricultural production. In the 10th and 11th centuries, peasants in Europe produced more goods more efficiently. At the same time, Europe experienced a virtual doubling of its population. This rise in population was physically evident in the growth of agricultural villages, towns, and cities and in the increase in arable land. Pushed by more lands and a bigger population with advanced tools and skills, the economy of Europe grew.

During the High Middle Ages, an agricultural revolution occurred in Europe. As people drained swamps, cleared forests, and built dikes to reclaim land from the sea, more land was brought under cultivation. At the same time, some peasants learned to cultivate their lands more intensely. Here, the key element was the rotation of cropped and fallow land. In medieval Europe fertilizers were so scarce that lands were often kept productive by letting them lie fallow (meaning uncultivated). Earlier systems of rotation worked on a two-field basis: one field was cultivated and the other left fallow. Now, beginning in the 8th century, a better three-field rotation took place. The simple change kept two-thirds of the cultivated land in use instead of one-half of the two-field system. Last, but not least, productivity of the lands was improved greatly by gradual improvements in agrarian technology. Among all the new tools, metal tools and the new sort of plow were crucial. This plow was driven by well-harnessed oxen or horses, and it was heavy enough to cut through rich soil. People of the High Middle Ages also learnt to harness the power of water and wind to do jobs formerly done by human or animal power. The watermill became widespread. Dams were constructed to increase waterpower. Where rivers were unavailable or not easily dammed, Europeans developed windmills to harness the power of the wind.

The development of agricultural production contributed to the revival of commerce and manufacturing. It continued until the mid-14th century, when commerce, as the driving force, boosted economies in Europe, for which the emergence of new manufacturing offered more types of goods. Meanwhile, the continuing population expansion stimulated an impressive expansion of trade and industry.

The medieval commercial revival was characteristic of the opening right from the start, breaking through the limitations of area. The merchants from Pisa, Genoa, and Venice frequently entered the market in the Eastern Mediterranean and brought a new vitality to the inland cities. At the same time, the development of East-West trade was also up. In the Central Middle Ages, a much wider array of goods moved through a much wider assortment of local, regional, and international networks. Thus market villages① and regional towns② came

---

① market villages：集市村，专门负责农村地区的贸易，每周组织农民进行各类物品的交易。

② regional towns：地区大镇，为满足居民更多生活需求，帮助其实现更远距离物品交易的贸易中心。

into being. Whether in small markets or big cities, commerce lubricated the high medieval economy with an ever-increasing flow of money, which supported the building of the cathedrals, financed the crusades, and gave substance to the magnificent religious culture of the 13th century—money and ardent faith.

The rise in productivity and upsurge of commerce were accompanied by a general reawakening of urban life. Towns had greatly declined in the Early Middle Ages, especially to the North of the Alps. Old Roman cities continued to exist but had dwindled in size and population. With the revival of trade, merchants, skilled craftsmen and artisans came to settle in these activated old cities. At the end of the 11th century, towns were developing rapidly across Europe. The European economy in the High Middle Ages remained fundamentally agrarian, but the towns, as centres of commercial and industrial enterprise, were the greatest economic catalysts of the era.

Christianity in the High Middle Ages With the dawning of the High Middle Ages there emerged a newly invigorated papacy, dedicated to ecclesiastical reform and the spiritual regeneration of Christian society.

But before the beginning of the papal reform in the mid-11th century, the realities of the contemporary society were far different from the papal theory of Christian society. Based on the venerable tradition running back to the 5th century, the pope was the monarch of the apostolic Church. And the properly ordered society, the truly Christian society was one dominated by the Church which, in turn, was dominated by the pope. Nevertheless, in the mid-11th century, the Church was under the control of aristocratic lay proprietors. The Church was a vital part of the early medieval society, but it was always subordinate to the lay ruling class. In order to regain the control over the continent, a series of reforming popes launched a movement for change.

During the 11th century, Gregory Ⅶ, the greatest of the reforming popes by then, who was convinced that he had been chosen by God to reform the Church, claimed that he was God's "vicar on earth" and that the pope's authority extended over all Christians, including rulers. With the elimination of lay investiture, the Church was freed from the interference of lords in the appointment of church officials. However, the claims of Gregory Ⅶ triggered new conflicts with King Henry Ⅳ of Germany, who had appointed high-ranking clerics, especially bishops for many years in order to use them as administrators. As one of the great conflicts between church and state in the High Middle Ages, the Investiture Controversy① between Henry Ⅳ and Gregory Ⅶ dragged on until a new German king and a new pope compromised and reached the *Concordat of*

---

① Investiture Controversy：主教续任权之争，指 11 世纪末至 12 世纪初，教皇与神圣罗马帝国皇帝之间的权力之争。始于教皇格列高利七世与皇帝亨利四世为主教及修道院长续任权属于谁而产生的争议，终于 1122 年，亨利五世与教皇卡利克斯特二世签订《沃尔姆斯宗教协定》，双方达成妥协。

*Worms*① in 1122. The agreement provided that in the future bishops should be "invested with the symbols of their political authority by the king and should take an oath of fealty to him as his vassals, but the archbishop had the right to invest them with the symbols of their spiritual functions."② The continued political and religious battle for decades was temporarily ended.

In the 12th century, the popes intended to consolidate their power and build a strong administrative institution. Papal authority over the European church had increased immeasurably and the dream of a papal monarchy came ever nearer to realisation. Revenues flowed into its treasury from all the states of Western Christendom; the traditional theory of papal supremacy over Christian society was magnified and elaborated by the canon lawyers; the papal curia served as a court of last appeal for an immense network of ecclesiastical courts. Meanwhile, a clearly organised hierarchical structure within the Church came into being. The pope and papal curia (staffed by high church officials known as cardinals, the pope's major advisers and administrators) were at the apex of the administrative structure. Below the pope and cardinals were hierarchically archbishops, bishops and priests.

The Church reached the peak of its political, intellectual, and secular power in the 13th century during the papacy of Pope Innocent Ⅲ from 1198 to 1216. Pope Innocent Ⅲ was regarded as history's most powerful pope, "a brilliant, astute diplomat, an imperious, self-confident aristocrat who, although genuinely pious was distinctly aloof from the surging religious emotionalism of the humbler folk of his age."③ He believed that the pope was the supreme judge of European affairs and intervened in politics everywhere, and virtually realised Gregory's dream of a unified Christian world.

Although it is true to a certain degree to say that the High Middle Ages were dominated by the institutional church, the Church sometimes functioned imperfectly and often fell short of its ideals. Worse, the Church was not free from corruption among its own personnel. However, the greatest shortcoming of the Church was not gross corruption but a mechanical attitude toward the Christian religious life. Although the popes in the 13th century won an overwhelming victory in power politics, their spiritual role was more and more obscured. As a result, the papacy's international religious mission was being steadily subordinated to its local political interests. Gradually, it lost

---

① *Concordat of Worms*：1122年，神圣罗马帝国皇帝亨利五世同罗马教皇卡利克斯特二世为解决主教续任权之争，在沃尔姆斯缔结的宗教协议。根据协约，皇帝放弃亲授戒指和法杖的权力，但保留了另外一个特权：在教皇授予戒指和法杖之前，用自己的权杖轻点未来的主教。

② Edward Mcnall Burns, *Western Civilizations*, Vol. Ⅰ, 7th Ed., New York: W. W. Norton & Company, Inc., 1968, p. 364

③ C. Warren Hollister, *Medieval Europe: A Short History*, 2nd Ed., New York: John Wiley & Sons, Inc., 1968, p. 198.

its hold on the heart of Europe.

Crusades between 1096 and 1272, as a curious mix of God and warfare, waves of zealous and adventuresome European Christians mounted crusades against the Muslims. Eight main crusades were launched, each lasting from one to four years, except the Seventh Crusade, which dragged on longer from 1248 to 1254. These campaigns gave the revived papacy of the Middle Ages another opportunity to demonstrate its influence over European society.

The crusading movement grew out of developments in both east and west. In the east, the balance of power between the Byzantine Empire and various Muslim Caliphates was upset by the 11th-century arrival of a new power: the Seljuk Turks① converted to the Islamic faith. In 1071, the Seljuks defeated a Byzantine army and occupied Asia Minor. That same year, they took Jerusalem too. In the west, the papacy, under the direction of the Gregorian movement regained its control over the emperors. When the West heard that Seljuk atrocities stood against Christian pilgrims to Jerusalem, the papacy grew concerned. And when the desperate Byzantine emperor appealed to the west for help, he wrote to Pope Urban Ⅱ instead of the holy Roman Emperor or any other existing monarch. The pope decided to respond to this challenge.

In 1095, Pope Urban Ⅱ summoned Christian warriors to take up the cross and reconquer the Holy Land. In the powerful address to the Frankish aristocracy, the pope called on the French warriors to avenge Seljuk atrocities and to drive the "the infidel②" from Jerusalem. He also promised that they would obtain the remission of their sins and be sure of the incorruptible glory of the Kingdom of Heaven. Enthusiastically, the French warriors poured into crusading armies, as did the peasants, townspeople, women, children, even the infirm and the aged. This army was poor, ill-equipped, disorganised, lacking in military discipline, and encouraged by simply religious faith. It was not strange that they were quickly cut down by the Seljuk troops; the survivors continued their dream by joining a more professional force that arrived the following year. This was later called the "Popular Crusade".

In 1097, another force, composed mainly of knights from France, Normandy, and Norman Sicily, came with a better preparation. From the very beginning, the crusaders and their Byzantine allies differed in objective. The crusaders were focused on nothing but the conquest of the Holy Land, while the Byzantines wanted only the recapture of the provinces of Asia Minor. So the crusaders soon broke with the Byzantines and hurled themselves across Asia Minor into Syria. In the summer of 1099 they conquered Jerusalem. The goal of the First Crusade had been achieved and in the Holy Land the

---

① Seljuk Turks:塞尔柱土耳其人,塞尔柱王朝突厥部族的人。

② infidel:不信仰基督的人,异教徒,在中世纪晚期主要指伊斯兰教徒。

crusaders celebrated their victory by plundering the city and cruelly slaughtering its Muslim and Jewish inhabitants. The conquered lands were organised into four crusader states: the county of Edessa, the principality of Antioch, the county of Tripoli, and the kingdom of Jerusalem. This is called the First Crusade.

The Second Crusade (1147—1148) was inspired by the powerful preaching of Bernard of Clairvaux (1090—1153) and led by the king of France and the Holy Roman Emperor. The campaign began with high hopes but ended in defeat and disaster at the hands of Seljuk Turks in Asia Minor. In 1187 Jerusalem was recaptured by the Muslims under Saladin, Sultan of Egypt, causing Emperor Frederick Barbarossa and the kings of France and England, Philip Ⅱ "Augustus" and Richard "the Lion-Hearted", to embark on the Third Crusade (1187—1192). This was a strong start, but the crusade quickly faltered. Eventually, Richard negotiated a settlement whereby Saladin agreed to allow Christian pilgrims free access to Jerusalem. However, on his way home, Richard fell into hostile hands and became the prisoner of Frederick Barbarossa's son, the Emperor Henry Ⅵ (1165—1197), until his mother, Eleanor, could raise the ransom to buy his freedom.

The 13th century witnessed a sequence of failures of various other crusades. The 4th Crusade initiated by Pope Innocent Ⅲ in 1193 ended with the fall of the Latin Empire of Constantinople. In Germany in 1212, a visionary, ill-organised enterprise known as the "Children's Crusade" ended in tragedy. The Fifth Crusade (1217—1221) attempted to recover the Holy Land by way of the powerful Muslim state of Egypt. The crusade achieved some early successes, but its ultimate failure marked an end to papal leadership of the Western crusaders. In the Sixth Crusade, the German emperor Frederick Ⅱ (1194—1250) led a largely peaceful expedition and obtained possession of Jerusalem by an agreement with the sultan of Egypt without papal support, which marked an important shift in crusading from papal to royal initiative. The last two major crusades, poorly organised by the pious king of France, Louis Ⅸ, were complete failures, especially after the fall of Acre, which marked an end of the crusader states in the Holy Land.

Several causes accounted for the ultimate failure of the Crusades. First, the campaigns were frequently badly organised and managed, showing a lack of unified command. Secondly, the ambitions of the campaigns' leaders conflicted. Some professed a desire to protect the Christian churches with the real purpose to conduct the territorial expansion, while others had the dream of a holy war of all of Latin Christendom to strengthen Latin Christianity, to exalt the papacy, and even to restore the union of the Eastern and Western churches. The rival leaders quarrelled, split, and even lost sight of the original purpose of conquering the Holy Land from the Turks. In addition, the motivation for the Crusades, especially in the beginning, came mostly from a wave of

religious fervour that brought nobles and commoners alike into the Crusader armies. Doubts about the spiritual significance of later wars also contributed to their decline.

The Crusades left a complex and troubling legacy in world civilisation. On the one hand, the greed, violence, and religious militancy at the heart of the crusading movement also fostered the growth of a persecuting mentality within Europe. On the other hand, however, the Crusades gave Europeans a new awareness of the world beyond their own local realms of religion and small-town economies. The interaction of Christian Europe with the Muslim world was actually both more intense and more meaningful in Spain and Sicily than in the Holy Land. Economically they surely promoted the economic growth of the Italian port cities, especially Genoa, Pisa, and Venice. It was certainly not the crusades that caused the trade recovery. Even without the crusades, Italian merchants would have established new trade relations with the Eastern world.

The Cultural and Intellectual World Europe in the High Middle Ages underwent a series of profound economic, religious and political changes, which were matched by deeply significant artistic and intellectual awakening. Significant creative work was done in literature, sculpture, law, philosophy, music, drama, and even in science. This was an age of spiritual renewal, as reflected in the brilliance of scholastic thought. The following will provide only a glimpse of the remarkable achievements of this fertile era.

The literature of the Central Middle Ages was abundant and richly varied. With the changing stages of social development, different types of literature formed their own characteristics gradually to meet the need of various social classes. There were mainly four types: religious literature, heroic epics, cavalier literature and literature of the urban classes.

There was a large number of religious literature works covering a wide range including the writings of Christian theologians. They performed great function in advocating religious belief and spreading religious doctrines. The earliest heroic epics were the *chansons de geste* (songs of heroic deeds)[①], while the most popular was the *Song of Roland*[②], the legendary account of a Muslim attack on Charlemagne's rearguard as it retreated across the Pyrenees. These heroic epics reflected the people's aspiration to break away from the national confusion and build a stable and wealthy society. Cavalier literature was widespread in West Europe in mainly two forms, lyric and romance, reflecting the ideals and poetic lives of nobles and knights. The romance

---

① songs of heroic deeds：英雄史诗，又称为武功歌，例如《罗兰之歌》。随着封建制度的开始形成，人们逐渐产生了国家统一的愿望。频繁的战争鼓励了尚武精神，促使了英雄史诗的形成。

② *Song of Roland*：中世纪法国英雄史诗《罗兰之歌》，分为 291 节，共 4002 行，用当时民间语罗曼语写成。主要是歌颂帝王的颂德歌，起初是口头流传，后来经收集后编成书。

flourished in 12th- and 13th-century France and among the French-speaking nobility of England. It spread also into Italy and Spain, and became a crucial factor in the evolution of vernacular literature in Germany. As the 13th century drew to its close, the French romance tended to become conventionalised and drained of inspiration. By the 13th century, the writings which undoubtedly made the strongest appeal to the urban classes were the fabliaux①. These stories were written not to edify or instruct but chiefly to amuse. Most of them were also strongly anti-clerical and indicated no high regard for the religious spirit.

The great masterpieces of medieval literary talent were respectively the *Romance of the Rose*②of Guillaume de Lorris and Jean de Meung, and Dante's *Divine Comedy*③. Each was a summary of late medieval civilisation in its own way.

As the early agglomerations of traders evolved into organised towns, the economy of town and country became able to support people devoted to a life of thought, so the informal exams of students and teachers developed into organised institutions of learning, and the intellectual horizon of Europeans began to open. The 12th and 13th centuries saw the new universities sprouting across Europe. Law and medicine became serious intellectual disciplines; steady advances were made in natural philosophy and theological studies. In the process, a world that had once seemed filled with uncertainties, mysteries and demons slowly changed into a world that seemed more knowable—built by God, structured by logic, and capable of human understanding.

The remarkable philosophic achievement of the late Middle Ages was the famous system of thought known as Scholasticism, which was usually defined as the attempt to harmonise reason and faith or to make philosophy serve the interest of theology. The primary development of the Scholastic philosophy began with the teachings of Peter Abelard(1079—1142), one of the most significant figures in the history of thought. The heyday of Scholasticism came in the 13th century, as a result of the labours of numerous intellectuals in various fields of learning. By the end of the 13th century Scholasticism④ began to decline, partly due to the teachings of the last of the Scholastics, John Duns Scotus, and partly because of the growing popularity of nominalism.

The late Middle Ages produced two great styles of architecture, the Romanesque

---

① fabliau 的复数，尤指流传于12～14世纪法国的世俗故事，又称"短篇俚语故事"、"讽刺性的寓言诗"、"小故事诗"。它以日常生活为描写对象，以教士为讽刺对象，经常描写农民的机智、美德和反抗精神，鞭挞丑恶思想，通常在篇末都有道德教训，总结全诗的意义。

② *Romance of the Rose*：13世纪法国寓言长诗《玫瑰传奇》，包括上下两卷。基洛姆·德·洛利思创作了上卷，共4000千多行，他用玫瑰比喻贵族妇女，写一位诗人怎样爱上玫瑰却受到阻碍的故事；另一位民间诗人续写下卷，约18000行，描述了诗人如何在理性和自然帮助下成功获得了玫瑰。

③ *Divine Comedy*：《神曲》，意大利诗人但丁的长诗。全诗为《地狱》、《炼狱》和《天堂》三部分。

④ Scholasticism：经院哲学是与宗教神学相结合的唯心主义哲学，属于欧洲中世纪特有的哲学形态，是天主教教会用来训练神职人员，在其所设经院中教授的理论，故名"经院哲学"。

and the Gothic. The Romanesque was mainly a product of the monastic revival. It attained its full development in the century following the year 1000. The great abbey churches that epitomised the Romanesque style reflected the monastic values of order, simplicity, and otherworldliness. There were regional differences as the form developed, but the Romanesque buildings shared fundamental characteristics, including a floor plan in the shape of a cross, the use of round arches and barrel vault, and heavy buttresses to support the legs of the arches.

In the late 12th and 13th centuries, the increase in wealth, the advancement of learning, the growth of secular interests, and the pride of the cities in the newly acquired freedom and prosperity led to a demand for a more elaborate architectural style to express the ideals of the new age, thus the Gothic architecture superseded the Romanesque in popularity. Gothic architecture was one of the most intricate of building styles, whose basic elements were "the pointed arch, groined and ribbed vaulting, and the flying buttress"①. Other features included "lofty spires, rose windows, delicate tracery in stone, elaborately carved facades, multiple columns, and the use of gargoyles, or representations of mythical monsters, as decorative devices"②. The greatest Gothic churches of the 13th century brought architecture, sculpture, stained glass, liturgical music to the single end of providing a majestic background for the central act of medieval Christian worship, the Mass.

Medieval thinkers failed to free science from its subservience to theology, but they pointed the way to a more accurate understanding of the physical universe. One of the greatest contributions was the awareness of the significance of observation and experiment when people explored the physical world. Influenced by Aristotle, both Albertus Magnus of Paris and Robert Grosseteste of Oxford first advocated the above methodology, leaving a profound impact on the exploratory behaviour of later generations until today.

Section Four The Decline of the Middle Ages (c. 1300—c. 1500)

The Great Plague From the end of the 13th century to the beginning of the 14th century, Europe experienced some extreme weather conditions. It was called the "little ice age"③ in history. Lower temperatures resulted in heavy storms and constant rainfalls. The growing seasons of crops were cut short, and harvests were reduced. There were serious food shortages between 1315 and 1317 in Northern Europe. Similar

---

① Edward Mcnall Burns, *Western Civilizations*, Vol. Ⅰ 7th Ed., New York: W. W. Norton & Company, Inc., 1968, p. 389.

② Edward Mcnall Burns, *Western Civilizations*, Vol. Ⅰ 7th Ed., New York: W. W. Norton & Company, Inc., 1968, p. 389.

③ little ice age：小冰河期，泛指 15 世纪到 19 世纪中叶气温偏低的时期。

weather conditions ravaged Southern Europe in the 1330s and 1340s. Famine was widespread throughout Europe. Some believe that the malnutrition resulted from the hanger in Europe increased the devastation of the "Black Death", as weaker body conditions of people made them more vulnerable to diseases.

The outbreak of the plague in the mid 14th century was the most disastrous as it not only devoured people's lives but also led to an economic, social, political, and cultural crisis. It was a natural disaster that wreaked humanistic havoc. Families abandoned each other. The dead remained unburied. People did not know what the future held, given the seemingly unstoppable plague.

Europeans were horrified by the plague especially because 14th century physicians and healers were at a loss to explain the process of infection. Some blamed earthquakes or fogs; some attributed it to mysterious forces; some even thought that Jews had poisoned the wells. Yet no one considered rats and rat control. Almost everyone agreed on one major cause: God's anger. They regarded the plague as a sure sign of God's anger.

Generally, the plague was primarily a combination of three related diseases: (1)Bubonic plague, which was the most common and most important form of plague, was carried by black rats and spread by the fleas the rats carry and infect. Symptoms of bubonic plague included high fever, aching joints, swelling of the lymph nodes, and dark blotches caused by bleeding beneath the skin. Bubonic plague was actually the least toxic form of plague, but, nevertheless, killed 50 to 60 percent of its victims; (2) Pneumonic plague was a respiratory infection. Bubonic plague is highly contagious as the victims cough severely. Very much like the SARS epidemic in the early 21st century, the coughing and sneezing symptoms made it spread very easily; (3) Septicemic plague added still another channel of contagion as it spread through blood and could be transmitted by fleas.

The first phase of the plague was from 1347 to 1349. The virus was first introduced to the European continent from the Middle East by merchants. Then it quickly spread to the whole of Europe in the path of the traders. It quickly reached the British Isles in the West, Scandinavia in the North and Russia.

Failing to explain and understand the cause of the plague, people were horrified. And the horrors became more violent because of the disgusting course of the disease. The victims of the plague suffered a gross death, horrible to see, to smell, and to nurse. So many people died so swiftly that proper burial became impossible. It has been estimated that the European population declined by 25% to 50% between 1347 and 1351, which means a death toll of 19 to 38 million people out of 75 million in four years.

However, the plague was not done-and would not be done for a long time. There were major outbreaks again in 1361—1362 striking especially hard at young people who were born since the Great Plague since they lacked any immunity from prior exposure.

Then the plague recurred regularly every ten years for the rest of the century and the next century. The European population did not start to recover until the end of the 15th century; not until the mid 16th century did Europe begin to regain its 13th century population levels. Even then, recurrences of the plague did not end until the beginning of the 18th century when a new species of brown rat began to replace the black rat.

The plague killed more than 30% of the whole population within two years, which resulted in a serious labour shortage. The once crowded rural villages and busy city streets were deserted. The problem of rural overpopulation was suddenly solved and those who were lucky enough to survive the plague then had sufficient land.

An Unsteady Society The plague caused serious economic and social troubles in Europe. The sudden decrease of population after the plague resulted in a severe shortage of labours, which in turn resulted in the dramatic increase of labour price. The decrease of population also reduced the demand for food, which caused an increase of agricultural produce.

Unhappy with their life situations, poor peasants of many European countries began to fight for their rights through rebellious uprisings, such as the 1358 French peasants' revolt and the 1381 English peasant rebellion. Similar farmers' uprisings also broke out in other European countries. Though most of these uprisings were suppressed quickly, the spirit would not be easily crushed. The British aristocrats had good reasons to fear as the peasants aimed at ending the aristocratic system which they thought was the origin of social inequality. The landowners also felt they needed to be nicer to their labourers and exploited them less.

The countryside was not the one and only place to find revolts. The towns and cities of Western Europe lost relatively large numbers of people to the Great Plague. Commercial and industrial activity suffered almost immediately from the catastrophe. An oversupply of goods and an immediate drop in demand led to a decline in trade after 1350. Some industries suffered greatly. Bourgeois merchants and manufacturers responded to a decline in trade and production by attempting to restrict competition and resist the demands of the lower classes. Tensions between "haves" and "have-nots" were especially high. Quickly the uprisings of workers began to terrorise commercially important big cities.

Although the peasant and urban revolts sometimes resulted in short term gains for the participants, the uprisings were easily crushed and their gains quickly lost. Geographically dispersed, rural and urban rebels were not united and had no long-range goals. Immediate gains were uppermost in their minds. Accustomed to ruling, the established classes easily combined and crushed dissent when faced with these social uprisings. Nevertheless, the rural and urban revolts of the 14th century ushered in an age of social conflict that characterised much of later European history.

Crisis in the World of Christianity The plague also served to intensify the crisis of the Christian Church. The late Middle Ages were featured by new strong expressions of Christian faith. For example, the Eucharist①, or the divine dinner, grew into a major Christian celebration. The Host, or the holy bread, was carried through town streets in a great procession. It was a time for the churches to raise money and a time to attack Jews. The many new practices of worship became the foundations for spiritual reform and spiritual revolt after the plague.

It is certainly true that the Great Plague had affected the religious practices in Europe severely. Many religious responses to the plague were beyond the church's control, such as the hysterical attacks that Christians launched against Jews. Worse, many times, the panicked people cast angry eyes at the Church. Why had the Church not warned the faithful of God's anger? Why were clergy dying in even greater numbers than the laity? In the 14th and 15th centuries, the church faced serious threats to its credibility and power.

Even during the glorious time of the High Middle Ages, the growing secular monarchies of Europe presented a challenge to papal claims of temporal supremacy. The conflict between Church and state in the Late Middle Ages reached its height in the struggle between Pope Boniface Ⅷ and King Philip Ⅳ (1285—1314) of France. In his desire to acquire new revenues, Philip expressed the right to tax the French clergy. Boniface Ⅷ claimed that the clergy of any state could not pay taxes to their secular ruler without the pope's consent. Underlying this issue was a basic conflict between the universal sovereignty of the papacy versus the royal sovereignty of the monarch.

The death of Gregory Ⅺ (1370—1378) in the spring of 1378 brought the beginning of the Great Schism②, the division of the Roman Church. At that time, the Church was dominated by the French, so the Romans feared that the French majority in the Church would result in the election of a Frenchman as the new Pope. And the new French Pope would move the papacy, office of the Pope, to Avignon, a French town. To prevent all this from happening, the Romans blackmailed the papal-election meeting, threatening that they would kill all the cardinals, high church officials just below the Pope, if they failed to elect a Roman or an Italian as the new Pope. Yielding to the pressure, the cardinals elected an Italian Pope, known as Pope Urban Ⅵ (1378—1389). However, the French side of the Church soon declared the election of Urban as illegitimate and invalid. They chose a French man as the Pope and quickly returned to Avignon. The French Pope was titled Clement Ⅶ. Thus, there began to be two Popes, Urban in Rome

① Eucharist：圣餐礼，是许多基督教会里的中心仪式，在“最后的晚餐”那天举行，仪式上奉献面包和葡萄酒来纪念耶稣之死。

② the Great Schism：15世纪基督教的大分裂，或称“宗教改革”，从罗马公教中分裂出了路德教派、英国国教以及加尔文教派等。详见第六章。

and Clement in Avignon. Each of the Popes had their own followers in Europe. France, Spain, Scotland, and Southern Italy supported Clement, and England, Germany, Scandinavia, and most of Italy supported Urban. As both Popes needed political support, the different political policies followed the religious division. Both Popes made political policies which were in the interests of their own supporting states. In their fight for legitimacy and power, both Popes condemned the other as the enemy of the Christ. Since the pope was believed to be the highest Christian leader and held the key to heaven, their fight against each other greatly damaged the faith of believers. The ordinary Christians were confused and did not know who to follow.

A Diverse and Dynamic Culture The Great Plague became the topic of many artistic and intellectual works in Europe. Those scholars who lived through the disaster collected many stories about the plague and retold them with great narrative skill. Among them stands the master storyteller Giovanni Boccaccio (1313—1373) who collected stories from many sources and completed the great work *The Decameron*①. The blood, the boils, the swellings, the quick deaths and the mass burials remained subjects for the great writers long after 1350. In 14th and 15th century Europe, death was, understandably, on everyone's mind. Thus the devastation of the massive death did not kill people's interest in art. Instead the aftermath of the Great Plague witnessed a revival of culture in Europe. In this period, more ordinary people were educated and became literate. People's higher levels of education and literacy resulted in the flourishing of such artistic forms as plays, songs or stories. The era produced literary and artistic giants such as Giotto di Bondone (1266—1337), Geoffrey Chaucer (c. 1340—1400), and Jan van Eyck (c. 1385—1440). In sum, the aftermath of the Great Plague in Europe was an era featured by diverse and dynamic intellectual and cultural developments. It was an era of great contrasts, as people mourned the deaths of the plague while celebrating the new life after the plague, as people fought against clericalism while still remaining faithful in the old faith, as artists tried to revive old artistic styles while introducing new styles.

Over the course of the 14th and 15th centuries, Latin stopped its domination as a language of artistic expression. Very similar to the New Culture Movement in the early 20th century in China, the spread of the use of vernacular languages increased people's access to knowledge and education. For example, the use of modern languages empowered women with broader exposure to the cultural and artistic lives in Europe.

---

① *The Decameron*:《十日谈》,意大利作家薄伽丘著。书中写到10个佛罗伦萨的年轻人为躲避瘟疫而隐居山庄,大家商定每人每天讲一个优秀动听的故事,以愉快地度过一天中最难熬的时光。他们共讲了10天,100个故事,收集成集命名为《十日谈》。故事描写和歌颂了现世生活,歌颂自由爱情的可贵,赞美爱情是才智和高尚的源泉等。详见第五章。

And the popularity of vernacular languages was initiated by the writing of literary works in vernacular languages. Dante and Chaucer's works virtually elevated regional dialects to national languages. In the late 15th and early 16th centuries, literary forms created in vernacular languages were able to rival Latin, and gradually triumphed and replaced Latin. The Gothic style in architecture was put to an end and the old Greco-Roman style was reborn. The pointed arches in the Gothic tradition were replaced by round domes and arches of the old Rome. Sculptors began to turn their attention to the perfect human body in the local Greco-Roman tradition. Donatello (1386—1466) incorporated styles of ancient sculptures in his creation *of David*①. Michelangelo (1475 — 1564) further developed the tradition Donatello started. Painters began to depict lifelike figures and landscapes, exploiting the new techniques of perspective②. The era also inspired much philosophical thinking. Philosophers and intellectuals pondered over old problems while new problems were presented to them. Some of them were inspired by Petrarch and looked back to Plato, while others followed Thomas Aquinas in the traditional framework of medieval universities and looked forward.

Moreover, in 1500 many new inventions and improvements—gunpowder, the water pump, eyeglasses, and mechanical clocks—were changing the ways people lived.

Chapter Review

This chapter mainly traced the emergence, development and height of the Medieval Ages till its decline. In a chronological order, the emergence of the Middle Ages was illustrated by a detailed description of the Islamic, Byzantine worlds. From 900 to 1150, European society assumed many of the distinctive features that it would still bear until the modern period. Governments grew in power, scope and sophistication rapidly and cultural horizons expanded too. But everything was fragile. The years after 1150 were more creative. In this period, powers like France, England and German realised the great promise which they had already shown before 1150. However, the papacy entered during the 13th century. Along with the crusades, the first large-scale social movements turned up. After the 13th century, the economy of Europe grew more complex because of the plague and demographic change. New patterns of trade and new manufacturing techniques appeared and spread throughout Europe. Promoted by the economic recovery, the social and political consciousness was looking forward to a new page.

---

① *David*：青铜雕像《大卫》，文艺复兴时期意大利杰出雕刻家多纳泰罗的代表作之一。多纳泰罗运用古希腊人创立的对应构图方式，向人们展现了一位形体比例和结构都十分准确的少年形象。是艺术史上最伟大的作品之一。详见第五章。

② perspective：透视法，是一种在二维平面上表现三维物体和深度关系的技术。

Exercise

Ⅰ. *According to the information provided in this chapter, choose the correct alternative among A, B, C, and D that can complete each of the following statements.*

1. What can the Middle Ages be called?

   A. "Age of Art". B. "Age of History".

   C. "Age of Science". D. "Age of Faith".

2. Who is a vassal?

   A. Business man. B. Military ruler.

   C. Slave. D. Feudal tenant.

3. In the feudalist relationship in the Middle Ages, who were at the bottom of the social hierarchy?

   A. The lords. B. The warriors. C. The nobles. D. The vassals.

4. What were the three classes of people of Western Europe?

   A. Pope, peasants and nobles. B. Kings, lords and monks.

   C. Clergy, lords and peasants. D. Warriors, peasants and priests.

5. What must a monk do before entering the monastery according to the Benedictine Rule?

   A. To abandon his wife.

   B. To be loyal to the Church.

   C. To study some knowledge of Benedictine Rule.

   D. To give up all his possessions.

Ⅱ. *Fill in the blanks with what you have learned in this chapter.*

1. In European history, the thousand-year period following the fall of ________ in the 5th century is called the Middle Ages.
2. Between ________ and ________, Western Europe was the scene of frequent wars and invasions during the Middle Ages.
3. The two great architectural styles that dominated the high middle age were ________.
4. On the Christmas day of 800 Pope Leo Ⅲ formally recognised his accomplishment by placing the imperial crown on his head, which was later called "________".
5. ________ was the centre of medieval life under feudalism. By the 12th century manor houses came to be called ________.

Ⅲ. *According to what you have learned, answer the following questions briefly in your own words.*

1. What happened in Western Europe after the decline of the Roman Empire?
2. What does feudalism mean in the Medieval Ages?
3. What were the cultural characteristics of the period from 500 to 1000?

4. What is the importance of the using of vernacular languages in Medieval literature?
5. In what ways did Gothic art differ from Romanesque art?

Ⅳ. *With critical analysis, answer the following essay questions in your own words.*

1. What kind of role did the crusades play? Please try to comment on its causes, process and effects.
2. What caused the decline of the Medieval Age? Please try to make some illustrations on the economic, social, and religious life.

Ⅴ. *Work in small groups, and make comparisons based on the following topic.*

While Christianity was spreading rapidly throughout Europe in Middle Ages, Buddhism was also favoured by the court of Tang Dynasty in the same period. Take the political and economical background into consideration, and try to explain why religions enjoyed a prosperous development in this period of human history.

Voices on Key Points

Medieval Civilisation

That is a Medieval way of drawing history, in which they do not respect the law and want the rest of the world to respect the law. That's not possible.

——Emir Kusturica

We owe to the Middle Ages the two worst inventions of humanity—romantic love and gunpowder.

——Andre Maurois

In the middle ages people were tourists because of their religion, whereas now they are tourists because tourism is their religion.

——Robert Runcie

Suggested Reading

1. (美)F. Bacon 著，易璐注释:《Medieval Days——中世纪》，商务印书馆 2007 年版。
2. (英)G. R. 埃文斯著，茆卫彤译:《中世纪的信仰》，北京大学出版社 2005 年版。
3. (法)吉尔松著，沈清松译:《中世纪哲学精神》，上海人民出版社 2008 年版。
4. (意)卢多维科·加托著，夏方林译:《中世纪:帝国时代》，四川人民出版社 2000 年版。
5. (法)雅克·勒高夫著，周嫄译:《钱袋与永生:中世纪的经济与宗教》，上海人民出版社 2007 年版。

Chapter Five　The Age of the Renaissance (14th—17th Century)

The Renaissance, then, was an age of transition that saw the rejection of certain elements of the medieval outlook, the revival of classical cultural forms, and the emergence of distinctly modern attitudes. ①

Learning objectives

After reading this chapter, you will be able to:

1. *Understand humanism and know some important representatives of humanism and their thinking;*
2. *Know some artists and how their artistic styles were influenced by humanism;*
3. *Know some literatures and their representative works;*
4. *Understand the pattern of politics in the Renaissance;*
5. *Know the development of science in that age.*

---

① Marvin Perry, et al., *Western Civilisation: Ideas, Politics & Society*, 5th Ed., Boston: Houghton Mifflin Company, 1996, p. 303.

蒙娜·丽莎的微笑以其神秘优雅而闻名于世，达·芬奇的巅峰之作《蒙娜·丽莎》以其无与伦比的艺术成就而被永久地珍藏于巴黎的卢浮宫，致使寻常大众或终其一生也无缘得见真迹。此佳作或许是文艺复兴的最佳代言，艺术家的思想解放及人文情怀在对那位城市贵妇的逼真刻画中得以酣畅淋漓地体现。

这场自14～17世纪在欧洲兴起的思想文化运动，成为中古时代和近代的分水岭。黑暗的中世纪终成历史，文学、艺术、哲学以及自然科学等一改往日的死气沉沉，焕发出令后人受益匪浅的勃勃生机。人文主义的冲击同时深入到城市生活、政治和经济等多个层面。1480～1520年文艺复兴进入鼎盛阶段，佛罗伦萨的中心地位被罗马取而代之。达·芬奇、米开朗基罗和拉斐尔并称为“三大艺术巨人”；但丁、彼特拉克、薄伽丘则并称为文学史上的“三颗巨星”。政治形势方面，意大利乃至欧洲处于动荡不安之中，意大利政治哲学家马基维利亚在其著作《君主论》中提出了现实主义的政治主张。在人文主义浸润之下，人们的创造力和好奇心得以张扬，对于文艺复兴时期自然科学的发展起到了极大的推动作用。总之，以意大利多个城市为中心而蓬勃发展起来的文艺复兴，如一夜春风，旋即吹遍整个欧洲。

Section One The Rise of the Renaissance (14th—15th Century)

The Renaissance is the rise of a new culture of the rising bourgeoisie from the early 14th century to 17th century in Europe. The word "Renaissance" is derived from French, meaning "rebirth". The "Dark Age" had passed, and the thinkers and artists believed they were experiencing a rebirth of cultural forms of Greece and Rome. Their contributions were not only the recovery and application of antiquity, or Greco-Roman civilisation, but also incorporated innovation and novelty to a large extent, thus marking a new age.

The cradle of the Renaissance—Italy The Renaissance originated in Italy in many of the developed urban city-states, such as Florence and Venice, where citizens lived a wealthy and liberal life, attempted to cultivate the arts, and enjoyed the fruits of worldly life.

Italy was surrounded by the Mediterranean Sea, and in the Renaissance period many commercial city-states of Italy were the pivots of the trades between Western Europe and Eastern countries. Hit severely by the plague, the Italian merchants lost their commercial pre-eminence by the 14th century; but by the 15th century they were experiencing a resurgence of a flourishing commerce.

Florence was the biggest handicraft industrial centre in Italy. The Florentine woollen industry began to experience a recovery in this period. The banking business and the silk industry of Florence had taken the lead in those industries simultaneously in Europe. At that time, the biggest banking house in Europe was solely owned and managed by the Medici family[1]. The domain of this banking house extended to Venice, Milan, Rome, Avignon, Bruges, London, and Lyons. Meanwhile, industries began to develop and expand in Italy, including glassware, hand worked items in metal, and precious stone industries. Other new industries, especially printing, mining, and metallurgy, began to compete with the textile industry in the 15th century.

The prosperous and rich urban industries promoted a variety of social communications and activities. The Italian citizens had to abide by a set of fixed rules of etiquette in order to be accepted in social life. Influenced by humanistic thinking, people also had to enhance their competence in rhetoric and debate so as to appreciate sophisticated written and oral arguments. People pursued worldly happiness and profits and became indifferent to religious beliefs. They held festival ceremonies, among which the "Carnival" retained its popularity until today.

Family life changed considerably with the influence of humanism and secularism[2] in the Renaissance. The Italians felt a sense of security with the family bond in the dangerous urban world of the Renaissance period. In order to keep the family bonds tight, people usually paid great attention to marriages. The marriages were often arranged by parents in order to strengthen business or family ties. The bride's dowry was one of the most essential elements of their marriage contact. However, people's attitudes towards marriage were changing gradually. They began to emphasise individual struggle, late marriage and late childbirth instead of early marriage and early childbearing.

The husband was expected to make important decisions and keep the wife and the children under control. He was the master of the Italian family. The wife, who was responsible for the housework and the care of the children, held a certain degree of autonomy in daily lives.

Social Changes in the Renaissance The flourishing development of commerce and industry forwarded some changes of social order in the Renaissance, although the tripartite division of society from the Middle Ages had continued. The clergy still made up the most superior estate; they believed that people should be guided to spiritual ends. The nobility was the second social estate because they were believed to provide security and justice for society. The peasants and inhabitants of the towns and cities constituted the lowest estate in the Renaissance society. Significant adaptations occurred in the second and third estates.

Early in the 14th century, the old nobility suffered from decreasing incomes and

① Medici family：美第奇家族，出了三个教皇（利奥十世、克莱蒙七世及利奥十一世）及两个法国皇后（凯琳·美第奇和玛丽·美第奇）的意大利贵族家庭。“大”科西莫（1389～1464）是这个家庭中第一个统治佛罗伦萨的人。

② secularism：现世主义，世俗化，指拒绝一切宗教教义或活动的社会组织体系。

increasing life expenses. But the survival of nobility and the participation of the new nobles maintained and extended the second estate. By the 15th century, with the infusion of new blood, the aristocracy class was reconstructed. The nobility, including the old and the new, held important military posts and political posts in society so as to continue to dominate society in Europe.

The nobles, or aristocrats, were expected to conform to certain ideals by 1500. They were expected to achieve military skills like the medieval knights, and were required to have a classical education and to master a certain artistic skill, such as playing a musical instrument or drawing and painting. Suffused with the secular lifestyle advocated by the civic humanists, the nobles were expected to expose themselves to military arts, education, the arts, and gracefully show off their accomplishments. These basic attributes of the nobility were elaborated in *The Book of the Courtier* written by Castiglione. The social ideal of the aristocracy was the Renaissance ideal of the well-developed personality. As to the purpose of these courtly standards, Castiglione said:

> Therefore, I think that the aim of the perfect Courtier, which we have not spoken of up to now, is so to win for himself, by means of the accomplishments ascribed to him by these gentlemen, the favour and mind of the prince whom he serves that he may be able to tell him; and that when he sees the mind of his prince inclined to a wrong action, he may dare to oppose him... so as to dissuade him of every evil intent and bring him to the path of virtue. ①

The third estate was mostly composed of the peasants who made up 85% to 90% of the total European population. By the 14th century, the manorial system of serfdom continued declining due to the economic crisis. The Black Death resulted in a drastic decrease of the peasantry, which sped up the conversion of servile labour into rents paid in money. More and more peasants were becoming legally free by the end of the 15th century in Western Europe.

Besides the peasants, the third estate also included the inhabitants of towns and cities. They were not completely equal in the society. The patricians took the first position among these people because they were wealthier due to their capitalistic enterprises in trade, industry and banking. The petty burghers made up the second group in this estate. They maintained their livelihood by selling goods and providing services in the local communities. Property-less workers and the unemployed were even inferior to them. So at that age, poverty was a serious social problem.

---

① Baldassare Castiglione, *The Book of the Courtie*, trans. Charles S. Singleton, Garden City, N. Y.: Doubleday & Company, Inc., 1959, pp. 288—289.

Humanism[①] **in Renaissance** The word "Humanism" could date back to the age of the ancient Rome. At that time, the formal education included seven subjects—grammar, rhetoric, logic, arithmetic, geometry, astronomy and music. Cicero named this kind of comprehensive education "humanitas". By the end of the 15th century, the "liberal arts"—grammar, rhetoric, poetry, moral philosophy or ethics, and history, based on the study of the classics, were called the humanities. And the teachers who taught these arts were called humanists.

Humanism is the most significant hallmark of the Renaissance Period, which is an educational and cultural programme based on the ancient Greek and Roman classics. In the humanists' eyes, ancient literature was distinct for its clear and graceful style and it was cherished for its insights into human nature. The humanist valued it for the sake of the above-mentioned thought, but not for the requirements of Christian doctrines.

Francesco Petrarch (1304—1374) was one of the early humanists and was sometimes regarded as the "father of humanism" because of his unparalleled devotion to the spread of humanism in the 14th century. He contributed greatly to the collection and spread of the Latin manuscripts, and he encouraged his pupils to study Greek so as to enhance their humanist learning. He followed Cicero's example and suggested that education should stress rhetoric and moral philosophy—wisdom with eloquence. That is, education should not only be the study of knowledge but also the proper use of it for public good and communication.

The Florentine intellectuals also took Cicero as a model. Leonardo Bruni (1370—1444), the distinguished humanistic historian, wrote a biography of Cicero entitled the *New Cicero*. In the book, he enthusiastically eulogised Cicero's contribution on politics and literature. Bruni also wrote the biographies of Dante and of Petrarch in order to publicise their humanistic thinking. At the beginning of the 15th century, the fusion of Florentine civic spirit and pride created a new wave for the humanist movement in Florence, which was later called "civic humanism" by the modern scholars. Civic humanism reflected the values of the urban society of the Italian Renaissance. Many humanists were involved in social and political events.

Florence was under the rule of Cosimo de' Medici in 1434. He intentionally led the humanists to heed this philosophy in order to solidify his power base. Byzantine scholars brought many studies of Plato to Italy. As a result, a dramatic conversion from active city life to Platonism[②] occurred in the second half of the 15th century. A large number

---

① Humanism：人本主义。文艺复兴时期的文化和知识运动，强调对世俗事物的关心，是对古希腊、古罗马的文学、艺术和文明的重新发现和研究的结果。

② Platonism：柏拉图哲学，柏拉图主义，尤指宣称理念形式是绝对的和永恒的实在，而世界中实在的现象却是不完美的和暂时的反映。

of scholars had committed themselves to philosophy, especially to the study of Platonic thinking. Among them, Marsilio Ficino (1433 — 1499) and Giovanni Pico della Mirandola (1463—1494) were two predominant representatives. Ficino devoted his life to translating Plato's works and to fully explain Neoplatonism① that was the Platonic philosophy in simple and plain words. He integrated Christianity and Platonism to prove the consistency of humanism, Christianity and Platonism. Giovanni Pico della Mirandola was the friend and pupil of Ficino. His most well-known work was entitled *Oration on the Dignity of Man*②. In the book, Pico offered a ringing statement of unlimited human potential: "To him it is granted to have whatever he chooses, to be whatever he wills." The significance of the book lies in its eloquent summation of the Renaissance interest in humans and the belief in the dignity of human life.

Section Two Arts and Literature in the Italian Renaissance (Mid-1400s—Late 1500s)

The age of the Renaissance is an age of great masters in art and literature. A large number of artists and scholars were emerging and an appreciable amount of artistic and literary works were being written. The merging of the arts and literature with the religious tradition brought about a completely new age.

Artists and Their Artistic Works Proportion, balance and harmony were the key points fashioned in the field of art in the Renaissance Period. The pursuit of nature and the focus on human beings became the primary goals of the Renaissance artists. Hence, Renaissance art was a significant symbol of humanism. From the artistic work at that time, people could appreciate the active and worldly life. This replaced medieval art that mainly played a religious role.

Florence was the birthplace of sculptures and paintings in the Renaissance Period. The Florentines played a leading role in the aesthetic transformation from the Medieval Ages to the Renaissance Period.

Giotto (1276—1337) was one of the most well-known painters at that time. He produced figures represented pictorially by alterations in light and shade and he developed techniques of perspective so as to make the figures three dimensional. His creativity broke with the old traditions. Instead of using the dull and simple golden or

---

① Neoplatonism：新柏拉图派哲学，古希腊文化末期最重要的哲学流派，并对西方中世纪中的基督教神学产生了重大影响。该流派主要基于柏拉图的学说，但在许多地方进行了新的诠释。新柏拉图主义流行于公元3～5世纪，被认为是以古希腊思想来建构宗教哲学的典型。虽然被归属于柏拉图主义阵营，但却带有折中主义倾向，与亚里士多德学说和斯多亚派有着明显的联系。其特点在于：建构了超自然的世界图式，更明确地规定了人在其中的位置，把人神关系置于道德修养的核心，强化了哲学和宗教的同盟，具有更浓厚的神秘主义色彩。

② *Oration on the Dignity of Man*：《论人的尊严》，意大利文艺复兴时期哲学家若望・皮科・德拉・米兰多拉，康科地亚伯爵的著作，被称为"文艺复兴时代的宣言"。

blue background found in the art of the Medieval Ages, he brought natural landscape settings into practice.

The most distinctive characters in his paintings are the emotional expressions of the figures and the depiction of the complication of human nature. He was later regarded as the "founder of the modern figure painting". His most distinguished achievement is reflected in church frescoes①. *Flight into Egypt*② is one of his best frescoes. It describes the Bible story of Maria and the Little Christ escaping to Egypt in order to avoid the persecution of Herod. In this fresco, the religious figures are endowed with earthly, full-blooded life.

Massaccio (1401 — 1428) followed in the step of Giotto and carried on his extraordinary artistic style. He also emphasised the laws of the perspective principle, including the figure's structure. He focused on the material and form of the figure making them appear strong and powerful. His fresco in the Brancacci chapel in Florence has been considered the first masterpiece of Early Renaissance art. He used religious themes representing the figures in a natural, realistic relationship with the landscape. In this fresco called *The Expulsion from the Garden of Eden*③, Adam and Eve ate the fruit of the tree of wisdom without permission and were driven out by God from the garden of Eden. Their mournful expression and repentant mind were depicted as genuine and touching by Masaccio. Painted in the Brancacci Chapel in the Church of Santa Maria del Carmine in Florence, *The Tribute Money*④ is another masterpiece by Massaccio. The realistic relationship between the biblical figures and their background is enhanced by the exquisite means of perspective by Massaccio. The story of the Bible is reproduced accurately and perfectly in this fresco. A good many artists in Florence in later ages followed the model of his massive, three-dimensional human figures.

In the 15th century, the artistic style of the Renaissance age was succeeded and advanced by Florentine painters. They enthusiastically experienced the process of experimentation and technical mastery. They further overcame the problems of perspective by carefully organizing the outdoor space and light using geometry and perspective. In addition, they experimented with movement in the anatomic structure. The two experimental techniques showed the important trends in the development of

---

① fresco：湿壁画法，用溶解于水的颜料在新鲜湿石灰上作画的方法。

② *Flight into Egypt*：《逃往埃及》，这是帕都亚的圣马利亚阿莱那礼拜堂中《圣母和基督传》37 幅壁画中最杰出的一幅。作者是文艺复兴时期意大利画家，雕刻家乔托。

③ *The Expulsion from the Garden of Eden*：《失乐园》，15 世纪意大利文艺复兴时期画家马萨乔的湿壁画之一，表现了亚当和夏娃因偷吃禁果而被上帝逐出伊甸园的圣经故事。

④ *The Tribute Money*：《纳税银》，马萨乔代表作之一，讲述了《新约》中的一个典故，即耶稣布道途中被收丁税的故事。这个宗教故事完全被画家描绘成真实的世俗场面，画面以中央的基督及其门人群像为主，全面透视焦点集中于基督头部，光线和礼拜堂窗口进光方向一致，构成了前所未有的富于真实感的效果。

Renaissance art. Painting the human nude, in a realistic way, became the top priority of the art at that time.

Indeed, the realistic portrayal of the human nude became one of the foremost preoccupations of Italian Renaissance art. The 15th century, then, was a period of experimentation and technical mastery.

Donate di Donatello (1386—1466) was one of the most outstanding sculptors in the Italian Renaissance and was called the founder of modern sculpture. In his artistic works, the essence of the ancient Roman art and distinct humanism spirits were harmonious. His art set the standard for all of his contemporaries. His best known statue is the life size bronze nude standing statue, *David*, created for the Medici in Florence. Donatello depicted David as a young hero who had defeated the enemy. In David, Donatello represented the strength and the dignity of human beings themselves. The statue later became the inspiration for Michelangelo's statue entitled *David*①.

One of the friends of Donatello, Filippo Brunelleschi (1377 — 1446), was a respected and gifted sculptor, who dedicated all his life to the creation and development of the Renaissance style. When in Rome with Donatello, he studied architectural monuments of Roman antiquity, which enabled his artistic works to be more creative. It was he who first redefined Gothic and Romanesque space with mathematical perspective, and who first created new rules of proportioning and symmetry. He developed techniques for lifting construction materials into position, and for creating a self-supporting upper shell for domes. He built many works of art in Italy, such as the church of San Lorenzo, the church of San Spirito, the Pazzi Chapel and the Cathedral of Florence. Among his outstanding works, the Cathedral② of Florence is best known for its dome. It was built according to the Roman models and was constructed without the support of scaffolding or pilasters③. Its classical columns, rounded arches and coffered ceiling were completely new architectural features.

During the mid-1400s, the Renaissance Period was surrounded by a Catholic counterattack. During this time, the artists continued their arts. This artistic prosperity ranged from 1490 to 1520 and was called the High Renaissance. By this time, Florence had lost its prominent position in politics, economics and art, and Rome had taken over its place becoming the cultural centre of Italy. By the end of the 15th century, the artists of Italy were using individualistic forms of creative expression and had become masters of new techniques for a scientific observation of their world. Leonardo da Vinci

---

① *David*：云石雕刻《大卫》，像高 2.5 米，连基座高 5.5 米。文艺复兴时期意大利雕刻家、画家、建筑家米开朗基罗的代表作。是艺术史上最伟大的作品之一，现藏于佛罗伦萨艺术学院美术馆。

② Cathedral：大教堂，主教控制的教区总教堂。

③ pilaster：壁柱，半露柱。有柱顶和底座的长方形柱子，作为装饰图案嵌入墙内。

(1452—1519), Michelangelo Bounaroti (1475—1564) and Raphael (1483—1520) were the three biggest artistic masters in the High Renaissance.

Leonardo da Vinci, a versatile genius, was a scientist, an engineer, as well as an artist. His constant observations, experimentation and insatiable hunger for knowledge contributed to his scientific and artistic works. His drawings were largely the records of his investigation of nature. Da Vinci often drew what he observed from the world around him, including human anatomy, animal and plant life, the motion of water, and the flight of birds. Da Vinci's *The Last Supper*①, on the end wall of the refectory of Santa Maria delle Grazie in Milan, is one of the most renowned paintings in its organisation of space and use of perspective to depict subjects three-dimensionally. In this painting, the dramatic reaction of the apostles—surprised, indignant, anxious and panicked—after being told that one of them would betray the Christ, was depicted vividly and in a lifelike manner. Da Vinci successfully revealed the figures' inner mind through their gestures and movement. *The Mona Lisa*② is an example of an artistic invention of Leonardo's—"what the Italians call sfumato③."④Da Vinci endowed this painting with an aura of mystery through the transition between dark and soft light. The figure's enchanting and ambiguous half smile has always attracted people in every corner of the world. The background is a deeply receding natural landscape with meandering rivers and rock formations, by which the painter explicitly expressed his distinct view of the natural world. In his eyes, everything was liquid, dynamic, and full of movement and energy.

Besides da Vinci, Michelangelo was another giant of the High Renaissance, who was not only a gifted painter, sculptor and architect but also a poet of superb talent. Enthusiastic and creative as he was, he filled his artistic works with incomparable majesty, dignity, energy and imagination. He made full use of his energy to paint the history of The *Old Testament* (covering more than 100 figures) on the central space of the ceiling of the Sistine Chapel in the Vatican. The figures he portrayed on the ceiling were all so muscular and graceful that they symbolised the perfect proportions of human beings. He spent almost four years completing this prominent masterpiece. His sculpture entitled *David*, created out of a marble block is well-known to the world as a young man with

---

① *The Last Supper*:《最后的晚餐》,达·芬奇的代表作之一,现藏米兰圣玛利亚德尔格契修道院。画作描绘的是《新约》中耶稣被犹大出卖的故事。在逾越节的晚餐上,耶稣说:"你们中间有一个人出卖了我。"言毕,众门徒顿时反应强烈,情态各异。达·芬奇通过自己对现实生活中不同人物个性的细微观察和炉火纯青的绘画技巧,惟妙惟肖地刻画了众门徒,尤其是犹大当时复杂的心理状态。

② *The Mona Lisa*:《蒙娜·丽莎》,达·芬奇的代表作之一,现存于法国卢浮宫。它是达·芬奇的最高艺术成就,成功地塑造了资本主义上升时期一位城市有产阶级的妇女形象。画中人物坐姿优雅,笑容微妙,背景山水幽深茫茫,淋漓尽致地发挥了画家那奇特的烟雾状"无界渐变着色法"般的笔法。画中人那如梦般的妩媚微笑,被不少美术史家称为"神秘的微笑"。

③ sfumato:[意](使素描中的明暗或色彩中的色阶有层次地调和的)渲染层次。

④ Marvin Perry, *Western Civilisation: A Brief History*, Boston: Houghton Mifflin Company, 2001, p. 222.

strong will. This "David" is considered far grander than Donatello's "David".

Another well-known painter, Raphael was best known for his many portraits of the Madonna① and for his large frescoes in the Vatican. The images of Madonna in his paintings are usually affable, majestic, poised and approachable and are quite different from the mysterious and stiff ones in Medieval religious works. *The Sistine Madonna*② is one of the marvellous renditions of his work. A union of balance, harmony and order is adequately reflected in his *The Alba Madonna*③. *The School of Athens*④ in the Vatican Palace exalts the philosophers of antiquity, including Plato, Aristotle, Socrates and Euclid and so on. The style of clarity and harmony is reflected in all his works.

Literatures and Works The Italian artists left an artistic treasure house for the later generations to appreciate and learn from. As a matter of fact, the Renaissance first took place in the field of literature. Alighieri Dante (1265—1321), Francesco Petrarch (1304—1374) and Giovanni Boccaccio (1313—1375), the three giants of Renaissance Literature composed the prelude of the Renaissance in Italy.

Dante was considered the greatest Italian poet and one of the most important writers of European literature. He received a thorough education in both classical and Christian literature. From 1295, he actively contributed to Renaissance literature in Florence but was exiled in 1302 to Italy. After 1302 he spent time travelling from one city to another. His *The Divine Comedy* was finished in the years of his exile. It is a 100-canto⑤(14233 lines) story-poem that shows the three worlds of the afterlife via the poet's journey through them. The three worlds are Hell, Purgatory⑥ guided by Vergil, and Heaven guided by Beatrice—Dante's beloved, to whom the poem was dedicated. *The Divine Comedy* portrayed an unchanging universe ordered by God but was written in a complicated pentameter⑦ form, which was an excellent synthesis of the medieval

---

① *Madonna*：圣母玛利亚(基督教中耶稣的母亲)，此处特指文艺复兴时期意大利画家拉斐尔的圣母像。

② *The Sistine Madonna*：《西斯廷圣母》，意大利画家拉斐尔代表作之一。它以甜美、悠然的抒情风格而闻名遐迩。这幅祭坛画，指定装饰在为纪念教皇西克斯特二世而重建的西斯廷教堂内的礼拜堂里的。最初它被放在教堂的神龛上，至1574年，一直保存在教堂里，故得此名。现为德国德累斯顿茨温格博物馆古代艺术大师馆收藏。

③ *Alba Madonna*：《阿尔巴圣母》，意大利画家拉斐尔代表作之一，现藏于华盛顿国立美术馆。因其收藏者阿尔巴公爵而得名。画作描绘圣母子与施洗约翰沐浴在暮色黄昏中时的亲情关系。圣母席地而坐，膝上坐着圣婴耶稣，身边坐着施洗约翰。圣母左手拿着刚刚合拢的《圣经》，右手搭在膝边的施洗约翰身上，以一种爱怜而静穆的目光，观望着两个幼儿的玩闹。

④ *The School of Athens*：《雅典学院》，又名《雅典学派》，意大利画家拉斐尔代表作之一。画作集古今著名哲学家于一堂，以雅典学者为主，背景衬以宏伟的古典大厅。

⑤ canto：长诗中的篇，相当于书中的"章"。

⑥ Purgatory：(罗马天主教)炼狱，那些在幸福中死去的人的灵魂必须去赎罪的地方。

⑦ pentameter：五音步格诗。英文诗歌中用得最多的便是抑扬格，90%的英文诗都是用抑扬格写成的。其中又以抑扬格五音步居多。如果一个音步中有两个音节，前者为轻，后者为重，则这种音步叫"抑扬格音步"，轻读是"抑"，重读是"扬"，一轻一重，故称抑扬格。如果一首诗的格律是"抑扬格五音步"(iambic pentameter)，即每行五步音，则称为"五音步格诗"。

outlook. In the long poem, which was a travel in spirit, the poet revealed the realm of the Christian God of that age.

Petrarch is an Italian scholar, poet, and is regarded as the founder of humanism. He was fascinated by both Christianity and classical culture. His works greatly affected the development of literature throughout Western Europe. He was devoted in the works of antiquity in collecting and remarking upon the classical works. Inspired by his beloved lady, Laura (some scholars believed she was a fancied character), he wrote the well-known poems called *Song Book*①. He was crowned as a poet laureate in Rome in 1341.

Giovanni Boccaccio was an Italian poet. He had been living in Florence and Naples up to 1350 where he was a productive writer who wrote a number of pastorals②, poems and prose tales. After that year, he was transferred as a diplomat to cope with some serious public affairs. At the same time, he concentrated on the opportunity to learn new knowledge and build new friendships. Taking advantage of the travel in Rome, Ravenna, Avignon and Brandenburg as ambassador of Florence, he became acquainted with Francesco and Petrarch and established a deep friendship with them. His distinguished work, the *Decameron*, which required more than ten years of writing, was finished in 1358. The summary of the story follows: in order to seek refuge from the plague at Florence in 1348, seven ladies and three gentlemen went to a country villa away from the city. And during the ten days of escape, they told one hundred stories to each other for the purpose of killing time. His excellent narrative skill and the abounding poetical sentiments encouraged his readers to sigh with admiration. The classical and the romantic traditions, which are both prominent characteristics in European literature, can be seen in *Decameron*.

Section Three The Pattern of Politics in the Renaissance (1494—Early 1600s)

The Italian States In the time of the Renaissance, Italy was in a state of disintegration, being ruled by five forces, including the Duchy of Milan, Venice, Florence, the Papal States and the Kingdom of Naples.

Central Italy was occupied by the Papal States. However, some cities and territories in central Italy were divorced from the domination of the popes with the papal residence in Avignon. The Duchy of Milan and Venice carved up Northern Italy. Southern Italy was always a feudal monarchy ruled by the Kingdom of Naples which strongly blocked the development of new art and literature. In 1494, the Kingdom of

---

① *Song Book*:《歌集》,彼特拉克的爱情诗集,共 366 首,其中 14 行诗 317 首,抒情诗 29 首,六行诗 9 首,叙事诗 7 首,短诗 4 首。全部诗集分上下两部分:《圣母劳拉之生》和《圣母劳拉之死》。

② pastoral:田园式作品,描绘或唤起乡村生活的文学或其他艺术作品,常采用理想主义手法。

Naples was invaded by the French army. Its independence came to an end. During the next thirty years, the wars aiming to occupy Italy between French and Spanish army raged in the Italian states. In 1527, Spain dominated Italy and this resulted in the end of the Italian Renaissance.

The glorious Renaissance culture was credited to be ruled by some enlightened ruling families who took control of a number of independent city-states. Isabella d'Este (1474—1539), called the "first lady of the world", was remarkable for her ruling power as well as her intelligence and political wisdom. She is the daughter of the duke of Ferrara and married Francesco Gonzaga, marquis of Mantua. She ruled Mantua successfully and made it an important cultural centre in the Italian Renaissance.

Besides Mantua, Urbino was another centre of culture in the 15th century. Federigo da Montefeltro ruled Urbino from 1444 to 1482. His good education enabled him to accept the new culture and art and his skills of fighting helped him to become not only a good ruler but an excellent condottiere①.

Machiavelli and the His Political Ideas Niccolo Machiavelli (1469—1527), once involved in overthrowing the Medici family's domination, was active in Italian political activities after the family was out of power. Through his diplomatic missions to France and Germany, he was deeply attracted by their unity and strong power. He was always thinking about the importance of Italian unity. He was expelled after the Medici family regained its power in 1512. The next year, he produced the famous political book *The Prince*②, which discussed how to keep and expand the state's power as a successful ruler.

He completely renounced the theory of divine right of a monarch that was the norm in the Medieval Ages, and expounded a new political theory that ascribed no divine origin to the state. In his point of view, the overriding purpose of a monarch was to maintain the survival of his state. Moral and religious considerations should have no place in a prince's thinking of ruling. His political ideas were far divorced from those of the previous political theorists and were more realistic and useful.

The European States Although the "new monarchies" that attempted to regain central power of monarchical governments in Europe were on the upswing in the second half of the 15th century, European states had always been in a state of upheaval in the Renaissance age. Like the monarchs in the Medieval Age, the Renaissance monarchs were fascinated with the centralisation of their political power. They made this tendency fiercer and more obvious although the expansion of royal authority showed different degrees in different areas. For example, decentralisation eclipsed centralisation in

---

① condottiere:雇佣军队长,14～16世纪雇佣军的头领。

② *The Prince*:《君主论》,文艺复兴时期政治家马基维利亚的著作,提出了现实主义的政治主张,以表达他对君王的忠诚与崇拜。全书有26章。

central and Eastern Europe. The Renaissance monarchs wanted to suppress the nobility, keep the church under their control, and compel their subjects to be loyal and obedient.

The French ruling class firmly resolved to enforce monarchical power and built a territorial state after the Hundred Years' War[①]. King Louis Ⅺ (1461—1483), regarded as the founder of the French national state, advanced the process of the state building and laid a firm basis for the later development of a strong French monarchy. In an attempt to keep a sufficient and regular income for the country, he greatly increased the taille[②], which was the annual direct tax on land or property and made it an on-going tax. The annexation of the nobility's possessions to the state's holding also expanded his power and territory.

The English were deeply influenced by the Hundred Years' War against the French. The economy was badly eroded not only by the cost of the Hundred Years' War, but also by the War of the Roses[③]. The civil war set the ducal house of Lancaster (symbolised by a red rose) and the ducal house of York (symbolised by a white rose) into direct opposition. It caused a great disturbance in England and many noble families were involved in the severe conflict. The war ended with the establishment of a new dynasty in 1485 when Henry Tudor, duke of Richmond, vanquished Richard Ⅲ (1483—1485), the last York king, at Bosworth Field.

The Habsburg Dynasty[④] obtained hegemony of the Holy Roman Empire. From the second half of the 15th century, this central European empire began to play an important part in European affairs.

Great disorder in Europe was caused by the struggle for strong monarch of many states. An ideal well-ordered world in Eastern Europe would not become true due to the existence of many multiethnic groups and religious differences. Hungary was governed by bishops and great territorial lords, which stood as an essential state in Europe. However, after the death of King Matthias Corvinus (1458 — 1490), the power of Hungary had been on the wane. Before the year 1480, Mongols had always held the power of Russia. Prince Ivan Ⅲ (1462—1505) built a new state, which was divorced from the control of the Mongols. The new state's capital city was known as Moscow.

---

① Hundred Years' War：百年战争，指英国和法国以及后来加入的勃艮第于1337～1453年间的战争，是世界最长的战争，断断续续进行了长达116年。

② taille：法国封建时代君主及领主征收的租税。

③ War of the Roses：玫瑰战争（1455～1487），指英国兰开斯特王朝（House of Lancaster）和约克王朝（House of York）的支持者之间为了英格兰王位的断续内战。兰开斯特王朝的家徽是红玫瑰，约克王朝是白玫瑰。

④ Habsburg Dynasty：哈布斯堡王朝，欧洲历史上最为显赫、统治地域最广的王室之一。

Section Four The Natural Science in the Renaissance (15th—17th Century)

The humanism in the Renaissance played an important role in the development of natural science. People were divorced from the bondage of Medieval theology and were expected to pursue ideological emancipation. People put more emphasis on reality, scientific experiments and exploration. Human creativity and curiosity were perpetually expanded and constantly satisfied in this period. The development of manufacturing encouraged the exploration into the natural science. Finally, the scientific and technical accomplishments of ancient Greece, Rome, Arabia and China provided enlightenment for European scientific development.

The Invention of Movable Printing Movable metal printing was invented in the 15th century. The art of printing made a profound impact on the life and studies of European intellectuals. It gave the scholars and scientists of that age more convenient access to the ancient literatures. It not only helped to widen the outlook and the knowledge of the intellectuals, but also made it possible to spread cultural and scientific communication among different countries as well. German printer Johannes Gutenberg (1400—1468) was responsible for the process of developing the movable type, and he was the first one to print Bible in such a type. In the period of the Renaissance, one of the largest industries in Europe was certainly the printing industry. Venice was well known as the printing centre and many other states including Italy, France and Spain were also powerful in printing at that time. The new printing system contributed a lot to the publication and spread of many religious books, Latin and Greek classics, medieval grammars, legal handbooks, philosophy books and popular romances.

The Development of Astronomy Astronomy was the starting point of the scientific revolution of the Renaissance Age. The earth-centred system was supported by the Catholic Church in Medieval Age but was doubted by the Renaissance scientists with the development of navigation.

Nicolaus Copernicus (1473—1543), a Polish astronomer, was regarded as the founder of modern astronomy. According to him, the earth was a mobile sphere that turned on its axis once a day. He became sceptical about the thought of geocentrism① (the centre of the universe is the earth) that had occupied the most important place in the field of astronomy and a dogma of the church. On the contrary, he thought that the centre of the universe was the sun. And all the planets, including the earth, revolved around it all day and all night. His bold assumption was acknowledged as the

① geocentrism：地心说，认为地球是宇宙的中心，而其他的星球都环绕着它而运行的一种学说。最初由古希腊学者欧多克斯提出，后经亚里士多德、托勒密进一步发展而逐渐建立和完善起来。

heliocentric (sun-centred) system. *The Revolutions of the Heavenly Bodies*① was his most well-known work in which he elaborately expressed his theory. His thinking became widespread and was the motive of the rapid development of modern science. In other words, he turned out to be a pioneer of a scientific revolution. Despite the revolutionary spirits of Copernicus, his theory had little immediate impact and a further step was made by the German scientist Johannes Kepler (1571—1630)②.

Tycho Brahe (1546—1601) was a Danish astronomer. He created perfectly precise astronomical measurements of the solar system and identified more than 700 stars. He kept astronomical observations for more than 20 years and recorded the planet activities in details, which provided Johannes Kepler (1571—1630) with accurate data for his research. Kepler was not only an astronomer but also a natural philosopher in Germany. He made his contribution to the formulation and the verification of the three laws of planetary motion later called Kepler's laws.

Giordano Bruno (1548—1600) was a faithful follower of theory of Copernicus. He openly and actively spread the heliocentricism③ theory of Copernicus in the decade of 1582 to 1592. He expressed his opposition against the church by his brave action. His pursuit for truth and his contempt for Christianity roused great indignation within the church. When sentenced to death by fire, he still attacked the church: "Perhaps you, my judges, pronounce this sentence against me with greater fear than I receive it." He died heroically for a worthy cause, and his insistence on truth always lived in people's hearts. But the fallacy of the church was overthrown by the telescope of Galileo.

Galileo Galilei④(1564—1642), the Italian physicist and astronomer, advanced the telescope in 1609. With the help of his powerful telescope, people could observe the Milky Way, the four largest satellites of Jupiter and the lunar craters for the first time. He recorded these findings in the book *The Starry Messenger*⑤ published in 1610. His most famous book, *The Dialogues*⑥, was published in 1632 in which he stated the fact that the earth revolves around the sun. His "treason" also offended the church. As a result, he was sent to jail, and finally he died of illness while under house arrest in 1642

① *The Revolutions of the Heavenly Bodies*:《天体运行论》,共6卷,波兰天文学家哥白尼的天文著作,书中提出了“日心说”,推翻了“地心说”。

② Kepler:开普勒,德国著名天体物理学家,提出著名的行星运动三大定律。详见第七章。

③ heliocentricism:日心说,也称为地动说,是关于天体运动的和地心说相立的学说。它认为太阳是银河系的中心,而不是地球。由波兰天文学家哥白尼提出。

④ Galileo Galilei:伽利略·伽利雷,意大利天文学家、物理学家和哲学家。参见第七章。

⑤ *The Starry Messenger*:《星际使者》,意大利物理学家伽利略的著作。该书记述并论证了他的一系列天文学发现,诸如月球表面凹凸不平、太阳上有黑子等。这些理论与亚里士多德的天体完美论点形成对立,使伽利略名噪一时。

⑥ *The Dialogues*:《对话》,意大利物理学家伽利略的著作,出版于1632年,又名《关于托勒密和哥白尼两大世界体系的对话》(*The Dialogue on the Two Chief Systems of the World*)。书中对哥白尼学说作出了理性论证。

because he never gave in to the excessive power of the church.

The Development of Medicine and Anatomy The ancient Greek anatomist, Galen, whose medical theories were in favour of religion, was replaced by some physicians and anatomists in the Renaissance time. They re-examined many medical classics and created many new therapies and new theories concerning the human nature.

Andreas Vesalius (1514—1564)①, a Belgian anatomist and physician, was among those who challenged Galen's teachings. Through his study, he pointed out that Galen's anatomical teaching which was based on the dissections of animals was not appropriate to be applied to human beings. His seven-volume book, *On the Fabric of the Human Body*②, is the description of the structure of the human body based on his dissections of the human body. He even made drawings himself in the book to illustrate his theories more clearly. He presented the process of the construction of muscles in layers and pointed out the errors in the previous theories of anatomy. His technical drawings and his brave challenge against the long-lasting old theories are regarded as a great breakthrough in the history of medicine.

William Harvey (1578—1657)③, an English doctor and anatomist, published the book *Anatomical Essay on the Motion of the Heart and Blood in Animals*④ which explained how blood was pumped from the heart throughout the body, returning to the heart and then recirculated. Harvey also conducted research in embryology, and he published *Essays on the Generation of Animals*⑤ as a result. He was regarded as a medical leader of that age although some people disregarded his unconventional anatomical theories. He was doctor to King Charles Ⅰ of England and was appointed doctor of physics at Oxford. His genius in medicine and science was highly praised and observed in the field of the European medical community after his death in 1657.

Chapter Review

This chapter mainly depicted the social changes and developments in the Renaissance age and the intellectuals and artists' new vision of humankind shown in their representative works. Their brilliant achievements were innovation and novelty

---

① Andreas Vesalius:安德烈·维萨留斯,著名解剖学家。参见第七章。

② *On the Fabric of the Human Body*:《人体结构》,比利时医生安德烈·维萨里发表于1543年。在著作中,他冲破了以盖仑为代表的旧权威们臆测的解剖学理论,以大量、丰富的解剖实践资料,对人体的结构进行了精确的描述。

③ William Harvey:威廉·哈维,英国科学家、生理学家和胚胎学家,其贡献是划时代的,标志着新的生命科学的开始,是16世纪科学革命的一个重要组成部分。参见第七章。

④ *Anatomical Essay on the Motion of the Heart and Blood in Animals*:《关于动物心脏与血液运动的解剖研究》,英国医生威廉·哈维发表于1628年。该书的问世标志着近代生理学的诞生,同时也奠定了哈维在科学发展史上的重要地位。

⑤ *Essays on the Generation of Animals*:《动物的生殖》,英国医生威廉·哈维在1651年发表的著作,标志着当代胚胎学研究的真正开始。

which made a new era. Humanism, the most prominent symbol of the Renaissance, was explored in this chapter, i. e. its origin, its representatives, and its profound impact on different fields of the society. The High Renaissance, which witnessed the shift of the cultural centre from Florence to Rome, also contributed to the accomplishments of the three artistic masters at the time. The situations of Italian and European states were presented, and, meanwhile, Machiavelli's political thinking was discussed. His ideas, shown in his book, *The Prince*, were far more realistic than those of the medieval forebears. The development of natural science of that age benefited largely from the spread of humanism. The previous achievements in science and the development of manufacture also contributed to the creativity of the natural scientists.

Exercise

Ⅰ. *According to the information provided in this chapter, choose the correct alternative among A, B, C, and D that can complete each of the following statements.*

1. The birthplace of the Renaissance is ________.

   A. England　　B. Spain

   C. The Holy Roman Empire　　D. Italy

2. Besides the peasants, the third estate in the Renaissance society also consisted of ________.

   A. the old nobles

   B. the new nobles

   C. the inhabitants of the towns and cities

   D. the clergy

3. ________ was called the founder of modern sculpture.

   A. Giotto　　B. da Vinci　　C. Donatello　　D. Masaccio

4. In the following forces, which one was NOT the ruling class in the Italian Renaissance?

   A. The duchy of Milan　　B. Rome

   C. The Papal States　　D. Florence

5. The marble sculpture *David* is depicted as a nude young man with strong will. This "David" is over 5 metres and produced by ________.

   A. Michelangelo　　B. Donatello　　C. Brunelleschi　　D. Dante

Ⅱ. *Fill in the blanks with what you have learned in this chapter.*

1. The most distinct characteristic of the Renaissance was ________.
2. *The Divine Comedy* written by Dante is the tale of the poet's journey through Hell, ________ and Heaven.
3. Polish astronomer Nicolaus Copernicus is best famous for his theory of ________.

4. In the book ________, Vesalius illustrates human structure and muscle with his own drawings.
5. At the beginning of the 15th century, the fusion of Florentine civic spirit and pride cut a new way for the humanist movement in Florence, which was later called "________" by the modern scholars.

Ⅲ. *According to what you have learned, answer the following questions briefly in your own words.*

1. What is the meaning of the Renaissance? Why do we call the time ranging from 14th century to 17th century in Europe Renaissance?
2. What reputation did Petrarch have? What is his contribution to the Renaissance?
3. Could you name the three artistic giants and tell their works that dominated the High Renaissance?
4. Who gave the best expression to the Renaissance preoccupation with political power? What is his opinion?
5. What is impact of the development of printing on the Renaissance?

Ⅳ. *With critical analysis, answer the following essay questions in your own words.*

1. Discuss the driving forces and the significance of the flourishing development of natural science in the Age of the Renaissance.
2. Humanism played a very important role in the Renaissance. Discuss how it runs through the fields of art, literature and natural science at that time.

Ⅴ. *Work in small groups and make comparisons based on the following topic.*

Renaissance, which means "rebirth" in French, is a cultural movement that involves in the recovery of antiquity. While the Renaissance scholars were experiencing the rebirth of culture in Europe, Chinese scholars in the Late Ming Dynasty and the Early Qing Dynasty were also undergoing a trend of thought in literature and art. For instance, they advocated the importance of Song poetry as well as that of Tang poetry and tried to bring freshness to poetry creation. Could you put forward your idea of the similarities or the differences between the trend of thought in literature and art in the Renaissance and that of the Late Ming Dynasty and the Early Qing Dynasty?

Voices on Key Points

Renaissance

In essence the Renaissance was simply the green end of onc of civilisation's hardest winters.

——John Fowles

The Renaissance of the 15th century was, in many things, great rather by what it designed that by what it achieved.

——Walter Pater

Arts and Literature in Italian Renaissance

The various forms of intellectual activity which together make up the culture of an age, move for the most part from different starting-points, and by unconnected roads.

——Walter Pater

Suggested Reading

1. Geraldine A. Johnson 著，李建群译：《文艺复兴时期的艺术》，外语教学与研究出版社 2008 年版。
2. Jerry Brotton 著，赵国新译：《文艺复兴简史》，外语教学与研究出版社 2007 年版。
3. Hopkins, Lisa & Matthew Steggle. *Renaissance Literature and Culture*. Shanghai: Shanghai Foreign Language Education Press, 2008.
4. 白秀兰等著：《文艺复兴巨子全传》，长春出版社 1995 年版。
5. (英)佩特著，李丽译：《文艺复兴》，外语教学与研究出版社 2010 年版。

Chapter Six Protestant Reformation (1517—Late 16th Century)

I now intend, by the help of God, to throw some light upon the wiles and wickedness of these men, to the end that when they are known, they may not henceforth be so hurtful and so great a hindrance. God has given us a noble youth to be our head and thereby has awakened great hopes of good in many hearts; wherefore it is meet that we should do our part and profitably use this time of grace. ①

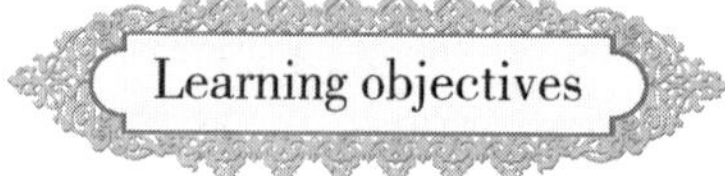

After reading this chapter, you will be able to:

1. *Understand the profound effects of the Reformation in history;*
2. *Know Martin Luther and his Lutheranism;*
3. *Know Calvinism and Zwingli' reformation in Zurich;*
4. *Know the Anabaptists and their radical thinking;*
5. *Understand the development of the Counter Reformation.*

---

① C. M. Jacobs, trans. "An Open Letter to the Christian Nobility of the German Nation Concerning the Reform of the Christian Estate," in *Works of Martin Luther*, Vol. Ⅱ, Philadelphia: Muhlenberg Press, 1915, p. 63.

马丁·路德，一位德国宗教改革家，以沸腾的热血和坚定的信念而流芳百世。

1517年10月31日，年轻的马丁·路德慷慨凛然地站在了维登堡城堡大教堂的门前，在门上张贴了著名的《九十五条论纲》，以学术辩论的方式来指责教会的诸多弊端，由此拉开了欧洲宗教改革运动的序幕。他提出了著名的"因信称义"观念，认为所谓的"义"来源于上帝的恩典和对上帝的虔诚信仰，而不在于自己的善行和功德，以此与教会针锋相对。继路德宗之后，加尔文宗、安立甘宗(英国国教)、再洗礼宗等新教宗派接踵而来，德国、法国、瑞士和英国等多个欧洲国家先后投入到这次沸沸扬扬的宗教运动当中。其中，加尔文宗与路德宗和安立甘宗并称新教三大主流派。在欧洲诸国的宗教改革运动中，英国的宗教改革是一场自上而下的运动。同时，天主教会的"反宗教改革"也迎头而上，耶稣会、异端裁判所和天特会议均是其重要组成部分。

Section One The Launch of the Reformation (Second Half of the 15th Century—1516)

The Reformation in the 16th century was not only a religious movement but also a spiritual revolution, which aimed at the institutional reform of the church and the protection of the interests of the peasants and the bourgeoisie. Apart from Martin Luther's reform movement, the reform of Christendom was one of the major goals of the Christian, or Northern Renaissance, Humanism.

Christian or Northern Renaissance Humanism Northern humanists, also called Christian humanists for their profound preoccupation with religion, stuck to the translations and editions of the classics to find a more humane morality than the theological arguments of the medieval scholastics.

Although regarded as naive, Christian humanists optimistically supported schools because they always believed the power of education. In their views, in order to carry out a reform of the church and society, human beings' competence to reason and improve themselves could not be disregarded. According to the famous humanist Desiderius Erasmus (1466—1536), the Holy Scripture should be translated into simple languages so that the common people, such as the lowliest women, the farmer and the weaver, could understand and appreciate true Christian piety or an inward religious feeling. He firmly held the view that the key of the reform was the change of human beings who composed the society.

Erasmus, the most distinguished Christian humanist, urged the religious reform by publicizing his conception of religion "the philosophy of Christ", which was based on a review of the gospel① of the *New Testament* (published in 1516 and annotated). He

① gospel:《圣经》福音书:《新约圣经》的前四本书之一，记载了耶稣的生平、死亡、复活和他的教导。

longed to restore Christianity through a programme of widespread education about early Christianity. In the New Testament, a more sensible conception of Christian doctrine was stated. The methods of the Scholastic theologians were completely rejected by Erasmus to make people free from frivolity and stupidity and the bookish way of thinking. His satire *The Praise of Folly*① was written in 1509 in which he presented his criticism of the abuses of the church and the corruption of the society.

With his works and all his efforts, Erasmus devoted considerate time to the preparation and promotion of the reformation; he disclosed the abuses of the church, and enhanced the "Revival of Learning". However, he was attacked by the Lutherans for his efforts to reform within the church. Unfortunately, his education programme resulted in nothing. All in all, despite his inconsistency with the Lutheranism②, his attempt to reform and his contribution to the formal reformation was a shining point in the period of the 16th century. However, when the Lutheran revolution came, he found himself in an embarrassing position. The Lutherans attacked him for his cowardice and inconsistency in refusing to follow up his opinions to their legitimate conclusions.

Church and Religion In the time from 1350 to 1480, the Renaissance popes' desires to demonstrate supremacy over kings and to offer spiritual leadership over all western Christendom had been cast off by theologians and political theorists. The failure of the popes led the church into a crisis and affected the spiritual life of all Christendom. Thus the rebellion against the church's authority, started by humanists and spread among the laypeople, was like an arrow in a bow.

At the same time, the atmosphere of the 14th and 15th centuries, with its uncertainty of life and quickness of death, created a yearning for meaningful religious expression and certainty of salvation③. This impulse expressed itself in two ways—either through external forces such as the veneration of relics and the buying of indulgences④ or through the mystical path (with the feature of a neglect of religious tenet and a desire to keep a life of internal piety based on the belief in Christ). More and more Christians only made pilgrimages to holy centres such as Rome and Jerusalem in pursuit of spiritual benefits and forgot all else.

In the 15th century, the outstanding feature of the revival of religious piety was that it adhered to the orthodox beliefs and practices of the Catholic Church. Impotent

---

① *The Praise of Folly*:《愚人颂》,尼德兰伊拉斯谟的教育著作。伊拉斯谟说,争取幸福作为生活目标是愚蠢的,因为为了幸福,我们要通过夸张欺骗,自恋奉承进行自欺欺人。

② Lutheranism:路德教义,是宗教改革家马丁·路德宣扬的宗教教义,强调"因信称义"的天主教准则。

③ salvation:(基督教科学派)超度,救度。生命、真理或爱是超越一切的认识和证明,随之毁灭一切罪恶、疾病和死亡的幻象。

④ indulgence:赎罪券,拉丁文意为"仁慈"或"宽免"。1313 年天主教会开始在欧洲兜售。教皇宣称教徒购买这种券后可赦免"罪罚"。

clergy failed to ensure people's certainty of salvation and their spiritual peace. The clergy showed little appreciation for the deepening of religious life in the second half of the 15th century, which set the stage for Luther's reformation.

Section Two German Protestant Reformation (1517—Early 16th Century)

In the late 15th century and the early 16th century, the capitalist economy of Germany was severely held back by the feudal separationist rule. The country was torn apart, which led to a lack of a unified domestic market. In the meantime, the Vatican took advantage of this split and tried to plunder the country. Armed revolts erupted one after another and the appeal for reformation grew day by day. In 1517, papal indulgences were sold under the instigation of Pope Leo X in order to raise money to build St. Peter's Cathedral in Rome. Martin Luther was totally disappointed with the church and attacked the abuse of the church power, and this marked the beginning of the reformation.

Luther and His Doctrine in the Early Age Little Martin, the future famous religious reformation leader, was born on November 10th, 1483. The great German religious reformer, Martin Luther (1483—1546), whose father was a miner in Mansfeld, was expected to become a lawyer and live a better and more respected life. With this expectation, young Luther's father sent him to the village school at Mansfeld, then to a school at Magdeburg, then to Eisenach. He was poor and was taken into a hospice to reside when at Magdeburg and Eisenach. In order to make a living, he also served as a chorister in a church and begged for food from the town people. The hardships suffered in his childhood laid a firm foundation for his later struggle against the tough church power.

In 1501, Luther entered the University of Erfurt. At that time, Erfurt was a famous university and considered the intellectual centre of Germany. Young Luther lived up to his father's expectation and studied law. He devoured the classical works thirstily and worked hard toward his law career. A large number of works in Latin were in his domain of reading and the study of Greek helped him to grasp the spirit of some classical works. Later on he turned to give more attention to questions in religion and did not involve himself in humanist lectures. Although becoming master in the liberal arts in 1505, he began to develop an interest in religion. He entered the Augustinian monastery at Erfurt. With regard to this, there was a story that in order to be rescued from a storm, Luther promised God he would be a monk, and he kept his word by entering the monastery. He also did not live up to his father's expectation because he hoped to assure his salvation in the monastery. Obtaining his doctorate of theology in Wittenburg in 1511, he was accepted by the University of Wittenburg as a professor of biblical theology.

Justification by faith was the core of Luther's teachings. According to him, the masses were just common beings. They were so weak and powerless that they could not promise sufficient good works to achieve salvation. Consequently, faith in the promises of God, but not good works, could help human beings ensure salvation. Justification was the act by which a person was made to deserve salvation. Luther redefined his thinking by carefully studying the Bible. Justification by faith became the most important doctrine of the Protestant Reformation with the Bible serving as a guide to explore religious truth and ethics.

In 1517, John Tetzel, a papal agent inspired by the Pope, promoted the selling of the indulgences in central Germany. This measure was aimed to amass funds for the church misleading the common people by assuring them of salvation. In response to the sale of the indulgences, Luther challenged the church officials openly and posted his *Ninety-Five Theses*① on the door of the Castle Church. These theses were first written in Latin, but soon translated into German and were posted throughout Europe. The Reformation began formally. And an essential thinking of Luther began to emerge in the *Ninety-Five Theses* and ran through his other works afterwards, and this was that he believed the Christian salvation should be achieved by contrition for sins and trust in God's mercy. Faith was undoubtedly a prerequisite to gain salvation, which was a gift from God.

Other works of Luther also served to promote the development of the reformation. In the short treatise *On the Freedom of a Christian Man*②, he expounded his main doctrine, justification by faith. "It is faith alone, not good works, which justifies, frees, and brings salvation through Jesus."③ However, this did not mean the Christian could be freed from good works; instead, Christians would want to do good works to show their gratitude to God. In the *Address to the Nobility of the German Nation*④ written in German, he appealed for the removal of the papacy in the country and advocated for the princes to set up a reformed German church. In his *The Babylonian Captivity of the Church*⑤, he fought against the sacramental system the pope of the church insisted upon. He further suggested reforming monasticism and assenting to clergies' marriages.

---

① *Ninety-Five Theses*:《九十五条论纲》。新教路德宗创始人马丁·路德将其张贴在维登堡城堡大教堂的门前,以学术辩论的方式来指责教会的诸多弊端,由此拉开了欧洲宗教改革运动的序幕。

② *On the Freedom of a Christian Man*:《论基督徒的自由》,新教路德宗创始人马丁·路德的文章。与《致德意志基督教贵族公开书》等文章一起痛斥了罗马教廷对德意志的专横和掠夺,并呼吁世俗君主建立不受罗马教廷控制的民族教会。

③ Jackson J. Spielvogel, *Western Civilisation: A Brief History*, Volume Ⅰ: *To 1715*, Belmont: Wadsworth, 1999, p. 369.

④ *Address to the Nobility of the German Nation*:《致德意志基督教贵族公开书》,新教路德宗创始人马丁·路德的文章。

⑤ *The Babylonian Captivity of the Church*:《教会被掳于巴比伦》,新教路德宗创始人马丁·路德于1520年所作。讲述了教会中世纪时被掳于教皇专权的黑暗权势之下,并呼吁宗教改革要回归《圣经》。

Luther's doctrines met with flat rejections from both the Pope and the emperor. He was sentenced as guilty of heresy in 1520 and was excluded by the church in 1521. Luther refused to reject the heretical doctrines he had espoused, and he was deprived of his civil rights. His German supporters saved him on his way back and secretly led him to a castle. He dedicated himself to the translation of the New Testament there, and it was spread among his followers.

The Development of Lutheranism Despite the complications he suffered, Luther led his religious movement to a revolution on a grand scale. His doctrines won approval throughout Germany and even spread over some other European countries during the early 16th century. The whole of Germany was permeated by the preaching of evangelical sermons around 1520s. Under the pressure of Lutheranism, a reform of the inner life of the church began.

Luther's reform was based on the support of the princes and magistrates in the country because he believed the authority of the state and its rulers were given by God to keep peace and order in order to spread the Gospel. So the Lutheran churches, advanced as state churches both in Germany and Scandinavia, were ruled by the state. The church members were all supervised and disciplined by the state. Luther also established new religious services to replace the Mass. Consequently, Luther did not live up to the peasants' expectation for supporting them against their lords in the peasants' war in June 1524.

In 1525, Luther married Katherina von Bora, a former nun, thus confirming his denunciation of clerical celibacy①. With this, he initiated the practice of marriage of the Protestant ministers.

Section Three Reformation Outside Germany (1520s—Late 16th Century)

Affected by the reformation in Germany, Lutheranism spread rapidly in European countries in the 16th century. Luther's reform gradually became the headspring of some more radical religious movements and social upheavals. For Catholics, Lutheranism and the later radical doctrines were all heresies. The correct interpretation of the Bible became the focus of the disputes between Catholics and Protestants. Because it was impossible for the two sides to be united in opinions on the issue, cruel warfare often kept company with fierce theological confrontations.

John Calvin and Calvinism② John Calvin(1509—1564) was born in a substantial family. He was offered the best education, provided the ecclesiastical patronage and was promised a hopeful future. It was hoped that he would become an employable priest

① celibacy：禁欲，指因为宗教誓言而禁止性关系。

② Calvinism：加尔文教派，法国著名宗教改革家、神学家约翰·加尔文毕生的许多主张的统称，在不同的讨论中有不同的意义。在现代的神学论述习惯当中，加尔文主义的意思是指“救赎预定论”和“救恩独作说”。

after he attained the chaplaincy[①] attached to the altar of La Gésine in the cathedral of Noyon in 1521, so that he could experience the tonsure[②]. Years later, in 1528, he went to the University in Orléans to study law under the rule of his strict father. Then in both Orléans and Bourges, he became more influenced by the thriving force of the religious reformation and by the charm of humanistic thinking. Being very interested in the classics and humanism, he delved into the study of classical works and of the Hebrew after he went back to Paris. Like Martin Luther in Germany, John Calvin gradually became a French Protestant theologian during the Reformation and founded Calvinism, which was a system of Christian theology.

In France, the humanists were promoting the rapid development of the Reformation and Calvin was excited and active in this group. He became a great reformer. Sometime in 1533, he met French followers of Luther and became convinced of the truth of the new theology. He began to spread its beliefs immediately after his conversion, and within a year he and his followers met with trouble from the civil and ecclesiastical authorities. Calvin was arrested, but was released because of insufficient evidence.

His well-known work—*Institutes of the Christian Religion*[③] was published in 1536. In this small treatise, Calvin gave a concise summary of the essential truths of the Christian religion. Originally in Latin, the treatise was published in French in 1541 to distribute it in French-speaking areas. In this work, Calvin further supported Luther's most famous doctrine—justification by faith. He stood on Luther's side on many important doctrines. Meanwhile, he also stressed the absolute sovereignty of God. On all accounts, the work was a masterpiece for the interpretation of Protestant doctrines and a guide for ecclesiastical organisation. Owing to this extraordinary treatise, Calvin occupied one of the posts as a new leader of Protestantism[④].

As mentioned above, Calvin believed in the absolute sovereignty of God, that is, the salvation or the damnation of human beings was predestined by God, which must not be changed by any means. He called it the "eternal decree". According to Calvin, "He has once for all determined both whom he would admit to salvation, and whom he would condemn to destruction."[⑤] Predestination[⑥], which was one of the most

---

① chaplaincy：礼拜堂牧师之职位或任期。

② tonsure：削发仪式，剃光头发或一部分头发，尤指成为神甫或和尚的入门仪式。

③ *Institutes of the Christian Religion*：《基督教要义》，16 世纪宗教改革代表人物约翰·加尔文的著作。本书以简明易懂的方式，系统地阐明了基督教神学的要义。全书共四卷，第一卷论述了人如何认识作为创造主的上帝；第二卷探讨了人如何认识作为救赎主的上帝；第三卷讨论了领受基督救恩的方式及其益处；第四卷阐述了教会的性质、治理和圣礼。

④ Protestantism：基督新教，简称"新教"，也经常被直接称为"基督教"，与天主教、东正教并列为基督宗教的三大派别。

⑤ Jackson J. Spielvogel, *Western Civilisation A Brief History*, Volume Ⅰ: *To 1715*, Belmont: Wadsworth, 1999, p. 382.

⑥ Predestination：宿命论，上帝已经预先注定万物的教义，尤指上帝已经选定给某些人永久的拯救。

important aspects of Calvin's doctrine of salvation, stood as a prominent doctrine of the development of Calvinism.

According to Calvin, salvation could be indicated by three tests: first, an open profession of faith; second, a decent and godly life and third, the participation in the sacraments[①] of baptism and communion. For sacraments, Calvin kept baptism and the Lord's Supper. To him, Christ's presence in the Lord's Supper was only on a spiritual level because his body was at the right hand of God.

Calvin believed it was the church that was responsible for supervising and disciplining its members. The church was a divine institution in which the words of God could be preached and the sacraments could be carried out. This thinking was implemented when he later had the opportunity to set up his church in Geneva.

Fortunately, Calvin met a good-willed protestant named Guillaume Farel (1489－1565) who helped him make a turning point in his reformation career in 1536. Calvin must have owed Farel a debt of gratitude for his recognition and appreciation of his talents because it was Farel who persuaded him with earnestness to stay in Geneva and further his study there. With the help of Farel, Calvin began to carry out his plan of reforming the city of Geneva. Not only did he recruit clergy but also some laymen to serve the church, forming a well-organised church order. He also established the Consistory[②] for enforcing moral disciplines by admonishing and correcting deviants. The moral life, the daily behaviour and the doctrinal orthodoxy of Genevans were all under the control of this court. But the Consistory went to an extreme with the expansion of its power. The early "fraternal corrections" became public penance and excommunication[③]. In order to practice his doctrine of the separation of church and state, Calvin kept the two institutions apart in Geneva and enabled the church, which he thought a divine institution, to work independently of state power.

The State was not supposed to interfere with the use of fonts, the unleavened bread in the Lord's Supper, and with the celebration of the church-festivals. Step by step, Genevan citizens could not tolerate Calvin and his firm and tough control, so he felt it hard to carry out his dramatic reform there. Consequently, Calvin, together with his faithful ally, Farel, was forced to leave Geneva in 1538.

Soon after John Calvin left, the city of Geneva went through a great change in the government. The city was split up into factions and was in a state of disunity. The firm ruling strategy of Calvin was later recalled by the city and then in 1540, the government

① sacrament：西方基督教的圣礼。大部分其他西派教会中由耶稣规定的可赋予人神圣恩典的有两项圣事——洗礼和圣餐。

② Consistory：教会议会。某些新教教会中管理当地教区全体教徒的机构。

③ excommunication：开除教籍。取消某人教籍的一种正式的教会的惩罚。

made a unified decision to persuade him to return and rule the city with his strong power. So in 1541, he was invited to return the city and continue to govern Geneva. Facing many adversaries and encountering many difficulties, he did not resign and he persevered.

The first step of Calvin's reform was to reorganise the Church after he made a correct assessment of the situation in Geneva. Under the reign of Calvin, government was carried out with a powerful church court in order to keep discipline. A consistory was formed after Calvin's proposal was passed unanimously in a conference in November in 1541. The members of the city churches had the right to put all the people under church rules, regardless of who they were. This stirred up public indignation and even made Calvin alienated from many of his supporters. Simultaneously, the government was modified by Calvin to become a mere skeleton only having the responsibilities of the selection of syndics, the staffing of some minor offices and the fixation of the wine price.

The reformation led by Calvin in Geneva developed vigorously and Geneva became a vital centre of Protestantism. All European countries welcomed the missionaries trained in Geneva. Calvinism laid a firm foundation in many states in Europe, such as France, Scotland and Netherlands. And even Lutheranism was taking root in the mid-16th century.

The Reformation in Zurich The reformation also had roots in the Swiss city of Zurich, in which Ulrich Zwingli (1484—1531) advocated a form of Christianity similar to that of Martin Luther, but more radical. First of all, he did his utmost to arouse Swiss nationalistic passions, strongly opposed their service in foreign military forces, and encouraged them to break away from the noble's political bondage. While gaining great authority among the masses, he disseminated his own thinking.

He became a priest in 1506 and was ordained a cathedral priest in the Great Minister of Zurich in 1518. Next year, he worked his way up to be nominated as the "People's Priest", which was the highest ecclesiastical position in the city of Zurich. Simultaneously, he accepted Martin Luther's reformation thinking and actively carried it out in the city. Like Luther, he resolutely fought against the selling of indulgences. According to his theology and morality, all Christians should believe in and obey nothing but those that had been expressed clearly and literally by the Bible. In the light of this guiding principle, he also opposed the fast① at Lent② in 1522 for it was not advocated in the New Bible. In an effort to gain popularity among the masses, he brought his ecclesiastical reform programmes into full play in Zurich by 1523. As a result, the city became a very important Protestant foundation where the Protestant

① fast：禁食，斋戒，特指宗教戒律。

② Lent：大斋节，封斋期。从圣灰星期三（大斋节的第一天）到复活节的40天为禁食和为复活节作准备进行忏悔的季节。

revolution took place throughout Switzerland.

With the impact of Zwingli, the city council announced the evangelical reforms in Zurich from 1524 to 1525. They abolished all relics and images; removed all paintings and decorations from the church walls. Scripture reading, prayer and sermons were added into a new liturgy[①]. Some old traditions of papal Christianity were abolished by the church, and the authority of the pope was removed.

Zwingli and his followers strongly emphasised the divine nature of Christ, which was extremely contrary to Luther's way of thinking—Jesus was not only the holy God but was a worldly human being at first, which made possible the transformation of the Eucharist into the physical body and blood of Christ. Consequently, Zwinglian Protestantism unanimously held their point of view and struggled against the human nature of Christ. As a result, they also took a stand against the Lutheran view of the Eucharist. Zwingli thought that the Eucharist was just the symbol of the body and blood of Christ. He and his inheritors objected to Luther's thinking that the bread and wine of the Eucharist was spiritually transformed into the body and blood of Christ. This was the biggest difference on their doctrinal issues. Zwingli gradually split from Luther's theories and began to carry out a more extreme reform by setting up a strict Protestant society in Zurich.

The Radical Reformation: The Anabaptists The word Anabaptist[②] means "re-baptiser." It is often used to refer to all "Radical Reformers", a diverse group that remained outside the mainstream of the Reformation.

The Anabaptists advocated a radical and absolute reform of the church. They resolutely claimed that the church and the state should be separated rather than be mixed. They did not advocate that the state punish or execute people for religious reasons; instead, they thought the most appropriate punishment for heresy was excommunication. In their teachings, the church was the congregation of the redeemed and was contrary to the world, to society as a whole. They also emphasised spiritual experience, practical righteousness, and obedience to divine standards. As a whole, they hoped to restore "primitive Christianity" in order to eliminate the oaths and capital punishment and to exclude the exercise of magistracy. As implied by their name, they did not admit the holy validity of infant baptism and they discarded the belief of "justification by faith" held by Martin Luther, because they could not find any hint of the two in the Scriptures. They believed in the primacy of the Bible and regarded baptism as an external witness of the believer's personal covenant of inner faith. For

---

① liturgy：礼拜仪式，基督教公开典礼的一种规定或一整套模式。

② Anabaptist：再洗礼派教徒。16世纪宗教改革激进运动的成员，相信《圣经》的权威性，相信政教分离、信徒和非信徒分离。

them, justification by faith in words, but opposition in action, was extremely unfaithful or immoral.

The radical movement of the reformation was carried forward rapidly in Europe. This was indeed a great shock to Zwinglian reformation, as well as that of Luther, at that time. In Switzerland, a group of Zwingli's associates shifted their focus to rebaptism, a profound challenge to his doctrines. The followers of this radical movement were mostly from the working classes and they grew steadily in many European countries.

When the waves of the radical reformation were surging forward dramatically, some extraordinary leaders emerged. Among them, Menno Simons (1496 — 1561) was a young and capable leader of the Anabaptists of the Low Countries. The members of his sect characterised particularly by simplicity of life, pacifism①, and non-resistance were called Mennonites. In his early thirties, he began to probe into the Scriptures in order to find the truth of transubstantiation②. His exploration of the sacred writings helped him win the name of "evangelical humanist". His outstanding and enduring efforts for the Anabaptist movement allowed for the further development of it.

The English Reformation The divorce of the King Henry Ⅷ (1509 — 1547) provided a chance for the reformation in England, so that the English Reformation was initiated by the king, not the church. Catherine, the queen of Henry Ⅷ, was unable to give birth to a son as their future heir, and the king grew more and more anxious and impatient. Accidentally and inevitably, in 1525, Henry fell in love with Anne Boleyn, the attractive young maidservant of the queen. Being adept at scheming, charming young Boleyn kept reserved without winning the title of Queen. Driven by the desire to have a male heir and infatuated with the charm of the maidservant, King Henry became quite in favour of the idea of annulment③.

But the King's request for annulment got no response from Pope Clement Ⅶ, who was not only under the power of the Holy Roman Emperor Charles Ⅴ, but also the nephew of Queen Catherine. Dissatisfied with the Pope's neglect and motivated by the strong desire to have a male heir, Henry Ⅷ decided to grant himself a divorce in England's ecclesiastical courts. Thomas Cranmer, the head of the court, declared the annulment in 1533 and affirmed the king's second marriage to Anne Boleyn soon after the annulment.

In England, all appeals to Rome were banned and penalties of praemunire④ against

---

① pacifism：和平主义，反战论。认为国家之间的争端应该而且能够被和平解决。

② transubstantiation：(神学) 圣餐变体论，认为尽管圣餐面包和葡萄酒的外表没有变化但已经变成了耶稣的身体和血。

③ annulment：宣告婚姻无效。法院对已发生或将发生的不完美婚姻作的无效宣告。

④ praemunire：蔑视王权罪，英国法律中因求助或遵从外国法庭而冒犯国王统治权的违法行为。

those who brought papal bulls[①] into England were demanded by the House of Commons. By any means, the paramount power of the king was largely promoted. In addition, the Church was not allowed to make any regulations without being assented to by the King. All the compulsory measures by the Commons against the Church infuriated Pope Clement, so that he announced that the King Henry and Thomas Cranmer were excommunicated from the Church, declared the annulment in 1533 to be invalid, and he refused to acknowledge Henry's marriage with Anne Boleyn.

Some laws were also enforced in order to protect the royalty in England. *The Act of Supremacy*[②] declared that the King was "the only Supreme Head in Earth of the Church of England". *The Ecclesiastical Appointments Act*[③] granted the Sovereign the power to nominate bishops. And according to *The Treasons Act*[④], anybody who refused to acknowledge the King would be punished by death as high treason.

Moreover, the papal nuncio[⑤] was forced to leave England and diplomatic relations with Rome were cut off. The Church of England was controlled by the King Henry, not by Rome.

After Henry Ⅷ died in 1547, he was succeeded by his son, Edward Ⅵ (1547—1553), who was a Protestant. As a result, the Church of England became Protestant in its doctrines via the efforts of Cranmer. With the New Acts of Parliament, the clergy was given the right to marry and a revised protestant liturgy was created using a new prayer book known as *The Book of Common Prayer*. These changes resulted in much opposition culminating in the actions of Mary, the next ruler of England.

In 1553, Edward Ⅵ was succeeded by Henry and Catherine's daughter, Mary (1516—1558), who was a devout Catholic. As soon as she rose to power, she did her utmost to carry forward the Roman Catholic faith in England again. She took decisive measures to fulfil her ambition, including abolishing the religious proclamations of Edward Ⅵ and putting down heresy with ruthless force. More than 300 persons, including Thomas Cranmer, were burned for heresy. Owing to her cruel and ruthless rule, she was nicknamed as "Bloody Mary". During her reign, she did not capture the confidence or the support of her subjects, because she constantly catered to the papacy and the Roman Catholic Church.

Like her father, Mary had been worried about the heir of her kingdom. With the

---

① papal bulls:(天主教)教皇的正式命令。

② *The Act of Supremacy*:《至尊法案》,1534 年颁布,宣布英王亨利八世不仅是世俗的最高统治者,也是宗教的最高统治者,英国所有教会不再听罗马教皇的指挥。

③ *The Ecclesiastical Appointments Act*:《教职任命法案》,英国宗教改革时期颁布的法案,规定教会必须根据英王指定的候选人推选主教。

④ *The Treasons Act*:《叛国罪法案》,英国宗教改革时期颁布的法案,规定不承认英王最高权威即是叛国罪,可判处死刑。

⑤ nuncio:罗马教皇的使节或代表。

motive to bring an heir to her throne, she married Prince Philip Ⅱ of Spain, the son of Charles Ⅴ, in 1590. Unfortunately, her countrymen all regarded Spain as a chief enemy of their country and their dislike of her grew more and more violent. Her marriage did not bring fortune to England. Her husband's return to Spain in 1558 precluded any hope of an heir. She reluctantly accepted Elizabeth, her half-sister, as the next queen of her country. Elizabeth, the daughter of Anne Boleyn and an Anglican[①] Protestant, successfully refused Mary's pressure to convert to Roman Catholicism, finally accomplished great achievements and heroic exploits and became the world-famous Elizabeth Ⅰ.

The Thirty-Nine Articles of Religion[②] was established at Queen Elizabeth Ⅰ's suggestion in 1567, which became the guiding principles of the Anglican doctrine of the English Church. The Church of England became the state religion. Standing up to great outside pressures, she also unified a Protestant England and defeated the Spanish armada in 1588. Under her reign, the national power of England was increasing day by day in every respect.

Section Four The Counter-Reformation (Mid-16th Century)

The reformation was in full swing by the mid-16th century and obtained the support and favour of the people from the peasants to the noble families. Lutheranism swept across Germany and Scandinavia and Calvinism across parts of Switzerland, France, Netherlands and Eastern Europe. The Roman Catholic Church underestimated the strong force of the Protestant Reformation. Its spread gradually put great pressure on the Church and eventually pushed the church power to seek a new religious order and to appeal for a counter reformation. The revival of Roman Catholicism was called the Catholic Reformation, and also, termed Counter Reformation.

The Society of Jesus The Society of Jesus, also known as the Jesuits, is a religious order founded by Saint Ignatius Loyola (1491—1556) in 1534. He wrote *The Spiritual Exercises*[③], a training work for spiritual development, and he made it a useful tool by which people would be taught to follow the glory of God through the Catholic Church. The Society was organised in the form of a military command with strict rules and disciplines to control the members. All members swore that they would show their allegiance and obedience to the papacy.

The Jesuits earnestly asked the papacy to raise an international movement for the

---

① Anglican：英国国教的；英国圣公会或与其起源和教派有关的教派。

② *The Thirty-Nine Articles of Religion*：《三十九条信纲》，英格兰圣公会的教义文献。在伊丽莎白一世统治时期公布。

③ *The Spiritual Exercises*：《神操》，耶稣会创始人圣依纳爵·罗耀拉的著作。该书表现了他的灵修思想，即帮助他人，不重蹈那些致命的覆辙，从而大觉大悟，最终获得心灵的解放。

revival of Christian universalism[①] and they carefully avoided local corruption. With sharp eyes and cool minds, they realised some of the imperfections of the Reformation, such as fragmentation and predestination. Countermeasures were taken to raise people's hope for life.

The Jesuit Constitutions written by Ignatius contributed to a centralised organisation, took emphasis of absolute self-abnegation[②] and advocated the obedience to Pope and superiors. Expanding in strength, they espoused three doctrines which enabled their organisation to gain popularity. (1) They founded schools in many countries in Europe. (2) The teachers recruited were required to have a good knowledge of classical studies and theology in order to educate their students in the struggle against the progress of Protestantism. (3) They made contributions to the revival of Catholicism in Germany and Eastern Europe.

A Revived Papacy Confronted with the Protestant Reformation and the corruptions of popes and cardinals, papal reform began in the 1540s under the influence of the hardliners. They viewed any compromise with Protestant theologies as heresy. When Cardinal Caraffa, an unwavering hardliner, came into power, he successfully encouraged Pope Paul Ⅲ(1534—1549) to establish a Roman Inquisition[③] in 1542.

The Roman Inquisition was a system of tribunals held in the Roman Catholic Church in the second half of the 16th century, directed to suppress heresy. Those who were thought to commit a large number of crimes, such as sorcery[④], blasphemy[⑤] and witchcraft were prosecuted by the Inquisition. Besides, the Roman Inquisition censored printed literature.

The power of the Inquisition was increased when Caraffa was appointed Pope Paul Ⅳ (1555—1559). In his reign, censorship[⑥] was increased and "dangerous books" were burned to prevent the spread of Protestant theologies. Known as the "first true pope of the Catholic Counter-reformation", Caraffa created an *Index of Forbidden Books*[⑦]. Books that were listed in the index were forbidden to the Catholics. All the works that were considered heretic, or were suspected of heresy, were included in this Roman catalogue.

The power of the tribunals affected most of the Italian peninsula but also extended into other parts of Europe, such as Avignon. In the mid-18th century, the Italian states

---

① universalism:(神学)宇宙神教;普救说。

② self-abnegation:克己,自我牺牲。

③ Roman Inquisition:罗马宗教裁判所。旨在镇压一切反教会、反封建,以及有异端思想或同情异端的人。

④ sorcery:巫术,魔法。通过鬼神的帮助而使用超自然的力量。

⑤ blasphemy:亵渎。亵污或玷污上帝或神明的行为、言辞或文字。

⑥ censorship:审查;审查制度。此处指教会对面向公众的文学、艺术等领域的检查筛选。

⑦ *Index of Forbidden Books*:《禁书索引》,又名《罗马索引》,由罗马教皇保罗四世颁布,由罗马宗教裁判所推动列出了许多天主教徒禁止阅读的书籍。

decisively suppressed the local tribunals and successfully prevented the prosecution of heresy of the Catholic Church. Consequently, the Inquisition faded away.

The Council of Trent The Council of Trent① was promoted by Pope Paul Ⅲ in 1545 in the city of Trent. The council established the foundations of the Counter Reformation. The 19th Ecumenical Council of the Roman Catholic Church was the general term of religious councils held from December 13, 1545 to December 4, 1563.

The Council's purpose was to oppose the reformation and eliminate the severe abuses. It declared that the Scripture in Latin by the Catholic Church was the only legal work and could only be interpreted by the Church. People should abide by tradition as well as by Scripture in religious matters. Not only faith but also good works were responsible for salvation. The Council stressed the importance of education in religion and advocated the construction of mission schools. In the Council, the Moderates, who advocated compromise, were defeated by the Conservatives, who insisted on the Catholic doctrines that completely opposed Protestant thinking. Thus, the traditional Catholic teachings were reaffirmed in the council. The seven sacraments (baptism, Eucharist, Reconciliation, Confirmation, Marriage, Holy Orders and Anointing of the Sick), the Catholic doctrine of transubstantiation, and clerical celibacy were all upheld. The efficacy of indulgences and the belief in purgatory were both strengthened. The Council of Trent affirmed the supremacy of the popes and the unification of the church. It was the most impressive embodiment of the ideals of the Counter-Reformation.

Chapter Review

This chapter mainly discussed the profound shocks experienced by the European states at the age of the Reformation. The abuse of power by the Church roused great indignation among people. The time was ripe for a challenge to the power of the church. Martin's Ninety-Five Theses marked the beginning of this great religious movement. Justification by faith was the core of Lutheranism. It was plain that the Catholic Church had underestimated the strength of Luther's reformation. With the support of political power, Lutheranism rapidly spread in European countries in the 16th century. It soon became the source of some more radical religious movements. Calvinism was carried out in Geneva vigorously and it occupied a prominent position in many states in Europe. In response to the vehement reformation, the church set off the Counter Reformation reaffirming the veneration of saints and the authority of the Pope.

---

① Council of Trent：天特会议，罗马教廷于北意大利的天特城召开的大公会议，旨在抵抗马丁·路德的宗教改革所带来的冲击。

Exercise

Ⅰ. *According to the information provided in this chapter, choose the correct alternative among A, B, C, and D that can complete each of the following statements.*

1. *The Praise of Folly* was a satire written by Desiderius Erasmus, in which he presented his criticism of ________.
   A. Lutheranism
   B. the abuses of the church and the corruption of the society
   C. Calvinism
   D. the Protestant Reformation
2. In the following works, ________ is NOT written by Martin Luther.
   A. *Address to the Nobility of the German Nation*
   B. *Ninety-Five Theses*
   C. *The Religious Pilgrimage*
   D. *The Babylonian Captivity of the Church*
3. In the following statements, ________ was NOT Calvin's test that might indicate possible salvation.
   A. an open profession of faith
   B. decent and godly life
   C. participation in the sacraments of baptism and communion
   D. the adult baptism
4. ________ was appointed "People's Priest" in 1519, the most powerful ecclesiastical position in the city of Zurich.
   A. Martin Luther　　B. Ulrich Zwingli
   C. John Calvin　　D. Guillaume Farel
5. ________ was the first protestant city beyond the boundary of Germany. From there the reformation swept across the map of Switzerland.
   A. Zurich　　B. Geneva　　C. Bern　　D. Basel

Ⅱ. *Fill in the blanks with what you have learned in this chapter.*

1. The Catholic Church made people believe that the buying of ________ could ensure their salvation.
2. The work ________ issued in 1536 immediately secured Calvin's reputation as one of the new leaders of Protestantism.
3. Most prominent among the means Calvin used to reform the city was ________.
4. The word ________ is a label often assigned to "Radical Reformers", which is a diverse group that remained outside the mainstream of the Reformation.
5. In England, the reformation was initiated by ________. The King was declared

as "the only Supreme Head in Earth of the Church of England" by *The Act of* ________.

Ⅲ. *According to what you have learned, answer the following questions briefly in your own words.*

1. How could people merit salvation according to Martin Luther?
2. How did John Calvin call one of his doctrines "predestination"? What did he mean by "predestination"?
3. Could you make a list of Calvin's reforms in Geneva that made him unwelcome by the Genevans?
4. On what doctrinal issues did Zwingli and Luther remain apart? Please comment on it.
5. Could you depict the development of the England Reformation carried out by the King?

Ⅳ. *With critical analysis, answer the following essay questions in your own words.*

1. Who was the most influential of all the Christian humanists? What did he contribute to the Reformation?
2. What is the response of the Catholic Church under the pressure of the widely-spread reformation?

Ⅴ. *Work in small groups and make comparisons based on the following topic.*

A religious reformation swept through so many European states in the 16th century. Among the reforms in different states, only the one in England was carried out by the royal power. In the same period of history, Wanli Reformation, also called Zhang Juzheng Reformation, was carried out during the Ming Dynasty in China. Could you make a comparison between them, especially in terms of their style, influence and ending?

Voices on Key Points

The Launch of Reformation

Reformation, like education, is a journey, not a destination.

——Mary Harris Jones

The Reformation did not directly touch the question of the true character of God's church.

——John Nelson Darby

And finally, it was Deuteronomy that brought about the historical result of Josiah's reformation.

——Julius Wellhausen

German Protestant Reformation

All who call on God in true faith, earnestly from the heart, will certainly be heard, and will receive what they have asked and desired.

——Martin Luther

Everything that is done in the world is done by hope.

——Martin Luther

Suggested Reading

1. (英)阿利斯特·麦格拉思著,蔡锦图、陈佐人译:《宗教改革运动思潮》,中国社会科学出版社 2009 年版。
2. (法)克利斯坦著,花秀林译:《宗教改革》,格致出版社 2003 年版。
3. 雷士理编著:《基督教图文百科》,陕西师范大学出版社 2008 年版。
4. (美)乔治著,王丽译:《改教家的神学思想》,中国社会科学出版社 2009 年版。
5. (美)威尔·杜兰著,台北幼狮文化公司译:《马丁·路德时代——名人与时代》,东方出版社 2007 年版。

Chapter Seven Early Modern Times[①] (c. 1419—1800)

Indeed, world history in the strict global sense did not begin until the voyages of Columbus and da Gama and Magellan.

Learning objectives

After reading this chapter, you will be able to:

1. *Be familiar with the motives and impacts of European Expansion ever since the 15th century;*
2. *Be clear about the connotation of Absolutism;*
3. *Understand the causes of the Scientific Revolution in the 17th century and the Enlightenment in the 18th century;*
4. *Be acquainted with the ideas of such philosophers as Montesquieu, Voltaire, and Diderot.*

---

① L. S. Stavrianos, *The World Since 1500: A Global History*, New Jersey: Prentice Hall, 1966, p. 3.

文艺复兴和宗教改革改变了欧洲人对生活的看法，促进了西欧各国民族文化和教育事业的发展，有利于资本主义的发展，同时也预示着海外扩张和君主专制时代的来临。

以达伽马、哥伦布和麦哲伦为代表的航海家们的航海活动，使得西方与东方发生了真正意义上的碰撞与接触，极大地促进了欧洲资本主义的发展和殖民帝国的形成，同时，也给被征服国家和地区带来了灾难。15 至 18 世纪的欧洲政治形势风云变幻，西欧许多国家专制主义盛行，尼德兰建立了资产阶级共和国，英国则建立了君主立宪制国家。科学革命和启蒙运动破除蒙昧，倡导理性，力图用理性之光驱散黑暗，将人们引向光明。启蒙运动本质上是一场宣扬资产阶级政治思想体系的运动。受启蒙运动思想影响的所谓“开明君主”，尽管试图以启蒙运动的理念进行改革，然而，他们中大部分人最关注的依然还是自身的统治问题，因而收效甚微。

Section One Expansion of European Powers (c. 1419—1800)

Exploring the New World The ruthless character of western civilisation was best shown in its endless expansion into the rest of the world. By the 16th century, the Atlantic seaboard had become an important commercial centre where Portugal and Spain and later the Dutch Republic, England and France were to play a dominant role. The age of expansion was a key factor in the shift of Europe from the agrarian economy to a commercial and industrial capitalism. Expansion also resulted in Europeans' new and lasting contacts with the rest of the world that initiated a new phase of world history in the 16th century.

Europeans have long been attracted to lands outside of Europe. In *The Travels of John Mandeville*① in the 14th century, the author depicted lands filled with precious stones and gold. What is worth special mentioning was the experience of Marco Polo, who travelled to China in the 13th century. An account of his experiences, the Travels, has long been regarded as the most informative of all the descriptions of Asia by Medieval European travellers. In the 14th century, however, with the conquest of Ottoman Turks② and then the collapse of the Mongol Empire, a number of people tried to reach Asia by sea to gain the spices and other precious items. Underlying the European expansion, therefore, was an apparent economic motive. Merchants, adventurers and government officials were expecting possibilities of finding precious metals and new areas of trade.

One Spanish conquistador explained that he and his contemporaries went to the new world to "serve God and his majesty, to give light to those who were in darkness, and

① *The Travels of John Mandeville*：《曼德维尔游记》，是欧洲中世纪一部极富想象力的散文体虚构游记。

② Ottoman Turk：奥斯曼土耳其人。

to grow rich, as all men desire to do"[1]. This statement actually indicates another major reason for the overseas voyages—religious desire. Herman Cortes, the conqueror of Mexico, asked his Spanish rulers if it was not their duty to ensure that the native Mexicans "are introduced into and instructed in their holy Catholic faith"[2]. As a matter of fact, religious and secular affairs are closely interwoven in the 16th century. It is certain that grandeur and glory, as well as plain intellectual curiosity and the spirit of adventure, also played a certain role in the European expansion.

If economic profit, religious zeal and glory are the motives, what made the long voyages possible? First of all, the expansion of Europe was connected to the growth of centralised monarchies during the Renaissance. By the second half of the 15th century, European monarchies had strengthened both their authority and their resources which enabled them to turn their energies beyond their borders. At the same time, by the end of the 15th century, European states had accomplished a certain level of wealth and technology that enabled them to go on a series of voyages outside Europe.

At the end of the 15th century, Europeans got one of the most important world maps, the map of Ptolemy, who was an astronomer of the 2nd century A. D. By the 15th century, a Latin version of his work, Geography, had come out. In addition to showing the oceans as much smaller than the landmasses, Ptolemy had also dramatically underestimated the circumference of the earth, which led Columbus and other voyagers to believe that they could sail west from Europe to Asia.

The Portuguese and Spanish Empires Portugal played a leading role in European expansion when it began to explore the coast of Africa under the sponsorship of Prince Henry the Navigator (1394—1460). He was trying to seek a Christian kingdom as an ally against the Muslims, acquire trade opportunities for Portugal, and extend Christianity.

In 1419, Portuguese fleets began exploring southward along the western coast of Africa. After the year 1460, Portuguese ships gradually crept down the African coast until Bartholomeu Dias finally rounded the Cape of Good Hope at the southern tip of Africa in 1488. Ten years later, another fleet led by Vasco da Gama circled the cape and stopped at several ports under the control of Muslim merchants along the coast of East Africa. After further probing, his fleet returned to Europe with the ships filled with ginger and cinnamon which brought the investors a profit of several thousand percent. Da Gama's successful voyage marked the beginning of an all-water trade route to India. Gradually, under the direction of viceroys[3], Portugal established an overseas empire.

---

① Jackson J. Spielvogel, *Western Civilisation: A Brief History*, Beijing: Peking University Press, 2006, p. 251.

② Jackson J. Spielvogel, *Western Civilisation: A Brief History*, Beijing: Peking University Press, 2006, p. 251.

③ viceroy:(国王任命统治殖民地、自治领等的)总督。

Basically, the secret of Portugal's success was brought about by its powerful arms and extraordinary nautical technology. After the voyage of Vasco da Gama to the Coast of India, the Portuguese established themselves finally on the Malabar Coast with colonies in Goa Calcutta and successfully challenged the Arabs and Venetians for control of the European spice trade.

While the Portuguese were sailing eastward to seek access to the spice trade of the Indies, the Spanish were endeavouring to reach the same destination by sailing westward across the Atlantic. Spain's great resources helped it to build a far greater overseas empire quite different from that of Portugal.

Deeply convinced that the earth was smaller than people had thought, Christopher Columbus, a great Italian in the history of Spanish exploration, believed that he was able to reach Asia by sailing directly west. Failing to get sponsorship from the Portuguese, he persuaded Queen Isabella of Spain to support his expedition. Columbus's fleet reached the Bahamas in October 1492 and then went on to explore the coastline of Cuba and later to the northern shores of Hispaniola. Although Columbus held on to the belief until his death that he had reached Asia, other explorers soon realised that he had discovered a new land.

Columbus's voyage of 1492 marked the beginning of more than three centuries of Spanish conquest, exploitation and administration of a vast American empire. Their sophisticated weapons, organisational skills, and exceptional determination made them seemingly invincible. Moreover, they also benefited from rivalries among the native peoples. Based on their superior weapons that were strange to the natives, and also benefiting from the small pox that cost the lives a large population of the natives, the Spaniards conquered the Aztec Empire and the Inca, where colonial control was established. Spanish policy toward the native peoples of the New World was a combination of confusion, misguided paternalism①, and cruel exploitation. Spanish colonists largely ignored the Spanish government and brutally used the Indians to pursue their own economic profits. Indians were forced to work on plantations and in the lucrative gold and silver mines. Forced work, starvation, and diseases took a dreadful death toll on Indians—perhaps 30 to 40 percent of them died. Hispaniola was badly devastated: of an initial population of 100,000 when Columbus arrived in 1493, only 300 natives survived by 1570.

After conquering the Aztecs in Mexico and the Incas in Peru brutally, the Spanish were able to make its civilisation dominate the natives. The Spanish and the Indians made some accommodations to each other, but in the end European values, religions, economic goals, and languages dominated. No group that retained indigenous religion,

---

① paternalism：家长式统治，家长式作风。

language, or values could become part of the new dominant culture of the political power elite. In that sense, the Spanish conquest of the early 16th century marked the beginning of the process whereby South America was transformed into Latin America.

Rise of Dutch, England and France Both Portugal and Spain had become great colonial powers by taking advantage of the age of exploration initiated in the late 15th century. In the 17th century, however, their European neighbours to the north—first the Dutch and then the French and British—grew to such an extent that they were to replace the Portuguese and Spanish to establish their own colonial empires.

The primary threat to the Portuguese in Southeast Asia came with the arrival of the Dutch and the English, who were better financed. In the early 18th century, the Dutch seized a Portuguese fort in the Moluccas and then gradually pushed the Portuguese out of the spice trade. In the following fifty years, the Dutch managed to occupy most of the Portuguese coastal forts along the trade routes throughout the Indian Ocean. Actually, the aggressive Dutch drove the English traders out of the spice trade as well.

In India, the Indian subcontinent was partitioned into several Hindu and Muslim kingdoms when a Portuguese fleet reached the port of Calicut in the spring of 1498. It was a foreign dynasty named the Mughals achieved a new age of unity. The founder of the dynasty was Babur, whose grandson, Akbar, brought Mughal rule to most of India, creating the greatest Indian empire since the Maryann dynasty nearly two thousand years ago. As is known, the Portuguese were the first Europeans to arrive in India. They controlled regional trade in the Indian Ocean then. But at the end of the 16th century, two other rivals, the British and the Dutch, came to compete with Portugal, and with each other, for domination in the region.

During the first half of the 17th century, the British presence in India steadily increased. British success in India, however, attracted rivals, including the Dutch and the French. The Dutch were mainly engaged in the spice trade in the middle of the 17th century, and the French set up forts on the east coast. For a short period, the French won the competition with the British, and even seized the British fort at Madras. Luckily, the British were saved by Sir Robert Clive, a military genius and an ambitious British empire-builder. He became the chief representative of the East India Company in India. Finally, the French were confined to the fort at Pondicherry and a few small territories on the south-eastern coast. Meanwhile, Clive started to tighten the British hold on Bengal. After the battle of Plassey in 1757, the British East India Company received the authority to collect taxes from lands in the area surrounding Calcutta. During the Seven Years' War (1756—1763), the British successfully forced the French to withdraw completely from India.

Change in World Economy Ever since the High Middle Ages, Europeans had conducted a commercial revolution that provided townspeople with new opportunities in a basically agrarian economy. The geographic discoveries and economic expansion in the 15th century led to even greater burst of commercial activity and the inception of a world market.

Inflation had long been a serious economic problem in the 16th and early 17th centuries. This alleged price revolution swept through the entirety of Europe, although different regions were affected at different times. The rapid increase in the price of foodstuffs as well as other products and the failure of the wages to keep up with price increases made wage earners, especially agricultural labourers and salaried workers in urban areas, see their living standards drop. At the same time, however, landed aristocrats, who could raise rents, managed to become rich. Commercial and industrial entrepreneurs also benefited from the price revolution because of rise in price, expansion in markets and relatively cheaper labour costs. Some historians regard this profit growth as a valuable stimulus to investment and the growth of capitalism, laying the foundation for the economic expansion and prosperity of the 16th century. Governments were also affected by inflation. Borrowing heavily from bankers, they had to impose new tax burdens upon their subjects, often arousing new grievances.

The European trade of the 16th century witnessed the greatest flourishing around three major areas: the Mediterranean in the south, the Low Countries and the Baltic region in the north and central Europe, whose inland trade depended on the Rhine and Danube rivers. However, as overseas trade expanded, the Atlantic seaboard became even more important in that it brought together the Mediterranean, Baltic, and central Europe in a market that was easily influenced by the price changes.

The commercial expansion of the 16th and 17th centuries was facilitated by the new forms of commercial organisations, especially the joint-stock trading company in which individuals bought shares and received dividends according to their investment while a board of directors made the important business decisions. During its first ten years, for instance, investors received 30% on their money from the Dutch East India Company, which opened the Spice Islands and Southeast Asia to Dutch activity. The joint-stock company made it easier to raise large amounts of capital for world trading ventures.

Traditional family banking firms, which were no longer able to supply the numerous services needed for the commercial capitalism of the 17th century, were gradually replaced by new institutions. The city of Amsterdam created the Bank of Amsterdam in 1609 as both a deposit and a transfer institution and the Amsterdam Bourse, or Exchange, where the trading of stocks replaced the exchange of commodities. By the first half of the 17th century, the Amsterdam Exchange had become the hub of Europe's business world, just as Amsterdam had replaced Antwerp as the greatest commercial and banking centre of Europe.

In spite of the fact that commercial capitalism developed rapidly, most of the

European economies were still to a great extent agrarian, which experienced few changes since the 13th century. At least 80% of Europeans still worked on the land. Almost all of the peasants of Western Europe were free of serfdom[①], although many still owed a variety of feudal dues to the landed nobility. Despite the expanding market and rising prices, European peasants experienced little or no improvement in their lot as they were subject to increased rents and fees and higher taxes imposed by the state.

According to mercantilists, state intervention in some aspects of the economy was desirable for the sake of the national good. Government efforts to ensure the superiority of export goods, to construct roads and canals, and to grant subsidies to create trade companies were all predicated on government involvement in economic affairs.

With the establishment of colonies and trading posts in South and North America and the East, Europeans began an adventure in international trade in the 17th century. Although some historians construe this period as a nascent world economy, it should not be overlooked that local, regional, and intra-European trade still predominated. What made the trade across the ocean virtually rewarding, however, was the value of the goods rather than the volume. Dutch, French and English merchants were bringing back products that were still consumed largely by the wealthy but were beginning to make their way into the lives of artisans and merchants. Pepper and spices from the Indies, West Indian and Brazilian sugar, and Asian coffee and tea were becoming more readily available to European households. Trade within Europe throughout the 18th century also boomed. From 1716 to 1789, total French exports increased by three fold; intra-European trade, which constituted 75% of these exports in 1716, accounted for only 50% of the total in 1789. This increase in overseas trade has led some of the historians to proclaim the advent of a global economy in its real sense in the 18th century. Trade patterns now interlocked Europe, Africa, the East and the Americas.

The Impact of European Expansion From 1500 to 1800, the Atlantic nations of Europe expanded to other parts of the world. The first had been Spain and Portugal, the two great powers of the 16th century, and later the Dutch, who built their colonial empire in the 17th century as Portugal and Spain declined. The Dutch, however, soon met rivalries from the British and the French, who outstripped the others in the 18th century. By the end of the 18th century, it seemed that the British would grow into the great European imperial power. European expansion made a great impact on both the conquerors and the conquered.

The native peoples of the New World, with their own qualities and traits, were brutally conquered and their civilisations inevitably destroyed. In addition to a drastic decrease in population due to European diseases, their established social and political

① serfdom：农奴制，封建社会中封建领主在其领地上建立起来的剥削、奴役农奴的经济制度。

structures were replaced by European institutions, religions, languages, and cultures. In Africa, European involvement in slave trade had devastating effects, especially in coastal areas. Portuguese trading posts in the East had little impact on native Asian civilisations, although Dutch control of the Indonesian archipelago was more invasive. China and Japan remained intact during this age while India was subject to ever-growing British encroachment.

European expansion to the Central and South America brought about great changes in the population structure of the natives. By 1501, Spanish rulers had authorised marriage between Europeans and Native American Indians. Another group of people brought to Spanish and Portugal America were the Africans who were forced to work the plantations. This also resulted in Latin America's multiracial character. The offspring of Africans and whites, called Mulattoes, and descendants of whites, Africans and native Indians, called mestizos①, created a unique society in Latin America.

The ecological condition of the conquered areas was also affected by the European expansion. Europeans brought horses and cattle to the Americas. Horses fundamentally changed the life of the native Indians. Europeans also brought new crops like wheat and cane sugar, which were to be cultivated by native or imported African slaves. The Europeans also contributed to the exchange of world agriculture by spreading New World plants to other parts of the world. In the 16th century, for instance, the Europeans introduced sweet potatoes and maize to Africa.

The course of European expansion was undoubtedly a process of religious conquest. It was noted in the preceding section that one of the most important motives of the European Expansion was religious zeal. Actually, since the beginning of their conquest of the New World, Spanish and Portuguese rulers were intending to Christianise the native peoples. Under the guidance of this policy, the Catholic Church played an important role in the New World. Catholic missionaries—especially the Dominicans, Franciscans, and Jesuits—spread to different parts of the Spanish Empire.

Christianity was not the only thing the missionaries brought to the New World, even though they were driven by a strong religious zeal. In addition to Christianisation, the Catholic Church also constructed hospitals, orphanages, and schools. Monastic schools② instructed Indian students in the elementary skills of reading, writing, and arithmetic. The Catholic Church also included nunneries, places of prayer and quiet contemplation, but religious women, many of whom had aristocratic background, often lived comfortably and run schools and hospitals outside their establishments.

Overseas expansion of European nations also changed the life of Europeans

① mestizo：指在中南美洲既有印第安血统又有欧洲血统的混血儿。

② monastic school：修道院学校。

themselves. For some Europeans, expansion abroad brought their hopes for land, riches, and social advancement. One Spaniard commented in 1572 that many "poor young men" left Spain for Mexico, where they hoped to get landed estates by which they could be called "gentlemen". Many ordinary European women found new opportunities for marriage in the New World because of the lack of white women. Indeed, as one commentator once bluntly put it, even "a whore, if handsome, can make a wife for some rich planter"①.

European expansion satisfied their strong desire for gold and silver as well as other precious metals. One Aztec commented that the Spanish conquerors "longed and lusted for gold. Their bodies swelled with greed, and their hunger was ravenous; they hungered like pigs for that gold."② Besides gold and silver, Europeans were taking new agricultural products such as potatoes, chocolate, corn, tomatoes, and tobacco back to Europe while bringing to the New World horses, cattle and wheat. With the arrival of these products, new foods and new drinks appeared in Europe. Chocolate, which had been brought to Spain from Aztec Mexico, became popular by 1700. The first coffee and tea houses opened in London in the 1650s and spread rapidly to other parts of Europe.

European Expansion led to fierce competition and bitter conflicts which were further intensified later. The Anglo-Dutch trade wars and the British-French rivalry over India and North America became part of a new pattern of worldwide warfare in the 18th century. Bitter competitions also resulted in state-supported piracy in which governments authorised private captains to attack shipping from other countries and keep part of the proceeds for themselves.

Expansion also dramatically altered the Europeans' view of the world. At the beginning of the travels in the 15th century, Europeans depended on maps that were sometimes fanciful and inaccurate. Their voyages and expansions helped them to create more accurate maps showing a realistic portrayal of the world. Map projection③, a new technique to represent the round surface of a sphere on a flat piece of paper, was devised to further help the voyagers.

In the course of European expansion, the New World natives experienced unexpected psychological buffeting, which, to a certain extent, helped determine the direction in which world history was to develop. The relatively easy European success in conquering and dominating native peoples reinforced Christian Europe's belief in the inherent superiority of European civilisation and religion, which was incessantly

① Jackson J. Spielvogel, *Western Civilisation: A Brief History*, Beijing: Peking University Press 2006, p. 268.

② Jackson J. Spielvogel, *Western Civilisation: A Brief History*, Beijing: Peking University Press 2006, p. 268.

③ map projection:地图投影,把地球表面的任意点,利用特定的数学法则转换到地图平面上的理论和方法。

bolstered in the following stages of history and pervaded Western civilisation's relationship with the rest of the world.

Section Two Social Disturbance (Early 17th—Early 18th Century) and the Age of Absolutism (c. 1550—1800)

Social Crises, War, and Rebellions The economic prosperity in the wake of overseas expansion did not last long. In the 1630s and 1640s, with the decline in the amount of silver imported from South and North America, economic recession intensified, especially in the Mediterranean area. Population trends of the 16th and 17th centuries also showed Europe's worsening conditions. European population expanded in the 16th century thanks to the warmer climate and increased food supplies. However, statistics showed that population leveled off by 1620 and even declined by 1650, especially in central and southern parts of Europe. War, famine and plague continued to affect population levels, and another "little ice age"[①] midway through the 16th century affected harvests and led to famines.

Europe after the early 1600s was a period of slaughter and devastations. For a while it seemed that nothing could bring the fighting to an end and a feeling of irresolvable crisis descended on international affairs. Religious divergences, especially the struggle between militant Catholicism and militant Calvinism, played an important role in triggering the Thirty Years' War, also known as the "last of the religious wars". As the war progressed, however, it became more and more evident that secular, dynastic-nationalist considerations were far more important. The Thirty Years' War broke out in 1618 in the Germanic lands of the Holy Roman Empire as a struggle between Catholic forces, led by the Hapsburg Holy Roman Emperors, and Protestant—primarily Calvinist—nobles in Bohemia who rebelled against Hapsburg authority. Initially a struggle over religious issues, it soon developed into a wider conflict determined by political motivations as both minor and major European powers—Denmark, Sweden, France, and Spain—made the war a European-wide struggle. The struggle between The Bourbon dynasty of France and the Hapsburg dynasties of Spain and the Holy Roman Empire for the leadership of Europe was fundamental to the war. Wide in range as the war was, most of the battles were fought on German soil, bringing about devastating results for the German people. Whereas some areas of Germany remained nearly intact, others were reduced to ruins.

---

① 详见第四章第四节。

The war was ended by *The Peace of Westphalia*[①] signed in 1648. Some powers gained new territories, and one of them, France, became the dominant nation in Europe. The more than three hundred states that constituted the Holy Roman Empire were virtually recognised as independent states because each received the power to conduct its own foreign policy. This meant the end of the Holy Roman Empire and ensured German disunity for another two hundred years until 1871. The Peace of Westphalia also made it clear that religion and politics are not inseparable. Political consideration became the leading factor in public affairs and religion moved closer to becoming primarily a matter of personal conviction and individual activity.

Before, during, and after the Thirty Years' War, a succession of rebellions and civil wars originating from the discontent of both nobles and commoners shook the stability of many European authorities. To strengthen their power, monarchs strived to extend their authority at the expense of traditional powerful elements that resisted the ruler's efforts. At the same time, increased taxes by the government to finance their wars placed even greater burden on the people, arousing their indignation.

Between 1590 and 1640, peasant and lower-class revolts occurred in central and southern France, Austria, and Hungary. Portugal and Catalonia rebelled against Spanish rule in 1640. Urban uprisings also occurred in Russia in 1641, 1645, and 1648. French nobles rebelled from 1648 to 1652 hampering the ever-growing royal power. The northern states of Sweden, Denmark, and Holland also underwent upheavals involving clergy, nobles, and mercantile groups. By far the best known and most far-reaching struggle, however, was the civil war and rebellion in England, commonly known as the English Revolution.

Absolutism in Western Europe The period from the 16th to the 18th century is known as the Age of Absolutism. Absolutism[②], also known as absolute monarchy, meant that the sovereign power or ultimate authority in the state rested in the hands of a king who claimed to rule by divine right[③]—that kings received their power from God and were responsible only to God. But what did sovereignty mean? According to Jean Bodin, a late 16th-century political theorist, sovereign power consisted of the authority to make laws, tax, mete out justice, control the state's administrative system, and

---

① *The Peace of Westphalia*：《威斯特伐利亚和约》，象征三十年战争结束而签订的一系列和约，签约双方分别是统治西班牙、神圣罗马帝国、奥地利帝国的哈布斯堡王室和法国、瑞典以及神圣罗马帝国内勃兰登堡、萨克森、巴伐利亚等诸侯邦国。

② Absolutism：专制主义，是与民主政体相对立的概念，指一个人或少数几个人独裁的政权组织形式，体现在帝位终身制和皇位世袭制上，其主要特征是皇帝个人的专断独裁，集国家最高权力于一身，从决策到行使军政财政大权都具有独断性和随意性。

③ rule by divine right：君权神授，一种政府组织形式。在这种形式下，国家主权和最高权力掌握在君主手里，而君主声称用神圣权力进行统治，因而只向上帝负责。

determine foreign policy. These powers made a ruler sovereign.

The growth of absolutism in France was the product of a gradual evolution. Some of its antecedents went back to the reigns of Philip Augustus, Louis Ⅸ, and Philip Ⅳ in the 13th and 14th centuries. These kings solidified royal power by hiring mercenary soldiers, substituting national taxation for feudal dues, arrogating themselves the power to administer justice and restricting the authority of the Pope to regulate ecclesiastical affairs in the kingdom. After the Hundred Years' War, the monarch of France was able to introduce new forms of taxation, to maintain a huge standing army, and to abolish the sovereignty of the feudal nobles.

Absolute monarchy in France attained its zenith during the reigns of the last three Bourbon kings before the Revolution. The first of the monarchs of this series was Louis ⅩⅣ (1643—1715) who epitomised the ideal of absolutism more completely than any other sovereign of his age. At the age of twenty-three, he expressed his determination to be real king and sole ruler of France:

> Up to this moment I have been pleased to entrust the government of my affairs to the Late Cardian. It is now time that I govern them myself. You [secretaries and ministers of state] will assist me with your counsels when I ask for them. I request and order you to seal no orders except by my command... I order you not to sign anything, not even a passport... without my command; to render account to me personally each day and to favour no one. ①

Louis ⅩⅣ was serious when he said so. He established a conscientious routine from which he seldom deviated. Louis and his court came to set an example for monarchies and aristocracies for the rest of the world. In spite of the fact that Louis seemingly believed in the theory of absolutism, the reality was that at the beginning of his reign, France still had a bewildering system of overlapping authorities in the 17th century. Provinces owned their regional courts, local Estates, and sets of laws. Members of the high nobility with their huge estates, and clients among the lesser nobility still exerted much authority. Both towns and provinces possessed privileges and powers seemingly since ancient times that they would not easily give up.

One of the keys to Louis's power was that he was able to restructure the central policy-making machinery of government. The royal court at Versailles served three major purposes: the personal household of the king, the location of central governmental machinery, the place where powerful subjects came to find favours and offices for themselves and their clients, and the main arena where rival aristocratic factions jostled for power. The greatest threat to Louis's personal rule came from the very high nobles and the royal princes who were virtually performing the policy-making

① Jackson J. Spielvogel, *Western Civilisation: A Brief History*, Beijing: Peking University Press, 2006, p. 276.

duty of the royal ministers. By removing them from the royal council, the chief administrative body of the king and overseer of the central machinery of government, and keeping them occupied with court life, Louis managed to eliminate the threat. Instead, Louis ran his country by depending on nobles from relatively new aristocratic families. His ministers were expected to be subservient; Louis said, "I had no intention of sharing my authority with them."

The desire of Louis to maintain religious harmony within the country, which had long been considered an area of monarchical power, led Louis to pursue an anti-Protestant policy, in hope of converting the Huguenots to Catholicism. In October 1685, Louis issued the *Edict of Fontainebleau*①. Apart from revoking the *Edict of Nantes*②, the new edict provided for the destruction of Huguenot churches and the closing of their schools.

The cost of building palaces, maintaining his court, and waging wars made finances a crucial issue for Louis XIV. Fortunately, he had the services of Jean-Baptiste Colbert (1619—1683) as controller-general of finances. Preoccupied with mercantilism, Colbert tried every possible means to decrease imports and increase exports. He started new luxury industries and granted special privileges, including tax exemptions③, loans and subsidies, to individuals who established new industries. By building roads and canals, he improved communications and the transportation of goods internally. At the same time, he raised tariffs on foreign manufactured goods to restrict imports.

With the increase in the power of the central government and his strong desire for military glory, Louis developed a professional army of 100,000 men in peacetime and 400,000 in time of war. To achieve the prestige and military glory befitting the Sun King④ and to ensure the control of his Bourbon dynasty over European affairs, Louis waged four wars between 1667 and 1713. His ambitions, viewed by other European states as threats to European balance of power, led other European states to form coalitions to seek security. Although he expanded France's north-eastern frontier by adding some territory and established a member of his own Bourbon dynasty in Spain, France was in poor condition and surrounded by enemies.

The growth of absolutism in Spain was swifter than was true of its development in France. The decay of the country, however, had been too apparent by the beginning of

---

① *Edict of Fontainebleau*:《枫丹白露敕令》,法国国王路易十四在1658年10月为统一法国人的宗教信仰而颁布的最为凶狠的敕令,使法国境内的大量新教徒被迫迁出法国。

② *Edict of Nantes*:《南特敕令》,法国国王亨利四世在1598年4月13日签署颁布的一条敕令。这条敕令承认了法国国内胡格诺教徒的信仰自由,并在法律上享有和公民同等的权利。这条敕令也是世界上第一份有关宗教宽容的敕令。

③ tax exemption:税务豁免,免税。

④ Sun King:"太阳王",指法国国王路易十四。

the 17th century. The country was void of treasury; Philip Ⅱ went broke in 1596 due to excessive cost on war, and so did his successor in 1607 by spending a fortune on his court. The armed forces were outdated, the government was incompetent and the commercial class was weak in the midst of a suppressed peasantry, a luxury-loving class of nobles, and an oversupply of priests and monks. During the reign of Philip Ⅲ (1598—1621), many of Spain's weaknesses became all too apparent. Being a monarch, Philip Ⅲ only indulged in court luxury or miracle-working relics. He appointed the greedy duke of Lerma as his first minister to run the country. Preoccupied with the greedy lust for power and wealth, Lerma filled important offices of the country with his relatives. At first, the reign of Philip Ⅳ (1621—1665) seemed to offer hope for a revival of Spain's greatness, especially thanks to the competence of his chief minister, Caspar de Guzman, the count of Olivares. This clever and dedicated statesman worked to rejuvenate the country. A series of domestic reform decrees, aimed at curtailing the power of the church and the landed aristocracy, were soon followed by a political reform programme whose purpose was to further centralise the government of all Spain and its possessions in the royal monarch. All of these efforts, however, ended in vain because both the population and the power of the Spanish aristocrats made them too strong to curtail.

At the same time, most of the efforts of Olivares and Philip were impaired by their desire to achieve Spain's imperial glory and by a series of internal revolts. Apparently the greatness of Spain as a nation was approaching its end. Involved in the Thirty Years' War, Spain was engaged in a series of frightfully expensive military campaigns that provoked internal revolts and years of civil war. Unfortunately for Spain, the campaigns also failed to produce victory. As Olivare wrote to King Philip Ⅳ, "God wants us to make peace; for He is depriving us visibly and absolutely of all the means of war."[①] The defeats in Europe and the internal revolts of the 1640s disillusioned those who were still hoping for the revival of Spain. Dutch independence was formally recognised by *The Peace of Westphalia* in 1648, and under *The Peace of the Pyrenees*[②] with France in 1659, Spain had to surrender some border regions to France.

Absolutism in Central and Eastern Europe The chief countries of Central and Eastern Europe where absolutism flourished on its most grandiose scale were Prussia, Austria and Russia. The Thirty Years' War was officially ended in 1648 by *The Peace of Westphalia*, which left each of the more than three hundred German states making up the Holy Roman Empire virtually independent. Of these states, two emerged in the

---

① Jackson J. Spielvogel, *Western Civilisation: A Brief History*, Beijing: Peking University Press, 2006, p. 278.

② *The Peace of Pyrenees*:《比利牛斯和约》。1659 年法西战争结束时,法王路易十四与西班牙王腓力四世之间的和约(1659 年 11 月 7 日)。它结束了 1648～1659 年的法西战争。

17th and 18th centuries as great European powers.

The founder of absolute rule in Prussia was Frederick William the Great Elector (1640 — 1688), a contemporary of Louis XIV. Keenly aware of the fact that Brandenburg-Prussia was small, open territory with no natural frontiers for defence, Frederick William built an army of forty thousand men, making it the 4th largest in Europe. To maintain the army, Frederick William set up the General War Commissariat to levy taxes to support the army and oversee its growth. The Commissariat soon developed into an agency for civil government as well. This became his new chief governing instrument and was directly responsible to the elector. Many of its officials belonged to the Prussian landed aristocracy, the Junkers, who were also officers in the all-important army.

The development of absolutism in Austria was evident during the reigns of Leopold I (1658—1705). By the end of the Thirty Years' War, realising the fact that the dream of establishing an empire in Germany was unlikely to be achieved, the house of Austria assembled a new empire in eastern and south-eastern Europe. In the 17th century, Leopold I encouraged the eastward expansion of the Austrian Empire, but he was bitterly challenged by the revival of Turkish power. The Turks eventually pushed westward and laid siege to Vienna in 1683. A European army led by the Austrians, however, counterattacked and decisively defeated the Turks in 1687. Austria took control of Hungary, Transylvania, Croatia, and Slovenia, thus establishing an Austrian Empire in southeast Europe. By the beginning of the 18th century, the house of Austria had acquired a new empire of considerable size.

Russia at the beginning of the early modern age was a composite of European and oriental characteristics. A new Russian state had emerged in the 15th century under the leadership of the Principality of Moscow① and its grand dukes. In the 16th century, Ivan IV (Ivan the Terrible) (1533—1584) was the first ruler to take the title of tsar. Ivan expanded the territories of Russia eastward as well as the autocracy of the Tsar by crushing the power of the Russian nobility. His dynasty ended in 1598 and was followed by a resurgence of aristocratic power in a period of anarchy which did not end until the Zemsky Sobor, or national assembly, chose Michael Romanov in 1613 as the new Tsar, beginning a dynasty that lasted until 1917. In the 17th century, Russian society was dominated by an upper class of landed aristocrats who, in the course of the 17th century, managed to keep their peasants bound to the land. Townspeople were also controlled. Many merchants were not allowed to move from their cities without government permission or to sell their businesses to anyone outside their class. In this period, despite various revolts and upheavals, Russia was experiencing more frequent

---

① the Principality of Moscow：莫斯科公国，13世纪由弗拉基米尔大公国分封而成，首都莫斯科。

contacts with the West, and western ideas were beginning to affect all walks of Russian society. At the end of the 17th century, Peter the Great noticeably accelerated this westernising process.

Peter the Great (1689 — 1725) was the first of the Tsars to attempt the Europeanization of Russia. After a trip to the West in 1697 — 1698, he was eager to introduce reform to Russia by drawing on the European practices, believing that it would give him the army and navy he needed to make Russia a great power. Peter reorganised the central government, partly following the practices of European countries. He also sought to gain state control of the Russian Orthodox Church by abolishing the position of patriarch① and creating a body called the Holy Synod as a decision-making agency. The Great Northern War (1701 — 1721) between Peter and Sweden testified to the improved power of Russia thanks to the reform efforts of Peter. The Peace of Nystadt in 1721 formally recognised what Peter had already achieved: the acquisition of Estonia, Livonia, and Karelia. Peter realised his dream and by his death in 1725, Russia had already become a great military power and an important European state.

It should be noted that in the 16th and 17th century, there was still a long way to go before absolutism took root in most parts of Europe. In 1700, government for most people still meant the local institutions that affected their lives: local courts, local tax collectors, and local organisers of armed forces. Kings and ministers issued policies and guidelines, but they still faced great difficulties ensuring their implementation with the presence of landed nobility, military officers, judges, officeholders and landowners.

Limited Monarchy in the Dutch Republic and England Almost everywhere in Europe in the 17th century, kings and ministers were in control of central governments. But absolutism was not widely accepted throughout the entirety of Europe. In Western Europe, two great states—the Dutch Republic and England—successfully resisted the power of hereditary monarchs.

The history of the Dutch Republic offered a model contrasting to absolutism, government dominated by aristocrats or merchants. As a result of the 16th-century revolt of the Netherlands, the seven Northern provinces, which began to call themselves the United Provinces of the Netherlands in 1581, became the core of the modern Dutch state, which was officially recognised by *The Peace of Westphalia* in 1648. Beginning with William of Orange and his heirs, the house of Orange occupied most of the stadholderates, an agency responsible for leading the army and maintaining the order. This aroused the dissension of representatives from the States General from various

① patriarch：宗主教，东正教按习惯翻译为“牧首”，是早期基督教在一些主要城市如罗马、君士坦丁堡、耶路撒冷、亚历山大和安条克对主教的称号。他们的威望和权力比一般的主教要高。在很多古老的东方教会中，宗主教实际上被称为大公牧首。

provinces. They advocated a decentralised or republican form of government. The death of William Ⅲ (1672—1702) without direct heirs enabled the republican forces to gain control of the government. The Dutch Republic would not be seriously threatened by the monarchical forces.

A better model for a non-absolutist regime was England, where the king and Parliament struggled to determine the role each should play in governing the nation. "Absolutism according to the French model probably never had a chance in England."① Conflicts between the king and Parliament over the monarch's power and the king's religious policy, as well as the king's attempt to pursue a course of "personal rule" made the outbreak of the civil war inevitable. The Parliament forces led by Oliver Cromwell defeated the pro-monarch forces② and executed King Charles Ⅰ in 1649. The victory of Cromwell was followed by his dictatorship until his death in 1658. The restoration of the royal family did not last long and in 1688, a group of prominent English noblemen invited the Dutch chief executive, William of Orange, husband of James's daughter Mary, to invade England. England experienced a "Glorious Revolution" almost bloodlessly. In January 1689, William and Mary accepted the throne Parliament offered together with the provisions of the Bill of Rights③ that affirmed Parliament's right to make laws and levy taxes. They laid the foundation for a constitutional monarchy④ by helping establish a system of government based on the rule of law and a freely elected Parliament.

The Flourishing of European Culture Despite the disturbance of religious wars and the growth of absolute monarchy, European culture, art and literature, continued to flourish.

In Italy, the artistic Renaissance came to an end when a new movement called Mannerism⑤ emerged in Italy in the 1520s and 1530s. Mannerism originated as a reaction to the harmonious classicism and the idealised naturalism⑥ of High Renaissance art as practiced by Leonardo, Michelangelo, and Raphael in the first two decades of the 16th century. In the portrayal of the human nude, the standards of formal complexity had been set by Michelangelo, and the norm of idealised beauty by Raphael. But in the

---

① Marvin Perry, et al., *Western Civilisation: Ideas, Politics, and Society*, Boston: Houghton Mifllin Co., 2000, p. 399.

② pro-monarch forces：王党军。

③ Bill of Rights:权利法案。

④ constitutional monarchy：君主立宪制。在保留君主制的前提下，通过立宪，赋予人民权利、限制君主权力，以实现事实上的共和政体。

⑤ Mannerism：风格主义，16世纪流传于西方的美术流派，也被称为"样式占有欲"和"矫饰主义"。它反对理性对绘画的指导作用，强调艺术家内心体验与个人表现，绘画精细，表明效果华丽，多戏剧性场面，用不对称和动荡取代拉斐尔式的统一风格。

⑥ naturalism:自然主义，文学艺术创作中的一种倾向。作为创作方法，自然主义崇尚单纯地描摹自然，着重对现实生活的表面现象作记录式的写照，并企图以自然规律特别是生物学规律解释人和人类社会。

artistic works of Mannerist successors, an obsession with style and technique in figural composition often outweighed the importance and meaning of the subject matter. The apparently effortless solution of intricate artistic problems was instead highly valued, such as the portrayal of the nude in complex and artificial poses. Finally mannerism was replaced by a new movement, the Baroque, which led the artistic world for another century and a half. Baroque was applied in general to anything elaborate and fanciful, in particular to the artistic style of the 17th century and early 18th century. Baroque artists sought to harmonise the classical traditions of Renaissance art with the intense religious feelings fostered by the revival of religion in the Reformation.

In the second half of the 17th century, France replaced Italy as the cultural leader of Europe. Unlike the Baroque style, which was regarded showy and overly passionate, the French remained committed to the classical values of the High Renaissance. In fact, the more extravagant aspects of Italian Baroque art never appealed greatly to French taste, which preferred elegance to display and restraint to emotion. French late classicism, with its emphasis on clarity, simplicity, balance, and harmony of design, was, however, a rather austere version of the High Renaissance style. The greatest French painter of the 17th century, Nicolas Poussuin (1593—1665), saw his own work as a kind of protest against the excess of the Baroque. Possuin's real and enduring enthusiasm was for the world of classical antiquity. His paintings often express a nostalgic yearning for "a long-vanished past". In the Dutch Republic, wealthy patricians and burghers of Dutch urban society commissioned works of art for their guild halls, town halls, and private dwellings. Following the wishes of these patrons, Dutch painters became primarily interested in the realistic portrayal of secular, everyday life.

The period between 1580 and 1640 witnessed an unprecedented flourishing of dramas in both England and Spain. The golden age of English literature is often called the Elizabethan era because much of the English cultural flowering of the late 16th and early 17th centuries occurred during the reign of Queen Elizabeth. Of all forms of Elizabethan literature, drama best expressed the energy and intellectual versatility of the era, and of all the dramatists, none is more famous than William Shakespeare (1564—1614), the author of 37 plays, two narrative poems, and 154 sonnets. The son of a prosperous glove maker from Stratford-on-Avon, William Shakespeare belongs to those rare geniuses of mankind who have become landmarks in the history of world culture. The works of Shakespeare are a great landmark in the history of world literature for he was one of the first founders of realism①, a master hand at realistic portrayal of human

① realism，现实主义，19 世纪 30 年代首先在法国、英国等地出现的文学思潮，以后波及俄国、北欧和美国等地，成为 19 世纪欧美文学的主流，也造就了近代欧美文学的高峰。由于现实主义文学具有强烈的社会批判性，高尔基称之为“批判现实主义”。

characters and relations.

The theatre was one of the most creative forms of expression during Spain's gold age. Beginning in the 1580s, the agenda for playwrights in Spain was set by Lope de Vega (1562 — 1635), an incredibly prolific writer. Almost one-third of his fifteen hundred plays survived. Lope de Vega was outspoken when he said that he wrote his plays to meet the needs and desires of the audience. Actually, in a treatise on drama written in 1609, he stated that the foremost duty of the playwright was to satisfy public demand.

The craze for drama in France began to dawn around 1630 and lasted well into the 1680s. Unlike Shakespeare in England and Lope de Vega in Spain, French playwrights wrote more for elite audience and were forced to depend on royal patronage. In France, three of the greatest names in the history of drama were active at the same time, all of them benefiting at one point or another from the patronage of Louis XIV. Jean-Baptiste Moliere (1622—1673), for instance, was favoured by the French court and benefited from the patronage of the Sun King. He wrote, produced, and acted in a series of comedies that often satirised the religious and social world of his time. In *The Misanthrope*①, he mocked the corruption of court society, while in *Tartuffe*②, he ridiculed religious hypocrisy. Pierre Corneille (1606 — 1684), who created French Baroque tragedy, mostly took as theme an event in classical history or mythology which was often used to express eternal truths about human behaviour. Jean Racine (1639—1699), however, was more concerned with the theme of self-destruction: the inability to control one's own jealousy, passion, or ambition, and the resulting inability to survive its effects.

Section Three The Scientific Revolution (1543—1700) and the Enlightenment (c. 1650—1800)

The Scientific Revolution By one of the strangest ironies of history, the period when arrogant absolutism bestrode nations of the European continent was also a period of stupendous intellectual achievements. The Scientific Revolution in the 17th century questioned and ultimately challenged conceptions and beliefs about the nature of the external world and reality that had crystallised into a rather strict orthodoxy by the Late Middle Ages. Derived from the works of ancient Greeks and Romans and grounded in Christian thought, the medieval world view had become almost overwhelming. However, the disintegration of Christian unity during the Reformation and the following

① *The Misanthrope*:《恨世者》,又译《愤世嫉俗》,是一部五幕诗体喜剧的杰作,它以整个贵族社会为讽刺对象,揭露贵族阶层的腐朽、堕落以及贵族社会内部的自私虚伪、勾心斗角。

② *Tartuffe*:《伪君子》是莫里哀的代表作,剧本以封建贵族和宗教势力为对象进行辛辣的讽刺和深刻的揭露。

religious wars had provided a more comfortable environment for Europeans to challenge both the ecclesiastical and political realms, which was soon followed by a challenge to intellectual authority of this era.

Briefly put, the chief difference between the intellectual attitudes of the Medieval Age and those in the Scientific Revolution was a turning-away from the contemplation of the absolute and eternal to a study of the particular and the perceivable. The traditional cosmological views of the Late Middle Ages had been built on the ideas of Aristotle, Claudius Ptolemy, and a Christian theology. According to them, the universe was viewed as a series of concentric spheres with a motionless earth as its centre. The spheres, made of a crystalline, transparent substance, surrounded and moved in circular orbits around the earth. Traditional cosmology claimed that the universe was finite with its fixed outer boundary in harmony with Christian thought and expectations. The long held belief in the Earth-centred conception, however, met with unprecedented challenges from the theories of Copernicus①, Kepler②, Galileo, and Newton.

Kepler made great contribution to the development of cosmology by making two fundamental changes to the theories of his predecessors: the ellipse replaced the circular model and the presumption that planets moved in their orbits at varying speeds. Kepler was keenly interested in Hermetic thought and mathematical magic. In a book written in 1596, he elaborated on his theory that the universe was constructed on the basis of geometric figures, such as the pyramid and the cube. Convinced that the harmony of the human soul was reflected in the numerical relationships existing between the planets, he devoted much of his effort to discovering the "music of the spheres".

Despite the blow of Kepler's theory to traditional cosmology, he left many questions unanswered. What were the planets made of and how does one explain motion in the universe? It was an Italian scientist who achieved the next important breakthrough to a new cosmology by answering the first question. The life and work of Galileo Galilei (1564—1642) was typical both of the progress made by science in the 17th century and of the problems it encountered. Galileo changed the scientific world in two ways: first, as the stargazer who claimed that his observation through the telescope proved Copernicus right, for which statement he was tried and condemned by the Inquisition and second as the founder of modern physics. Galileo destroyed yet another aspect of the traditional cosmology in that the universe seemed to be composed of a material substance similar to that of earth rather than an ethereal or perfect and unchanging substance.

By viewing the whole universe as a giant machine, Isaac Newton (1642—1727), the

---

① Copernicus：(尼古拉)哥白尼，出生于波兰，提出了日心说，代表作是《天体运行论》。详见第五章。

② Kepler：开普勒，参见第五章。

English scientist, provided an answer to the question as to what led to the motion in the universe. In his *Mathematical Principles of Natural Philosophy*, Newton spelled out the Mathematical proofs demonstrating the universal law of gravitation. Newton's work was the culmination of the theories of Copernicus, Kepler, and Galileo. The universal law he demonstrated served as one that could explain all motion in the universe. At the same time, the Newtonian synthesis created a new cosmology in which the world was seen largely in mechanical terms.

At the same time fundamental changes took place to astronomy and mechanics, which led to new perception of the Universe and Nature, Medicine, a third field that had been dominated by Greek thought in the Late Middle Ages, also experienced a revolutionary transformation. Later Medieval medicine was dominated by the teachings of the Greek physician Galen, whose influence on medicine in anatomy, physiology, and disease was incredibly enormous. But with animal, rather than human, dissection, Galen worked out a picture of human anatomy that was quite inaccurate in many aspects. His belief that there were two separate blood systems, one controlling muscular activities and containing bright red blood and the other governing the digestive functions and containing dark red blood proved to be wrong.

Two major figures associated with the changes in medicine in the 16th and 17th centuries were Andreas Vesalius and William Harvey. A Belgian physician, Andreas Vesaliu (1514—1564)[①]revolutionised the study of biology and the practice of medicine by his careful description of the anatomy of the human body. Basing his observations on dissections he made himself, he wrote and illustrated the first comprehensive textbook of anatomy. Vesaliu's hands-on approach to teaching anatomy enabled him to overthrow some of Galen's most glaring errors. For instance, he did not hesitate to claim that the great blood vessels originated from the heart rather than from the liver. Nevertheless, Vesalius was not able to free himself from some of Galen's wrong assertions, including the belief of the flow of two kinds of blood in the veins and arteries. Only after William Harvey's[②] work on the circulation of the blood had come out was that Galenic misperception corrected. Harvey (1578—1657) studied at Cambridge University, and later he obtained a doctoral degree in medicine at Padua in 1602. He discovered the true nature of the circulation of the blood and the function of the heart as a pump. Based on meticulous observations and experiments, Harvey rejected the ancient Greek's contentions. He demonstrated that the heart was the beginning point of the circulation of blood in the body, that the same blood flows in both veins and arteries, and that the blood makes a complete circuit as it passes through the body. Harvey's works proved a

---

① Andreas Vesalius:安德烈·维萨留斯,参见第五章。

② William Harvey:威廉·哈维,参见第五章。

heavy blow to Galen's theories. His ideas were not generally recognised until the 1660s, when capillaries① were discovered.

The Enlightenment in the 18th Century The climax of the Scientific Revolution was a movement known as the Enlightenment. Few other movements in history have had such profound effects in moulding men's thoughts or in shaping the course of their actions.

The Paths to Enlightenment. The transition of the intellectual world from the Scientific Revolution to the Enlightenment would not have been possible without the important role played by a number of popularisers of the scientific ideas. Although the intellectuals of the 18th century were largely indebted to the scientific ideas of the 17th century, they did not always acquire knowledge directly from the original sources. As a matter of fact, scientific ideas were spread more by popularisers than by scientists themselves. Of special importance to the links between the Scientific Revolution in the 17th century and the Enlightenment in the 18th century was Bernard de Fontenelle (1657—1757). In his *Plurality of Worlds*, he used the form of a casual conversation between a lady aristocrat and her lover to present a detailed account of the new mechanical universe. A number of the educated elite of Europe learned the new cosmology in this way.

Scepticism toward the Medieval perceptions played an incalculable role in the arrival of the Enlightenment. With the arrival of the Scientific Revolution, the dogmatic controversies, religious intolerance②, and religious warfare led many Europeans to call into question the traditional religious truths and values. With the overturn of medieval cosmology and the advent of scientific ideas and rational explanations in the 17th century, many Europeans became sceptical about what they used to consider right. Scepticism about religion and a growing secularisation③ of thought were important factors in the emergence of the Enlightenment.

Besides scepticism, travel literature also played an important role in the advent of the Enlightenment. In the course of the 17th century, traders, missionaries, medical practitioners, and explorers began to publish an increasing number of travel books that gave account of many different cultures. In addition to that, the new geographical adventures of the 18th century explorers, especially the discovery in the Pacific of Tahiti, New Zealand, and Austria by British explorer James Cook, presented life scenes of "natural man" that were much happier than many Europeans. One intellectual once wrote:

> The life of savages is so simple, and our societies are such complicated machines! The Tahitian is close to the origin of the world, while the European is closer to its old age... They understood

---

① capillary：毛细血管。

② religious tolerance：宗教宽容，允许个人选择并非国家认可的宗教信仰形式的政策。

③ secularisation：世俗化，去宗教化。

> nothing about our manners or our laws, and they are bound to see in them nothing but shackles disguised in a hundred ways. Those shackles could only provoke the indignation and scorn of creatures in whom the most profound feeling is the love of liberty![1]

The travel literature of the 17th and 18th centuries also made Europeans realise the fact that there are nations and cultures quite different from themselves in the rest of the world. Some serious Europeans began to re-evaluate their own civilisation relative to others.

The inspiration for the Enlightenment came partly from the rationalism[2] of Descartes, Spinoza and Hobbes, but the real founders of the movement were Newton and John Locke (1632—1704). Newton had long been praised as the "greatest and rarest genius that ever rose for the ornament and instruction of the species". Newton's view of the world as a huge machine governed by universal laws led many other intellectuals to strive to apply his approach to investigation of the society. Newton's greatest achievement was to bring the whole world of nature under a precise mechanical approach. From this it was an easy step to the conclusion that every event in nature is governed by universal laws, which can be formulated as precisely as mathematical principles. More importantly, Newton deprived God of His power to guide the stars in their courses or to command the Sun to stand still. John Locke's theory of knowledge had a great impact on 18th century intellectuals. Maintaining that all of men's knowledge originates from sense perception, Locke developed Hobbes's sensationalism in systematic form. In his *Essay Concerning Human Understanding*, Locke denied the assumption that human beings' knowledge derived from heredity. Instead, he maintained that every person was born with a blank mind and that people and their perception of the world and the society were moulded by the environment in which they were brought up and by their own experiences. Taken together, the ideas of Newton and Locke seemed to offer the hope of a "brand new world" built on reason.

The Intellectuals and Their Ideas. The intellectuals of the Enlightenment were known by the French term the philosophes, although not all of them were French and only a few were philosophers. Despite the shared common bonds that combined the intellectuals together, they often disagreed. A few of them, however, dominated the movement completely, the three French giants—Montesquieu, Voltaire, and Diderot.

The Enlightenment blossomed forth in its fullest glory in France during the 18th century under the leadership of Voltaire (1694—1778) and other like-minded critics of

---

① Jackson J. Spielvogel, *Western Civilisation: A Brief History*, Beijing: Peking University Press, 2006, pp. 308—309.

② rationalism：理性主义是建立在承认人的推理可以作为知识来源的理论基础上的一种哲学方法。公元17～18世纪间主要在欧洲大陆上得以传播，本质上体现资产阶级的科学和民主，是启蒙运动的旗帜。

the established order. Voltaire epitomised the Enlightenment in somewhat the same way as Luther did the Reformation or Leonardo da Vinci the Italian Renaissance. Voltaire was especially well-known for his criticism of traditional religion and his strong attachment to the ideal of religious toleration. In his *Treatise on Toleration* in 1763, he argued that religious toleration had created no problems for England and Holland and reminded governments that "all men are brothers under God". As he grew older, Voltaire became even more strident in his denunciations of religious fanaticism①, intolerance, and superstition. Throughout his life, Voltaire championed not only religious tolerance, but also deism②, a religious outlook shared by most other philosophes. Deism was built on the Newtonian world-machine, which implied the existence of a mechanic(God) who had created the universe. To Voltaire and most other philosophes, God had no direct involvement in the world he had created and allowed it to run according to its own natural laws.

Charles de Secondat, the baron de Montesquieu (1689—1755), was renowned for his attack on traditional religion, the advocacy of religious toleration, the denunciation of slavery, and the use of reason to liberate human beings from the darkness of the Medieval ages. His most famous work, *The Spirit of the Laws*, published in 1748, was a comparative study of governments in which Montesquieu attempted to apply the scientific method to the social and political arena to ascertain the "natural laws" governing the social relationships of human beings. Montesquieu distinguished three basic kinds of governments: republics, suitable for small states and based on citizen involvement; monarchy, appropriate for middle-sized states and grounded in the ruling class's adherence to law; and despotic government③, apt for large empires and dependent on fear to inspire obedience. The translation of his work into English two years after publication made it available to American philosophes who incorporated its principles into the American constitution.

Among the other major philosophers of the Enlightenment in France were Denis Diderot (1713—1784) and Jean d'Alembert (1717—1783), both of whom were the chief members of a group known as the Encyclopaedists, so called from their contributions to the *Encyclopaedia*, which was intended to be a complete summation or the philosophic and scientific knowledge of the age. The *Encyclopaedia*, "undertook to explore the whole world of knowledge from the perspective of the philosophes."④

---

① religious fanaticism：宗教狂热。

② deism：自然神论，17～18 世纪英国和 18 世纪法国出现的一个哲学观点。认为虽然上帝创造了宇宙，但是在此之后上帝并不再对这个世界的发展产生影响。

③ despotic government：专制政府。

④ Richard E. Sullivan, et al., *A Short History of Western Civilisation Since 1600*, New York: McGraw-Hill, Inc., 1994, p. 469.

Culture and Society in an Age of Enlightenment Even the most determined cultural historians acknowledge serious difficulty in categorising the 18th century. Although it has been called the Age of the Enlightenment or the Age of Reason, these labels—which do, in fact, describe some of its aspects—failed to encompass the full spirit of the age. In fact, the 18th century presents an immense variety of artistic and intellectual ideas, seeming contradictory yet in fact coexistent.

New Developments in Art, Music, and Literature. The leading arts to be developed during the Age of Enlightenment were architecture and painting. The heavy and pompous architectural style of Louis XIV gave way to the Rococo architecture in France. Emphasising grace and gentle action, Rococo had a fondness for curves; it liked to follow the wandering lines of natural objects, such as seashells and flowers. It made much use of interlaced designs coloured in gold with delicate contours and graceful curves. Its lightness and charm are indicators of the pursuit of pleasure, happiness, and love. Some of Rococo's appeal is evident in the work of Antoine Watteau (1684—1721), whose lyrical views of aristocratic life-refined, sensual, and civilised, with gentlemen and ladies in elegant dress, revealed a world of upper-class pleasure and joy.

For the most part, music in the 18th century retained a serious purpose, and was untouched by the mood of Rococo. In France, many of Francois Couperin's (1668—1733) compositions for keyboard emphasise grace and delicacy at the expense of the rhythmic drive and intellectual rigour of the best of Baroque music. The works of Carl Philip Emanuel Bach (1714—1788) have considerable emotional range and depth, opening up new musical possibilities with their rich harmonies and contrasting moods. Classical, the musical style that developed in the middle of the 18th century, reached its fulfilment in the works of Wolfgang Amadeus Mozart (1756—1791). Mozart's discontent with the overly demanding archbishop of Salzburg forced him to move to Vienna where his failure to find a permanent patron made his life wretched. Nevertheless, he was a prolific composer who wrote string quartets, sonatas, symphonies, concerti, and operas—until he died at thirty-five, a debt-ridden pauper. Mozart composed with an ease of melody and a blend of grace, precision, and emotion that arguably no one has ever excelled. Haydn remarked to Mozart's father that "your son is the greatest composer known to me either in person or by reputation".

The 18th century also saw the great development of the novel. The English are considered to have established the "modern novel as the chief vehicle" for fiction writing. With no rigid rules, the novel was open to much experimentation. It also proved especially attractive to women readers and women writers. Henry Fielding (1707—1754) wrote novels about people without scruples who survived by their wits. In *The History of Tom Jones, A Foundling*, a lengthy novel about the adventures of a young scoundrel, Fielding presented a panoramic view of English life from the hovels of

London to the country houses of the English aristocracy. Although he attached more importance to action rather than inner feeling, Fielding embedded his moralising in the attacking of the hypocrisy of his age.

The High Culture and Popular Culture. The Enlightenment was merely one dimension of Europe's cultural life. Europe's economic expansion and relative prosperity were matched by a marked increase in publishing activity that served diverse audiences and by the creation of new cultural forms and institutions. Although the aristocracy still dominated society, men and women of lesser social status participated prominently in social life, resulting in the coexistence of high culture and popular culture.

High culture, also known as Elite culture, refers to the culture of the educated and wealthy, the numerically small and influential elites. By the 18th century, European high culture consisted of a learned world of theologians, scientists, philosophers, intellectuals, poets, and dramatists, for whom Latin remained an international language. Their work was supported mainly by the landed aristocracy and the wealthier upper classes in the cities. European high culture was noticeably cosmopolitan. In addition to Latin, French had become an international language of the cultural elite. Even King Frederick Ⅱ of Prussia favoured French over German. Whatever the effects of Frederick's attitude might have been, the wide spread of knowledge of French meant that ideas and literature could circulate easily past language barriers. Especially noticeable in the 18th century was an increase in both reading and publishing. With the development of magazines came daily newspapers. Filled with news and special features, the newspapers were relatively cheap and thus available to most of the Europeans.

Popular culture refers to the often unwritten and unofficial culture committed to the lives of artisans, peasants and the urban poor. In these sectors of the society, culture primarily meant recreation and was essentially public and collective. Group activity often occurs in a variety of celebrations: family festivals, such as weddings; community festivals in Catholic Europe that celebrated the feast day of the local patron saint[①]; annual festivals, such as Christmas and Easter that go back to medieval Christianity; and Carnival[②], the most spectacular form of festival, which was celebrated in the Mediterranean states of Spain, Italy, and France as well as in Germany and Austria. Characterised by great indulgence, all of these festivals were celebrated in a secular fashion: chatting, drinking, singings, etc., even though they were supposed to fulfil religious functions. It should be noted that popular culture was not entirely based on an

---

① patron saint：主保圣人，守护神。

② carnival：嘉年华，欧洲一个传统的节日。最早起源于古埃及，后来成为古罗马农神节的庆祝活动。多年以来，嘉年华逐渐从一个传统的节日，到今天成为包括大型游乐设施在内，辅以各种文化艺术活动形式的公众娱乐盛会。

oral tradition; there was a popular literature as well. So-called chapbooks①, printed on cheap paper, were short brochures including both spiritual and secular material as well as lives of saints and inspirational stories. They were sold by itinerant peddlers to the lower classes.

Section Four The Last Phase of the Old Order (1715—1789)

The 18th century, or to be more exact, the years from 1715 to 1789, has long been considered the last phase of old order in Europe, which was to be ended by the violent upheaval of the French Revolution. The European societies were still mostly agrarian and dominated by kings and landed aristocrats, a basic pattern that had prevailed in Europe since medieval times. Thanks to the Scientific Revolution in the 17th century and the Enlightenment in the 18th century, however, demographic, economic, and social patterns were beginning to change in ways that heralded the emergence of a modern new order.

The European States Despite the flourishing of absolute monarchy in most European States in the 17th century, this style of reign based on the assumption of divine rights gradually gave way to influential utilitarian arguments in the 18th century. Whereas spirits of the Enlightenment met with strong resistance from some states, they produced enormous impact on others, particularly Prussia, Austria, and Russia in Central and Eastern Europe.

France and England. In the 18th century, the French monarchy was unwilling to accept ideas of the philosophes and resisted reforms while the French aristocracy grew stronger. Louis XIV left France with large territories, an enormous debt, and an unhappy populace. Louis XIV's successors, Louis XV (1715—1774) and Louis XVI (1774—1792), also professed to rule by divine right. But neither of these kings had the desire to emulate the Grand Monarch in his enthusiasm for work and his meticulous attention to the business of state. Louis XV was lazy and incompetent and allowed himself to be dominated by a succession of mistresses. Problems of government bored him incredibly and when obliged to preside at the council table, he opened his mouth, said little, and thought not at all. Louis XVI, his grandson who succeeded him, was weak in character and mentally dull. Indifferent to politics, he amused himself by shooting deer from the palace window and playing at his hobbies of lock-making and masonry. Incompetent as they both were, the two kings maintained a government which was at least more arbitrary than had ever been the case before.

The significance of the Glorious Revolution of 1688—1699 was profound. It spelt the doom of absolute monarchy in England. The 18th-century British political system

① chapbook:印有歌谣、故事等的廉价书。

was characterised by a sharing of power between the king and Parliament, with Parliament gradually gaining the upper hand. (The United Kingdom of Great Britain was founded in 1707 when the governments of England and Scotland were united; the term British was used to refer to both English and Scots.) The king chose ministers responsible to himself who set policy and guided Parliament; Parliament had the power to make laws, levy taxes, pass the budget, and indirectly influence the king's ministers. The 18th-century British Parliament was dominated by two groups of a landed aristocracy: the peers, who sat for life in the House of Lords, and the landed gentry, who sat in the House of Commons. Both of the two groups were made up of landowners with similar economic interests, and they frequently intermarried. In the House of Commons, most of the deputies were chosen from the boroughs and counties but not by popular voting. Although all owners of property worth at least forty shillings a year could vote, the eligible voters in the boroughs varied wildly, enabling wealthy landed aristocrats to obtain support by patronage and bribery. This resulted in a number of "pocket boroughs"① controlled by a single person. The same was true with the county delegates, two from each of England's forty counties.

When Queen Anne (1702—1714) died in 1714 without an heir, the Elector of Hanover, a German prince who succeeded Anne, founded the new Hanoverian Dynasty and became George Ⅰ (1714—1727). Because George Ⅰ did not speak English and neither George Ⅰ nor his successor, George Ⅱ (1727—1760), knew the British system well, their chief ministers were responsible for Parliament. This exercise of ministerial power was an important step in the development of the modern cabinet system in British government. The 18th-century England witnessed the emergence of new forces when growing trade and industry led an ever-increasing middle class to favour expansion of trade and world empire. William Pitt the Elder became prime minister in 1757 and acquired Canada and India in the Seven Years' War. Despite his successes, however, Pitt the Elder was dismissed by the new king George Ⅲ (1760—1820) in 1761 and replaced by the king's favourite, Lord Bute.

Central and Eastern European States. Of the five major European powers, three were located in central and eastern Europe and came to play an increasingly important role in European international affairs.

The work of the Great Elector, the founder of absolute rule in Prussia, was continued and extended by his grandson, known as Frederick William Ⅰ (1713—1740), since he now had the title of King of Prussia. The king established the General Directory as the chief administrative agent of the central government to supervise military, police,

---

① pocket borough：口袋选区，被英国的地主贵族操控的一些小选区。他们大多内定出候选人，然后再由选民"选出"。

economic, and financial affairs. He endeavoured to keep a highly efficient bureaucracy of civil service workers who were obliged to obey, respect and serve the king. By using nobles as officers and thus maintaining a close bond between the nobility and the army, the king ensured the loyalty of the nobility to the absolute monarch. At the same time, because of its size and reputation as one of the best armies in Europe, the Prussian army was the most important institution in the state.

The most noted of the Prussian despots was Frederick II (1740—1786), commonly known as Frederick the Great. An earnest disciple of reformist doctrines of the new rationalist philosophy, Frederick was the leading figure among the "enlightened despots" of the 18th century. Declaring himself not the master but merely the "first servant of the state", he made Prussia the best-governed state in Europe. Frederick's benevolence in governing the state, however, was not carried over into foreign relations. After the War of the Austrian Succession and the Seven Years' War, he acquired the Polish territory between Prussia and Brandenburg and thus created greater unity for the scattered lands of Prussia. By the end of his reign, Prussia was recognised as a great European power.

The Austrian Empire had become one of the great European powers by the beginning of the 18th century. The full bloom of absolutism came during the reign of Maria Theresa (1740—1780), who established a national army, and curtailed the power of the church in the interest of consolidated government. The reforms of Maria Theresa were extended, at least on paper, by her son, Joseph II (1780—1790), who was determined to remake his empire in accordance with the highest ideals of justice and reason. Ambitious as he was, most of his magnificent plans ended in failure. Joseph II was not a practical reformer but a doctrinaire idealist. He alienated the nobility and the church by freeing the serfs and attacking the monastic establishment respectively. His attempt to rationalise the administration of the empire by imposing German as the official bureaucratic language alienated the non-German nationalities.

Another noted "enlightened despot"① was Catherine the Great (1762—1796), who became the ruler of all the Russians after Peter III, the last of the series of six successors of Peter the Great, was murdered by a faction of nobles. The former German princess was an intelligent ruler strongly committed to reform. She wished to reform Russia based on the ideas of the philosophes of the Enlightenment, but she was shrewd enough to realise that she could not carry out her reform at the price of alienating the nobility.

Catherine's subsequent policies strengthened the landholding class at the expense of all others, especially the Russian serfs, which led to even worse conditions for the

① enlightened despot：开明君主。

Russian peasantry. On the whole, by increasing Russia's territory westward into Poland and southward to the Black Sea, Catherine proved a worthy successor to Peter the Great.

Whereas Joseph Ⅱ sought truly radical changes based on Enlightenment ideas, neither Frederick Ⅱ nor Catherine the Great were seriously affected by Enlightenment thought. Joseph, Frederick, and Catherine were all primarily concerned for the power and well-being of their states. In their desire to build stronger state systems, however, these rulers did pursue such enlightened reforms as legal reform, religious toleration, and the extension of education, establishing a path to modern nationhood.

International Relations While rulers built up their states by enlarging bureaucracies, strengthening governmental institutions, and expanding resources, they also had to consider how best to deal with their neighbours. Leaders like Frederick Ⅱ of Prussia and William Pitt of Britain tried to shape their diplomacy according to what they considered the needs of their states. "Reasons of state" centred on security, which could be guaranteed only by force. Thus, the search for defensible borders and the weakening of rivals became obvious goals. The 18th century international relation in Europe was characterised by the intensified rivalry for more territories and an increased number of conflicts and warfare, as evidenced by the War of Austrian Succession and the Seven Years' War.

The War of Austrian Succession. The War of the Austrian Succession, in which France fought on the side of Prussia against Britain and Austria, was mainly a duel between Prussia and Austria. After the death of the Hapsburg emperor Charles Ⅵ (1711—1740), King Frederick Ⅱ of Prussia took advantage of the succession of Maria Theresa to the throne of Austria by invading Austrian Silesia. France also entered the war against its traditional enemy, Austria. Maria Theresa made an alliance with Great Britain who feared French hegemony over continental politics. More quickly than expected, the Austrian succession had produced a worldwide conflagration. During the War of the Austrian Succession (1740～1748), Prussia seized Silesia and France occupied the Austrian Netherlands. The war was officially ended in 1748 by the peace treaty of Aix-la-Chapelle, which provided for the return of all occupied territories to their original owners except for Silesia. Prussia's refusal to return Silesia led later to another war, at least between the two hostile central European states of Prussia and Austria.

The Seven Years' War (1756—1763). The most important of the wars among the European States in the 18th century was the Seven Years' War (1756—1763), known in American history as the French and Indian War①. The war was a climax of a struggle for supremacy in the development of overseas trade and colonial empires, which had been going on for nearly a century. Initially a dispute over possession of the Ohio

---

① the French and Indian War: "七年战争",在美洲历史上被称作"法国和印第安人战争"。

Valley, the conflict turned into the whole question of British or French domination of the North American Continents. Later the rivalry between Prussia and Austria over Silesia merged with the existing conflict between Britain and France. The Severn Years' War thus reached the proportions of a world war, with France, Spain, Austria and Russia arrayed against Britain and Prussia in Europe, and with English and French colonial forces striving for mastery not only in America but also in India.

The outcome of the Seven Years' War was exceedingly important for the later history of Europe. Forcing Maria Theresa to surrender all claims to Silesia, Prussia increased its territory by more than a third, raising the Hohenzollern kingdom to the status of a first-rank power. In the struggle for colonial supremacy, the British emerged with sensational triumph, giving her an abundance of raw materials which enabled her to take the lead in the Industrial Revolution. Losing most of its overseas colonies, France was crippled almost beyond hope of recovery, which had much to do with preparing the ground for the Great Revolution of 1789.

Social Change and Order Ever since the 18th century, Europe witnessed noticeable economic changes that eventually had a strong impact on the rest of the world. The new economic pattern was characterised by rapid population growth, an agricultural revolution, industrialisation, and an increase in worldwide trade.

Population and Food. Europe's population began to grow around 1750 and continued a slow upward movement possibly due to the falling death rate, an improved living standard of the people, and the availability of more plentiful food. The sharp reduction of the death rate came about as a result of several causes. Probably the most important was the effective control of smallpox as a consequence of inoculation and vaccination. A second factor was the establishment of maternity hospitals, which, in combination with improved obstetrical methods, reduced the mortality among infants by a large margin in the second half of the 18th century. Finally, progress in sanitation, together with the adoption of more hygienic habits by people of all classes, also contributed to the conquest of various diseases and to increasing the life-span of average people.

The improvement in living standard of Europeans in the 18th century is evidenced by the increasing per capita consumption of sugar, chocolate, coffee and tea, which were not merely substituted for other foods and drinks, but were additions to the diet. The growing demand for linen and cotton cloth and for such articles of luxury as mahogany was also evidence of economic prosperity.

Thanks to increased farmland, healthier and more abundant livestock, increased yields per acre, and an improved climate, 18th-century agriculture underwent unprecedented growth. The increased productivity in agriculture was also brought about by the role played by new techniques. In the 18th century, the English took the lead in

adopting the new techniques that have been characterised as an agricultural revolution. This early modernisation of English agriculture with its noticeable increase in productivity made possible the feeding of an expanding population about to enter a new world of industrialisation and urbanisation.

New Methods of Finance and Industry. The economic development of Europe in the 18th century was shown in and also benefited from the advent of new method of finance and industry. The establishment of new public and private banks and the acceptance of paper notes made possible an expansion of credit in the 18th century. The Bank of England was founded in 1694. In addition to receiving deposits and exchanging foreign currencies, the Bank of England also made loans. In return for lending money to the government, the bank was allowed to issue paper "bank notes" backed by its credit. These soon became negotiable and provided a paper substitute for gold and silver currency.

The most important product of European industry in the 18th century was textiles, most of which were still produced by traditional methods in cities as textile centres. A shift in textile production to the countryside was spreading to parts of Europe. Industrial production in the countryside was done by the "cottage industry", truly a family enterprise in which both spinners and weavers did their work on spinning wheels and looms in their own cottages. But in the second half of the century, significant changes began to occur that would soon revolutionise industrial production.

Toward A Global Economy. In the 18th century, while there was only a slight increase in intra-European trade, which still made up a dominant proportion of total trade volumes, overseas trade boomed. This increase in overseas trade led to the emergence of a global economy in its strict sense. Economies of individual states were no longer separate from each other and the world economy has developed into an entirety. Spain, Portugal, and the Dutch Republic, which had earlier dominated overseas trade, were increasingly superseded by France and Britain, the two great western European powers.

Global economy in this era refers to the patterns of trade that interlocked Europe, Africa, the Far East, and the American continents. In an example of triangular trade, British goods were shipped to Africa, where they were traded for a cargo of slaves, which were then shipped to Virginia and paid for by tobacco, which in turn was shipped back to England where it was processed and then sold in Germany for cash.

Social Order. Even though the Enlightenment produced widespread impacts on European states in the 18th century with its emphasis on liberty, reason, and justice, the pattern of Europe's social organisation underwent little change. Social station was still largely determined by heredity and quality. Although Enlightenment intellectuals attacked these traditional distinctions, they were difficult to eliminate. Despite the domination of conventional practices, some forces of change were at work in this traditional society. Reformers argued that the idea of an unchanging social order based on birth was contrary to the spirit of social progress. Moreover, with the emergence of new economic patterns, especially the growth of larger industries, the old structures were more difficult to maintain. In fact, the old order finally began to disintegrate at the end of the 18th century.

On the continent, peasants continued to work their small plots of land—whether owned or rented—in the village of their ancestors. Accounting for as much as eighty-five percent of Europe's population, the peasantry made up the largest social group. The most important distinction, at least legally, was between the free peasant and the serf. Neither legally free peasants nor tenant farmers①, however, were free from compulsory services, owing a variety of dues and fees to their landed owners. In Eastern Europe, for instance, the peasants' status was still defined by a system of serfdom similar to what prevailed in Western Europe during the Middle Ages. Serfs could not marry, move away, or enter a trade without their lord's permission. This personal servitude ensured that peasants would be available to provide the labour that the lord required. In the local villages that remained the centres of peasants' social lives, richer peasants proved highly resistant to innovations.

In the 18th century Europe, nobles, who constituted about two or three percent of European population, were still the dominant power of the society. They enjoyed legal privileges including judgment by their peers, immunity from severe punishment, and exemption from many forms of taxation. Nobles also held important positions in military and government affairs. Moreover, the 18th-century nobility played a significant role in the administrative machinery of state, and in most of Europe, the landed nobility controlled much of the life of their local districts.

Chapter Review

This chapter presented the fundamental economic, political and intellectual changes that took place to the Western World between the 15th and the 18th centuries. The European Expansion, which took the form of voyages and conquests, confronted the New World with the major European powers. The period from the 15th to the 18th centuries witnessed the development and flourishing of Absolutism in Western Europe and limited Monarchy in the Dutch Republic and England. The Scientific Revolution in the 17th century altered people's view of the universe, while the Enlightenment was dedicated to liberating human beings from the darkness of the medieval ages.

---

① tenant farmer：佃农，西欧封建领主制经济下承租份地的农民。

Exercise

Ⅰ. *According to the information provided in this chapter, choose the correct alternative among A, B, C, and D that can complete each of the following statements.*

1. Which of the following two countries played the dominant role in the first stages of European Expansion?
   A. Portugal and Spain.
   B. Spain and the Dutch Republic.
   C. England and France.
   D. Portugal and France.
2. The Thirty Years' War was officially ended by ________ in 1648.
   A. the *Peace of Paris*
   B. the *Peace of Westphalia*
   C. the First Continental Conference
   D. the Second Continental Conference
3. ________ was determined to transform Russia into a great political and military power after returning from a trip to the West in 1697—1698.
   A. Ivan Ⅳ the Terrible   B. Peter the Great
   C. Nicholas Ⅰ   D. Alexander Ⅱ
4. A Polish astronomer, ________ proposed that the planets have the Sun as the fixed point to which their motions are to be referred.
   A. Aristotle   B. Kepler   C. Ptolemy   D. Copernicus
5. The 18th-century-Europe saw the great development of the novel. In *The History of Tom Jones, A Foundling*, ________ presented a panoramic view of English life.
   A. John Defoe   B. Henry Fielding
   C. Charles Dickens   D. John Donne

Ⅱ. *Fill in the blanks with what you have learned in this chapter.*

1. In the British Revolution in the 17th century, the Parliament forces led by ________ defeated the Pro-monarch forces and in 1649 executed ________.
2. The golden age of English literature is often called ________ because much of the English cultural flowering of the late 16th and early 17th centuries occurred during the reign of Queen Elizabeth.
3. William Harvey discovered the true nature of ________ and the function of the heart as a ________.
4. The intellectuals of the Enlightenment were known by the French term ________, although not all of them were French and a few were philosophers.

5. The most important product of European industry in the 18th century was ________, most of which were still produced by traditional methods in cities. On the other hand, there were also production in the countryside, where the ________ was the major form of production.

Ⅲ. *According to what you have learned, answer the following questions briefly in your own words.*

1. What were the major motives of European voyages and expansions initiated from the 16th century?
2. What factors led to the arrival of the Enlightenment in the 18th century?
3. What were the characteristics of popular culture?
4. Why did Joseph Ⅱ's changes in Austria end in failure?
5. What does "Glorious Revolution" refer to? What's the significance of the emergence of "Bill of Rights" in Britain?

Ⅳ. *With critical analysis, answer the following essay questions in your own words.*

1. What impact did European Expansion initiated in the 16th century have on the conquered and the conquerors respectively?
2. What was the purpose of the Enlightenment? What were the major contentions of Voltaire?

Ⅴ. *Work in small groups and make comparisons based on the following topic.*

Compare Columbus's voyages with that of Zheng He in China's Ming Dynasty.

Voices on Key Points

The Scientific Revolution and the Enlightenment

One can not impede scientific progress.

——Mahmoud Ahmadinejad

We are redefining and we are restating our socialism in terms of the scientific revolution.

——Harold Wilson

Our society is the product of several great religious and philosophical traditions. The ideas of the Greeks and Romans, Christianity, Judaism, humanism and the Enlightenment have made us who we are.

——Jan Peter Balkenende

Our freedoms were born in the ideals of the Enlightenment and the musket fires of an historic revolution.

——John Boehner

Suggested Reading

1. Hanley, Ryan P. & Darrin McMahon (Ed.). *The Enlightenment*. New York: Routledge, 2010.
2. Israel, Jonathan. *A Revolution of the Mind: Radical Enlightenment and the Intellectual Origins of Modern Democracy*. Princeton: Princeton University Press, 2010.
3. 晏立农主编:《图说科学与启蒙运动》,吉林人民出版社 2009 年版。
4. 严仲仪编著:《法国杰出的启蒙运动学者孟德斯鸠》,商务印书馆 1984 年版。
5. 翟宇:《现代理性的成长:科学革命与启蒙运动》,长春出版社 2010 年版。
6. 张箭:《地理大发现研究:15～17 世纪》,商务印书馆 2002 年版。

Chapter Eight The Age of the Revolution and Industrialisation (1775—1860)

After 1800 *the public life of both France and Europe hinged to an unparalleled degree on the will of a single man.* ①

Learning objectives

After reading this chapter, you will be able to:

1. *Identify the causes of the French Revolution*;
2. *Be familiar with the different stages of the French Revolution*;
3. *Be acquainted with the highlights of Napoleon's domestic policies*;
4. *Be familiar with great changes brought about by the Industrial Revolution*.

---

① Mortimer Chambers, *The Western Experience*, Volume Ⅱ: *Since the 16th Century*, Boston: McGraw-Hill College, 1998, p. 727.

法国中央集权的封建君主专制政治经过其发展的鼎盛时期，到18世纪后半期却导致了越来越多的社会冲突，而启蒙运动的思想对人们反对封建专制制度的斗争起到了极大的鼓舞和推动作用。另一方面，在资本主义最早发展起来的英国，海外扩张为资本家们积累了大量的原始资本，庞大的殖民帝国又提供了广阔的商品销售市场。在这样的背景下，在英国最先掀起了工业革命的浪潮。

始于1789年的法国大革命是欧洲历史的转折点，它推翻了法国的封建专制统治，建立起了资产阶级的政治统治，传播了资本主义自由、民主、平等的进步思想，为日后欧洲的民主制度奠定了基础。发端于英国的工业革命，继而扩展到欧美各国，乃至整个西方世界，带来了大量的新技术、新体制，改变了欧洲社会的经济和政治结构。但是，一些社会问题也不可避免地随之而来。随着工业革命的进一步加深和扩展，这些问题也逐步激化起来。

Section One The Revolutionary Era (1775—1815)

Everywhere in the 18th century Europe, monarchs sought to enlarge their bureaucracies to raise taxes to maintain the new standing armies and support the intensified conflicts brought about by the rivalries among the powers. At the same time, the sustained population growth, dramatic changes in finance, trade, and industry, and the growth of poverty created tensions that undermined the traditional foundations of the old order. The inability of that old order to deal meaningfully with these changes led to a revolutionary outburst at the end of the 18th century that marked the beginning of the end for the old order.

The American Revolution The revolutionary era began in North America when the thirteen British colonies[①] along the Eastern seaboard revolted against their mother country. Despite their differences, the colonists found ways to create a new government based on liberal principles that made an impact on the "old world".

Causes of the Revolution. The immediate causes of the American Revolution were Britain's response to its victory over France in the Seven Years' War (1756—1763), known as the French and Indian War in America. With the British treasury drained by the war, the Parliament members thought it the duty of the colonists to pay for the expense of guarding the new North American territories. In 1765, the British Parliament enacted *The Stamp Act*[②], which attempted to levy new taxes on the colonies. Although riots quickly led to the statute's repeal, the next tax imposed that

① the thirteen British colonies：北美13殖民地，包括罗德岛、康乃狄格、马里兰、特拉华、宾夕法尼亚、马萨诸塞、弗吉尼亚、新罕布什尔、北卡罗来纳、南卡罗来纳、纽约、新泽西、佐治亚。

② *The Stamp Act*：《印花税法案》。1756年，英国议会通过一项法案，向北美殖民地征税。所有报纸，法律和商业文件都要购贴印花税票。

led to the rise in the price of many everyday articles aroused and intensified grievance among the colonists.

Behind the American Revolution as a complex movement was one fundamental fact: significant differences had arisen between the American and British political worlds. Whereas representation in Britain was indirect in that the members of Parliament did not speak for local interests but their entire kingdom, in the colonies representation was direct and representatives were not only expected to reside in and own property in the communities electing them, but also to represent the interests of their local districts. Long before 1776, they had extended the representative institutions to include small property owners, who probably could not have voted in England. The colonists had come to expect representative government, trial by jury[①], and protection from unlawful imprisonment. Each of the thirteen colonies had an elected assembly that acted as a miniature parliament; in these assemblies, Americans gained political experience and quickly learned self-government.

The rapidly growing population had created a booming economy in the American wilderness. Underlying the economy was a diverse agricultural establishment, ranging from small, independently owned family farms in New England and the Middle Atlantic colonies to great plantations worked by slaves in the Southern colonies. The colonies also attached great importance to commerce and industry. Despite formidable obstacles, colonial merchants, especially in New England and the Middle Atlantic colonies, slowly developed commercial exchanges within America and then extended their transactions to Great Britain, the West Indies, and continental Europe. Moreover, by 1776, the colonists had produced considerable amounts of manufactured goods, sometimes in defiance of British mercantilist regulations. American entrepreneurs were increasingly intent on expanding their economic interests and minimising external constraints.

Of great importance to the outbreak of the Revolution was the growing awareness of independence of the Americans. By the 1760s, the American colonists had developed a sense of common national identity. The British society was seen by the American colonists as old and decadent in sharp contrast to the youthfulness and vitality of their own. This sense of superiority led to a desire for independence. While the British envisioned the empire including the American colony as a single unit with the Parliament as the supreme authority throughout, the Americans had developed their own peculiar view of the British Empire. They argued that neither the king nor the Parliament had any right to interfere in the internal affairs of the colonies since they had their own representative assemblies.

---

① trial by jury：陪审团审判制度，是指特定人数的有选举权的公民参与决定是否起诉嫌犯、并对案件作出判决的制度。

Another source of hostility toward established authority among the American colonists was their religious traditions, particularly Puritanism[①], which viewed the Bible as the law of the state. Like their counterparts in England, the American Puritans challenged political and religious authorities who, in their view, contravened God's law. Thus, the Puritans acquired two habits that were crucial to the development of political liberty: dissent and resistance. When transferred to the realm of politics, these Puritan tendencies led the Americans to resist authority that they considered unjust.

One crisis followed another in the 1770s. The colonies' desire to take collective action against Britain's actions led to the First Continental Congress, held in Philadelphia in September 1774. The more militant members refused to compromise and urged the colonists to "take up arms and organise militias". When the British army under General Gage attempted to stop the rebel mobilisation in Massachusetts, fighting erupted at Lexington and Concord between the colonists and redcoats[②] in April 1775.

Course of the Revolution. On July 4, 1776, the Second Continental Congress approved the *Declaration of Independence* drafted by Thomas Jefferson. The stirring document affirmed the Enlightenment's unalienable rights of "life, liberty, and the pursuit of happiness" and declared the colonies to be "free and independent states absolved from all allegiance to the British crown". The war for American independence had formally begun.

The war against Great Britain was not an easy one. Britain had long been a strong military power in Europe with enormous financial resources. The Second Continental Congress had authorised the formation of a Continental Army under the leadership of George Washington. Compared with the British forces, the Continental Army was made up of undisciplined amateurs whose terms of service were usually very brief. Although 400,000 men served in the Continental Army and the militias during the war, General Washington never had more than 20,000 troops available for any single battle.

By the eve of the Revolution, a strong aspiration for national independence had been ubiquitous throughout the 13 colonies. Pioneering, courageous and with a strong sense of solidarity, the colonists in North America were willing and eager to achieve freedom and independence at any price. Therefore, they were passionately involved in putting into practice the ideals of liberty, equality and democracy.

Of great importance to the Revolution was the assistance provided by other European countries that tried to gain revenge for their defeats in earlier wars against the

---

① Puritanism：清教，基督教新教派别之一。16世纪出现于英国。该派要求以加尔文学说为依据改革英国国教会，承认《圣经》为唯一权威，反对国王和主教的专制。主张清除国教会所保留的天主教旧制度，简化仪式，提倡过勤俭清洁的生活。它是美国主流价值观的基础，铸造了美国的民族特性。

② redcoat：英国军人，尤其指美国独立战争期间的英国军人，因其制服为红色而得名。

British. The French were particularly generous in supplying arms and money to the American colonies from the beginning of the war. Despite victories in most of the battles, the British were in danger of losing the war. When the army of General Cornwallis was forced to surrender to a combined American and French army and French fleet under Washington at Yorktown in 1781, the British surrendered. After extensive negotiations, the *Treaty of Paris* was signed in 1783. It recognised the independence of the American colonies and granted the Americans' control of the Western territory from the Appalachians to the Mississippi River. After a good start, the Americans soon showed signs of political disintegration.

Toward A Federation. Although the thirteen American colonies showed little interest in establishing a united nation with a centralised authority after the revolution, there was an increasingly urgent demand for a stronger government to deal with severe economic troubles and such radical movements as Shay's Rebellion①. In the summer of 1787, fifty-five delegates attended a convention in Philadelphia to devise a new Constitution.

The proposed Constitution created a central government different from and superior to the governments of the individual states. The national government was entitled to levy taxes, raise a national army, regulate domestic and foreign trade, and establish a national currency. Following Montesquieu's principle of a "separation of powers" to provide a system of "checks and balances"②, the central or federal government fell into three branches, each with certain power to check the functioning of the others. A president would serve as the chief executive with the power to execute laws, veto③ the legislature's acts, make judicial and executive appointments, supervise foreign affairs, and direct military forces.

After fierce debates, the Federalists, who favoured the new Constitution, won by a slim margin thanks to their promise to add a *Bill of Rights* to the Constitution. Accordingly, in March 1789, the new Congress enacted the first ten amendments④ to the Constitution, later known as the *Bill of Rights*⑤. These guaranteed freedom of religion, speech, press, petition, and assembly, as well as the right to bear arms, protection against unreasonable searches and arrests, trial by jury, due process of law,

---

① Shay's Rebellion：谢司起义。

② checks and balances：制约和均衡。

③ veto：否决权，指某一组织或个人有权力单方面决定停止一项立法工作。最早出现在古罗马。在英国和大多数君主立宪制国家，君主有否决议会所通过的法案的权力，但很少使用；在美国，总统也有权否决国会通过的法案，但不是绝对的：若参众两院均以三分之二多数通过该法案，总统则无法否决，若法案只是以简单多数通过，总统则可以考虑动用否决权。

④ amendment：修正案，立法机关对于现有法律的修改，从而避免重新立法，节省资源，也不会改变现行法律的总条数，有利于法律的稳定性。主要用于法典性法律。

⑤ *Bill of Rights*：《人权法案》，指的是美国宪法中第一至第十条宪法修正案。

and the protection of property rights.

The American Revolution created the first state governments, and ultimately a national government in which the exercise of power was grounded not on royal sovereignty or traditional privilege but on the participation and consent of male citizens. Even more important as a historical precedent, it (to a certain extent) triggered the outburst of the French Revolution.

The French Revolution From the standpoint of the broad sweep of history, the French Revolution emerged as part of a larger, middle-class revolutionary movement. It began six years after the American War of Independence ended, and lasted for a decade. The French Revolution of 1789 proved to be a turning point in European history. Its sheer radicalism, creativity, and claims of universalism made it unique. Its ultimate slogan, "Liberty, Equality and Fraternity"① became the foundation of modern Western civilisation.

Causes of the Revolution. Of great importance to the outburst of the Revolution was the despotic rule of the Bourbon kings, with their illogical and unsystematic character of government, and the disastrous wars into which France was plunged during the 18th century. After 1614, the Estates General, a kind of parliament, was no longer summoned, which meant that the king was the sole repository of sovereign power. Confusion reigned in nearly every department and inefficiency, waste and graft became the ruling qualities of the government. France's defeat in the Seven Years' War and its burden of debt resulting from its involvement in the American Revolution led to quarrels between the king and the middle class and to the consequent outbreak of the Revolution.

The rise of the middle class to a position of extraordinary affluence and prestige played a dominant role in the outbreak of the Revolution. Before the Revolution, the French population had been divided into three estates. The clergy constituted the first estate, the nobility the second estate, and everyone else belonged to the third estate. About 8 percent, or 2.3 million people, constituted the bourgeoisie or middle class who owned about 20 to 25 percent of the land. This group included merchants, bankers, and industrialists who controlled the resources of trade, finance, and manufacturing and benefited from the economic prosperity after 1730. The bourgeoisie also included professional people—lawyers, holders of public offices, doctors, and writers. The bourgeoisie regarded themselves as the most productive force in the society. They were annoyed by economic restrictions which they saw as largely designed to protect the interests of the nobility and the crown. The opposition of these elites to the old order ultimately led them to take drastic actions against the monarchical regime.

Every great social upheaval of modern times, including the French Revolution, has

---

① liberty, equality and fraternity：自由，平等，博爱。

developed out of a background of intellectual causes. The intellectual causes of the French Revolution were mainly an outgrowth of the Enlightenment. One underlying theory of the Revolution was that of John Locke. According to his liberal theory, for instance, if the government exceeds or abuses the authority explicitly granted in the political contract, it becomes tyrannical, and the people then have the right to dissolve it or to rebel against it and overthrow it. The theories of Locke, together with that of such philosophers as Rousseau and Voltaire, paved the way in an intellectual sense for the Revolution.

The immediate cause of the French Revolution was the near collapse of the government finances. In 1789, the Parisians organised a popular force and on July 14 attacked the Bastille, the fall of which quickly became a popular symbol of triumph over despotism. Louis's acceptance of that reality signalled the collapse of the royal authority.

The Breakdown of the Old Regime. The course of the French Revolution was marked by three great stages, the first of which extended from June 1789 to August 1792. During most of this period, the destiny of France was in the hands of the National Assembly, constituted by the Third Estate. In the main, this stage was a moderate, middle-class stage. One of the first acts of the National Assembly was to destroy the relics of feudalism and lay an ideological foundation for its actions and provide an educational device for the nation by adopting the *Declaration of the Rights of Man and of the Citizen*. ①

The next of the main accomplishments of the National Assembly was the secularisation of the church. In November 1789, the National Assembly resolved to confiscate the lands of the church and to use them as collateral② for the issue of paper money. In July 1790, the Civil Constitution of the clergy was enacted, providing that all bishops and priests should be elected by people and should be subject to the authority of the state.

By 1791, the National Assembly had finally completed a new constitution that provided for a limited, constitutional monarchy. The lawmaking powers were bestowed upon a Legislative Assembly chosen indirectly by people through a process similar to that by which the President of the United States was originally supposed to be selected. This new system, although far removed from absolute monarchy, was decidedly not a government the mass could claim as their own. The new Legislative Assembly held its first session in October 1791.

---

① *Declaration of the Rights of Man and of the Citizen*：《人权和公民权宣言》，简称《人权宣言》，宣布"社会的目的就是共同幸福"，提出"主权在民"，并且表示如果政府压迫或侵犯人民的权力，人民就有反抗和起义的权力。

② collateral：抵押品。

The Radical Revolution. In the summer of 1792, the French Revolution entered a second stage, which lasted for about two years. On August 10th, the Legislative Assembly voted to suspend the king and ordered the election of a National Convention to draft a Constitution. The destiny of France in this period was in the hands of extremists representing the proletariat of Paris. The liberal philosophy of Voltaire and Montesquieu was now replaced by the radical and equalitarian[①] doctrines of Rousseau. This period was characterised by uncontrollable violence and bloodshed. This was the period not only of the execution of the king, but also of the September Massacres (1792) and of the reign of terror from the summer of 1793 to the summer of 1794.

The Third Stage. In the summer of 1794, the reign of terror came to an end, and soon afterward the Revolution passed into its third and final stage. The execution of Robespierre on July 28, 1794 represented the completion of a circle. The Revolution came once more to reflect the interests of the bourgeoisie. In 1795, the National Convention adopted a new constitution which established a national legislative assembly composed of two chambers: a lower house, known as the Council of 500, which initiated legislation, and an upper house, the Council of Elders, which accepted or rejected the proposed laws. The Council of Elders elected five directors as the executive committee or Directory. The period of the Directory was an era of stagnation, corruption, and graft. At the same time, the government of the Directory was faced with political enemies from both the left (Jacobin) and the right (royalists). Unable to find a definitive solution to the country's economic problems, and still carrying on the wars left from the Committee of Public Safety, the Directory increasingly relied on the military forces to maintain its power. This led to a coup d'état in 1799 in which the successful and popular military general Napoleon Bonaparte seized power.

Reign of Napoleon. In the autumn of 1799, the Revolution in France came to a close. The event that marked its end was the coup d'état of Napoleon Bonaparte on the 18th of Brumaire (November 9).

Domestic Policies of Napoleon. Napoleon placed almost unchecked authority in his own hands. In 1804, he proclaimed himself hereditary Emperor, and his thinly disguised autocracy reached its climax. Many of his reforms, however, proved to be progressive.

Napoleon's religious policies promoted tranquillity at home and a good image abroad. After arduous negotiations, Napoleon and the pope signed the Concordat of 1801, according to which the Catholic Church was no longer an enemy of the French government. Moreover, the agreement also reassured those who had acquired church lands during the Revolution that they would not be stripped of the lands, which obviously made them become supporters of the Napoleonic regime. The balance of

---

① equalitarian：平均主义的。

church-state relations tilted firmly in the state's favour, for Napoleon intended to use the clergy as the major supporter of his regime.

Napoleon's greatest achievement was the codification of law, a task begun during the Revolution. Napoleon completed seven codes of law, of which the most important was the *Civil Code* (or *Code Napoleon*)①. The Civil Code, along with other codes of criminal and commercial law, covered all aspects of civil life from birth to death, all civic aspects related to family and property, contractual responsibilities, and civil liberties. It clearly reflected the revolutionary aspirations for a uniform legal system, legal equality, and protection of property and individuals.

Napoleon was well aware of the significance of science. To assure French predominance, he supported important work in the areas of physics and chemistry, and made science a pillar in the new structure of higher education.

Napoleon also worked on optimising the bureaucratic structure of France by developing a powerful, centralised administrative machine. Administrative centralisation required a bureaucracy made up of capable officials, and Napoleon worked hard to develop one. Promotion in civil and military offices was to be based not on birth but only on demonstrated abilities.

Napoleon's Conquest. After giving France a new government, Napoleon's first task was to defeat the second European coalition② of Russia, Great Britain, and Austria. Having realised the need for a pause, Napoleon achieved a peace treaty in 1802 that left France with new frontiers and a number of territories from the North Sea to the Adriatic, but the peace was ended by a new war in 1803 with Britain, who was soon joined by Austria, Russia, and Prussia in the Third Coalition. In a series of battles at Ulm, Austerlitz, Jena, and Eylau from 1805 to 1807, Napoleon's Grand Army defeated the continental members of the coalition, giving him the opportunity to create a Grand Empire made up of the French Empire, dependent states, and allied states. Although the internal structure of the Grand Empire varied outside its inner core, Napoleon viewed himself as the leader of the whole.

Seemingly as formidable as Napoleon's army was, his empire collapsed almost as rapidly as it had been formed. Underlying the fall of Napoleon's empire were two fundamental reasons: Britain's survival and the sense of a national identity. Based on its unparalleled sea power, Britain was almost invulnerable to military attack. Although Napoleon considered an invasion of Britain and even collected ships for it, he met the defeat of a combined French-Spanish fleet by the British at Trafalgar in 1805. Napoleon

---

① *Civil Code*:《民法典》,也称《拿破仑法典》。一部典型的近代民法法典,是第一部以资本主义经济制度为基础的资本主义国家民法典。

② European coalition:反法联盟,1792 年至 1815 年间欧洲各国为了对抗新兴的资产阶级法国而结成的同盟。

then turned to his Continental System[1] to defeat Britain, but failed again.

A second important factor in the defeat of Napoleon was nationalism. Nationalism consisted of the unique cultural identity of a people based on common language, religion, and national symbols. The spirit of nationalism, which had made possible the mass armies of the revolutionary and Napoleonic eras, was also spread to states other than France. Napoleon's conquest aroused the patriotism of people in the invaded countries. A Spanish uprising against Napoleon's rule, aided by British support, kept a French force of 200,000 pinned down for years.

Fall of the Empire. With the foreign wars, Napoleon spread the idea of the French Revolution, which objectively accelerated the collapse of the feudal system in Europe. However, he went too far militarily, not only plundered and enslaved the people of Europe, but also violated the independence of many countries, causing resistance everywhere, which eventually led to the downfall of the Napoleonic Empire. Napoleon's biggest mistake was to invade Russia in June 1812.

After the war broke out, the Russian troops fell back in retreat. It was a strange war, one that pulled the French army to Moscow. When Napoleon's troops entered Moscow in September, they found a city in flames. Lacking food and supplies, Napoleon abandoned Moscow late in October and made the "Great Retreat" in terrible winter conditions. Only 40,000 out of the original army managed to straggle back to Poland in January 1813. This military disaster then led to a war of liberation all over Europe, culminating in Napoleon's defeat in April 1814.

In June 1815, Napoleon met his ultimate defeat at Waterloo. With his defeat, a new expression, "to meet one's Waterloo",[2] entered the language to describe devastating, permanent, irreversible downfall. Napoleon was exiled to the inhospitable Island of Saint Helena in the South Atlantic. An era had come to an end.

Section Two The Era of the First Industrial Revolution (1750—1860)

During the period from 1300 to about 1700, the modern civilisation passed through its first great economic upheaval. This was the Commercial Revolution[3], which completely destroyed the semi-static economy of the Middle Ages and replaced it with a dynamic capitalism dominated by merchants, bankers and shopkeepers. However, the Commercial Revolution was soon followed by an Industrial Revolution which transformed the economic and social structure of Europe.

---

① Continental System：大陆制度，拿破仑战争期间拿破仑出台的一项贸易封锁政策。

② meet one's waterloo：遭遇滑铁卢，彻底失败，一败涂地。

③ the Commercial Revolution：欧洲商业革命，主要表现为欧洲资本的流通范围和海外贸易的地域急剧扩大，进出口商品的种类、数量和贸易额迅速增加，由此导致了商业的性质和经营方式的改变。

The Industrial Revolution referred to the vast economic and social changes initiated in Great Britain during the last few decades of the 18th century and spreading to the Continent and other parts of the world during the 19th and 20th centuries. What was most revolutionary about the Industrial Revolution was the wave after wave of technological innovation, from the great breakthrough inventions such as the steam engine, to the hundreds of adjustments in technique that applied new ideas in one industry to another and solved problems. In the process of industrialising, nations experienced rapid population growth and a general shift from a feudal society based on agriculture to an urban society based on manufacturing.

The Industrial Revolution in Great Britain The British Industrial Revolution took its origin in central England in the 18th century. It led to a succession of economic growth and changes in many countries and affected the entire European continent. Strictly speaking, the industrial revolution could not be counted among the real revolutions, because it did not overthrow any regime or class, but it promoted the rapid progress in both society and technology.

Why Britain First? Britain possessed several favourable conditions enabling it to produce the first Industrial Revolution, the most important of which was its abundant gains and benefits from overseas expansion. Around 1750, Britain was on the brink of a golden age of power and prosperity. She had already acquired the most valuable colonies in the Western Hemisphere, and she was soon to clinch her commercial supremacy by defeating the French in the Seven Years' War. A large proportion of Britain's gains from overseas trade provided sufficient capital for productive investment.

As the leading capitalist nation in the early 18th century, Britain had the most highly-developed joint-stock company and perhaps the best banking system in Europe. Trading in securities was organised as a legitimate business when the London Stock Exchange was chartered in 1698. By 1700, London was able to compete with Amsterdam as the financial capital of the world.

It is evident that the availability of markets gave British industrialists a ready outlet for their manufactured goods. In the course of its wars and conquests, Britain had developed a vast colonial empire. A crucial factor in Britain's successful industrialisation was the ability to produce cheaply those articles most in demand abroad. Britain's machine-produced textile industry fulfilled that demand. On the other hand, the British domestic market should not be overlooked. Britain had the highest standard of living in Europe and a rapidly growing population. This demand from both domestic and foreign markets and the inability of the old system to meet it led entrepreneurs to seek and accept the new methods of manufacturing that a series of inventions provided.

The Agricultural Revolution of the 18th century was also important in accounting for the beginning of the Industrial Revolution in Britain. Even ordinary British families

did not have to use most of their income to buy food, giving them the potential to purchase manufactured goods. At the same time, a rapid growth of population in the second half of the 18th century provided a pool of surplus labour who could no longer earn a living for their families on the land.

A few other causes must be added to complete the picture. Britain possessed an effective central bank and well-developed, flexible credit facilities. Besides, Britain was rich in important mineral resources needed in the manufacturing process. Britain being a small country, the relatively short distances made transportation readily accessible. In addition to abundant rivers, from the mid-17th century onwards, Britain had constructed a large number of new roads, bridges, and canals based on national and individual investments.

New Technologies and Systems. The initial stage of the Industrial Revolution witnessed a phenomenal development of the application of machinery to industry that laid the foundations of the modern mechanical civilisation. In the 1770s and 1780s, the cotton textile industry took the first major step toward the Industrial Revolution with a series of innovations in technology. The development of the flying shuttle had quickened the process of weaving on a loom and enabled weavers to double their output. This, however, led to shortages of yarn until James Hargreaves's spinning jenny① allowed spinners to produce yarn in greater quantities. Edmund Cartwright's power loom②, invented in 1787, made it possible for the weaving of cloth to keep up with the spinning of yarn.

Few single inventions had greater influence upon the history of modern times than the steam engine invented by a Scottish engineer, James Watt (1736—1819). Watt's steam engine received its first practical application in the iron industry. Wilkinson became one of the largest customers for steam engines, using them for pumping, moving wheels, and ultimately increasing the power of the blast of air in the forge. It revolutionised the production of cotton goods and caused the factory system to spread to other areas of production, thereby creating new industries.

Apart from technological innovation and mechanisation in industry, the Industrial Revolution was also marked by the great improvement in transportation and communication. In 1804, Richard Trevithick invented the first steam-powered locomotive on an industrial rail line in South Wales. Later, the engines built by George Stephenson and his son proved superior, and in their workshops in Newcastle upon Tyne, the locomotives for the first modern railways in Britain were built. George

---

① spinning jenny：珍妮纺纱机，由詹姆斯·哈格里夫斯发明的纺纱机械（1770年获得专利），可以同时操作多个纱锭。

② power loom：动力纺织机。

Stephenson's Rocket was used on the first public railway line, which opened in 1830, extending thirty-two miles from Liverpool to Manchester. Like the Duke of Bridgewater's canal, it was designed to move coal and bulk goods, but surprisingly its most important function came to be moving people. Within twenty years, locomotives reached fifty miles per hour, an incredible speed to contemporary passengers. At the same time, new companies were formed to build additional railroads as the new industry proved to be technically and financially successful. As a cheaper and faster means of transportation, the railroad contributed significantly to the success of the Industrial Revolution and to sustained economic growth. The great productivity of the Industrial Revolution enabled entrepreneurs to reinvest their profits in new capital equipment, further expanding the productive capacity of the economy.

The Spread of Industrialisation Britain took the first step along the road to an industrial economy and it was not long before other Western states followed suit. The process of industrialisation initiated in Britain soon spread to the continental countries of Europe and the United States at different times and speeds during the 19th century. Not until after 1850 did the Industrial Revolution spread to the rest of Europe and other parts of the world.

Industrial Revolution on the Continent. Industrialisation on the Continent faced numerous hurdles, and thus followed a path that was somewhat different from that in Britain. Lacking technological knowledge, European ministers and entrepreneurs went to visit British factories and mines with the hope of borrowing the key industrial secrets that would unlock the prosperity of a new age. Despite the British efforts to prohibit the outflow of artisans and export of important machinery and machine parts, none of the path-breaking inventions remained a secret for long. By the 1840s, a new generation of skilled mechanics from Belgium and France was spreading their knowledge East and South. More importantly, continental countries, especially France and the German states, began to establish a wide range of technical schools to train engineers and mechanics.

A second difference between the British and continental industrialisation lies in the role that the government plays in the Industrial Revolution. Governments in most of the continental countries were accustomed to playing a significant role in economic affairs. Governments bore the cost of technical education, awarded grants to inventors and foreign entrepreneurs and in some places even financed factories. Governments also played an active role in infrastructure construction by bearing the cost of building roads and canals, deepening and broadening river channels, and constructing railroads. By 1850, a network of rails had spread across Europe.

The industrialisation of Europe did not go as rapidly. In France, it was a slow and gradual development that took advantage of traditional skills and occupation and gradually modernised the marketplace. In Germany, the process of industrialisation was faced with the political divisions of the Empire, and the economic isolation of the petty states, and the wide dispersion of the vital resources. In Eastern Europe, most states remained untouched by the Industrial Revolution and soon became sources of raw materials for their industrial neighbours.

Industrial Revolution in the United States. From 1800 to the eve of the Civil War, the United States witnessed its Industrial Revolution, accompanied by a process of urbanisation.

Like the continental states in Europe, the Americans began their industrialisation by borrowing from Great Britain. A British immigrant, Samuel Slater, established the first textile factory using water-powered spinning machines in Rhode Island in 1790. By 1813, factories with power looms similar to those in Britain were being established. Soon thereafter, however, the Americans began to catch up with or even surpass their British counterparts. The Harpers Ferry arsenal, for example, built muskets with interchangeable parts, enabling the Americans to avoid the more costly system in which skilled craftsmen fitted together individual parts made separately.

A country with a large territory, the United States lacked a good system of internal transportation needed to ensure sustained economic development. This was gradually remedied, however. Thousands of miles of roads and canals were built to link East and West. The steamboat facilitated transportation on the Great Lakes①, Atlantic coastal waters, and rivers. The railroad was the most important of all in the development of an American transportation system.

Despite its deficiency in workers, the United States had a rapidly expanding farm population whose size in the Northeast soon outstripped the available farmland. While some of this surplus labour force, especially men, went West, others, mostly women, found work in the new textile and shoe factories of New England. When a decline in rural births threatened to drain this labour pool in the 1830s and 1840s, the European immigrants, especially poor and unskilled Irish, English, Scottish, and Welsh, poured in to work in the factories. By 1860, the United States was well on its way to being an industrial nation.

Impact of the Industrial Revolution A large variety of far-reaching social changes were related to the Industrialisation. Although much of Europe remained bound by its traditional ways, already in the first half of the 19th century, the social impact of the Industrial Revolution was being felt, and future avenues of growth were becoming apparent. Dramatic changes in the number of people and where they lived were already

① the Great Lakes：五大湖区，北美洲中部的五个大湖，包括休伦湖、安大略湖、密歇根湖、伊利湖和苏必利尔湖。

extremely evident.

Factory System. With the advent of new inventions and technologies, the appearance and development of the factory system during the Industrial Revolution changed the life style of most Europeans. Industrial capitalists realised that it was much more efficient to bring workers to the machines and organise their labour collectively in factories than to leave the workers dispersed in their cottages, hence the advent of the factory system. The rise of the factory system resulted in a tremendous growth of productivity in manufacturing and a seemingly fantastic increase of manufactured goods. This factory system was the origin of the modern mill town and industrial city, which played an important role in the urbanisation process in Europe.

Population Growth. Population growth, which had already begun in the 18th century, became increasingly dramatic in the 19th century. In Great Britain, for instance, the population increased from about nine million in 1780 to almost 21 million in 1850. The substantial drop in the number of deaths from famines, epidemics and wars ensured an extended life-span of most Europeans, greatly contributing to the population growth in the 19th century. During this era, the death rate declined as a general increase in the food supply, already evident in the agricultural revolution of Britain in the late 18th century, spread to more areas. Famine largely disappeared from Western Europe, although there were certain exceptions in isolated areas.

All the European nations in the 19th century had an ascending population with Ireland as an exception. In the summer of 1845, the peasants of Ireland had a poor harvest of potatoes, the crop most Irish people lived on. As a result, the failure of the harvest caused the Great Famine, which led to a dramatic drop in the Irish population. More than 1 million died of starvation and diseases while almost 2 million emigrated to the United States and Britain. The flight of so many Irish to America reminds us that the traditional solution to overpopulation has always been emigration. Between 1821 and 1850, the number of emigrants from Europe averaged about 110,000 a year. As an alternative to migrating to other nations, however, the rural masses sought a solution to their poverty by moving to towns and cities within their own countries to find work. This well accounted for the process of rapid urbanisation in the first half of the 19th century.

Urbanisation. A more direct result of the Industrial Revolution was the shift of population from rural to urban areas and the growth in size and number of cities. In the Industrial Revolution, cities were no longer solely centres for princely courts, government and military offices, churches, and commerce. By 1850, especially in Great Britain and Belgium, they had become places for manufacturing, mining, and industry, growing in number, size and population. More than 50 percent of the British population lived in towns and cities by 1850. London alone grew from less than one million inhabitants in 1800 to over 2.5 million by 1850.

Despite the sharp increase of towns and cities in size and number, living conditions were miserable for many of the inhabitants. Already overcrowded, devoid of mass transportation facilities, and equipped at best with vastly inadequate sanitation facilities, the cities became more densely packed and unhealthy each year. Rich and poor alike suffered in this environment of diseases, crimes, and ugliness, although the poor obviously bore the brunt of these evils. As a general rule, the farther one lived from the central city, the wealthier one was. Wealthy middle-class inhabitants often lived in suburbs or the outer ring of the city where they could have individual houses and gardens. In the inner ring of the city stood the small row houses of the artisans and lower middle class. Finally, located in the centre of most industrial towns were the row houses of the industrial workers.

The overcrowded cities, with the diseases, crimes and ugliness, certainly alarmed many of the well-to-do middle class, who considered the condition of the workers in cities a clear threat to the stability of the society. Some observers, however, wondered if the workers could be held responsible for their fate. One of the best-known of a new breed of urban reformers was Edwin Chadwick (1800—1890), who devoted his whole life to sanitary reform in Britain. Chadwick advocated a reformed modern sanitary system including efficient sewers and a supply of piped water. Six years after his report, Britain's first Public Health Act established a National Board of Health to form local boards in charge of setting up modern sanitary systems. This legislation embodied his belief that public health should be administered locally so as to encourage the people to participate in their own protection.

Changes in Social Structure. One of the most important impacts of the Industrial Revolution on the social structure is that it pushed the industrial and commercial middle class to the dominant position in the society. The Industrial Revolution destroyed forever the old division of society into clergy, nobility, and commoners. The development of industry and commerce caused a corresponding development of a bourgeoisie, a middle class comprising people of common birth who engaged in trade and other capitalist ventures. From the 18th century onwards, as industry and commerce developed, the middle class grew in size, first in England and then throughout Europe. The new industrial entrepreneurs—the bankers and owners of factories and mines—came to amass much wealth and play an important role alongside the traditional landed aristocracy of their societies. As the new bourgeoisie bought great estates and acquired social respectability, they also sought political power, and in the course of the 19th century, their wealthiest members would hold high offices in many European countries and merge with those old elites.

The Industrial Revolution simplified the class structure of the society by reducing it into a sharpened distinction between the middle class and the labouring class, or the industrial proletariat. Ruthlessly exploited by factory owners, workers in the new industrial factories faced wretched working conditions. Factories were filled with foul language, filthiness, poor health, ignorance and promiscuity. The workroom, hot in summer and cold in winter, was usually kept moist so that taut thread would break less readily. The workday usually began at 5:30 or 6:00 in the morning and lasted for twelve hours of work plus whatever time was allocated for meals and for recesses. The notorious fact is that well-constituted men were rendered old and past labour at forty years of age and children were rendered decrepit and deformed; furthermore, thousands upon thousands of children died of consumption (tuberculosis) before they reached the age of sixteen.

Ruthless exploitation and wretched working conditions led workers to seek means of change and improvement. Despite government opposition, new associations known as trade unions① were organised by skilled workers in a number of new industries, including the cotton spinners, ironworkers, coal miners, and shipwrights. The purpose of these unions was mainly to preserve their own workers' positions by limiting entry into their trade and to gain benefits from the employers. These early trade unions aimed only at improvements for the members of their own trades. The largest and most successful was the Amalgamated Society of Engineers, formed in 1850.

Violence was another type of collective reaction by workers in the early decades of the Industrial Revolution. The winter of 1811 — 1812 saw the most outspoken and violent movement directed against the Industrial Revolution. Due to the reduction of wages and the replacement of experienced employees with unskilled labourers by the manufacturers, it was launched by Luddites②, the machine breakers.

The industrial workers' efforts to change the current situation and improve their working and living conditions were better shown in the movement known as the Chartism③. Organised by the London Working Men's Association, the movement sought to achieve political democracy. A People's Charter drawn up in 1838 demanded universal male suffrage④ and payment for members of Parliament. Two national petitions incorporating these points, affixed with millions of signatures, were presented to Parliament in 1839 and 1842. Although the movement broke up by mid-century without having achieved its goals, it was not a total failure. Its true significance lay in

① trade union：工会，工人阶级的群众组织，最早产生于18世纪中叶的英国，以后在其他国家相继建立，并大多争得了合法地位。工人们在反抗资本家压迫和剥削的斗争中，认识到必须团结起来，才能维护自身的利益，取得斗争的胜利，因而产生了工会。

② 卢德分子，原指19世纪初在英国反对工业革命，捣毁机器的手工业工人，后来泛指反对技术进步的人。

③ Chartism：宪章运动，19世纪30～40年代英国发生的争取实现人民宪章的工人运动，是世界三大工人运动之一。工人们要求取得普选权，以便有机会参与国家的管理。

④ universal male suffrage：男性普选制。

its ability to arouse and organise millions of working-class men and women, giving them a sense of working-class consciousness that they had not really possessed before.

Reformers and government efforts to improve the conditions of the industrial workers also came from outside the ranks of the working class. Reform-minded individuals protested against the evils of the industrial factory, especially condemning the abuse of children. Their efforts eventually met with success, especially in the decades of the 1830s and 1840s.

Chapter Review

This chapter presented the two fundamental revolutions, the French Revolution and the Industrial Revolution, as well as the impacts and changes the two revolutions brought about. Characterised by sheer radicalism, creativity, and claims of universalism, the French Revolution was a turning point in European history, constituting the foundation of modern Western civilisation. The Industrial Revolution, which started in Britain and later spread to other parts of the Western world, witnessed the emergence of a large number of new technologies and systems, transforming the economic and social structure of Europe in a less dramatic and rapid manner. Social problems, however, still arose and were even intensified with the furthering of the Industrial Revolution.

Exercise

Ⅰ. *According to the information provided in this chapter, choose the correct alternative among A, B, C, and D that can complete each of the following statements.*

1. The *Declaration of Independence* affirmed the Enlightenment's unalienable rights of ________.
   A. life, liberty, and the pursuit of happiness
   B. life, democracy, and the pursuit of happiness
   C. freedom, democracy, and the pursuit of happiness
   D. life, property, and the pursuit of happiness
2. Before the revolution, which group of the population constituted the first estate of the French society?
   A. The nobility. B. The clergy.
   C. The peasants. D. The professionals.
3. The Industrial Revolution simplified the class structure of the society by reducing it into a sharpened distinction between ________.
   A. the nobility and the middle class
   B. the nobility and the clergy

C. the middle class and the industrial workers

D. the clergy and the peasants

4. In the 1770s and 1780s, the ________ industry took the first major step toward the Industrial Revolution with a series of innovations in technology.

A. steel B. iron

C. woollen textile D. cotton textile

5. Trade unions were organised by skilled workers with the purpose to ________.

A. protest against the Industrial Revolution

B. achieve political democracy and demand universal male suffrage

C. preserve their own workers' positions and gain benefits from the employers

D. give working-class men and women a sense of working-class consciousness

Ⅱ. *Fill in the blanks with what you have learned in this chapter.*

1. The *Treaty of Paris* signed in 1783 recognised the independence of the American colonies and granted the Americans control of the Western territory from the ________ to ________.

2. In March, 1789, the American Congress enacted the first ten amendments to the Constitution, later known as ________.

3. What enhanced cotton industry to even greater heights of productivity was the invention of the steam engine in the 1760s by a Scottish engineer, ________.

4. The development of industry and commerce caused a corresponding development of a ________, a middle class comprising people of common birth who engaged in trade and other capitalist ventures.

5. Like the continental states in Europe, the Americans began their industrialisation by borrowing from Great Britain. A British immigrant, Samuel Slater, established the first textile factory using water-powered spinning machines in ________ in 1790.

Ⅲ. *According to what you have learned, answer the following questions briefly in your own words.*

1. What factors led to the outbreak of the American Revolution in 1770s?

2. Why did Britain lose the war in the American Revolution?

3. What is the difference between the Industrial Revolution in Britain and that in the Continent?

4. The Industrial Revolution was followed by a rapid process of urbanisation. What were the problems that came with the process?

5. What were the means by which workers sought improved working and living conditions?

Ⅳ. *With critical analysis, answer the following essay questions in your own words.*

1. Napoleon Bonaparte played an important role in French and European history. Present your comments on his feats and faults.

2. What were the major changes brought about by the Industrial Revolution?

Ⅴ. *Work in small groups and make comparisons based on the following topic.*

Compare two of the most prominent conquerors in the world, Napoleon and Genghis Khan in terms of their merits and faults.

Voices on Key Points

The Revolutionary Era

A revolution can be neither made nor stopped. The only thing that can be done is for one of several of its children to give it a direction by dint of victories.

——Napoleon Bonaparte

No real social change has ever been brought about without a revolution... revolution is but thought carried into action.

——Emma Goldman

The Era of the Industrial Revolution

Only since the Industrial Revolution has most people worked in places away from their homes or been left to raise small children without the help of multiple adults, making for an unsupported life.

——Martha Beck

The Industrial Revolution was another of those extraordinary jumps forward in the story of civilisation.

——Stephen Gardiner

When the Industrial Revolution of the 19th century brought a rapid increase in wealth, the demand of workers for a fair share of the wealth they were creating was conceded only after riots and strikes.

——John Boyd Orr

The industrial revolution has tended to produce everywhere great urban masses that seem to be increasingly careless of ethical standards.

——Irving Babbit

Suggested Reading

1. Anderson, James M. *Daily Life during the French Revolution*. Westport: Greenwood Press, 2007.
2. Hanson, Paul R. *Contesting the French Revolution*. Malden: Wiley-Blackwell, 2009.
3. 刘大明:《"民族再生"的期望:法国大革命时期的公民教育》,中国社会科学出版社 2005 年版。
4. 张美、鞠长猛:《现代世界的引擎:工业革命》,长春出版社 2010 年版。
5. 张苏黎:《法国大革命演义》,四川大学出版社 1997 年版。

Chapter Nine Modernity in Europe (1815—1914)

Only by joining forces had the European powers been able to defeat Napoleon, and a system of alliances continued to be needed even after the battles were over. ①

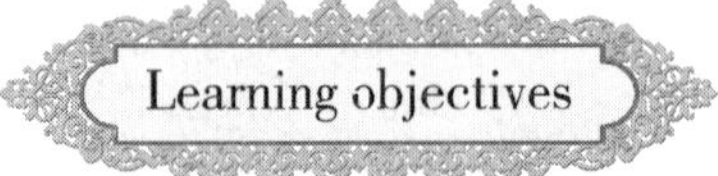

After reading this chapter, you will be able to:

1. *Know the meaning of such ideologies as liberalism, nationalism, and early socialism;*
2. *Know the spirits of Romanticism and Realism and be familiar with their manifestations in literature and art;*
3. *Be familiar with the thoughts of Marxism;*
4. *Understand the term "Mass Society" and be acquainted with its features;*
5. *Identify the inner relationship between the sense of anxiety in cultural development ever since the end of the 19th century and the tension among European powers before 1914.*

---

① Mark Kishlansky, Patrick Geary & Patricia O'Bnen, *Civilisation in the West*, Volume C: *Since 1789*, London: Longmans, 2001, p. 771.

法国大革命极大地动摇了欧洲的封建统治，也引起了欧洲各国封建统治者的集体恐慌。随着拿破仑的被流放和他所建立的帝国的瓦解，欧洲的保守派们渴望寻求和平和秩序，甚至要求将欧洲恢复到 1789 年法国大革命之前的状态。然而，随着自由、平等、民族主义等思想的兴起和发展，一些变革思潮逐步显示出自己的力量，回归 1789 年之前的状态已经完全没有可能。

这一时期的欧洲历史大致可以分为四个阶段：1815～1850 年为第一阶段，保守派的控制和压迫不断激起反抗，欧洲各国起义和革命此起彼伏；1850～1871 年为第二个阶段，民族主义思潮深入人心，许多民族渴望建立属于自己民族的国家，其中尤以德国和意大利完成统一为典型代表；1871～1894 年为第三阶段，以稳定和繁荣为特征，却很快被第四阶段的紧张局势所取代；1894～1914 年为第四阶段，与政治形势的发展相对应的是，欧洲的文化和艺术也经历了一个由浪漫主义到现实主义再到混乱的发展轨迹。

Section One Suppression, Revolution, and Romanticism (1815－1850)

Following the downfall of Napoleon and his empire, an overwhelming desire for peace and order seized the minds of the conservative classes in the victorious countries. Some sought to restore the old order to a Europe ravaged by war. In some quarters there was a desire to undo the work of the Great Revolution and return to the condition of 1789. But the western world had been changed. Inspired by the revolutionary principles of liberty, equality, and fraternity, the forces of change gave rise first to the revolts and revolutions that periodically shook Europe in the 1820s and 1830s and then to the widespread revolutions of 1848. By 1850 it was apparent the days of the old order were numbered.

The Conservative Order (1815－1830) After the defeat of Napoleon in 1815, efforts were made by European rulers to suppress the revolution and the revolutionary forces by restoring much of the old order. But the triumphant rulers also realised that it was impossible for them to return to the way things were in 1789.

The Peace Settlement. Most of the work of deciding the future of France and the fate of Europe after the long war which had involved nearly the whole of the Western world was done at the so-called Congress of Vienna.

In September 1814, the great powers—Great Britain, Austria, Prussia, and Russia—met at a congress in Vienna to arrange a final peace settlement after the Napoleonic wars. The congress was dominated by the Austrian foreign minister, Prince Klemens von Metternich (1773－1859). His greatest obsession was the hatred of political and social changes. He claimed that he was guided at Vienna by the principle of legitimacy, according to which the dynasties of Europe that had reigned in pre-Revolutionary days should be restored to their thrones, and that each country should regain essentially the same territory it had held in 1789. Despite its disregard for the wishes of the people and ignoring or even repressing the ideologies of nationalism and liberalism, the Congress of Vienna established a European order that managed to avoid a general European conflict for almost 100 years.

The Principle of Intervention. The peace arrangements of 1815 were only the beginning of a conservative reaction determined to crush the liberal and nationalist forces unleashed by the French Revolution.

Most conservatives preferred obedience to political authority, hated revolutionary movements, and accepted neither the liberal demands nor the nationalistic desires generated by the French revolutionary era. One way the great powers employed to keep the newly established status quo was the Concert of Europe① in which Great Britain, Russia, Prussia, Austria, and later France agreed to meet regularly to discuss their common interests and examine measures to preserve the stability of Europe.

The principle of intervention, meant to prevent revolution, could also be used to support revolution if the great powers found it favourable to themselves. In 1821, a revolt against the Turkish rulers broke out in Greece. In 1827, a combined British and French fleet went to Greece and defeated a large Turkish fleet. A year later, Russia declared war on the Ottoman Empire and invaded its European provinces of Moldavia and Wallachia. In 1830, the Turks had to allow Russia, France, and Britain to decide the fate of Greece. Greece then became an independent kingdom.

Conservative Order in Internal Affairs. Between 1815 and 1830, the conservative order of Europe was evident not only in the international relations but also in domestic affairs.

In 1815, British Parliament was mainly dominated by two political factions, Tories② and Whigs③. The Tories represented the old landed gentry and the Whigs were the aristocratic representatives of the Bourgeoisie, the industrial and the commercial middle class. Tory ministers remained dominant until 1830 and refused to change the existing political and electoral system. Demands for electoral reforms were responded to by suppression and minor changes that still kept the Tories in their conservative dominant position.

In 1814, the Bourbon family was restored to the throne of France in the person of

---

① Concert of Europe：欧洲协调，也称欧洲大国协同体。

② Tories："托利"起源于爱尔兰语，意为"不法之徒"。在此为托利党，产生于17世纪末的英国政党，19世纪中叶演变为英国保守党。

③ Whigs："辉格"一词起源于苏格兰的盖尔语，意为"马贼"。在此为辉格党，英国政党，产生于17世纪末，19世纪中叶演变为英国自由党。

Louis XVIII (1814－1824). He maintained Napoleon's Concordat[①] with the pope and accepted Napoleon's Civil Code with its recognition of the principle of equality before the law. The property rights of those who had purchased confiscated lands during the Revolution were also preserved. In 1824, Louis died and was succeeded by his brother, who became Charles X (1824—1830). Charles attempted to restore the old order as far as possible, and by 1830, France was on the verge of another revolution.

In Germany, secret societies and stormy agitation against hated regimes led Metternich to adopt a programme of repressive measures. Metternich ordered that every university should have a government supervisor; rebellious professors should be removed from their positions; student societies should be dissolved; and the press should be subject to a strict censorship. Thereafter, Metternich and the cooperative German rulers maintained the conservative status quo.

Although the Austrian Empire was composed of different peoples under the Hapsburg Emperor, Metternich managed to keep the empire under control by suppressing nationalism and preventing independence. The Germans, though only a quarter of the population, were economically the most advanced and played a leading role in governing Austria. Although these national groups, especially the Hungarians, claimed national rights of their own, Metternich managed to repress the nationalist forces and hold the empire together.

Tsar Alexander I (1801－1825), initially an enthusiast for new ideas, turned reactionary by 1820. Alexander had been one of the most enlightened monarchs of Europe, but after the defeat of Napoleon, his government reverted to strict and harsh censorship. Alexander was succeeded by his younger brother Nicholas I (1825－1855), who turned Russia into Europe's strongest pillar of reaction by his example at home and his willingness to use force abroad. Nicholas gave his closest attention to the army and the police and established a more effective bureaucracy by making it more directly responsible to the state and less attached to the nobility.

Opposition to Conservative Order The system of Metternich characterised by repression in domestic affairs by the great powers and suppression of revolutions led to a great number of uprisings against it. In Great Britain, the rule of the government for the benefit of the landed aristocracy evoked powerful opposition from the poets Shelly and Byron, and from the new industrial classes. In France, the modest compromise with progressive ideas which Louis XVIII incorporated in his Charter of 1814 proved to be more than his followers were willing to stand. As a result, the period from 1815 to 1820 was

---

① Concordat：宗教协定，作为罗马天主教领导人的教皇和世俗(国民)政府之间的协定。宗教协定通常规定在涉及两派的事件时的宗教和民事的权限。1801 年，教皇庇护七世和拿破仑·波拿巴签订了一个协议，恢复法国革命之前罗马天主教在法国的地位。

fraught with savage and sometimes bloody strife between ultra-royalists[①] and their liberal opponents.

Uprisings against the system of Metternich also occurred in colonies of European states, especially in Latin America. After the Bourbon monarchy of Spain was overthrown by Napoleon, Spanish authority in its colonial empire was weakened. By 1810, the disintegration of royal power in Argentina had led to that nation's independence. Simon Bolivar and his armies freed Colombia in 1819 and Venezuela in 1821. Jose de San Martin, another great leader, liberated Chile in 1817 and then, in 1821, moved on to Lima, Peru, the centre of Spanish authority. He was soon joined by Bolivar who crushed the last significant Spanish army in 1824. Mexico and the Central American provinces also achieved their freedom, and by 1825, after Portugal had recognised the independence of Brazil, almost all of Latin America had been freed of colonial domination.

Ideologies for Change Although the conservative forces were seemingly dominant throughout Europe during the period between 1815 and 1830, this age also witnessed the development of powerful movements for change. These movements had their roots in the rise of such political, economic, and social philosophies as liberalism, nationalism, and early socialism.

Liberalism[②]. One of these ideologies was liberalism that was unleashed in the Enlightenment of the 18th century and the American and French revolutions at the end of that century. It was grounded on the belief that human beings should be as free from restraint as possible. This opinion was evident in both economic liberalism and liberal politics.

Economic liberalism can be traced well back to Adam Smith's argument that government intervention in the free play of the market restricted economic forces which, if left to themselves, would increase productivity and prosperity. Bourgeois liberals thought that the economy, like the state, should proceed according to natural laws rather than the arbitrary decrees of rulers. A free economy, which they was thought to be as important as political freedom, benefited both the individual and the community. The economic philosophy of Economic Liberalism can be described thusly: Driven by self-interest, people would work harder and more efficiently. Self-interest and natural competitive impulses would increase economic activities producing more and better goods at the lowest possible prices for the well-being of the whole nation.

Liberal political thought was rooted in the writings of John Locke and of his

① ultra-royalists：极端保皇主义者。

② liberalism：自由主义，19 世纪初开始出现的资产阶级政治思潮。提倡以私有财产权为核心的个人权利，主张个人活动和发展的完全自由，实际上是奉行金钱的特权和垄断权。

philosophies. Liberals in the 19th century believed that their progress would contribute to the perfection of individuals and progress of the society. Liberals believed that individuals were entitled to equality before the law, to engage in careers they chose, and should be ensured freedoms such as freedom of the press, of speech, and of assembly, while government's powers should be limited. Moreover, most liberals advocated for religious toleration for all, an extension of the jury system, and separation of church and state.

Nationalism[①]. Nationalism may be defined as feelings of common cultural identity and loyalty to one's country. The essential components of nationalism emerged during the French Revolution. The Revolution asserted the principle that sovereignty derived from the people as a whole and that the state was not the private possession of the ruler but the embodiment of the people's will.

Nurtured by the French Revolutionary ideal of fraternity, modern nationalism was one of the most powerful forces that moulded the history of the Western world between 1830 and 1914. Divided people, such as the Germans, wanted national unity, while subject peoples, like the Hungarians, wanted the right to establish their own autonomy.

Nationalism soon spread to most European states. In the decades following the Napoleonic era, industrialisation and policies toward industrialisation were becoming connected with nationalism. By mid-century, nationalism had become closely tied with the central political, economic, and social forces of modern times. Despite its evil influence after 1848, nationalism did play an important role in opposing the conservative order.

Early Socialism. Socialist thought offered a radical alternative to conservative and liberal ideologies, varied as each of those were. The early socialists were romantics, for they dreamed of a new social order, a future utopia, where each individual could find happiness and self-fulfilment. They preferred cooperation to competition. Their being impractical in political ideals led them to be labelled as Utopian Socialists[②] by later Marxists.

One of the most notable of early socialists was Robert Owen (1771—1858). He believed that humans would reveal their true natural goodness if they lived in a cooperative environment. He devoted himself to his dream of establishing ideal communities. At New Lanark in Scotland, he was successful in transforming a dirty factory town into a flourishing, healthy community. Productivity rose, and profits

---

① nationalism：民族主义，即指将自我民族作为政治、经济、文化的主体而置于至上至尊价值观考虑的思想或运动。

② utopian socialist：空想社会主义者，又称“乌托邦社会主义者”，信仰空想社会主义。

increased. Visitors from all over Europe went to see the miracle of New Lanark. But Owen's attempt to create a self-contained cooperative community at New Harmony, Indiana, USA in the 1820s failed because of disagreement among the community. By the time of his death in 1858, Owen, who had converted to spiritualism, was largely ignored by the world he had sought to remake.

Revolution and Reform (1830—1850) In 1830, the forces of change, particularly nationalism, began to shake the conservative order of Europe, more successfully in some places than in others. Finally, in 1848, a wave of revolutions swept through Europe, causing liberals and nationalists everywhere to think that they were on the brink of creating a new order.

Political conflicts developed in France in the late 1820s. Charles Ⅹ's (1824—1830) attempt to restore the old regime as far as possible led to a revolt by liberals in 1830 known as the July Revolution. The bourgeoisie, students, and workers rebelled. They hoped to establish a republic, but the wealthy bourgeois who took control of the revolution feared republican radicalism. Therefore, they offered the throne to Louis-Philippe (1830—1848), a cousin of Charles Ⅹ. Charles Ⅹ fled to Britain and a new monarchy was established.

Compared with France, the growth of liberalism in Britain was less dramatic. In the 1820s, the moderate steps liberalism had taken toward reform failed in reaching the goal of broadening the franchise①. In 1830, the more liberal Whigs came to power. The Whig government realised that revolution was not a better way, so, in 1832, the new prime minister, Earl Grey, enacted the Reform Bill. This legislation helped deter revolutionary disturbances in Britain during 1848.

The revolutions in 1830 did not shake the basis of the conservative order established in 1815. The forces of nationalism and liberalism, however, never ceased to grow. With the development of the Industrial Revolution, more and more people showed their desire for political and social changes. Agitation of the middle class for democracy and reform, together with the severe famine in 1846 and growing demand for national autonomy in Central, Southern, and Eastern Europe triggered a revolutionary fever that swept through nearly every European state.

In France, as Louis-Philippe's government continued to refuse to make changes, opposition grew and finally the monarchy was overthrown on February 24, 1848. A Constitution was drawn up in November, 1848 by the national constituent assembly② elected by universal manhood suffrage. This constitution created the Second French Republic modelled upon the United States of America form of government. Thus an

① franchise：权利，尤其指公民权和选举权。

② constituent assembly：国民大会。

executive branch of government was created and led by a President.

In December 1848, Louis-Napoleon Bonaparte (1808—1873), an ambitious and clever politician, won an overwhelming victory in the first presidential election. It took him only three years to overthrow the republic in the violent coup d'état of December 2, 1851.

The Age of Romanticism① The age of reaction and revolution witnessed the emergence and development of a new intellectual movement known as romanticism. Unlike the Enlightenment's preoccupation with reason in discovering truth, the romanticists stressed the importance of feeling, emotion, and imagination as sources of knowing. Romanticism emphasised the individual, the subjective, the irrational, the imaginative, the personal, the spontaneous, the emotional, the visionary, and the transcendental②.

Romanticism in Literature. Above all, and in spite of variations, romantics shared similar beliefs and a common view of the world. Romanticists strongly opposed the confinement of classical forms and refused to accept the supremacy of reason over emotion. The leading romanticists were the English poets William Wordsworth (1770—1850) and Samuel Taylor Coleridge (1772—1834). *Lyrical Ballads* (1798), a collection of poems by Coleridge and Wordsworth, illustrates the essence of romanticism which is that poetry should be the reflection of human beings' spontaneous feelings rather than a formal and highly disciplined intellectual exercise.

Tragic sentiment was also a major concern of romantic literature. An important example was Johann Wolfgang von Goethe (1749—1832). His novel *The Sorrows of the Young Werther*, describes how an idealistic young man comes to feel increasingly disillusioned and frustrated by life, develops a hopeless passion for a happily married woman, and ends his agony by killing himself.

To the focus on emotion and sentiment of the romanticists could be added an attraction to the bizarre③ and unusual. In an exaggerated form, this preoccupation gave rise to so-called Gothic literature④, as shown in the short stories by the American author Edgar Allan Poe (1808—1849) and in *Frankenstein* by Mary Shelley. The latter is the story of a mad scientist who brings into being a humanlike monster who goes berserk.

---

① romanticism：浪漫主义，与现实主义同为文学艺术上的两大主要思潮。作为创作方法，浪漫主义在反映客观现实上侧重从主观内心世界出发，抒发对理想世界的热烈追求，常用热情奔放的语言、瑰丽的想象和夸张的手法来塑造形象。

② transcendental：先验的，超自然的。

③ bizarre：奇异的。

④ Gothic literature：哥特式文学。兴盛于维多利亚时代，其内容有着浓厚的恐怖色彩，大部分都被列入恐怖文学及魔幻小说的行列。

English romantic poetry of the first half of the 19th century marks a climax in the history of English literature. Percy Bysshe Shelley (1792—1822), expelled from school for advocating atheism[①], set out to reform the world. His *Prometheus Unbound*, completed in 1820, is about the revolt of human beings against the laws and customs that oppress them. Lord Byron (1788 — 1824) dramatised himself as the melancholy romantic hero he described in his own work, *Childe Harold's Pilgrimage*. He participated in the movement for Greek independence and died in Greece fighting the Turks.

Romantic poetry gave full expression to one of the most important characteristics of romanticism: love of nature, especially evident in William Wordsworth, who was often called the founder of the Romantic Movement in English poetry. His major theme was the relationship between human beings and nature. To Wordsworth, nature contained a mysterious force that the poet could perceive and learn from. Nature served as a mirror into which humans could look to learn about themselves. As he wrote, "one impulse from a vernal wood may teach you more of man of moral evil and of good than all the sages can."[②]

Romanticism In Art And Music. Like literature, artistic works of the 19th century burst beyond classical forms. Despite the varieties, romantic artists had in common at least two fundamental characteristics: view of artistic expression as a reflection of the artist's inner feelings, and the belief that a painting should mirror the artist's vision of the world and be the instrument of his own imagination. Moreover, the romanticists abandoned classical restraint for warmth, emotion, and movement.

The foremost champion of romanticism in France was Eugene Delacroix (1798 — 1863), who gloried in portraying struggles for freedom and other dramatic and sometimes violent scenes from history. The early life experiences of Caspar David Friedrich (1774—1840) left him with a lifelong preoccupation with God and nature. His vast, mysterious landscapes and seascapes proclaimed man's helplessness against the forces of nature and did much to establish the idea of the sublime as central concerns of the Romantic Movement.

Many romanticists consider music as the most romantic of all the artistic forms since it can penetrate into the inner feelings and emotions of human beings. Although music historians called the 18th century an age of classicism and the 19th the era of romanticism, there was much carryover of classical forms from one century to the next. One of the greatest composers of all time, Ludwig van Beethoven, served as a bridge

---

① atheism：无神论。

② William Wordsworth, "The Tables turned," in Andrew. J. George ed., *The Complete Works of Wordsworth*, Boston: Houghton Mifflin, 1904, rev. ed. 1982, p. 83.

between classicism and romanticism.

Born in Bonn Germany, Beethoven (1770—1827) dominated a period of musical history as no one else before or since. Rooted in the classical traditions of Joseph Haydn and Mozart, his art reached out to encompass the new spirit of humanism and incipient nationalism expressed in the works of Goethe and Friedrich von Schiller. He revealed more vividly than any of his predecessors the power of music to convey a philosophy of life and in certain of his compositions was to be found the strongest assertion of the human will in all music. He became the fountainhead of the romanticists who followed him, especially in his ideal of programme or illustrative music, which he defined in connection with his Sixth (Pastoral) Symphony as "more an expression of emotion than painting".

Section Two Nationalism and Realism (1850—1871)

Many changes sought by the liberals and nationalists during the first half of the 19th century came true. Examples of such changes include Louis-Napoleon Bonaparte's great contributions to French economic growth, the national unification in Germany and Italy by the early 1870s, and many European states changing to constitutional monarchy governmental forms.

The France of Napoleon Ⅲ Elections in France had left the Second Republic ruled by a president, Louis Napoleon, and a Chamber of Deputies in which a majority were monarchists who had not wanted a republic at all.

The Second Napoleonic Empire. Keeping his uncle's defeat in mind, Louis Napoleon, Napoleon Ⅲ prepared for his family's restoration as rulers of France. When the National Assembly rejected his proposal to revise the constitution and allow him to stand for re-election, Louis initiated a coup d'état and seized control of the government in 1851. He was both the first titular president and the last monarch of France.

Thanks to Napoleon's policies, French economy prospered in the 1850s. Industrialisation and economic growth were boosted by more railroad construction, public works, and financial institutions. Meanwhile, a major renovation of Paris was carried out that created the outline of the modern city, including a new sewer system, new beautiful parks, and new wide boulevards.

The Crimean War. France's revived national glory reached its peak during the Crimean War (1854—1856). Napoleon Ⅲ turned France's resources to foreign affairs allying France with other nations to fight against Russia's invasion of Ottoman Empire.

A war erupted between the Russians and Turks in 1853 when the Russians demanded the right to protect Christian shrines[①] in Palestine, a privilege that had

① Christian shrine：基督教神殿。

already been extended to the French. When the Turks refused, the Russians invaded Turkish Moldavia and Walachia. Failure to resolve the dispute by negotiations led the Turks to declare war on Russia on October 4, 1853. In the following year, on March 28, Great Britain and France, fearful of Russian gains at the expense of the disintegrating Ottoman Empire, declared war on Russia.

Russia lost its domination of the Black Sea. In 1855 the allies took Sebastopol on the Crimean Peninsula. The Russians soon sued for peace. By the Treaty of Paris, signed in March 1856, Russia was forced to give up Bessarabia at the mouth of the Danube and accept the neutrality of the Black Sea. In addition, the Danubian principalities of Moldavia and Walachia were placed under the protection of all the great powers.

The Crimean War signified an important shift in the European balance. In 1856, the conservative alliance of Austria, Prussia, and Russia that had dominated the Continent had broken up over competing ambitions in the Balkans and Germany and in the meantime the European international situation remained fluid. Those willing to pursue the "politics of reality"① found themselves in a situation rife with opportunity. It was this new international situation that made possible the unification of Italy and Germany.

National Unification: Italy and Germany While leading people in other places to seek independence and establishment of their own national states, the rise of nationalism virtually helped to promote the unification of Italy in 1870 and Germany in 1871.

For centuries Italy had been politically divided into various city-states, kingdoms, and provinces. The arduous task of uniting Italy required the work of a great political leader. He soon appeared: Camillo Benso, Count of Cavour (1810－1861), prime minister of Sardinia. Under the joint efforts of Cavour and Giuseppe Garibaldi, the most colourful of all the makers of the Italian nation, the Kingdom of Italy was formally declared in 1861, with Victor Emmanuel Ⅱ as the king. The remaining two provinces, Venezia and Rome, were joined to the Kingdom in 1866 and 1870 respectively, when first Austria and then France were defeated by Prussia. In 1870, Italy completed its national unification and Rome became the new capital of the united country.

During the 1850s both liberalism and nationalism began to make rapid headway in the German states. In 1858, the unstable reign of Frederick William Ⅳ gave way, and his younger brother, who three years later became King William Ⅰ, assumed leadership of the Prussian government as regent②. William Ⅰ later nominated as the chancellor③

① politics of reality：现实主义政治，关注于实际利益而不是抽象理论或道德伦理的政治。

② regent：摄政王，即代替或代表出国的、年幼的、生病的或神志不清的君主行使国家领导权的人。

③ chancellor：德国、奥地利等国家的总理或首相。

Otto Eduard Leopold von Bismarck (1815—1898), a figure who played a decisive role in the unification of Germany. In 1867, Bismarck established the North German Confederation under the leadership of Prussia. After the Franco-Prussian war was ended with the defeat of France in 1871, Germany achieved its unification and replaced France as the dominant power on the European continent.

The National State in Mid-Century While Italy and Germany were in the course of achieving their unification, other states in the Western world were also undergoing transformations.

The Austrian Empire: Toward A Dual Monarchy. Of all the states of Europe, Austria alone lacked a single ethnic group that identified with the empire fully. Military defeats in Italy and then at the hands of Prussia proved that changes were seriously needed. The result was the negotiated *Ausgleich*[①], or *Compromise*, of 1867, which created the dual monarchy of Austria-Hungary. Each part of the empire now enjoyed autonomous governments. What the two parts shared were a single monarch and common policies for defence and diplomacy. Ruled by the Dual Monarch, the Austrian Empire lasted for fifty years as one of Europe's great powers.

Imperial Russia. In Russia, defeat in the Crimean War made domestic reforms an urgent issue. Nicholas' son, Alexander Ⅱ (1855—1881), who came to power in the midst of the Crimean War, quickly initiated reforms and declared his intention to abolish serfdom.

On March 3, 1861, Alexander issued his emancipation edict. By the Tsar's decree, more than twenty-two million serfs in Russia gained legal rights and were promised title to the land they worked or its equivalent. Alexander Ⅱ also attempted other reforms in the army and the educational system. In 1864, he instituted a system of zemstvos, or local assemblies, to oversee public welfare and to keep the peace.

These steps were part of a process that made Russia more like other European states. However, the wave of reforms did not last long. Each reform uncovered more that needed to be done, and leaders remained fearful. By 1870, Russia was witnessing increasing levels of dissatisfaction. After Alexander Ⅱ was killed by a bomb in March, 1881, his son and successor, Alexander Ⅲ (1881—1894), turned against reform and returned to the traditional methods of repression and reaction.

Great Britian: The Victorian Age. As revolutions ravaged Continental Europe in 1848, Britain managed to maintain its social calm and sustained economic growth. British statesmen were not reluctant to point out to the rest of the world that Britain had achieved industrial growth without rending the social fabric. In spite of slums, poverty,

---

① *Ausgleich*:(德语)妥协。1867 年 2 月 8 日达成的一项旨在协调奥地利和匈牙利之间的关系的协议,奥匈帝国就是根据该协议建立起来的。

diseases, and famines that ravaged the kingdom, Britain avoided revolutions or civil wars.

One of the reasons for Britain's stability was its sustained economic growth. Thanks to the Industrial Revolution, Britain had an enormously productive capitalist economy by 1850. The British sense of national pride was well reflected in Queen Victoria (1837 — 1901), the last of the House of Hanover. The Victorian Age, as Britain during the reign of Queen Victoria has been known ever since, was characterised by a pious complacency.

Another explanation for Britain's relative calm lay in the development of democracy in this kingdom. Built on an established political culture emphasising liberty, the British Parliament was able to adapt to the demands of an industrialising society. One important issue was the extension of voting rights. The British political system was democratised, although slowly, after 1832, when the *Reform Bill* was passed. In 1867, the introduction of the *Second Reform Bill* doubled the electorate, giving the vote to a new urban population of shopkeepers, clerks, and workers. In 1884, farm labourers were enfranchised.

The United States: Civil War. While leading Germany and Italy to complete their national unifications, the force of nationalism helped the United States to prevent a possible national disintegration in the first half of the 1860s. Disputes over the future of slavery arose and intensified between the North and the South. The attempt to maintain them in the course of the first half of the 19th century led the South to become increasingly isolated. At the same time, the growth of an abolitionist movement in the North challenged the southern order and created an "emotional chain reaction" that led to civil war.

In 1860, the Republican Party that advocated for the abolishment of slavery won the presidential election and Abraham Lincoln (1809—1865) became president. The ten southern states seceded from the union and formed the Confederate States of America. In March, civil war broke out when Lincoln ordered troops to defend federal territory and property.

In the war the North gained overwhelming advantages over the South. On January 1, 1863, Lincoln's *Emancipation Proclamation* made most of the nation's slaves "forever free". The increasingly effective Union blockade of the South combined with a shortage of fighting men made the Confederate cause desperate by the end of 1864. In 1865, the South surrendered and the North won complete victory, which meant the end of the confederacy and of slavery in the United States. As in Italy and Germany, the nation-state had defeated sectional interest.

The Emergence of A Canadian Nation. To the north of the United States, nation building was also making progress. By the *Treaty of Paris* in 1763, Canada passed into

the hands of the British. By 1800, most Canadians desired more autonomy, although the colonists failed to agree on the form this autonomy should take. Upper Canada (now Ontario) was predominantly English-speaking while Lower Canada (now Quebec) was dominated by French Canadians. Increased immigration to Canada after 1815 also fuelled the desire for self-government.

The head of Upper Canada's Conservative Party, John Macdonald, became an avid apostle for union and self-government. Fearful of American desires on Canada during the American Civil War, the British government finally capitulated to Macdonald's demands, and in 1867, Parliament established a Canadian nation—the Dominion of Canada—with its own constitution. John Macdonald became the first prime minister of the Dominion.

Industrialisation and the Marxist Response In the period 1850—1871, Industrial Revolution on the European Continent further developed. Technological innovations increased productivity and lowered the cost of production. As a result, the growth of industry made this period an age of considerable economic prosperity.

The Industrial Revolution brought about the rise of industrial and commercial middle class, the bourgeoisie. However, it also led to the class struggle between the middle class and the industrial workers. Although workers formed trade unions to fight for improved working conditions and increased wages, they tended to represent only a small part of the industrial working class. Violent struggles such as the Luddite Riots proved ineffective. Real change for the industrial proletariat would only come with the development of socialist parties and socialist trade unions. These emerged after 1870, but the theory that made them possible had already been developed by mid-century in the work of Karl Marx.

The beginning of Marxism can be found in 1848 with the publication of a short treatise entitled *The Communist Manifesto*[①], written by two Germans, Karl Marx (1818—1883) and Friedrich Engels (1820—1895). It was an important symbol of the birth of Marxism. According to Marx, the capitalists and the workers were two opposing classes in a modern capitalist society. Through a revolution by the working class, capitalism would inevitably be replaced by a more advanced socialist system.

Marx never stopped writing during the 1850s, 1860s, and 1870s, and in 1867, he published his most important work, *Das Kapital*, a critical and thorough analysis of capitalism. Another great contribution by Marx was his work with union organisers to form the International Working Men's Association (the First International) in 1864, which served as an umbrella organisation for working-class interests. Marx was the

---

① *The Communist Manifesto*:《共产主义宣言》,卡尔·马克思和弗里德里希·恩格斯为共产主义者同盟起草的纲领,国际共产主义运动第一个纲领性文献,马克思主义诞生的重要标志,由马克思执笔写成。

dominant personality on the organisation's General Council and devoted much of his time to its activities. Like the Paris Commune[①], this organisation did not last long, either, but it did play a role in spreading Marx's ideas of socialism, particularly in Germany. In 1889, six years after Marx's death, the Second International was established by Engles and other socialists. Continuing the unfinished work of the First International, it helped to spread socialism, maintain doctrinal purity, and develop socialist strategies. The Second International disintegrated in 1914.

Science and Culture in an Age of Realism As an age of democratisation, economic prosperity, and national unity, the period from 1850 to 1870 was one marked by the rapid growth of scientific knowledge and the shift of art and literature from romanticism, an obsession with the emotion, sentiment, and inner feelings of human beings, to realism with its focus on the external, material world.

A New Age of Science. Compared with all preceding epochs, the period from 1850 to 1870 marked the zenith of scientific progress. Each of the older branches of science was greatly developed, and a dozen or more new ones were added to the list. Despite the change brought about by the Scientific Revolution of the 16th and 17th centuries, the intellectual developments had remained the preserve of educated elite and few of the discoveries and progresses were translated into real productivity. Moreover, the technical advances of the early Industrial Revolution had depended more on the practical experiments of technologically oriented amateur inventors than on the development of pure science. During the period from 1850 to 1870, however, an increasing number of people came to take interest in pure science, which was gradually accepted as the only worthwhile source of knowledge. This resulted in a number of basic scientific discoveries that were soon transformed into technological improvements that affected all Europeans.

The development of the steam engine encouraged scientists to work out its theoretical foundations, an obsession that led to the study of thermodynamics, the science of the relationship between heat and mechanical energy. In chemistry, the Russian Dmitri Mendeleev in the 1860s classified all the material elements then known on the basis of their atomic weights and provided the systematic foundation for the periodic law. In about 1865, James Clerk Maxwell (1831—1879) showed that light appeared to behave in much the same way as electromagnetic waves do, thus making a great contribution to the study of electromagnetics[②]; Louis Pasteur (1822—1895) laid the basis for the science of bacteriology by his epochal attack upon the theory of

---

① Paris Commune：巴黎公社，成立于 1871 年 3 月 18 日，是人类历史上第一个无产阶级政权。

② electromagnetics：电磁学，物理学的一个分支，主要探讨电性与磁性的交互关系。其研究对象包括电磁波、电磁场、电荷以及带电物体的动力学等。

spontaneous generation. Pasteur succeeded in convincing the scientific world that living organisms develop only from other living organisms. That was his famous Law of Biogenesis①. Considered the "Father of Antiseptic Surgery"②, Joseph Lister (1827—1912) achieved sensational results in preventing infection by cleaning wounds and surgical instruments with carbolic acid③ and by introducing carbonised catgut for surgical sewing.

The scientific progress in almost all branches of science revolutionised the method of scientific research and contributed greatly to the secularisation process. The widespread acceptance of the scientific method, based on observation, experiment, and logical analysis, as the only path to objective truth and objective reality, undermined the faith of many people in religious revelation and truth. Therefore, the 19th century saw an increasing secularisation, particularly evident in the growth of materialism, the belief that everything mental, spiritual, or ideal was simply an outgrowth of physical forces. According to Ernest Heinrich Haeckel (1834—1919), for instance, nothing spiritual exists and the universe was composed of matter alone in a process of constant change from one form into another. The importance of materialism was strikingly evident in the most important scientific achievement of the 19th century, the development of the theory of organic evolution according to natural selection. A picture of humans as material beings that were simply part of the external world could be built on the theories of Charles Darwin.

The Theory of Organic Evolution. Charles Darwin (1809—1882) was renowned for his theory of Organic Revolution contained in his *On the Origin of Species*④(1859). Also known as the theory of Natural Selection, this hypothesis involves the idea that it is nature, or the environment, that selects those variants among the offspring that are to survive and reproduce. Darwin pointed out that the parents of every species begot more offspring than could possibly survive. Consequently, a struggle took place among these offspring for food, shelter, warmth, and other necessities for life. In this struggle certain individuals have the advantage because of the factor of variation, which means that no two of the offspring are exactly the same. It is those favoured members of the species that win out in the struggle for survival; the others are eliminated generally before they have lived long enough to reproduce.

Initially Darwin applied his theory only to plant and animal species. Later, he attempted to show that his theory could also be applied to human beings. In *The Descent*

---

① Law of Biogenesis：生源说定律，又称"生源律"，认为生命只能由生命而来。

② antiseptic surgery：消毒法外科。

③ carbolic acid：石碳酸。

④ *On the Origin of Species*：《物种起源》，达尔文论述生物进化论的重要著作，出版于1859年11月24日。

of Man[①], published in 1871, he argued for the animal origins of human beings: "man is the co-descendant with other mammals of a common progenitor." Humans were not an exception to the rule governing other species.

Although Darwin's ideas were eventually accepted, they were initially objected by some people for their debasement of humans. Some of Darwin's claims even provoked the most profound opposition. Some were disillusioned by Darwin's view of human beings as offspring of apes rather than unique beings of nature while others upset by his claim of life as a struggle for survival. Gradually, however, Darwin's theory was accepted by scientists and other intellectuals and thus deeply influenced modern Western society and thought.

Realism in Literature. Started in France, realism was ushered in by the Industrial Revolution and growing nationalism in the world. Realism attempts to portray the speech and mannerisms of everyday people in everyday life and tends to focus on social and domestic problems. The term refers, sometimes confusingly, to a more general attitude that rejects idealisation, escapism, and other extravagant qualities of romanticism in favour of recognizing soberly the actual problems of life.

Realism in literature is a mode of writing that gives the impression of recording or reflecting faithfully an actual way of life. It seeks to describe life without any idealisation or romantic notions. In its pure form, realism is a down-to-earth and precise representation of human life and social conditions. As a dominant literary trend, it is associated chiefly with the life of the middle or lower class people in which the problems of ordinary people in unremarkable circumstances are rendered with close attention to the details of physical setting and to the backgrounds of social life. Realism sought to avoid sentimental language and realists advocated careful observation and accurate description, an approach that led them to prefer prose and novels to poetry.

One of the leading novelists of the 1850s and 1860s was the Frenchman Gustave Flaubert (1821—1880). His contempt for bourgeois society found best expression in his portrayal of Emma Bovary, who tried to discover in her own provincial life the romantic love she read about in novels. Her shoddy affairs and increasing debts led to an inevitably dramatic conclusion. William Thackeray (1811—1863) wrote extensively about contemporary society. With *A Novel without a Hero* as the subtitle of his *Vanity Fair*[②], Thackeray deliberately deviated from the Romantic conventions. Perhaps the greatest of the Victorian novelists was Charles Dickens (1812—1870). With striking

---

① *The Descent of Man*:《人类的由来》,首次出版于 1871 年,此书重点阐述了人类是怎么由低等生物进化而来的,并对他的性选择理论作了更多细节上的描述。

② *Vanity Fair*:《名利场》是萨克雷的成名作品,辛辣地讽刺了买卖良心和荣誉的"名利场"中各种丑恶现象,并运用深刻的心理描写和生动的细节勾勒刻画人物,是一部现实主义杰作。

force and truthfulness, he created pictures of bourgeois civilisation, describing the misery and sufferings of common people and uncovering social problems that occurred in the course of the Industrial Revolution. In *Hard Times*, for instance, he wrote of the evils of industrialisation.

Realism in Art. Realism also established itself as an important trend in art in the second half of the 19th century. Among the most important characteristics of realism are a desire to accurately depict the everyday life of ordinary people, peasants, workers, or prostitutes; an attempt at photographic realism①; and an interest in the natural environment. Realism rejects imaginative idealisation in favour of a close observation of outward appearances. The French took the lead in realist painting.

One of the first realist artists was Honore Daumier (1808—1879), who used his work to criticise the evils of society in general and government in particular. In *Belly*, he produced a powerful image of the greed and corruption of political opportunists.

Gustave Courbet (1819—1877) was the most famous artist of the realist school. Courbet rebelled against the romantic painting of his day, turning to everyday events for his subject matter. One of his famous works, *The Stonebreakers*, painted in 1849, shows two road workers engaged in the deadening work of breaking stones to build a road. This representation of human misery was a scandal to those who objected to his "cult of ugliness".

A French painter renowned for his peasant subjects, Jean-Francois Millet (1814—1875) was preoccupied with scenes from rural life, especially peasants labouring in the fields, although his realism still contained an element of romantic sentimentality. In *The Sower*, a peasant, energetically scattering seeds in a field, became a symbol of new life and the symbiotic relationship between humans and nature.

Section Three The Age of Progress (1871—1894)

By 1871, the spread of industrialisation and the wealth of scientific and technological achievements had led to extensive optimism among the Europeans. After the revolutionary and military upheavals of the mid-century decades, many Europeans believed that they stood on the verge of a new age of progress.

The Second Industrial Revolution About 1860, the industrialisation of the modern world entered a new phase so different from what had gone before that historians are disposed to call the Second Industrial Revolution. Whereas the first Industrial Revolution had given rise to textiles, railroads, iron and coal, in the Second Revolution, steel, chemicals, electricity, and petroleum led the way to new industrial frontiers.

New Products and New Markets. One of the major features that distinguished the

① photographic realism：照相写实主义，超级写实主义。

Second Industrial Revolution from the first was the rise of steel as the basic industrial material. With the development of new method of rolling and shaping, steel almost entirely supplanted iron for railroad rails, for the framework of large buildings, for bridges, and for other purposes where a cheap metal with a high degree of tensile strength was desired.

The Second Industrial Revolution was characterised by the wide use of electricity and a range of new products that came with it. The electricity was produced by a generator and then converted by electric motors into mechanical energy which was in turn put into use in industrial production. New inventions followed the wide use of electricity. The telephone was invented in 1876 by Alexander Graham Bell and the wireless telegraph by Guglielmo Marconi in 1895. The invention of wireless telegraph paved the way for the emergence of radio, the wireless telephone, and television. The first commercially practical generators of electrical current were developed in the 1870s.

The Second Industrial Revolution was also marked by the partial replacement of coal by gas and oil as principal sources of power as well as the invention of the internal combustion engine①. The processing of oil and gasoline made possible its widespread use as a source of power in transportation. An oil-fired engine was made in 1897, and by 1902, the Hamburg-American Line had switched from coal to oil on its new ocean liners.

The value of the internal combustion engine was more evident in the development of automobile and the airplane. In 1900, the whole world produced only 9,000 cars; by 1906, Americans had surpassed the initial lead of the French. The car industry was revolutionised by an American, Henry Ford, when he introduced the mass production of the Model T. By 1916, Ford's factories were producing 735,000 cars a year. In the meantime, air transportation was also transformed when the Wright Brothers, Orville and Wilbur, made the first flight in 1903 at Kitty Hawk, North Carolina.

Another typical feature of the Second Industrial Revolution was the introduction of automatic machinery, an enormous increase in mass production, and a division of tasks of labour into minute segments of the manufacturing process. Machines were invented to direct and operate other machines and to complete whole series of manufacturing processes that formerly required much human labour. The development of precision tools led to the creation of assembly line production. First used in the United States for small arms and clocks, the assembly line production technique had moved to Europe by 1850.

New Patterns in Economy. One of the changes brought about by the Second Industrial Revolution was that it led to the division of Europe into two economic zones by 1900. Great Britain, Belgium, France, the Netherlands, Germany, the western part

---

① the internal combustion engine：内燃机，一种通过在自身内部燃烧燃料而产生能量的发动机。

of the Austro-Hungarian Empire, and northern Italy constituted an advanced industrialised core that enjoyed a high standard of living and relatively healthy and educated populations. The little industrialised areas to the south and east, consisting of southern Italy, most of Austria-Hungary, Spain, Portugal, the Balkan kingdoms, and Russia, were still largely agricultural and served the function of providing food and raw materials for the industrialised countries.

The economic prosperity of the late 19th century and the revolution in transportation and communication produced a true world economy with Europe at its centre. This pattern was one in which Western needs were met and investment were widely made abroad. By 1900, Europeans were importing beef and wool from Argentina and Australia, coffee from Brazil, nitrates from Chile, iron ore from Algeria, and sugar from Java. With its capital, investment, industries, and military might, Europe dominated the world economy by the end of the 19th century.

Socialist Parties and Trade Unions. To improve their working and living conditions, many industrial workers organised political parties and labour unions. One of the most important of the socialist parties was formed in Germany in 1875. Under the direction of its two Marxist leaders, Wilhelm Liebknecht and August Bebel, the German Social Democratic Party (SPD) grew rapidly. In 1890, it received 1.5 million votes and thirty-five seats in the Reichstag[①], the German Parliament. When it received 4 million votes in the 1912 elections, it became the largest single party in Germany.

Toward the end of the 19th century, Marxist parties split into two factions. Some insisted that the attainment of socialism should be based on the imminent breakdown of capitalism and that the teaching of Marxism should be strictly followed. Others, however, believed that the theories of Marx should be revised to adapt to changing conditions. They were, therefore, referred to as revisionists. As the most prominent revisionist, Eduard Bernstein (1850 — 1932) asserted that capitalism was not on the verge of collapse, capital was not being amassed by fewer and fewer persons, the middle class was not disappearing, and the working class was not afflicted by "increasing misery". While spouting revolutionary slogans, many socialist parties followed Bernstein's revisionist approach.

Apart from political parties, trade unions were also founded to improve the working class's conditions. Attempts to organise the workers did not come until unions had won the right to strike in the 1870s. Strikes proved necessary to achieve the workers' goals. By 1900, two million workers were enrolled in British trade unions, and by the outbreak of World War Ⅰ in 1914, this number had risen to between three and four million.

The Emergence of Mass Society The new patterns of industrial economy, mass

---

① Reichstag：德国议会。

consumption and working-class organisation that identified with the Second Industrial Revolution were only one aspect of the new mass society that emerged in Europe after 1871. Apart from that, the mass society of Europe was also characterised by a larger and vastly improved urban environment, mass education, and mass leisure.

Transformation of the Urban Environment. One of the most important consequences of industrialisation was urbanisation. In the course of the 19th century, urban residents came to account for an ever-increasing proportion of the European population. In 1800, they constituted 40 percent of the population in Britain, 25 percent in France and Germany, and only 10 percent in Eastern Europe. By 1914, urban inhabitants had increased to 80 percent of the population in Britain, 45 percent in France, 60 percent in Germany, and 30 percent in Eastern Europe. The explosion of population was paralleled with the enlargement of cites. Between 1800 and 1900, London's population grew from 960,000 to 6,500,000. The sanitary conditions of city dwellers were greatly improved in the Second Industrial Revolution. During the First Industrial Revolution, the towns and cities were filled with filth and diseases and workers were living in wretched conditions. In the 1840s, however, a number of urban reformers, such as Edwin Chadwick in England and Rudolf Virchow and Solomon Neumann in Germany, pointed to filthy living conditions as the primary cause of epidemic diseases and urged sanitary reforms to correct the problem. In 1875, the *Public Health Act* was promulgated① in Britain, requiring that all new buildings have running water and an internal drainage system. For the first time in Western History, the role of governments touched upon detailed regulations for the improvement of the living conditions of urban residents.

Sufficient attention was also paid to the housing condition of the industrial workers. Overcrowded, disease-ridden slums were considered dangerous not only to physical health but also to the political and moral health of the entire nation. It was held by many that good housing was a prerequisite for stable family life, and without stable family life one of the "stabilizing elements of society" would be dissolved, much to society's detriment.

After the efforts of private enterprises to solve the housing crisis had failed, governments by the 1880s realised, reluctantly, that they could no longer act as onlookers. In 1890, a British housing act empowered local town councils to construct cheap housing for the working classes. Similar activity had been set in motion in Germany by 1900. In housing as in many other areas of life in the late 19th and early 20th centuries, the liberal principle that the government that governs least governs

---

① promulgate：公布，传播，发表。

best[①] proved untrue.

Education and Leisure in the Mass Society. In the mass society, education came to be viewed as an issue of paramount importance due to the vital role it played in propelling social advancement and personal achievement. The Second Industrial Revolution called for more skilled labourers, making education an urgent issue. The expansion of voting rights that necessitated a more educated electorate also sped up the development of education.

Ever since the 1870s, governments' role in offering and regulating education was more and more clear. Primary schools became available and professional teachers were trained. Between 1870 and 1914, most Western governments began to offer at least primary education to both boys and girls between the age of six and twelve. Governments also took up responsibility for the quality of teachers by establishing teacher-training schools. By 1900, state-financed primary schools, salaried and trained teachers, and free, compulsory mass elementary education had been available in many European states. As a result, more and more people were able to read and write. For the first time in Western history, in the wealthier nations at least, a majority of the adult population could read and write.

The increase in literacy brought about by mass education gave rise to mass newspapers after 1871. These newspapers, such as *Evening News* (1881) and *Daily Mail* (1896), were written in an easily understood style and tended to be extremely sensational. Specialty magazines, such as *Family Herald* for the entire family began to appear in the 1860s. Literature for the masses was but one feature of a new mass culture; another was the emergence of new forms of mass leisure.

In the mass society, entertainment seemed to have become professionalised. Although the new amusements were important for improving people, it was self-evident that they served primarily to provide entertainment and distract people from their work. The new mass leisure also represented a significant change from earlier forms of popular culture. Festivals and fairs were based on active and spontaneous community participation, whereas the new forms of mass leisure were businesses, standardised for largely passive mass audiences and organised to make profits.

Something similar happened to sports. Unlike the old rural games, they were becoming strictly organised with sets of rules and officials to enforce them. In Britain, soccer had its Football Association in 1863, and rugby had its Rugby Football Union in 1871. In the United States, the first national association to recognise professional baseball players was formed in 1863. Moreover, sports were emphasised by Britain's elite schools, who believed that they inculcated the "many virtues of perseverance,

① the government that governs least governs best:管得最少的政府是管得最好的政府。

sacrifice for the team, and playing by the rules". Soon sports demonstrated the capacity to promote communal identity on a much broader civic and national scale. Competition could invoke both individualism and nationalism, as it did in the modern Olympic Games established in 1896 through the efforts of Baron Pierre de Coubertin of France.

New technology played a role in the emergence and development of mass leisure activities. The new technology created new experiences for leisure, such as the Ferris wheel[①] at amusement parks, and the mechanised urban transportation systems of the 1880s meant that even the working classes could make their way to athletic games, amusement parks, and dance halls. Railways could take people to the beaches on weekends.

The National State In the late 19th-century Western Europe, considerable progress was made in achieving such liberal practices as constitutions, parliaments, and individual liberties and in reforms that encouraged the expansion of political democracy through voting rights for men and mass political parties. In Central and Eastern Europe, however, these developments were strongly resisted because the old political forces remained strong.

Western Europe: The Growth of Political Democracy. From Russia to Spain, European nations had adopted parliamentary systems and until the end of the 19th century, Britain provided the model of how such a system was supposed to work. Much advanced by the *Reform Act of 1867*, the voting right was further extended during the second ministry of William Gladstone (1880—1885) with the passage of the Reform Act of 1884. By giving the vote to all men who paid regular rents or taxes, it largely enfranchised the agricultural workers, a group previously excluded. Beginning in 1911, members of the House of Commons were paid salaries, which at least opened the door to people other than the wealthy. The British system of gradual reform through parliamentary institutions had become the way of British political life.

In France, political conflict revolved around the form of government following the fall of the Second Empire. After the defeat of Louis Napoleon's armies and his capture, National Assembly was elected and a provisional republic was set up which later came to be called the Third Republic. The government established by the *Constitution of the Republic* was about as democratic as any in the world. This constitution formed a legislature with an upper house, the Senate, and a lower house, the Chamber of Deputies. New elections in 1876 and 1877 strengthened the hands of the republicans who managed by 1879 to institute ministerial responsibility and establish the power of the Chamber of Deputies. The prime minister and his ministers were now responsible not to the president but to the Chamber of Deputies. The President of France was about

① Ferris wheel: 摩天轮。

the nearest approach to a nonentity that it would be possible to find among heads of state. His every act had to be approved by a member of the ministry.

Italy's liberal monarchy was committed to modernising the nation through modest reforms, but the political system in which only the well-to-do could vote made it hard to win broad popular support. Economically, Italy was still weak despite the completion of national unification. This weakness was worsened by the sectional differences between the poverty-stricken south and the industrialising north. The Italian government was unable to deal efficiently with the chronic turmoil between workers and industrialists because of widespread corruption among government officials and the lack of stability created by ever-changing government coalitions. Even the granting of universal male suffrage in 1912 did little to correct the extensive corruption and weak government.

Central and Eastern Europe: Persistence of the Old Order. Whereas the development of political democracy was evident in Western Europe, Germany, Austria-Hungary, and Russia witnessed little progress in political democracy. Authoritarian forces, especially powerful monarchies and conservative social groups remained strong.

Bismarck had given Germany a constitution that established representative institution but left power in the hands of a conservative monarch. Although elected on the basis of universal male suffrage, the lower house of the parliament, the Reichstag, did not have ministerial responsibility. The chancellor and the ministers were responsible not to the parliament but to the emperor. The emperor was no figurehead; he was vested with extensive authority over the army and navy, over foreign relations, and over the enactment and execution of the laws. Besides, he could declare war if the coasts or territory of the Empire were attacked. Although the creation of a parliament elected by universal suffrage presented opportunities for the development of a real democracy, it failed to grow in Germany before World War Ⅰ since the army and Bismarck served as the two major defenders of monarchy and aristocracy.

In the 1870s, the liberal values of the bourgeoisie dominated the Austro-Hungarian Empire, and the Hapsburg monarchy adjusted to constitutional government. However, Emperor Francis Joseph (1848—1916) largely ignored it and proceeded to rule by decree when parliament was not in session. At the same time, the problem of the minorities continued to trouble the empire. The granting of universal male suffrage in 1907 led many nationalities to lobby[①] in the parliament for autonomy. This led prime ministers after 1900 to ignore the parliament and increasingly rely on imperial emergency decrees to govern.

In Russia, after the assassination of Alexander Ⅱ in 1881, his son and successor, Alexander Ⅲ (1881—1894) quickly turned to the repressive measures of earlier tsars.

① lobby：游说。

Believing that his father's death was the result of too much talk about further reform following the abolition of serfdom, he sought to achieve stability by using the Orthodox Church and the police. Advocates of a constitutional tsar and social reform, and revolutionary groups were persecuted. After the death of Alexander Ⅲ, his weak son and successor, Nicholas Ⅱ (1894—1917), was convinced that the absolute power of the autocracy should be preserved.

Section Four Anxiety and Tension (1894—1914)

Even though many Europeans in the last decade of the 19th century still believed that they were living in an age of stability and prosperity, there had been widespread anxieties and tensions throughout the Western World. With the rise of New Imperialism and creation of empires, rivalries intensified and world conflicts were impending. The unrest of the age was best embodied in the intellectual and cultural developments, characterised by confusion and anxiety.

The cultural life of Europe in the decades before 1914 reflects similar dynamic tensions. Despite the appearance of progress, European philosophers, writers, and artists were advancing cultural expressions that questioned traditional ideas and values and undermined public confidence. By 1914, many intellectuals had a sense of unease about the direction in which society was heading and a feeling of imminent catastrophe. They proved incredibly prophetic.

Intellectual and Cultural Developments Ever since the last decade of the 19th century, a new mood of cheerfulness began to make itself felt in the Western world. Economic growth, improved living standards, and development of education made people believe that they were living in an age of certainty and prosperity. But the apparent gaiety was only superficial. Near the end of the century, an alternative view of the physical universe, new views of human nature, and radically innovative forms of literature and art broke through old beliefs and opened the way to a modern consciousness. They provoked a sense of confusion and anxiety before 1914 that would become even more evident after the war.

Development in Sciences. The 19th century was an era that witnessed unprecedented scientific progress. Many people believed that by applying already known scientific laws, human beings would be able to achieve a complete understanding of the physical world and an accurate picture of reality. The new physics dramatically altered that belief.

By the end of the 19th century, serious challenges emerged to the principal intellectual foundation of the 19th century, the Newtonian view of the universe as a giant machine in which time, space, and matters were objective realities and the belief that matters were composed of indivisible and solid material bodies called atoms. By the

end of the century, some scientists discovered that atoms were not simply hard, material bodies but small worlds containing such subatomic particles as electrons and protons that behaved in a seemingly random and inexplicable fashion.

The greatest challenge to the Newtonian synthesis came from the *Theory of Relativity* by Albert Einstein(1879－1955). Albert Einstein put forward the *Special Theory of Relativity*① in 1905. In this theory, Einstein discussed the relationship of matter and energy and formulated an equation to explain the relationship: $E=mc^2$②. He held that neither space nor time had an existence independent of human experience. Moreover, matter and energy reflected the relativity of time and space. In 1916, Einstein advanced his other famous theory, *General Theory of Relativity*③, in which he formulated a new view of the universe. He frowned on Newton's theory of gravitation and theorised that gravity is a geometric property of space and time. He showed that the curvature of space-time is directly related to mass, momentum, and energy.

Sigmund Freud and Psychoanalysis. Although poets and mystics had revealed a world of unconsciousness, most intellectuals under the impact of the Enlightenment continued to believe that human beings responded to conscious motives in a rational manner. At the end of the 19th and beginning of the 20th centuries, the Viennese doctor Sigmund Freud(1856－1939) put forth a series of theories that undermined belief in the rational nature of the human mind. His major ideas were published in 1900 in his *The Interpretation of Dreams*④, which contained the basic foundation of what came to be known as psychoanalysis.

According to Freud, human behaviour was strongly determined by the unconscious, by former experiences and inner forces of which people were largely oblivious. A human being's inner life was a battleground of three contending forces: the id, the ego, and the superego⑤. The id was the centre of unconscious drives ruled by what Freud termed the pleasure principle. The id contained all kinds of lustful drives and desires as well as crude appetites and impulses. The ego was the seat of reason and hence the coordinator of the inner life. It was governed by the reality principle, which meant that people at times rejected pleasure so that they might live together in society. The superego was the

---

① *Special Theory of Relativity*：狭义相对论

② $E=mc^2$：质能等价理论，能量＝ 质量×光速的平方。

③ *General Theory of Relativity*：广义相对论。

④ *The Interpretation of Dreams*：《梦的解析》，心理学的经典书籍，是西格蒙德·弗洛伊德的著作之一。该书开创了弗洛伊德的"梦的解析"理论，被作者本人描述为"理解潜意识心理过程的捷径"。

⑤ the id, the ego and the superego：本我，自我和超我。the id：为本能冲动的根源，按照快乐原则行事，强烈要求得到自我满足；the ego：自我，弗洛伊德人格结构理论中的概念之一。自我指自己可意识到自我思考、感觉、判断或记忆的活动，其机能是寻求"本我"冲动得以满足，它遵循的是"现实原则"，为本我服务；the superego：超我，弗洛伊德人格结构理论中的概念之一。超我在人格结构中代表理想的部分，它是个体在成长过程中通过内化社会道德规范和文化环境的价值观念而形成的，其机能主要在监督管束自己的行为。超我的特点是追求完美。

locus of conscience and represented the inhibitions and moral values that society, in general, and parents, in particular, imposed on people. The superego served to force the ego to curb the unsatisfactory drives of the id.

Freud's explorations of the world of the unconscious had a profoundly upsetting impact on Europeans' conception of themselves. Freud himself viewed his theories as a great blow to human pride, to "man's craving for grandiosity".

Social Darwinism and Racism. In the second half of the 19th century, the application of Darwin's principle of organic evolution to the social order led to the emergence of Social Darwinism①. According to the theory, persons, groups, and races are subject to the same laws of natural selection as Charles Darwin had perceived in plants and animals in nature. According to the theory, which was popular in the late 19th and early 20th centuries, the weak were diminished and their cultures delimited, while the strong grew in power and in cultural influence over the weak. Social Darwinists believed that human life in society was a struggle for existence according to the theory of "survival of the fittest"②, a phrase put forward by the British philosopher and scientist Herbert Spencer.

The emergence and development of social Darwinism revived racism, which was far from being new in Western civilisation. Perhaps nowhere was the combination of extreme nationalism and racism more evident than in Germany where racist nationalism was expressed in volkish thought. The concept of the Volk③(nation, people, or race) had been an underlying idea in German history since the beginning of the 19th century. According to Houston Stewart Chamberlain (1855—1927), a British-born Germanophile④ political philosopher, modern-day Germans were the only pure successors of the Aryans⑤ who were portrayed as the true and original creators of Western culture. The Aryan race, under German leadership, must be prepared to fight for Western civilisation and save it from the destructive assaults of such inferior races as Jews, Negroes, and Orientals. Chamblain's theory had a great impact on pan-German and German nationalist thought, particularly Adolf Hitler's National Socialist movement.

The Culture of Modernity. At the same time as Freud, social thinkers were breaking with the Enlightenment view of human nature and society, artists and writers were rebelling against traditional forms of artistic and literary expression, thus giving

---

① Social Darwinism：社会达尔文主义，19 世纪的社会文化进化理论，因和达尔文生物学理论有关系而有此名。

② survival of the fittest：适者生存。

③ Volk：（德语）民族，人民。

④ Germanophile：亲德派。

⑤ Aryan：雅利安人，属高加索人种（白色人种）。该人种身材较大，皮肤浅白，面长多毛，鼻骨高，瞳孔颜色浅，发色多变。原居于今天俄罗斯南部乌拉尔山脉附近的古代部落，使用印欧语系的语言，被认为是印欧语系民族的共同祖先。

rise to the great cultural revolution called Modernism[①].

Throughout much of the late 19th century, literature was dominated by Naturalism[②] which applied scientific reasoning to the realistic world. In literature, it extended the tradition of realism, aiming at an even more faithful, unselective representation of reality without moral judgment. Naturalism differed from realism in its assumption of scientific determinism, which led naturalistic authors to emphasise man's accidental, physiological nature rather than his moral or rational qualities. Individual characters were described as helpless victims of heredity and environment, motivated by strong instinctual drives from within and distressed by social and economic pressures from without. Naturalism is a type of "realism" usually characterised by a pessimistic world view.

At the turn of the century, a new group of writers, known as the symbolists, reacted against realism. As a school for poetry creation, symbolism was characterised by its distinctive consciousness of modernity. Symbolism[③] called for the poets to reject the demand of naturalist literature. Poetry, they argued, should seek the reality of the heart, and bestow abstract conception with specific forms. In the works of the symbolist poet, W. B. Yeats, poetry ceased to be part of popular culture because only through a knowledge of the poet's personal language could one hope to understand what the poet was saying.

Impressionism[④] was an art movement which stemmed from France in the late period of 19th century and reached its summit in the 1870s influencing all of Europe. Impressionist painters like Pissarro sought to accurately and objectively record visual reality in terms of transient effects of light and colour. They put priority to the visual sense and pursued the instant feeling in the painting process. These artists recorded the flickering shadows on canvas in a seemingly casual way. Throughout his long career, Claude Monet (1840—1926), founder of impressionism, retained a total fidelity to visual perception. His preoccupation with the effects of light and colour reached its most complete expression in his numerous paintings of water-lilies in his garden. In many of his paintings, he tried to capture in paint the effect of the shimmering, ever-changing appearance of water, leaves, and blossoms.

---

① Modernism：现代主义，20世纪以来具有前卫特色、与传统文艺分道扬镳的各类美术派别和思潮，又称现代派。

② Naturalism：自然主义，源自卢梭等，主张教育应返归自然，应与自然的人类相结合，重视活动与经验的学习，自我的陶冶。

③ Symbolism：象征主义，19世纪末产生于法国的文学艺术运动。它在巴黎的知识界影响很大，并对20世纪美学的发展起了一定的推动作用。

④ Impressionism：印象主义，19世纪后半期到20世纪初期流于法国及欧美乃至世界的一种艺术流派和文艺思潮。

Postimpressionism emerged by the end of 19th century and extended beyond impressionism. The artists from this school pursued pure emotional experience in their artistic creation. The postimpressionists recorded their personal feeling of reality rather than copied objects. A famous post-impressionist was the tortured and tragic figure, Vincent van Gogh (1853－1890). For van Gogh, art was a spiritual experience. He maintained that artists should paint what they felt. In his *Starry Night*①, he painted a sky alive with whirling stars that overwhelmed the huddled buildings in the village below.

The Spanish artist Pablo Picasso (1881－1973) and the French painter Georges Braque (1882－1963) developed a new style in painting between 1909 and 1914, which was called cubism. Like the impressionists and postimpressionists, the cubists sought to express the reality based on their emotion. Moreover, they probed into the interaction between the flat canvas and the tridimensional world. Picasso's 1907 work *Les Demoiselles d'Figure*② was called the first cubist painting.

The modern artist's flight from "visual reality" reached a high point in 1910 with the beginning of abstract painting. A Russian who worked in Germany, Vastly Kandinsky (1866－1944), was one of the founders of abstract expressionism③. As is evident in his *Painting with White Border*, Kandinsky sought to avoid representation altogether. He believed that art should speak directly to the soul. To do so, it must avoid any reference to visual reality and concentrate on colour.

About the same time painters in France were developing the style we call impressionism. Claude Debussy (1862－1918), a young French composer, began to break new musical ground. Abandoning the concept of the development of themes in a systematic musical argument which lay behind classical sonata④ form and romantic symphonic structure, he aimed for a constantly changing flow of sound.

At the beginning of the 20th century, developments in music paralleled those in painting. Expressionism in music was a Russian creation, the product of the composer Igor Stravinsky (1882－1971) and the Ballet Russe⑤, the dancing company of Sergei Diaghilev (1872－1929). Together they revolutionised the world of music with Stravinsky's ballet

---

① *Starry Night*:《星夜》,凡·高的代表作之一。

② *Les Demoiselles d'Avignon*:《阿维农姑娘》,毕加索作品,被认为是立体主义的第一幅作品。

③ abstract expressionism: 抽象表现主义,二战后直到20世纪60年代早期的一种绘画流派。"抽象表现主义"这个词用以定义一群艺术家所作的大胆挥洒的抽象画。他们的作品或热情奔放,或安宁静谧,都是以抽象的形式表达和激起人的情感。

④ sonata:奏鸣曲。

⑤ Ballet Russe: 俄罗斯芭蕾舞团。俄罗斯艺术活动家谢尔盖·佳吉列夫(Sergei Diaghilev)于1909年在巴黎创立了俄罗斯芭蕾舞团。在20世纪初的世界歌剧史上,俄罗斯芭蕾舞团是一个重要的艺术团体,它的演职人员包括作曲家德彪西、斯特拉文斯基等人,毕加索曾任剧团的布景设计。

The Rites of Spring[①]. Constantly changing, immensely complex, and frequently violent, his rhythmic patterns conveyed a sense of barbaric frenzy that was enhanced by the weight of sound obtained from the use of a vast orchestra. At the premiere on May 29, 1913, the pulsating rhythms, sharp dissonances, and unusual dancing overwhelmed the Paris audience and caused a riot at the theatre.

Politics: New Directions and New Uncertainties The period between 1894 and 1914 was one when progress slowed and uncertainties intensified. After 1894, liberals in the Western society moved in new directions. With their newfound voting rights, workers elected socialists who called for new reforms when they took their places in legislative bodies. In central and eastern Europe, tensions increased as authoritarian governments refused to satisfy the demands of reformers. Outside Europe, a new giant emerged in the Western world: United States.

Great Britain: The Transformation of Liberalism. Under the pressure of trade unions and the Labour Party, liberalism in Britain experienced noticeable transformations. Both the British trade unions and Fabian Socialism[②](a doctrine that came into being around 1884) advocated evolution toward a socialist state by democratic means. In 1900, representatives of the trade unions and Fabian Socialists united to form the Labour Party. By 1906 twenty-nine members were elected to the House of Commons.

The Liberals, who held the government from 1906 to 1914, realised that they would have to enact a programme of social welfare, otherwise they would lose the support of the workers. Under the leadership of David Lloyd George (1863—1945), the Liberals voted for a series of social reforms. Liberalism, which had been based on the principle that the government that governs least governs best, was transformed.

Growing Tensions in Germany. With the expansion of industry and cities came the general call for further steps to democratisation. However, conservative forces, especially the landed nobility and representatives of heavy industry, two of the powerful ruling groups in Germany, tried to block it by supporting William Ⅱ's (1888—1918) activist foreign policy of finding Germany's "place in the sun"[③]. Expansionism would distract people from further democratisation.

The tensions in German society brought by the conflict between modernisation and traditionalism were also embodied in a new, radicalised, right-wing politics. A number of nationalist pressure groups emerged to support nationalistic goals. Such groups as the

① *The Rites of Spring*：斯特拉文斯基的芭蕾舞剧《春之祭》，被评为对西方音乐历史影响最大的五十部作品之首。

② Fabian Socialism：费边社会主义，19世纪后期，流行于英国的一种主张采取渐进措施对资本主义实行点滴改良的资产阶级社会主义思潮。

③ place in the sun：太阳下的地位，显要的地位。

Pan-German League stressed strong German nationalism and advocated imperialism as a tool to overcome social divisions and unite all classes. They were also anti-Semitic① and denounced Jews as the destroyers of the national community.

Industrialisation and Revolution in Russia. In the process of industrialisation, which occurred to Russia late, an industrial working class came into being and socialist parties were established, wishing to overthrow the tsarist regime and establish peasant socialism. Their growing opposition to the tsarist authority, together with Russia's defeat at the hands by the Japanese in 1904—1905, finally led to revolution in 1905. After the revolution, Nicholas Ⅱ (1894—1917) issued the *October Manifesto*, in which he promised to guarantee civil liberties, freedom of speech, press, and assembly, to establish a broad franchise, and to create a legislative body, the Duma②, whose members would be popularly elected and whose approval would be necessary before the enactment of any legislation. However, a real constitutional monarchy proved short-lived. By 1907, the tsar had curtailed the power of the Duma, and he fell back on the army and bureaucracy to rule Russia.

Rise Of The United States. During the period from 1865 to 1914, the United States witnessed dramatic changes. By the eve of World War Ⅰ, the country had completed its transformation from an agrarian economy to a mighty industrial power. By 1914, the United States had become the world's richest nation and enjoyed a high degree of urbanisation.

Despite the social progress and industrial prosperity, there were serious problems, posing threat to social stability of the United States. The gap between the rich and the poor became increasingly wide. In 1890, the richest 9 percent of the Americans owned an incredible 71% of all the wealth. Labour unrest over unsafe working conditions, strict work discipline, and periodical cycles of devastating unemployment led workers to organise. By the turn of the century, the American Federation of Labour was established to represent labour's voice.

Growth of Canada. Canada faced problems of national unity at the end of the 19th century. At the beginning of 1870, the Dominion of Canada consisted of four provinces: Quebec, Ontario, Nova Scotia, and New Brunswick. After two more provinces in 1871—Manitoba and British Columbia—were added, the Dominion of Canada extended from the Atlantic to the Pacific.

Real unity was difficult to achieve, however, because of the distrust between the

---

① anti-Semitic：反犹太主义的，对仇恨犹太人或犹太教的思想与行为的总称，在各个不同历史时期有不同的动机和表现形式。虽然犹太人与阿拉伯人同属闪族，但通常反闪族主义指的是反犹太主义。剥削阶级仇视排斥和迫害犹太人的种族主义思想和政策，表现为对犹太人的歧视、限制和隔离，乃至排斥、驱逐和灭绝。

② Duma：杜马，沙俄议会下院，第一届杜马是沙皇尼古拉斯二世在1906年成立的。

English-speaking and French-speaking peoples of Canada. Wilfred Laurier (1896－1911), who served as the first French-Canadian prime minister in 1896, succeeded in reconciling Canada's two major groups. During his administration, industrialisation boomed and immigrants from Europe helped to populate Canada's vast territories.

The New Imperialism Between 1880 and 1914, Western powers started imperial expansion, "new imperialism", to satisfy their demand for control over new territories in Asia, Africa, and the Pacific. They gained increasing dominance over much of the rest of the world, taking with them Western culture and institutions to the indigenous societies.

The economic motivation for the new imperialism was clearly seen. Due to the rapid expansion of industry in Europe and the United States, the West was engaged in imperial expansion hoping that they could find new markets, new sources of raw materials, and new investment outlets for surplus capital.

Nationalism was probably a greater drive behind the new imperialism. As European affairs grew tense, ambitious European states competed to establish colonies abroad that served as ports and fuelling stations for their navies. These new ports also served to demonstrate international power.

Then, too, imperialism was tied to Social Darwinism and racism. Social Darwinists proposed that nations that were strong and successful at expanding industry and empire would survive while others would not; they maintained that superior races should control inferior ones by military force indicating national strength and power.

Religious zeal also played an important role in the shaping of new imperialism. Most Europeans considered it their duty to "civilise" "ignorant" peoples. This notion of the "white man's burden"[①] helped at least the more idealistic individuals to rationalise imperialism in their own minds. Nevertheless, the belief that the superiority of their civilisation obligated them to impose modern industry, cities, and new medicines on supposedly primitive nonwhites, even if they had to be killed to do so, was yet another form of racism.

For many reasons the new imperialism had a dramatic effect on Africa and Asia as European powers competed for control over these two continents.

International Rivalry and the Coming of War Between 1871 and 1914, the Western world was characterised by a period of long peace. This state of international relationships featuring calm and stability was brought about mainly by Bismarck, the Iron Chancellor of Germany. When he was forced to resign in 1890, Europe grew out of control and a world war was impending.

---

① white man's burden：白种人的责任，种族主义辩护者声称，将西方教育与文明传播给被视为落后的民族是白种人的责任。

Aware of the fact that the unification and later the rise of Germany as the most powerful state had endangered the European balance of power, Bismarck became preoccupied with protecting his country by making allies and isolating France. He entered into a pact with Austria-Hungary in 1879. The inclusion of Italy in 1882 transformed the pact into a Triple Alliance. This committed Germany, Austria-Hungary, and Italy to support the existing political order while providing a defensive alliance against France. In 1887, Bismarck bullied Russia into signing a secret agreement, the Reinsurance Treaty, which guaranteed neutrality in the event of a war with France. The Bismarckian system of alliances succeeded initially in preserving peace and the status quo. But it proved short-lived when Emperor William Ⅱ dismissed Bismarck in 1890 and began to chart a new direction for Germany's foreign policy.

Between 1890 and 1907, Europe went through a diplomatic revolution. The Germans lost the friendship of Russia and Italy. In 1894, France and Russia concluded a military alliance. Britain abandoned her isolation to enter into agreement with Russia and France. In 1907, Britain and France concluded a similar agreement with Russia, thereby forming the so-called *Triple Entente*①. Europe became divided into two opposing camps that became more and more unwilling to compromise. When the members of the two alliances became involved in a new series of crises between 1908 and 1913 over the struggle for the control of the remnants of the Ottoman Empire in the Balkans②, the emphasis was no longer on avoiding a war but on preparing for one.

Crises in the Balkans (1908—1913) After 1890 closely allied enemies surrounded Germany due to its diplomatic policies. Emperor William Ⅱ's efforts to enhance German power by finding Germany's rightful "place in the sun" finally led to crisis in the Balkans.

Austria was concerned that Serbia had become a dangerous antagonist and was fearful that Turkey's influence in the Balkans would grow following the revolution in 1908 by the Young Turks③ who determined to modernise their nation. Austria-Hungary decided to annex Bosnia and Herzegovina. That move outraged nationalists in Russia, who believed that Russia should defend the interests of Slavs④ everywhere. They demanded an international conference, a proposal agreed by Britain and France.

---

① *Triple Entente*：三国协约，指1970年至第一次世界大战爆发期间，英、法、俄三国为对抗德、奥、意军事集团而形成的军事协议。

② the Balkans：巴尔干半岛，一个历史和地理上的名词，指欧洲的东南隅位于亚得里亚海和黑海之间的陆地。巴尔干半岛与伊比利亚半岛、亚平宁半岛并称为南欧三大半岛。

③ Young Turks：土耳其青年组织。土耳其国内各改革派集团组成的联盟，领导了国内反对奥斯曼苏丹阿卜杜勒·哈米德二世集权统治的革命运动，并最终在土耳其建立了立宪制政府。

④ Slavs：斯拉夫人，欧洲各民族和语言集团中人数最多的一支。其主要分布在欧洲东部和东南部，少数居于亚洲北部和太平洋地区。语言属印欧语系。

When William Ⅱ intervened and demanded that the Russians accept Austria's annexation of Bosnia and Herzegovina or face war with Germany, the Russians, who were weakened from their defeat in the Russo-Japanese War[①] in 1904 — 1905, were afraid to risk war and backed down. Humiliated, the Russians vowed revenge.

European attention returned to the Balkans in 1912 when the members of the Balkan League[②]—Serbia, Bulgaria, Greece, and Montenegro—defeated the Ottoman Empire in the first Balkan war. Montenegro opened hostilities by declaring war on Turkey on Oct. 8, 1912, and the other members of the league followed suit 10 days later. Before the victorious allies were able to agree on how to divide the conquered Ottoman territory, the Second Balkan War broke out. Serbia, Greece, and Romania attacked and defeated Bulgaria in June, 1913. The Second Balkan War was ended by a treaty, according to which Serbia got most of Macedonia and Greece and gained southern Macedonia as well as western Thrace and the Island of Crete.

The Balkan wars further damaged the balance between European powers and finally led to the outbreak of World War Ⅰ. Bulgaria, frustrated in Macedonia, looked to Austria for support, while Serbia, which had been forced by Austria to give up its Albanian conquests, regarded Vienna with greater hostility than ever. The heightened tensions in the Balkans reached their climax in World War Ⅰ, which was sparked by the assassination of the Austrian heir-apparent by a Serb[③] in Sarajevo, Bosnia, on June 28, 1914.

Chapter Review

This chapter was dedicated to the different orientations in which political, diplomatic and cultural developments were advancing between 1815 and 1914. Despite efforts made to restore old orders from 1815 to 1850, Europe was occasionally shaken by revolts and revolutions. The spirit of revolution was also evident in the rise of Romanticism in literature and art. The age from 1850 to 1870 was a period of nationalism, in which many changes sought by the liberals and nationalists during the first half of the 19th century came true. The same period also witnessed the rapid development of science and the shift of literature and art from Romanticism to Realism. The brief period of progress from 1871 to 1894 was immediately followed by the tension and anxiety before 1914, which was evident in the confusion in scientific, literal and artistic developments.

---

① Russo-Japanese War：日俄战争。1905～1905年，日本与沙皇俄国为了侵占中国东北和朝鲜，在中国东北的土地上进行了一场帝国主义战争，史称“日俄战争”，以沙皇俄国的失败而告终。

② Balkan League：巴尔干同盟。保加利亚、塞尔维亚、希腊和黑山为反对土耳其而建立的政治军事联盟。

③ Serb：塞尔维亚人，南斯拉夫人的一支，主要聚居在巴尔干半岛和中欧。塞尔维亚人是塞尔维亚的主要民族，黑山、波斯尼亚和黑塞哥维那的主要民族之一，也是克罗埃西亚、马其顿共和国和斯洛文尼亚的主要少数民族。

Exercise

Ⅰ. *According to the information provided in this chapter, choose the correct alternative among A, B, C, and D that can complete each of the following statements.*

1. Which of the following statements concerning early socialism is false?
   A. Early socialism is a force for change.
   B. The early socialists were romantics.
   C. The early socialists wanted to introduce equality into the society.
   D. Early socialists were for private property.
2. Romantic writers emphasised emotion and sentiment in their works. An important example for Romantics was the tragic figure in *The Sorrows of the Young Werther*, a novel by the great German writer ________.
   A. John Wolfgang von Goethe　　B. Walter Scott
   C. Gustave Flaubert　　D. William Wordsworth
3. Which of the following statements concerning *The Communist Manifesto* is wrong?
   A. It was published in 1848.
   B. It was an important symbol of the birth of Marxism.
   C. It advocated peaceful means in fighting against capitalism.
   D. It was written by Karl Max and Friedrich Engels.
4. Which of the following statements about Jean-Francois Millet is false?
   A. He was French.
   B. He was preoccupied with rural scenes.
   C. He was a sheer romanticist.
   D. He was especially interested in peasants labouring in the fields.
5. According to Freud, the three contending forces in human beings' inner life do not include ________.
   A. the id　　B. the ego
   C. the superego　　D. the unconscious

Ⅱ. *Fill in the blanks with what you have learned in this chapter.*

1. One method used by the great powers to maintain the new status quo after the Napoleonic war was ________, according to which Great Britain, Russia, Prussia, and Austria (and later France) agreed to meet periodically in conferences to discuss their common interests.
2. To the focus on emotion and sentiment of the romantics could be added an attraction to the bizarre and unusual. In an exaggerated form, this preoccupation gave rise to so called ________ literature, as shown in the short

stories by the American Edgar Allan Poe.

3. Literary realists in the mid-19th century sought to avoid sentimental language and advocated careful observation and accurate description, an approach that led them to prefer ________ and ________ to poetry.
4. According to the ________ theory of Albert Einstein, neither space nor time had an existence independent of human experience.
5. The defeat of the Russians by the ________ in 1904—1905 led anti-government forces to rebel against the tsarist regime. After a general strike in October 1905, the government capitulated.

Ⅲ. *According to what you have learned, answer the following questions briefly in your own words.*

1. What is the political contention of liberalism?
2. Why was early socialism also known as Utopian socialism?
3. Why did some people initially object to Darwin's theory of Organic Evolution?
4. What is naturalism? What is the difference between naturalism and realism?
5. What impact did social Darwinism have on Adolf Hitler's National Socialist movement?

Ⅳ. *With critical analysis, answer the following essay questions in your own words.*

1. What distinguished the Second Industrial Revolution from the First?
2. What gave rise to the New Imperialism?

Ⅴ. *Work in small groups and make comparisons based on the following topic.*

Compare Freud's psychoanalysis and his *Interpretation of Dreams* with *Zhou Gong's Dictionary on Interpretation of Dreams* (《周公解梦》) in China's West Zhou Dynasty.

Voices on Key Points

Suppression, Revolution, and Romanticism

Whatever the immediate gains and losses, the dangers to our safety arising from political suppression are always greater than the dangers to the safety resulting from political freedom. Suppression is always foolish. Freedom is always wise.

——Alexander Meiklejohn

To say the word Romanticism is to say modern art—that is, intimacy, spirituality, colour, aspiration towards the infinite, expressed by every means available to the arts.

——Charles Baudelaire

In Romanticism, the main determinant is the mood, the atmosphere. And in that regard, you could also describe Schubert as a Romantic.

——Dietrich Fischer-Dieskau

Age of Nationalism and Realism

Extreme nationalism and Bolshevism have broken up the old world, a new world is in the making. It is literally true that old things are passing away; all things may become new, granted we have wise, unselfish, and determined guides.

——John Raleigh Mott

Nationalism—in other words, the dividing of the church into bodies—consisting of such and such a nation, is a novelty, not above three centuries old, although many dear children of God are found dwelling in it.

——John Nelson Darby

Nations whose nationalism is destroyed are subject to ruin.

——Muammaral-Gaddafi

True realism consists in revealing the surprising things which habit keeps covered and prevents us from seeing.

——Jean Cocteau

I believe realism is nothing but an analysis of reality. Film scripts have a synthetical constitution.

——Manuel Puig

Suggested Reading

1. Sisman, Adam. *The Friendship: Wordsworth and Coleridge*. New York: Viking, 2007.
2. 陈伯通:《法国浪漫主义文学旗手雨果》,商务印书馆 1984 年版。
3. 杜瑞清等:《欧洲浪漫主义文学》,陕西人民出版社 2002 年版。
4. 石昭贤等编:《现当代外国现实主义文学四十讲》,贵州人民出版社 1984 年版。
5. 赵克毅、辛益编著:《意大利统一史》,河南大学出版社 1987 年版。

Chapter Ten World Wars and Post-war Era (1914—2000)

The armed conflict that raged throughout Europe from 1914 until 1918 put to rest forever the notion that war was a heroic rite of passage conferring nobility and glory. ①

Learning objectives

After reading this chapter, you will be able to:

1. *Be acquainted with the causes and impacts of World War Ⅰ and World War Ⅱ;*
2. *Understand the chaotic and irrational features of cultural and intellectual developments from 1914 to 1945;*
3. *Identify the underlying conflicts and tensions that finally led to the Cold War;*
4. *Be familiar with new developments in art and literature in Western World after World War Ⅱ, which was characterised by great diversity.*

① Lawrence S. Cunningham & John J. Reich, *Culture & Values*, Volume Ⅱ: *A Survey of the Humanities with Readings*, Boston: Wadsworth, Cengage Learning, 2009, p. 531.

19世纪后期欧洲的稳定和进步并没能持续太久,欧洲乃至整个西方世界被冲突和战争的阴云所笼罩。第二次工业革命之后,欧洲列强经历了不同程度的发展,然而,正是这种各国经济实力和军事实力发展的不均衡,加之扩张主义思潮的推波助澜,最终使欧洲列强从冲突走向了战争。

1914～1945年两次世界大战期间,野蛮的阴影始终笼罩着欧洲,其毁灭性无法估量。此外,经历过两次世界大战之后,欧洲国家大都被严重削弱,世界舞台的重心也相应地由西欧转移到了美国和苏联。二战结束之后,美、苏两国之间在意识形态领域的冲突加剧,两国进入旷日持久的冷战,直至1991年苏联解体才结束。与此同时,欧洲各国正逐步向政治和经济一体化的方向迈进。两次世界大战期间,文化和艺术领域也呈现了相应的发展趋势。两次世界大战给人们带来的幻想破灭感使文学家和艺术家们痴迷于荒诞主义题材,并关注人的无意识领域,而战后的西方文化和艺术则呈现出一种明显的多元化的发展态势。

Prior to 1914, the dominant mood in Europe was one of pride in the accomplishments of Western civilisation and confidence in its future progress. Advances in science and technology, the rising standard of living, the spread of democratic institutions, and Europe's position of power in the world all contributed to a sense of optimism. However, the mythic power of nationalism and the primitive appeal of conflict were driving European civilisation to the abyss. The two world wars rocked the 20th century and changed Europe and the world as a whole.

Section One Wars and Revolutions (1914—1945)

What many Europeans liked to call their "age of progress" in the decades before 1914 was also an age of anxiety and uncertainties. The feverish competition for colonies markedly increased the existing rivalries among the European states. After 1914, Europeans began to demolish their civilisation on the battle grounds of Europe in World War Ⅰ and World War Ⅱ.

World War Ⅰ Though not really the "first world war", World War Ⅰ had an impact far exceeding the Seven Years' War, the Napoleonic Wars, and other previous global war fares. It quickly became a "people's war" in which civilians as well as soldiers participated in violent demands for extermination of the enemies. It bore fruit in an epidemic of revolutions. In such ways it settled the pattern for an age of violence that continued through the greater part of the 20th century. Even more extraordinary was the fact that World War Ⅰ marked the close of a long era of peace.

Causes of the War. On June 28, 1914, in Sarajevo, the capital of the Austro-Hungarian province of Bosnia, a nineteen-year-old Serb assassinated Archduke Franz Ferdinand, heir to the Austrian throne. Austria declared war on Serbia and World War Ⅰ broke out. Although the assassination immediately led to the War, there were also

other underlying forces that were driving Europeans toward the war.

A major inner cause that led to the outbreak of World War Ⅰ was the uneven economic and political developments of European powers by the end of the 19th century. A young unified state, Germany had surpassed such European powers as Britain and France by 1914 in industrial production. Therefore, the German Empire was eager for more dominance to match the greatness of its economic strength.

National, imperial, and economic rivalry underlay the developments that led to the outbreak of World War Ⅰ. The increasingly militant nationalism that had been growing since the mid-19th century encouraged nations to view one another as dangerous rivals in the struggle for national power and prestige. The outburst of imperialism in the decades before 1914 pitted these nationalistic rivals against one another in the race to acquire colonies and expand their international influence. The growth of industrial and financial capitalism created a context of competitive economic struggle.

Course and Impact of the War. Despite the initial remarkable enthusiasm, the war proved a bloody disaster for soldiers from both sides. In 1916 and 1917, millions of young men were sacrificed in the search for the elusive breakthrough. In ten months at Verdun, 700,000 men lost their lives over a few miles of terrain.

The entry of the United States in the war transformed it into an ideological conflict between democracy and autocracy when President Wilson told the American people that they were fighting to "make the world safe for democracy". In 1917, German hostility brought the United States into the conflict in Europe. After the war ended in 1918, the *Treaty of Versailles*① was singed declaring the formal surrender of German and Austrian forces. However, World War Ⅰ forever changed modern warfare, introducing the concepts of total warfare and weapons of mass destruction②.

One of the most important consequences of the World War Ⅰ was the emergence of Socialist Russia. After the Romanov dynasty was overthrew in the February Revolution in 1917, a provisional government was established. In November, however, the Soviets under the direction of Lenin overthrew the provisional government and established the first communist regime in the world.

The Peace Settlement An assembly of nations was held in Paris from January to June 1919 for the purpose of drawing up the new European peace. Great powers like France, Britain, Italy and the United States undertook the primary task of the peace settlement, and small states, newly-formed states and non-European states also contributed to the deliberations.

---

① *Treaty of Versailles*:《凡尔赛条约》或《凡尔赛和约》,是第一次世界大战后,战胜国(协约国)对战败国(同盟国)的和约,它的主要目的是惩罚和削弱德国。

② total warfare and weapons of mass destruction:全面战争和大规模杀伤性武器。

The final peace settlement of Paris produced five separate treaties with the defeated nations—Germany, Austria, Hungary, Bulgaria, and Turkey. According to the *Treaty of Versailles* with Germany, signed on June 28, 1919, Germany had to: (1) make a down payment of £5 billion against a future bill, (2) hand over a significant proportion of their merchant ships, including all vessels of more than 1600 tons, (3) give up all German colonies, and (4) deliver coal to neighbouring countries.

The separate peace treaties made with the other Central Powers (Austria, Hungary, Bulgaria, and the Ottoman Empire) extensively redrew the map of Eastern Europe. Territorial rearrangements were also made in the Balkans. Romania acquired extra lands from Russia, Hungary, and Bulgaria. Serbia formed the centre of a new South Slav State, Yugoslavia, which joined Serbs, Croats, and Slovenes together.

Despite the end of the war, the peace settlement at Paris was far from enough to ensure sustained peace. The Germans viewed the *Treaty of Versailles* as a heavy blow and humiliation of their national pride. Many Germans viewed the *Peace of Versailles*① as a dictated peace and vowed to seek its revision. On the other hand, principal designers of the peace, Russia, the United States, and Britain backed off from guaranteeing enforcement of the peace treaties. The exclusion of Russia from the peace settlement, unwillingness of the United States to enforce the treaty, and the fact that Britain declined to guarantee it, meant that France had to stand alone to face its old enemy. The peace settlement was hoped, nevertheless, to be the basis for a lasting peace.

Resurgence and Economic Depression Taking into consideration the real ability of reparation of Germany, an international commission produced a new plan for reparations, named the Dawes plan②, in August 1924, which sought to end inflation and restore the economy in Germany. The plan drew up a more modest and realistic schedule of payments for Germany and extended loans of $ 200 million from American banks to set the plan in motion. The plan helped create a new era of European prosperity between 1924 and 1929.

The resurgence and stability of European economy was paralleled with new developments in European diplomacy. A spirit of international cooperation was fostered by the foreign ministers of Germany and France, Gustav Stresemann (1878—1920) and Aristide Briand (1862—1932), respectively, who concluded the *Treaties of Locarno*③ in 1925. According to these treaties, Germany, France, and Belgium promised never again

① 即 *Treaty of Versailles*。

② Dawes plan：道威斯计划，道威斯委员会提出解决德国赔款问题的报告。

③ *Treaties of Locarno*：洛迦诺公约，1925 年 10 月 16 日英、法、德、意、比、捷、波七国代表在瑞士洛迦诺举行的会议上通过的 8 个文件的总称。

to go to war against each other and to respect the demilitarised zone[①] that separated them. The borders of all three countries were "guaranteed" by Britain and Italy, who also took the responsibility of ensuring integrity of the demilitarised zone. After the conclusion of the treaty, "a spirit of Locarno", a friendly atmosphere initiated by the treaty, took effect and gave promise for a new age of security.

The economic prosperity of 1920s vanished overnight when Europe was stricken by the Great Depression[②] between 1929 and 1933, one of the most shattering experiences in the economic history of the modern world. The depression resulted mainly from a downturn in domestic economies and an international financial crisis created by the collapse of the American stock market in 1929.

The Great Depression resulted in an economic situation more chaotic than the governments were able to handle. Governments seemed powerless to deal with the crisis. The depression led to greater government intervention in the economy, even in countries like the United States that had a strong laissez-faire tradition. Protective tariffs were raised and a state-controlled economy became increasingly popular. Another effect was a renewed interest in Marxist doctrines since Marx had predicted that capitalism would destroy itself through overproduction. Communism took on new popularity, especially with workers and intellectuals. Finally, the Great Depression resulted in the rise of such dictatorial doctrines as militant expansionism and Fascism[③]. Militant expansionism was directed toward the conquest of neighbouring territories as a means of solving economic problems. Fascism was extreme right-wing dictatorial political system. Promising a way out of the Great Depression, Fascism came to win increasing popularity in the 1930s.

World War Ⅱ Hopes for Western civilisation progress turned out to be groundless since plans for economic reconstruction yielded to inflation and to an even more devastating Great Depression at the end of the 1920s. Likewise, confidence in political democracy was soon shattered by the rise of authoritarian governments. Authoritarian regimes in Germany and Italy finally led to the outbreak of World War Ⅱ, an even more devastating catastrophe. The 20th-century crisis, begun in 1914, seemed only to be worsening in 1939.

The Course of the War. Using Blitzkrieg[④], or lightning war, Hitler stunned

---

① demilitarised zone：非军事区。

② Great Depression：大萧条，1929～1933年之间全球性的经济大衰退。

③ Fascism：法西斯主义，是一种结合了社团主义、工团主义、独裁主义、极端民族主义、中央集权形式的社会主义、军国主义、反无政府主义、反自由放任的资本主义、反共产主义和反自由主义的政治哲学，可以视为是极端形式的集体主义。

④ Blitzkrieg：闪电战，也叫闪击战，是二次世界大战期间德军首创的一种战术。其特点是充分利用飞机、坦克的快捷优势，以突然袭击的方式制敌取胜。

Europe with the speed and efficiency of the German attack. On September 1, 1939, a long column of German tanks crossed the Polish border. After Hitler turned a deaf ear to a joint warning by Britain and France to Germany that she must cease her aggression, Neville Chamberlain (1937—1940) made a radio announcement that Britain was at war with Germany. Later France also entered the war.

Even though Britain and France declared war on Germany, they both followed the policy of appeasement① and Poland received little military assistance. In less than three weeks, Warsaw had been captured.

The war was widened when Hitler turned to the east and invaded the Soviet Union On June 22, 1941. The United States entered the war when Japanese carrier-based aircraft attacked the United States naval base at Pearl Harbour on December 7, 1941. After the Anti-Fascist Alliance was established, Hitler's failure was doomed. He committed suicide on April 30, 1945, two days after Mussolini had been shot by partisan Italian forces. On May 7, German commanders surrendered. The war in Europe was over. When the Americans dropped the newly developed bombs on Hiroshima and Nagasaki, the Japanese surrendered unconditionally on August 14. The war was over.

World War Ⅱ was one of the great watersheds of 20th-century geopolitical history. It led to the extension of the Soviet Union's power to Eastern European nations, enabled a communist movement eventually to take power in China, and marked a major transfer of power in the world from the Western European states to the United States and the Soviet Union.

Culture in an Era of Wars and Revolutions The two world wars struck people in the Western society with a strong sense of pessimism and despair. European intellectuals felt that they were living in a "broken world"②. The period between 1914 and 1945, characterised by wars and upheavals, threatened the destruction of some of the most basic ideals and institutions. Rumblings of a distant thunder forced men to question the inherently good and rational nature of human beings. Passions of war distorted the thinking of countless individuals and led them to conceive of their world as chaotic and irrational. Sense of despair, view of human beings as irrational and the world as chaotic were also evidenced by new cultural and intellectual trends during the period from 1914 to 1945.

Nightmares and New Vision: Art and Music. Artistic trends after 1914 were

① policy of appeasement：绥靖政策，第二次世界大战前夕欧美列强对希特勒的侵略行为所采取的政策。特点是姑息纵容后者的要求而不予制止。

② Marvin Perry, et al., *Western Civilization: Ideas, Politics, and Society*, New York: Houghton Mifflin Harcourt Publishing Company, 2008, p. 809.

largely a working out of the implications of pre-war developments. Abstract expressionism, for example, became more popular as many pioneering artists of the early 20th century matured between the two world wars. In addition, pre-war fascination with the absurd and the unconscious seemed even more appropriate after the nightmare landscapes of battlefronts. This gave rise to both the Dada Movement and Surrealism①.

Dadaism② was a movement to protest the madness of the war and its senseless slaughter. With nonsensical language, dissonant music and a completely iconoclastic③ attitude to the great masterpieces of the traditional culture, it explored a way to resist the "rational" warmongers and politicians, and it critically scrutinised tradition. The 1918 Berlin Dada Manifesto maintained that "Dada is the international expression of our times, the great rebellion of artistic movements". In the hands of Hannah Hoch (1889—1978), however, dada became an instrument to comment on women's roles in the new mass culture. Dada had far-reaching effects on the art of the 20th century. Its nihilistic④, antinationalistic critiques of society and its unrestrained attacks on all formal artistic conventions found no immediate inheritors, but its preoccupation with the bizarre, the irrational, and the fantastic bore fruit in the Surrealist Movement.

One of the most representative and creative of the dada artists was Marcel Duchamp (1887—1968). Duchamp originated two ideas in sculpture: sculpture with moving parts (mobiles) and sculptures constructed from pre-existing fabricated material originally intended for other purposes (ready-mades). Duchamp also gained notoriety for his whimsically irreverent attitude toward art, illustrated by his gesture of exhibiting a urinal at an art show as well as his humorous but lacerating spoofs of high culture, the most "dada" of which is his famous defacement of the *Mona Lisa*.

In the 1920s, a new stream called Surrealism came to the fore. Surrealists sought a reality beyond the material, sensible world and found it in the world of the unconscious through the portrayal of fantasies, dreams, or nightmares. Surrealism's emphasis was not on negation but on positive expression. The movement represented a reaction against what its members saw as the destruction wrought by the "rationalism" that had guided European culture and politics in the past and that had culminated in the horrors of World War Ⅰ. As stated by the major spokesman of the movement, the poet and

---

① Surrealism：超现实主义，在法国开始的文学艺术流派，源于达达主义，1920～1930年间盛行于欧洲文学及艺术界中。它的主要特征是以所谓"超现实"、"超理智"的梦境、幻觉等作为艺术创作的源泉，认为只有这种超越现实的"无意识"世界才能摆脱一切束缚，最真实地显示客观事实的真面目。

② Dadaism：达达主义艺术运动是1916～1924年流行于西方的一种虚无主义文艺流派。达达主义是一种无政府主义的艺术运动，它试图通过废除传统的文化和美学形式发现真正的现实。

③ iconoclastic：打破旧习的。

④ nihilistic：虚无的，无政府主义的。

critic André Breton (1896—1966), "surrealism was a means of reuniting conscious and unconscious realms of experience so completely that the world of dream and fantasy would be joined to the everyday rational world in 'an absolute reality, a surreality'."① Drawing heavily on theories adapted from Sigmund Freud, Breton saw the unconscious as the wellspring of the imagination. He defined genius in terms of accessibility to this normally untapped realm, which, he believed, could be attained by poets and painters alike.

By employing logic to depict the illogical, the surrealists created disturbing and evocative images. In its later period, Salvador Dali (1904—1989), a Spanish artist, joined the movement. Dali's artistic style derived mainly from his discovery of Sigmund Freud's writings on the erotic significance of subconscious imagery, and his affiliation with the Paris Surrealists, a group of artists and writers who sought to establish the "greater reality" of man's subconscious over his reason. In *The Persistence of Memory*②, Dali portrayed recognizable objects that have been divorced from their normal context. By placing these objects into unrecognizable relationships, Dali created a disturbing world in which the irrational had become tangible.

The move to Functionalism③ in modern architecture also became more widespread in the 1920s and 1930s. Functionalism meant that in architecture, the form of a building should be determined by practical considerations such as use, material, and structure, as distinct from the attitude that plan and structure must conform to a preconceived picture in the designer's mind. Frank Lloyd Wright (1869—1959) "championed an architecture that produced buildings designed for their specific function with an eye focused on the natural environment in which the building was to be placed and with a sensitivity to what the building should say"④. Under the doctrine of functionalism, art and engineering were to be unified, and all unnecessary ornamentation was to be stripped away. Especially important in the spread of functionalism was the Bauhaus school, founded in 1919 at Weimar, Germany, by the Berlin architect Walter Gropius who combined two schools, the Weimar Academy of Arts and the Weimar School of Arts and Crafts.

Modern art forms did not go unchallenged during the period from 1914 to 1945. Many traditionalists viewed modern arts as degeneracy and decadence. This was especially evident in the totalitarian state of Nazi Germany. In the 1920s, Weimar

---

① *Merriam Webster's Encyclopedia of Literature*, Springfield: Merriam-Webster, Incorporated, 1995.

② *The Persistence of Memory*:《记忆的永恒》是萨尔多·达利在1931年创作的油画作品。

③ Functionalism:功能主义(建筑)。功能主义就是要在设计中注重产品的功能性与实用性,即任何设计都必须保障产品功能及其用途的充分体现,其次才是产品的审美感觉。

④ Lawrence S. Cunningham & John J. Reich, *Culture & Values*, Volume Ⅱ: *A Survey of the Humanities with Readings*, Boston: Wadsworth Cengage Learning, 2008, p. 584.

Germany was one of the chief European centres for modern arts and sciences. Hitler and the Nazis rejected modern art as "degenerate" or "Jewish" art.

The revolution in art was paralleled to great changes in music initiated by Igor Stravinsky. But Stravinsky still wrote music in a definite key. The Viennese composer Arnold Schonberg (1874—1951) created a new method of composition based on a row, or series, of 12 tones—a method called atonality[①]. He was also one of the most influential teachers of the 20th century. Among his most significant pupils were Alban Berg and Anton Webern.

The Search for the Unconscious. Literary movements during the period of depression and the two world wars showed tendencies similar to those in art and music. The major novelists, poets, and dramatists came to be deeply concerned about the feelings, uncertainties, unconscious motives as well as the hope and destiny of human beings. Many were particularly interested in probing into the hidden secrets of the mind. These developments led to a searching of new methods and techniques in literary writing. One of its most apparent manifestations was in a "stream of consciousness"[②] technique in which the writer presented an interior monologue or a report of the innermost thoughts of each character.

The most famous example of "stream of consciousness" was written by James Joyce (1882—1941), an Irish exile, T. S Eliot (1888—1965), an American expatriate in London, and Virginia Woolf (1882—1941), an English novelist and critic. In the works of both James Joyce and T. S. Eliot, there was fragmentation of line and image, the abandonment of traditional forms, and overwhelming sense of alienation and homelessness. Many features of Virginia Wolf's novels like *Mrs. Dalloway* (1925), *To the Lighthouse* (1927), and *The Waves* (1931) have been highly praised. Particularly appreciated are her keen sense of narrative, wise and sophisticated perception of time shifts, rich and buoyant style of lyric poetry, and deep and thorough understanding of the textures of modern life.

The shift of focus from the conscious to the unconscious also led to greater popular interest in psychology. By the 1920s, Freud's ideas had been widely accepted. Psychoanalysis even developed into a major profession, especially in the United States. But Freud's ideas did not go unchallenged, even by his own pupils. One of the most prominent challenges came from Carl Jung.

A disciple of Freud, Carl Jung (1856—1961) proposed and developed the concepts

---

① atonality：无调性音乐，属于现代主义音乐的创作手法之一。它由19世纪后期音乐中变音体系的极度发展、调性的频繁变化、和弦结构的复杂化以及功能联系的消失等因素而逐步形成的。在无调性音乐中，音乐在任何一个音上开始或结束，无所谓主音与属音。

② stream of consciousness：意识流。文学作品中人物意识流动状态的描述手段。

of the extraverted and the introverted personality, archetypes[①], and the collective unconscious[②]. Jung's study of dreams led him to diverge sharply from Freud. Whereas for Freud the unconscious was the seat of repressed desires or appetites, for Jung, it was an opening to deep spiritual needs and ever-greater vistas for humans. Jung viewed the unconscious as twofold: a "personal unconscious" and a "collective unconscious", which existed at a deeper level of the unconscious. The collective unconscious was the repository of memories that all human beings share and consisted of archetypes, mental forms or images that appear in dreams. The archetypes are common to all people and have a special energy that creates myths, religions, and philosophies. Jung's work proved influential in psychiatry and in the study of religion, literature, and related fields.

The Heroic Age of Physics. The pre-war revolution in physics initiated by Albert Einstein and other scientists continued in the era of world wars and revolution. In fact, Ernest Rutherford (1871—1937), the British physicist who laid the groundwork for the development of nuclear physics, dubbed the 1920s the "heroic age of physics".

Instead of challenging only traditional physics, Einstein practically rocked the entire structure of science before his age. It had a major influence in precipitating other developments in physics. In 1927, the German physicist Werner Heisenberg (1901—1976) published his indeterminacy, or uncertainty, principle[③], upon which he built his philosophy and for which he is best known. In essence, Heisenberg posited that the old mechanistic principle of universal causation was no longer entirely valid. The phenomena of the subatomic world could not be predicted with certainty but could be dealt with only in terms of possibility. This principle shattered confidence in predictability and dared to propose that uncertainty was the underlying principle of all the physical laws.

Section Two The Cold War and the New Era of the Western World (1945—2000)

World War Ⅱ was ended, but only after tremendous sacrifices and costs. Much of European civilisation lay in ruins, and the old Europe had disappeared forever. Even before the last battles had been fought, the United States and the Soviet Union had arrived at different visions of the post-war world. Immediately after the war was ended,

---

① archetype：原型，荣格理论下集体无意识的主要内容，这一概念对于社会心理学有着深远的意义。在荣格看来，人们的个体行为和集体行为在很大程度上都是由无意识的原型所决定的。

② collective unconscious：集体无意识，瑞士心理学家、分析心理学创始人荣格的分析心理学用语。指影响个人观念的长期以来代代相传潜移默化产生的集体观。

③ indeterminacy principle：测不准原理，不确定性原理。

their differences led to an even more devastating conflict known as the Cold War. World War Ⅱ also destroyed Europeans' supremacy in world affairs. The rapid collapse of the colonial empires of the European nations signalled the end of an old era and the beginning of a new one.

The Cold War After World War Ⅱ, the work of reconstructing destroyed cities and returning economies to their peacetime functions went forward against a background of tension between the Soviet Union and the Western Democracies. This period was the most confrontational period of the Cold War, during which the superpowers extended their rivalry to more and more regions of the globe. Churchill's famous words produced a high-coloured description of the situation in those days, "from Stettin in the Baltic to Trieste in the Adriatic, an iron curtain has descended across the Continent."①

The Cold War adequately embodied the incompatible political ambitions of two nations—the United States and the Soviet Union based on their divergent historical experiences. It was not only the outcome of the ideological conflicts between the two powers, but also a product of their increasing desires for hegemony in the world. During the war years, both the capitalist and socialist countries worked together to fight against the Fascist forces. When the war was ended, however, the conflicts came to the fore.

Beginning with the disagreement on settlement of the Eastern Europe, the United States and the Soviet Union avoided direct military confrontation in Europe and engaged in actual combat operations only to keep allies from defecting to the other side. Thus the Soviet Union sent troops to preserve communist rule in East Germany (1953), Hungary (1956), Czechoslovakia (1968), and Afghanistan (1979). For its part, the United States helped overthrow a left-wing government in Guatemala (1954), supported an unsuccessful invasion of Cuba (1961), invaded the Dominican Republic (1965) and Grenada (1983), and undertook a long (1964—1975) and unsuccessful effort to prevent communist North Vietnam from bringing South Vietnam under its rule.

The Cold War began to break down in the late 1980s during the administration of Soviet leader Mikhail S. Gorbachev (1985—1991). Gorbachev's internal reforms had weakened his own Communist Party and allowed power to shift to Russia and the other constituent republics② of the Soviet Union. In late 1991 the Soviet Union collapsed and fifteen newly independent nations were born from its corpse, including a Russia with a democratically elected, anti-communist leader. The Cold War had come to an end.

Recovery and Renewal Within a few years after the defeat of Germany and Italy, economic revival brought renewed growth to the European society, although major differences remained between Western and Eastern Europe.

---

① 出自丘吉尔 1946 年 3 月发表的"铁幕"演说。

② constituent republics:(前)苏联的加盟共和国。

The Soviet Union: From Stalin to Khrushchev. Stalin's policy for economy succeeded to promote growth of heavy industry, but failed to pay sufficient attention to light industry and people's living standards. Consumer goods were scarce and housing remained a serious problem. In politics, during the time when Stalin was in power, he remained the undisputed master of the Soviet Union. He exercised sole authority and pitted his subordinates against one another.

After Stalin's death on March 5, 1953, a new collective leadership succeeded Stalin until Nikita Khrushchev (1894 — 1971) emerged as the chief Soviet policy-maker. Khrushchev extended the process of de-stalinisation by reducing the powers of the secret police and closing some of the Siberian prison camps. Economically, Khrushchev tried to attach more importance to light industry and consumer goods. However, his attempts proved less successful and damaged his reputation within the party. These failures, combined with increased military spending, hurt the Soviet economy. Foreign policy failures caused additional damage to Khrushchev's reputation among his colleagues. In 1964, he was forced out of office and the real power rested in the hands of Leonid Brezhnev (1906—1982), the "trusted" supporter of Khrushchev who had engineered his downfall.

Western Europe: The Revival and Unity. Within the context of the Cold War struggle, Western Europe survived the difficult years immediately following World War Ⅱ, recovered by the 1950s, and grew in new directions in the following decades.

The history of France from 1958 to 1969 was dominated by one man, Charles de Gaulle (1890—1970). In 1958, de Gaulle established the Fifth Republic as a presidential regime with an indirectly elected chief executive. de Gaulle rejuvenated French economy and increased French prestige among the Third World countries by consenting to Algerian independence. However, people's dissatisfaction with the inability of the government to deal with large government deficits and increasing cost of living finally forced de Gaulle to resign from office in April, 1969.

In Britain, the Labour Party swept to victory in elections held in July 1945, just as the war was coming to an end. The new Labour government, under Clement Atlee (1883—1967), the new prime minister, proceeded to enact the reforms that created a modern welfare state. The British welfare state became the norm for most European states after the war. The cost of building a welfare state at home forced the British to reduce expenses abroad. Economic necessity brought an end to the British Empire.

In the context of continuing economic problems, the Conservatives returned to power from 1951 to 1964. They extended the welfare state by determining to improve housing condition of the British. The British economy had recovered from the war at a slower rate, which masked a long-term economic decline. Underlying the problems was a deeper issue. As a result of World War Ⅱ, Britain had lost much of its pre-war

revenues from abroad but was left with a burden of debt from its many international commitments.

By the end of World War Ⅱ, Germany was divided into four occupation zones. In 1949, the three western zones were united into the Federal Republic of Germany, also known as Western Germany. Under Konrad Adenauer's (1876—1967) chancellorship, the West German Federal Republic experienced the "economic miracle". It was largely guided by the minister of finance, Ludwig Erhard. By 1955 the West German gross national product exceeded that of pre-war Germany. Real wages doubled between 1950 and 1965 even though work hours were cut by 20 percent. Unemployment fell from 8 percent in 1950 to 0.4 percent in 1965.

Europe after World War Ⅱ was moving in a direction of economic and political unity. The European Coal and Steel Community (ECSC) was formed in 1951 by the Netherlands, Belgium, Luxembourg, France, Italy and West Germany. Afterwards, the establishment of a "common market" in coal and steel among the member states of ECSC proved a major success. In 1957, the members of European Coal and Steel Community created the European Atomic Energy Community (EURATOM) to further European research on the peaceful uses of nuclear energy. In the same year, the same six members established the European Economic Community and collaborated to expand their integrated markets. This collaboration became known as The Common Market and worked to create a free flow of labour and capital, the eradication of restrictions on trade, joint investment practices and coordinated social welfare programmes.

Eastern Europe: Behind the Iron Curtain. Although Eastern Europe was also involved in the general European recovery from World War Ⅱ, their recuperation was slow and did not attain the remarkable results seen in Western Europe. One reason was the fact that Eastern Europe had not established a solid economic foundation before the war; as a result, the nations there had to surmount more difficulties than Western Europe during their recovery.

Eastern Europe achieved economic modernisation and boosted living standards during the 1950s and 1960s. Steady employment was ensured, the basic social services were extensive, inexpensive housing, and access to health and educational facilities were provided.

The pattern of economic and political developments in Eastern Europe was initially defined by the Soviet Union. Indeed, in the late 1950s and 1960s, the Soviet Union made it clear, particularly in Poland, Hungary, and Czechoslovakia, that it would not allow its Eastern European satellites to become independent of Soviet control.

The Emergence of a New Society A complex mixture of continuity and transformation characterised social and cultural trends in the years following 1945. The disillusionment and anxiety which marked the earlier decades of the 20th century still existed, yet a new sense of experimentation of productivity developed. Different from the trends generated in the difficult decades prior to World War Ⅱ, the subsequent productivity experimentation reflected the reality that the social turmoil had subsided and a greater sense of stability existed.

After World War Ⅱ, the social structure of European countries was changed. In addition to traditional groups such as businesspeople and professionals in law, medicine, and universities, a new group of managers and technicians became members of middle class. Changes also occurred to the lower classes. The number of industrial workers ceased increasing and even dwindled in certain regions. At the same time, a substantial increase in their real wages enabled the working classes to seek the consumption patterns of the middle class, leading to what some observers have called the "consumer society".

Increased incomes, together with shorter working hours, created an even greater market for mass leisure activities. All aspects of popular culture—music, sports, media—became commercialised and offered opportunities for leisure activities including concerts, sporting events, and television viewing. The post-war era also saw the growth of mass tourism. After the war, the combination of more vacation time, increased prosperity, and the flexibility provided by package tours with low-budget rooms enabled millions to realise their dreams of travels.

The 1960s witnessed a growing youth movement that questioned authority and fostered rebellion against the older generation. Spurred on by the Vietnam War and out of a growing political consciousness, the youth rebellion became a youth protest movement by the second half of the 1960s. After World War Ⅱ, European states began to create greater equality of opportunity in higher education by eliminating fees, and universities experienced an influx of students from the middle and lower classes. But it also brought problems. Classrooms with too many students, irresponsibility of professors to their courses, lack of democracy in university administration, and too many outdated courses led to an outburst of student revolts in the late 1960s. For many students, the calls for democracy within the universities were a reflection of their deeper concerns about the direction in which Western society was heading. Although student revolts fizzled out in the 1970s, the larger issues they raised were increasingly revived in the 1990s.

The End of the Cold War Mikhail Gorbachev, who came to power in the Soviet Union in 1985, eventually brought a dramatic end to the Cold War. His "New Thinking"① opened the door to a series of stunning changes.

---

① New Thinking：新思维，苏共中央总书记戈尔巴乔夫在任期间在政治、经济、外交领域提出的一系列改革思想。

Gorbachev's openness pleased neither Communist party hardliners nor Western-oriented supporters of capitalism. In a coup d'état staged in 1991, Gorbachev was replaced. Boris Yeltsin (1931 — 2007), who was elected President of the Russian Republic, held firm against the coup d'état. In October, the Soviet Union collapsed and was replaced by the loose Confederation of Independent States.

The fall of communism and the collapse of the Soviet Union meant the end of the Cold War, making any renewal of the global rivalry between two competing superpowers impossible. No one could know the implications of such fundamental changes, but it was clear that domestic politics, economic policies, and international relations would all now be different.

Eastern Europe: After the Fall. The collapse of Communist governments in Eastern Europe during the revolutions of 1989 brought a wave of euphoria① to Europe. In 1989 and 1990, new governments throughout Eastern Europe sought to scrap the remnants of the old system and introduce the democratic procedures and market systems.

But most Eastern European countries had little or virtually no experience with democratic systems. Ethnic divisions made political unity almost impossible and the rapid conversion to market economies also proved unsuccessful. Unemployment climbed. Wages remained low while prices skyrocketed. For both political and economic reasons, the new non-Communist states of Eastern Europe faced dangerous and uncertain futures. Nevertheless, by 1998, some of these states, such as Poland and the Czech Republic, were making a successful transformation to both free markets and democracy.

Western Europe: The Winds of Change. In Western Europe, two decades of amazing economic growth was followed by severe recessions in the mid-1970s and early 1980s. Prices rose and unemployment rate increased. The substantial increase in oil price that followed the Arab-Israeli conflict in 1975 was a major cause. Moreover, due to the economic recession throughout the world, demand for European products went down. The economic situation of Europe was thus worsened. In the 1980s, European states managed to make their economies recover, even though there were still many problems.

After 1970, Europe was moving toward further integration. The European Economic Community established in 1957 expanded when Britain, Ireland, and Denmark joined the organisation in 1973. The European Economic Community was now called European Community (EC) by its members. On January 1, 1994, the European Community became the European Union (EU). The "Euro", a common currency of the

---

① euphoria：精神欢快，欣快。

union, was introduced in 2002.

In West Germany, Willy Brandt (1913 — 1992), the first Social Democratic chancellor, was especially successful with his "opening toward the east", for which he received the Nobel Peace Prize in 1972. Brandt's successor, Helmut Schmidt (b. 1918) was successful in eliminating a deficit of 10 billion marks in three years. In 1982, the Free Democrats joined with the Christian Democratic Union of Helmut Kohl (b. 1930) to form a new government. A clever politician, Helmut Kohl benefited from the reunification of Germany in October 1990 and made the new Germany the leading power in Europe. However, the recovery of East Germany economy, which virtually collapsed, took more money than expected. The government's decision to raise taxes as a way-out, combined with high levels of unemployment, led to widespread grievances.

In Britain, between 1964 and 1979, neither Conservatives nor Labour, who alternated in power, could solve the fighting between Catholics and Protestants in Northern Ireland, a series of dramatic terrorist acts staged by the Irish Republican Army (IRA)[①], or Britain's ailing economy.

In 1979, the Conservatives returned to power under Margaret Thatcher (b. 1925). The "Iron Lady" used austerity measures to control inflation. Her economic policies improved the British economic situation but at a price. Whereas the south of England, for example, prospered, the old industrial areas of the Midlands and north declined and were beset by high unemployment and poverty.

In 1990, Thatcher's attempt to replace local property taxes with a flat-rate tax payable by every adult to his or her local authority meet with different degrees of opposition. At the end of November, a revolt within her own party caused Thatcher to resign and be replaced by John Major (1990—1997). Unable to capture the imagination of most Britons, however, his government was replaced by the Labour Party led by Tony Blair (1997—2007) in 1997.

The French economy declined after the 1973 economic depression. In 1981, Francois Mitterrand (1916 — 1995), the Socialist leader, was elected President of France. Mitterrand's efforts to freeze prices and wages to reduce high budget deficit and high inflation, as well as his liberal measures to aid workers largely failed. The government had to return some of the economy to private enterprise. During his second term from 1988 to 1993, France's economic decline continued. In May, 1995, the Conservative mayor of Paris, Jacques Chirac (b. 1932), was elected President.

The United States: The American Domestic Scene. In 1968, Richard Nixon (1968 — 1974) was elected President of the United States. Nixon, ended American involvement in Vietnam, improved diplomatic relationship with China, and sought to

---

① the Irish Republican Army (IRA)：爱尔兰共和军，由爱尔兰民族主义者组成的激进组织。

rejuvenate the economy by curbing inflation. His paranoia, however, led him to the Watergate Scandal and finally his resignation on August 9, 1974. After Nixon's resignation, Vice President Gerald Ford (b. 1913) became President, only to lose in the 1976 election to Jimmy Carter (b. 1924).

Both Ford and Carter faced severe economic problems of high inflation, high unemployment, and low earnings. Carter's loss to Ronald Reagan (b. 1911) in the election of 1980 brought forward a new political order.

The Reagan administration consisted of a number of new directions. Budget cuts, expenditure on the Star Wars①, as well as the supply-side economics② were economic policies of the government. Despite economic upturn in the short run, the spending policies of the Reagan administration produced record government deficits.

The inability of George Bush (b. 1924), Reagan's successor, to deal with the deficit problem enabled Bill Clinton (b. 1946) to become President in November 1992. Clinton favoured a number of the Republican policies of the 1980s. This was a clear indication that the rightward drift in American politics was by no means ended by this Democratic victory. In fact, Clinton's re-election in 1996 was partially due to his adoption of Republican ideas and policies.

The Development of Canada. In 1968, the Liberal government of Pierre Trudeau (b. 1919) came to power. The government passed the *Official Languages Act*, making both English and French Canada's official languages. High inflation and Trudeau's efforts to impose the will of the Federal government to the provincial governments cost his popularity and support. In 1984, Brian Mulroney (b. 1939), leader of the Progressive Conservative Party, came to power. Mulroney made great efforts to privatise Canada's state-run enterprises. His free trade agreement with the United States led to the reduced popularity of his government. In 1993, the Liberal leader, Jean Chretien, became Prime Minister.

Governments of both Trudeau and Mulroney had to face the problem of the French-speaking province of Quebec. Some separationists sought the secession of Quebec from the rest of Canada, even by terrorist bombings. Even though their schemes were foiled in 1995, debate over Quebec's status continued to divide Canada in the late 1990s.

The World of Western Culture Developments in culture and science in post-war Europe were characterised by great variety. Many pre-war modern trends continued, and new movements emerged.

---

① the Star War：星球大战计划，美国总统里根于1983年提出的一项国防计划，旨在使用最新的现代化技术为美国建立一个不可摧毁的导弹防御系统。

② the supply-side economics：供应面经济政策，美国总统里根推行的一系列经济政策，包括降低所得税率，降低利率，抑制通货膨胀，扩大军费开支，增加财政赤字等。

Recent Trends in Art. For the most part, the United States played a dominant role in the art world after World War Ⅱ. Many believed that the 20th century was the American century, not only in economic power, but also in art. New ideas and styles emerged first in America and then spread to Europe and the whole world. New York has become the cultural capital of the Western World.

Abstractionism[①], especially abstract expressionism, emerged as the artistic mainstream. Despite variety in styles, abstract expressionist paintings share several broad characteristics. They are basically abstract, i. e., they depict forms not drawn from the visible world. They emphasise free, spontaneous, and personal emotional expression and they exercise considerable freedom of technique and execution to attain this goal, with a particular emphasis laid on the exploitation of the variable physical character of paint to evoke expressive qualities (e. g. sensuousness, dynamism, violence, mystery, and lyricism). They show similar emphasis on the unstudied and intuitive application of paint in a form of psychic improvisation akin to the Automatism[②] of the surrealists, with a similar intent of expressing the force of the unconscious in art. They display the abandonment of conventionally structured composition built up out of discrete elements and their replacement with a single unified, undifferentiated field, network, or other image that exists in unstructured space.

American exuberance in abstract expressionism is evident in the enormous canvases of Jackson Pollock (1912—1956). His swirling forms and seemingly chaotic patterns broke all conventions of form and structure. During his lifetime he received widespread publicity and serious recognition for the radical poured, or "drip" technique[③] he used to create his major works. Among his contemporaries, he was respected for his deeply personal and totally uncompromising commitment to the art of painting. His work had enormous influence on his contemporaries and on many subsequent art movements in the United States. He is also one of the first American painters to be recognised during his lifetime and after as a peer of 20th-century European masters of modern art.

The early 1960s saw the emergence of Pop Art[④], which took images of popular culture and transformed them into works of fine art. Andy Warhol (1930—1987) was the most famous of the pop artists. His mass-produced art apotheosised the supposed banality of the commercial culture of the United States. An adroit self-publicist, he projected a concept of the artist as an impersonal, even vacuous, figure who is nevertheless a successful celebrity, businessman, and social climber.

---

① Abstractionism：抽象主义，或抽象派，又称抽象表现主义(Abstract Expressionism)。

② Automatism：自动主义，在艺术中为表现无意识的创造力而运用的方法。

③ "drip" technique：滴色画法。

④ Pop Art：通俗艺术，20 世纪 50 年代美国的一种艺术派别，特点是模仿商业艺术的技法以及通俗文化和大众传媒的风格。

When artists pushed the modernist world view to its extreme limit, a new trend in art, known as Post-modernism[①], emerged. It was built on what modernism has accomplished, but it had its own voice too. Post-modernism prefers "utilizing tradition", whether that includes more styles of painting, or elevating traditional craftsmanship to the level of fine art. Weavers, potters, glassmakers, and furniture makers gained respect as artists.

Literature. The most significant new trend in post-war literature has been called the "Theatre of the Absurd". In this view, human beings were struggling vainly to find a purpose and to control its fate. Humankind is left feeling hopeless, bewildered, and anxious. Language in an absurdist play is often dislocated, full of clichés, puns, repetitions, and non sequiturs[②]. Its most famous proponent was the Irishman Samuel Beckett (1906－1990). In one of his plays, *Waiting for Godot*[③] (1952), Beckett explored an absurdist world beyond logic, decency, and the certainty of language itself. Critics were in accord with the judgment that *Waiting for Godot* is a classic statement about language, human relations, and the ultimate significance of the world.

The sense of meaninglessness that inspired the Theatre of the Absurd also underscored the philosophy of Existentialism[④] which was rooted in the disillusionment of the late 19th century, the atmosphere of anxiety in the early 20th century brought about by the two world wars, the Great Depression, and the tensions of the Cold War. Two of the most celebrated exponents of existentialism were Albert Camus (1913－1960) and Jean-Paul Sartre (1905－1980). According to Camus, the world was absurd and without meaning; humans, too, are without meaning and purpose. The theme he touched on was the anguish of individuals struck by awareness of God's nonexistence and of an impending engagement with nothingness which would exist through eternity. However, in terms of the responses to this absurdity of existence, Camus stood firm against suicide and nihilism. Life may be absurd, but this is not justification for resignation. The other leading light of existentialism, Sartre, described himself as an atheist who viewed existentialism as an approach to the consequences of the world without God. He argued that there is no meaning in existence; consequently, there are no final rights and wrongs in life. Individuals are just born, simply exist, and are free. Therefore, they themselves are responsible for making decisions, taking actions, laying

---

① Post-modernism：后现代主义，20世纪80年代的一种艺术流派，特征为新旧形式的奇妙混合，也称"后现代派"。

② non sequitur：不合逻辑的推论。

③ *Waiting for Godot*：《等待戈多》，爱尔兰剧作家塞缪尔·贝克特的两幕悲喜剧。1952年用法文发表，1953年首演。《等待戈多》是戏剧史上真正的革新，也是第一部演出成功的荒诞派戏剧。

④ Existentialism：存在主义，当代西方哲学主要流派之一。存在主义以人为中心、尊重人的个性和自由，认为人是在无意义的宇宙中生活，人的存在本身也没有意义，但人可以在存在的基础上自我造就，活得精彩。

down their own standards and rules by which they abide in their life. Ultimately, death comes to all.

Religion. Western world after World War Ⅱ witnessed the revival of religions. The Enlightenment in the 18th century and the great progress in science and technology in the 19th century led to the secularisation of the Western society. However, the two world wars and the Great Depression brought about renewed passion in religious faiths.

Great efforts were made by such theologians as the Protestant Karl Barth (1886—1968) and the Catholic Karl Rahner (1904 — 1984) to adapt traditional Christian teachings to the contemporary life. Karl Barth appealed for reaffirmation of the Christ who is the inspiration of faith. He also affirmed the uniqueness of Christianity and reasserted the spiritual power of divine revelation. History is, as Barth saw it, an arena where the individual's faith is always being tested. Karl Rahner attempted to revitalise traditional Catholic theology by incorporating aspects of modern thought. He is best known for his work in Christology and for his integration of an existential philosophy of personalism with Thomistic realism, by which human self-consciousness and self-transcendence are placed within a sphere in which the ultimate determinant is God.

In the Catholic Church, attempts at religious renewal also came from two charismatic popes—John XXIII and John Paul Ⅱ. Pope John XXIII (1881—1963) called the Second Vatican Council (1962—1965) in the spirit of Christian tolerance and unity. The Council liberalised a number of Catholic practices. The Mass was henceforth to be celebrated in the vernacular languages rather than Latin. John Paul Ⅱ (b. 1920), a Pole, was the first non-Italian to be elected pope since the 16th century. His numerous travels around the world helped strengthen the Catholic Church throughout the non-Western world. He projected an updated image of the Catholic Church, which embodied dynamism and activism. However, he held a conservative attitude towards faith and morals by turning down the liberalisation of church policy on theological doctrines, the priesthood, the family and sex.

Science and Technology. Western world after World War Ⅱ experienced a new wave of revolution in science and technology, which fundamentally promoted the development of social productivity, helped improve people's living standards, and changed their way of thinking.

During World War Ⅱ, university scientists were recruited to develop new weapons and practical instruments of war, such as radar system, self-propelled rockets, jet airplanes, and computers. In spite of the fact that most wartime devices were created for destructive purposes, they could easily be adapted for civil uses. The first computer, for instance, which was invented in 1946 to compute values for artillery range tables, proved to be an instrument that revolutionised people all over the world. As the core of the new revolution, information technology, including microelectronics, computing technology, communication, and network technology had become the fundamental assets of the fast-paced civilisation.

The most exciting discoveries in the biological sciences were in the field of genetics. The term genetics generally refers to the artificial manipulation, modification, and recombination of DNA or other nucleic acid molecules in order to modify an organism or population of organisms. In 1953, the nature of the complicated DNA molecule, which controls the pattern of all living things, was discovered by an American biochemist and a British physicist. In 1980, the first genetically modified mouse came into being. Later, the gene cloning technology became an integral part of genetics. Cloning, a method of asexual reproduction, produces an individual with the same DNA as another. In 1996, Dolly, the first cloned sheep, was born in Edinburgh, an event that shocked the whole world.

Despite the advances that were produced by the alliance of science and technology, they also brought problems. The optimistic assumption that scientific knowledge enables human beings to manipulate the environment for their benefit was questioned by some in the 1960s and 1970s who believed that some technological advances had far-reaching side effects on the environment. The threat of global warming and the widespread proliferation of dying forests and lakes made environmental protection one of the important issues of the 1990s.

Popular Culture. The 20th century saw an explosion of popular culture, characterised by the tremendous variety and availability of popular literature, art and music. These changes were enabled by dramatic developments in many aspects of society. Communications were substantially expanded, from cheap newspapers and paperback novels to radio, cinema and television; lots of large public facilities such as museums, concert halls, and stadiums were constructed; the level of mass education was generally upgraded, which gave rise to people's greater interests in cultural activities; the urban classes led a life of abundance with a good deal of leisure time, a fact that enabled more people to make full use of cultural offerings for their own gains.

Distinct from the elite culture, popular culture usually produces many forms of communication including newspapers, television, advertising, comics, pop music, radio, cheap novels, and cinemas. These aspects of popular culture were considered as commercial entertainment for the lower classes. However, the line between the two blurred. For example, cinema was probably the most creative form of art in the 20th century. As a sophisticated, innovative and artistic medium, the potential of cinema was revealed in the works of filmmakers like Ingmar Bergman (b. 1918) in Sweden and Federico Fellini (b. 1920) in Italy. However, numerous popular films were released year after year despite the incisive criticism of being undistinguished. Cinemas, as well as other industries that disseminated cultural materials such as television, publishing industries and news media, became the major attractions in the old popular culture throughout the decades of the 20th century.

Americanisation. Despite the pluralism after World War Ⅱ spawned by an age of instant communication and ever-growing technology, the United States has been the most influential force in shaping popular culture in the West and, to a lesser degree, the entire world. Many people, not always admiringly, spoke of the "coca-colonisation" of the world. Through its music, movies, and television, the powerful country has spread its culture, way of living, particular values and the American Dream① to millions of people around the world.

Movies and televisions were the primary means by which the United States spread its popular culture throughout the world after World War Ⅱ. Movies of the United States took the lead and thus dominated both European and American markets. In 2000, movies in the United States attained a box office of $ 7.7 billion, a record high in history. American television productions have also demonstrated remarkable wide appeal. The television series Dallas was as popular and well-known in Europe as in the United States.

The United States also dominated popular music since the end of World War Ⅱ. Popular music is rooted in the tribulation of urban blacks, the traditionalism of rural whites, the protest of activists, and the hopes and aspirations of the common people. All the forms, folk music, R&B, country and western, and the various shades of rock, soon spread to the rest of the world, where local artists transformed them in their own ways.

The leading role the United States played in popular culture after World War Ⅱ was also evident in the development of sports. Support from the government and craze of the American people made sports boom in the country. Most people were engaged in sports activities or simply watch the games. Basketball, baseball, American Football, and rugby are among the most popular games in the country. Due to the development of satellite television and various electronic breakthroughs as well as the United States' efforts to extend its overseas market, sports as part of the popular culture has also spread to the rest of the world. Basketball players like Michael Jordan (b. 1963) and Kobe Bryant (b. 1978) enjoy the same popularity in other countries of the world as in the United States. More and more foreign players entering NBA also mean that the league has had an increasingly important impact on the whole world.

---

① American Dream：美国梦。长久以来美国人持有的一种信仰，即任何人都可以通过自己的聪明才智和辛勤劳动实现自己的奋斗目标，比如豪华汽车、宽敞住宅等。

Chapter Review

This chapter presented a panoramic view of the Western World in and after the two world wars. Europeans' sense of progress was shattered by the two world wars, which cost the lives of millions of people. The profound sense of despair and disillusionment brought about by the two world wars was paralleled by development in art and music featuring an intensified fascination with the absurd and the unconscious. The Cold War, which stemmed from the ideological conflict between the United States and the Soviet Union, ended with the collapse of the Soviet Union in 1991. After World War Ⅱ, literature and art took on a new look characterised by remarkable diversity.

Exercise

Ⅰ. *According to the information provided in this chapter, choose the correct alternative among A, B, C, and D that can complete each of the following statements.*

1. Which of the following statements concerning the peace settlement in Paris after World War Ⅰ is false?

   A. It was made in 1919.

   B. It consisted of five separate treaties with the defeated nations.

   C. It ensured sustained peace.

   D. It was seen by many Germans as a humiliation to Germany.

2. The move to ________ in modern architecture, which meant that in architecture, the form of a building should be determined by practical considerations, became more widespread in the 1920s and 1930s.

   A. functionalism　　B. existentialism　　C. realism　　D. romanticism

3. Which of the following is not a writer of "stream of consciousness"?

   A. James Joyce.　　B. Virginia Woolf.

   C. T. S. Eliot.　　D. William Shakespeare.

4. After Nixon resigned the presidency in 1974, Vice-President ________ became president, only to lose in the 1976 election.

   A. Bill Clinton　　B. Gerald Ford

   C. George Bush　　D. Ronald Reagan

5. The most significant new trend in post-war literature has been called ________. In this view, human beings were struggling in vain to find a purpose and to control its fate. One of the best-known examples is the play *Waiting for Godot* by Samuel Beckett.

   A. post-modernism　　B. surrealism

   C. Theatre of the Absurd　　D. modernism

Ⅱ. *Fill in the blanks with what you have learned in this chapter.*

1. Using Blitzkrieg, or ________, Hitler stunned Europe with the speed and efficiency of the German attack.
2. In the 20th century, the focus of literature tended to shift to a more subjective point of view and to the feelings, uncertainties, and unconscious motives of individuals. One of its most apparent manifestations was in a ________ in which the writer presented an interior monologue or a report of the innermost thoughts of each character. One of the best-known examples is James Joyce.
3. The pre-war revolution in physics initiated by Albert Einstein and other scientists continued in the era of wars and revolution. In fact, Ernest Rutherford dubbed the 1920s the ________.
4. After World War Ⅱ, a substantial increase in their real wages enabled the working classes to seek the consumption patterns of the middle class, leading to what some observers have called the ________.
5. In 1957, the members of European Coal and Steel Community created ________ to further European research on the peaceful uses of nuclear energy.

Ⅲ. *According to what you have learned, answer the following questions briefly in your own words.*

1. Why was the ending of World War Ⅱ followed by a Cold War between Soviet Union and the United States?
2. What led to the youth movement? What was this movement about?
3. Why did the economic, political, and social developments prove to be unsuccessful in Eastern European countries?
4. What are the characteristics of abstractionism?
5. What were the problems brought about by the technological advances after World War Ⅱ?

Ⅳ. *With critical analysis, answer the following essay questions in your own words.*

1. How did existentialism and the church respond respectively to the despair generated by the apparent collapse of civilised values in the 20th century?
2. Give some examples to prove that the United States had played a leading role in spread of popular culture after World War Ⅱ.

Ⅴ. *Work in small groups and make comparisons based on the following topic.*

China's table-tennis teams are almost unparalleled in the world, while American basketball teams have proved second to none. What do you think ensured China's dominance in table-tennis and America's success in basketball?

Voices on Key Points

Wars and Revolution

After two world wars, the collapse of fascism, nazism, communism and colonialism and the end of the cold war, humanity has entered a new phase of its history.

——Hans Kung

The international order established at the end of World War Ⅱ could certainly have been worse. However, this order did contain certain factors which bore within them the seeds of instability.

——Eisak Sato

After the First World War the economic problem was no longer one of production. It was the problem of finding markets to get the output of industry and agriculture dispersed and consumed.

——John Boyd Orr

Cold War and the New Era of Europe

During the Cold War, we lived in coded times when it wasn't easy and there were shades of grey and ambiguity.

——John Le Carre

During the Cold War, we gathered information by listening to the Soviets, taking pictures of the Soviets, and we allowed our human intelligence to decline.

——Bob Graham

The Cold War isn't thawing; it is burning with a deadly heat. Communism isn't sleeping; it is, as always, plotting, scheming, working, fighting.

——Richard M. Nixon

Suggested Reading

1. Dorman, Andrew & Greg Kennedy (Ed.). *War & Diplomacy: From World War I to the War on Terrorism*. Washington, D.C.: Potomac Books, 2008.
2. 刘雪莲主编:《欧洲一体化与全球政治》,吉林大学出版社 2008 年版。
3. 萨缪尔·贝克特著,施咸荣译:《等待戈多》,人民文学出版社 2002 年版。
4. 王缉思等主编:《冷战后的美国外交》,时事出版社 2008 年版。
5. 文聘元:《两次世界大战的故事:从第一次世界大战到第二次世界大战》,上海社会科学院出版社 2009 年版。
6. 许海云:《他们制造了冷战》,人民日报出版社 2009 年版。

Culture Link

1. The history of the system of writing

- Proto-literate symbol systems (roughly from 3400—3200 B. C.):

  The Sumerian archaic cuneiform script and the Egyptian hieroglyphs.

  True alphabetic writing (around 2000 B. C.) includes:

- Phoenician Alphabet dated back to 1050 B. C. and gradually died out during the Hellenistic period, which records only consonant sounds.

The Phoenician Alphabet

𐤀	Aleph	Ox	‘	𐤈	Tet Wheel	Heavy	T	𐤐	Pe	Mouth	P
𐤁	Beth	House	B	𐤉	Yodh	Hand	Y	𐤑	Tsade	Hunt Heavy	S
𐤂	Gimel	Camel	G	𐤊	Kaph	Palm of a Hand	K	𐤒	Qoph	Needle Head	Q
𐤃	Daleth	Door	D	𐤋	Lamedh	Goad	L	𐤓	Resh	Head	R
𐤄	He	Window	H	𐤌	Mem	Water	M	𐤔	Shin	Tooth	Sh
𐤅	Waw	Hook	W	𐤍	Nun	Serpent	N	𐤕	Taw	Mark	T
𐤆	Zayin	Weapon	Z	𐤎	Samekh	Fish	S				
𐤇	Heth	Wall	H	𐤏	Ayin	Eye	’				

Note: In the above table there are four parts in each column:

the Phoenician sign

the Phoenician name

the English meaning

the English phone

- The Greek alphabet is derived from the Phoenician alphabet. The phonology of Greek differed greatly from that of Phoenician: it notes both vowels and consonants with separate symbols.

The Greek Alphabet

Α	α	alpha	Ι	ι	iota	Ρ	ρ	rho
Β	β	beta	Κ	κ	kappa	Σ	σ, ς	sigma
Γ	γ	gamma	Λ	λ	lambda	Τ	τ	tau
Δ	δ	delta	Μ	μ	mu	Υ	υ	upsilon
Ε	ε	epsilon	Ν	ν	nu	Φ	φ	phi
Ζ	ζ	zeta	Ξ	ξ	ksi	Χ	χ	chi
Η	η	eta	Ο	ο	omicron	Ψ	ψ	psi
Θ	θ	theta	Π	π	pi	Ω	ω	omega

Note: In the above table there are three parts in each column:

(1)the upper-case Greek letter

(2)the lower-case Greek letter

(3) the Greek letter name

The Roman alphabet, also called Latin alphabet, is the most widely used alphabet system in modern time.

Majuscule Forms

ABCDEFGHIJKLMNOPQRSTUVWXYZ

Minuscule Forms

abcdefghijklmnopqrstuvwxyz

2. Bible

The Bible is the main religious text of Judaism and Christianity. The Hebrew or Jewish bible, also called Tanakh, is composed of three parts: the Torah ("Teaching", also known as the Pentateuch or "Five Books of Moses"), the Prophets, and the Writings. It was primarily written in Hebrew.

The Christian Bible consists of the Hebrew Scriptures, which have been called the *Old Testament*, and some later writings known as the *New Testament*, which were originally written in Greek.

3. Homer

- Life 8th century B. C.
- Works The *Iliad*, The *Odyssey*, *Epic Cycle*, *Homeric Hymns*
- Dialect an archaic version of Ionic Greek
- Style single, unified theme or action in the epic cycle

4. **Greeks' Philosophy**

- Pre-Socratic philosophy was advocated by ontologists who rejected mythological explanations for reasoned discourse.
- Classic Greek philosophy, one of the most influential branches of philosophy, was made known to the world by three great philosophers—Socrates, Plato and Aristotle.
- Hellenistic philosophy is the period of Western philosophy that was developed in the Hellenistic civilisation following Aristotle and ending with Neoplatonism, and is composed of various schools like Platonism, Peripateticism and Cynicism.
- Transmission of Greek philosophy under Islam was an event that transformed the intellectual life of Western Europe. It consisted of the discovery of many original works, such as those written by Aristotle in the classical period, commentaries by Hellenistic philosophers written in late Antiquity, and commentaries from early Muslim philosophers in the Arab world, or Muslim world, written during the Islamic Golden Age from the 9th to 12th centuries.

5. **The word "Roman" may remind one of the following terms**

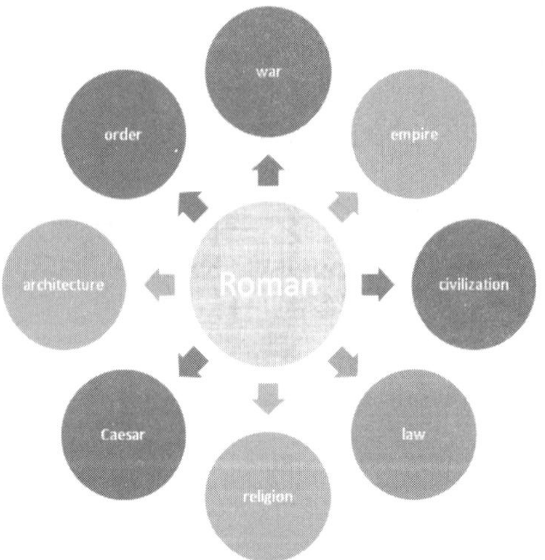

6. **Ancient Roman Memorabilia**

Time	Event
753 B. C.	Roman was founded.
509 B. C.	The Roman Republic was founded.
218—201 B. C.	The Second Punic War
73—71 B. C.	Slave rebellion led by Spartacus
44 B. C.	Caesar was assassinated.
27 B. C.	The Roman Empire was founded.
235—284	Military Anarchy

续表

Time	Event
395	The Roman Empire was divided into western and eastern parts.
476	The Western Roman Empire fell to ruin.
1453	The Eastern Roman Empire fell to ruin.

7. The historical changes contributing to Roman's prosperity

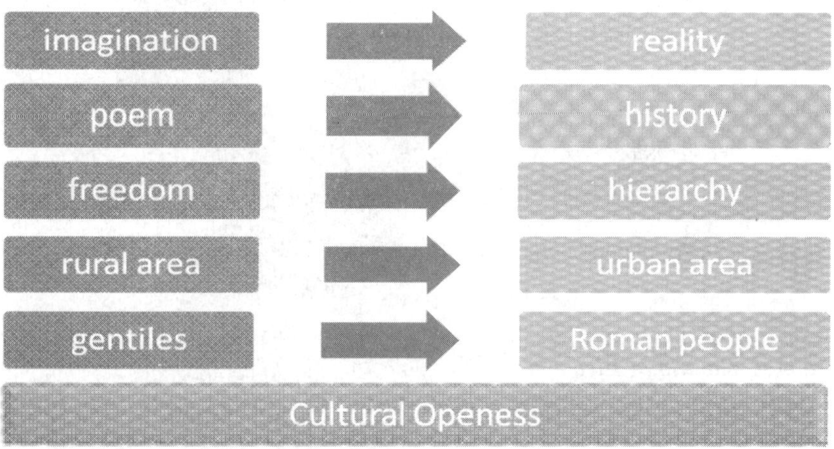

8. Roman's ruin is due to

9. The Beliefs of Christianity

This Christian group advocates the infallibility of the pope and the hierarchical nature of the religious order as represented by church organisation.

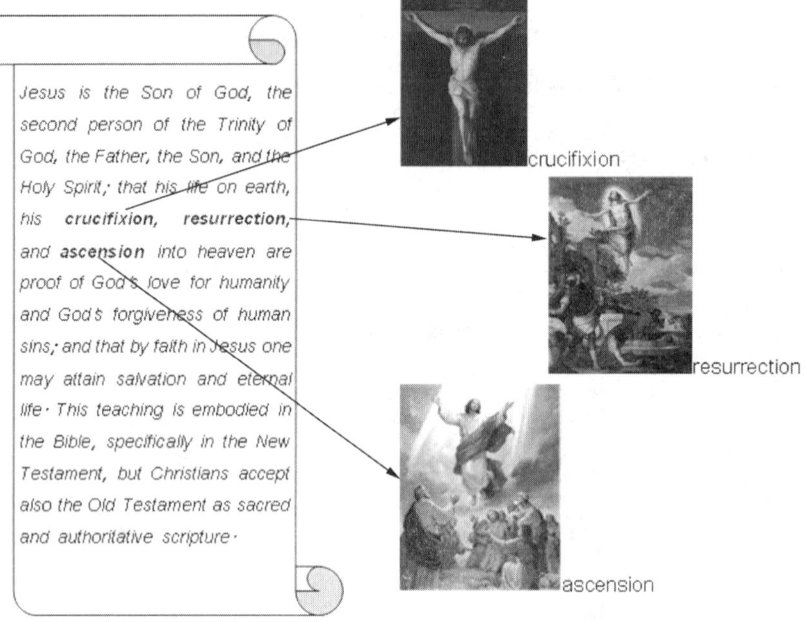

10. Timeline of *The Mona Lisa*

1503	Leonardo begins painting *The Mona Lisa*, which he will work on for four years.
1519	Leonardo dies at the age of sixty-seven at the manor of Cloux near Amboise.
1530s	Francois Ⅰ displays *The Mona Lisa* in a semi-public art gallery at Fontainebleau, his favourite chateau.
1800	*The Mona Lisa* is hung in Napoleon Bonaparte's bedroom in the Tuileries.
1804	*The Mona Lisa* is installed in the Grand Gallery of the Louvre.
1914	*The Mona Lisa* is sent to her new place in the Louvre's Salon Carré on January 4.
1963	*The Mona Lisa* is seen by one million six-hundred-thousand visitors in the United States for seven weeks, first at the National Gallery of Art in Washington, D. C., and then at the New York Metropolitan Museum of Art.
1974	*The Mona Lisa* visits the Tokyo National Museum and then the Pushkin Museum in Moscow, where she is seen by more than 2 million viewers.

11. Level of Church

Level one: Chapel

Level two: Church

Level three: Cathedral

Level four: Basilica

12. Top Eight Famous Churches in Europe

• Santo Maria del Fiore

The Basilica di Santa Maria del Fiore is the cathedral church (Duomo) of Florence, Italy, started in 1296 in the Gothic style to the design of Arnolfo di Cambio and completed structurally in 1436.

• Temple Expiatori de la Sagrada Familia

The Temple Expiatori de la Sagrada Família, often simply called the Sagrada Família, is a massive, privately-funded Roman Catholic church that has been under construction in Barcelona, Catalonia, Spain since 1882 and is not expected to be complete until at least 2026.

• Piazza del Duomo

The Piazza del Duomo ("Cathedral Square") is a wide, walled area at the heart of the city of Pisa, Tuscany, Italy, recognised as one of the main centres for medieval art in the world. In 1987, the whole square was declared a UNESCO World Heritage Site.

• Assumption Cathedral

Assumption Cathedral, also called Dormition Cathedral, consists of a number of Cathedral churches dedicated to the Dormition of the Theotokos in the Orthodox tradition and Assumption of Mary in the Roman Catholic tradition.

• Cathedral of Santiago de Compostela

Located in Santiago de Compostela in Galicia, Spain, Santiago de Compostela Cathedral is the reputed burial-place of Saint James the Greater, one of the apostles of Jesus Christ. It is the destination of the Way of St. James, a major historical pilgrimage route since the Middle Ages.

• Mosteiro dos Jerónimos

The Jerónimos Monastery, another World Heritage Site located in the Belém district of Lisbon, Portugal, is made entirely out of limestone. It was built to thank God for the safe return of all those Portuguese explorers who had ventured out on dangerous exploits.

• Notre Dame de Paris

Notre Dame de Paris ("Our Lady of Paris" in French) is a Gothic cathedral situated on the eastern half of the Île de la Cité in the 4th arrondissement of Paris, France, with its main entrance to the west. Notre Dame de Paris is widely considered one of the finest examples of French Gothic architecture.

• Helsinki Cathedral

Helsinki Cathedral is an Evangelical Lutheran cathedral of the Diocese of Helsinki, located in the centre of Helsinki, Finland. The church was originally built as a tribute to the Grand Duke, Nicholas Ⅰ, the Tsar of Russia and until the independence of Finland in 1917, it was called St. Nicholas' Church.

13. European Art

Art Movement	Age	Features	Notable painters and their works
Mannerism	1520—1580	Intellectual sophistication; Artificial qualities	Jacopo da Pontormo's *Joseph in Egypt* Jocopo Tintoretto's *Last Supper*
The Baroque	17th century to the early 18th century	great drama, rich, deep colour and intense light and dark shadows	Peter Paul Rubens's *Judgement of Paris* Frans Hals's *Gypsy Girl*
Rococo	mid-18th century	shell-like curves and focus on decorative arts	Jean Antoine Watteau's *Pilgrimage on the Isle of Cythera*

14. American Political System

- American political system is based on federalism. To provide a system of "checks and balances" in accordance with Montesquieu's principle of a "separation of powers", the federal government is divided into three branches—the executive branch led by the President, the legislative branch dominated by a bicameral Congress consisting of the Senate and the House of Representatives, the judicial branch headed by the Supreme Court. The three branches examine and check the functioning of each other.
- America employs two-party system, the Democratic party and the Republican party, whose main function is to manipulate the presidential election. The two parties take turns in governing the country.
- American federal government is superior to the state government but the latter still enjoys considerable independence.

15. French Political System

Since the French revolution of 1789, France has undergone a complicated alternation among the constitutional monarchy, the republic and the empire before the birth of the Third Republic in 1875 established the republic institution.

The government is a semi-presidential system determined by the French Constitution of the Fifth Republic, which is divided into an executive, a legislative and a judicial branch. The President, head of state, and the Prime Minister, head of government, controlled the power in an executive branch. The Parliament of France, making up the legislative branch, consists of two houses: the National

Assembly and the Senate. The French judicial system has the distinctive feature that it consists of judicial and administrative streams. The judicial stream of courts adjudicates civil and criminal cases while Courts of administrative law adjudicate on claims and suits against government offices and agencies.

16. Enlightenment

The Age of Enlightenment, or simply The Enlightenment, is a term used to describe a time in Western philosophy and cultural life centred upon the 18th century, in which reason was advocated as the primary source and legitimacy for authority.

The movement developed at about the same time in Germany, France, Great Britain, the Netherlands, Italy, Spain, and Portugal and spread through much of Europe, including the Polish-Lithuanian Commonwealth, Russia and Scandinavia as well as in America. It could be argued that the signatories of the American *Declaration of Independence*, the United States *Bill of Rights*, the French *Declaration of the Rights of Man and of the Citizen*, and the Polish-Lithuanian Constitution of May 3, 1791, were motivated by "Enlightenment" principles.

17. Enlightenment Philosophers and Their Theory

Philosopher	Theory	Representative Works
John Lock (1632—1704)	Theory of religious tolerance Liberal theory	*Two Treatises of Government* (1689) *An Essay Concerning Human Understanding* (1690)
Montesquieu (1689—1755)	Philosophy of history Political views like Separation of Powers	*Considérations sur les causes de la grandeur des Romains et de leur décadence* (1734) *De l'esprit des lois* (1748)
Voltaire (1694—1778)	Religion Freemasonry	*Lettres philosophiques sur les Anglais* (1733), revised as *Letters on the English* (circa 1778) *Treatise on Tolerance* (1763)
Jean Jacques Rousseau (1712—1778)	Theory of nature man Political theory Education and child rearing	*The Social Contract*, *Discourse on Inequality* (1754) *Émile: or, on Education* (1762)

18. American Dream

Traditionally, Americans have sought to realise the American dream of success, fame and wealth through thrift and hard work. However, the industrialisation of the 19th and 20th centuries began to erode the dream, replacing it with a philosophy of "get rich quick".

19. Romanticism, Naturalism and Realism

Romanticism	A literary movement in Europe and the United States in the last half of the 19th century and the early years of the 20th century.
	The spirit of realism lies in the literary area.
	The realist literary focus on novel writing.
	It lays emphasis on fidelity to actual experience.
	The realist's language was usually simple, clear and direct.
Naturalism	The naturalistic novel is a record of men and manners.
	To the naturalists, the novel is a demonstration of social law.
	The language used by naturalists must be the actual language used by people.
Realism	It expresses the concern for the world of experience, of the commonplace, for the familiar and the low.
	The Realism writers wrote about what they observed and knew. They believed that representation of life should be the main object of the novel, and offered an objective rather than an idealised view of human nature and experience.
	Realism reacts against Romanticism's emphasis on intuition, imagination, a dreary sense of wonder, idealism, and faith in nature and general optimistic belief in the goodness of things.

20. Nine Aliens in Western Culture

- Elf

  They often appear in the supernatural stories, not so terrible. Legends say they come and go in the jungle, and sometimes will steal little children.

- Devil

  It's for the "soul of the evil". The devil can be any kind of evil spirit, from the depraved angels to the followers of Satan. As the only incarnation of evil, they always appear in the literature.

- Stone Animal

  The image of stone animal often appears in fine church buildings. From the 13th century, they are carved on the church for the discharge of roof water. They are carved to protect the church from evil forces.

- Zombie

  Zombie often appears in movies. Zombie evolves from the voodoo worship, even today some people still believe that after death people will wake up and be able to walk.

- Werewolf

  The legends of werewolves can be traced to ancient Greece. In the Middle Ages, when people cannot explain a murder case, they always regard werewolves as suspects.

- Halloween's Pumpkin

  Pumpkin is a Halloween sign, with which to drive ghosts away.

- Vampire bat

  Vampire bats hide in the dark of cliffs. They will use their sharp teeth taking blood of life. Sometimes they attack humans.

- Witch

  In the past, people believe that witches had supernatural magic. In Churches witches were thought evil. In Medieval Europe, to catch witches was considered to be unusual thing, and in the United States it was still the case until the 17th century.

- Vampire

  Vampire leads a living by sucking human blood. For thousands of years, the vampire's image appears in various cultures, which was allegedly from Eastern Europe in the 18th and 19th century.

Proper Names

Abbasid：(阿拉伯帝国)阿巴斯王朝(750～1258)的统治者

Abou Simbel Rock Temple：古埃及第十九王朝法老拉美西斯二世在阿布辛贝勒的岩石中建造的巨大神殿

Abraham：亚伯拉罕，希伯来族长。

Achilles：阿基里斯，海洋女神忒提斯(Thetis)与国王佩琉斯(Peleus)的儿子。他是所有英雄之中最耀眼的一位，也是战无不胜的。

Actium：(希腊西部沿海)阿克兴海角，公元前31年罗马内战期间，安东尼和屋大维在此进行了一场海战。

Adolf Hitler：阿道夫·希特勒，奥地利裔德国政治人物，1921年成为纳粹党党魁，1933年被任命为德国总理，1934年成为德国元首。第二次世界大战期间，他兼任德国武装力量最高统帅。他被公认是二战的主要发动者。

Adrianople：阿德里安堡，Edirne的旧称，位于土耳其。

Adriatic：亚得里亚海，地中海的一个大海湾。在意大利与巴尔干半岛之间，通过南端的奥特朗托海(Otranto)与爱奥尼亚海(Ionian Sea)相通。

Aegean Islands：爱琴群岛(希腊)

Aegean Sea：爱琴海，地中海一部分，在希腊和土耳其之间。

Aeneas：埃涅阿斯，希腊女神阿佛洛狄忒(罗马神话中称维纳斯)之子，在希腊人占领特洛伊城之后来到意大利，是特洛伊战争中的勇士。

Aequi：埃魁人，古意大利民族，曾长期与罗马为敌。

Aeschylus：埃斯库罗斯，古希腊的一位戏剧家，被尊称为“悲剧之父”。

Afghanistan：阿富汗

Agamemnon：阿伽门农，特洛伊战争中希腊军队的统帅。

Ahmose：阿赫摩斯法老

Ahura：阿诃罗神，波斯人信奉的天神。

Akhenaten：埃赫那吞，即阿蒙霍特普四世。

Akkad：阿卡德，人类历史上第一个帝国，早于该地区后来出现的巴比伦和亚述帝国。

Alaric：阿拉里克，西哥特人首领。一般认为他是西哥特王国的缔造者。

Albert Camus：阿尔贝·加缪，法国小说家、哲学家、戏剧家、评论家

Albert Einstein：阿尔贝·爱因斯坦(1879～1955)德裔美籍物理学家，犹太人，现代物理学的开创者和奠基人，相对论的提出者。相对论深刻揭示了时间和空间的本质属性，是物理学领域的重大革命。

Albertus Magnus：大阿尔伯图斯，德国经院哲学家，神学家和科学家，在亚里士多德影响下提出了"自然宗教"与"启示宗教"的区别。由于知识渊博，被称作"全能博士"。

Alexander the Great/Alexandria：亚历山大大帝(前356～前323)，世界古代史上有名的帝王，他的启蒙老师是著名的哲学家亚里士多德，他一生酷爱古希腊文化，继位时才20岁，继位后首先果断地镇压了宫廷阴谋，接着平定了希腊的反马其顿情绪，于公元前334年，率3万步兵、5千骑兵开始了世界古代史上有名的东侵。

Alexandria：亚历山大，埃及最大海港和第二大港口城市，位于尼罗河以西一条东北一西南方向伸展的狭长地带上，西北临地中海、东南靠迈尔尤特湖。

Alfred：阿尔弗烈德，英格兰韦塞克斯王国国王(871～899)、学者及立法者，曾击败丹麦人的侵略并使英格兰成为统一的王国。

Allah：阿拉，伊斯兰教上帝。

Alps：阿尔卑斯山

Amarna：阿玛纳，法老埃赫那吞在此城建立首都。

Amorites：阿摩利特人，也称"古巴比伦人"。

Amos：阿摩司，《圣经》所载公元前8世纪的希伯来先知。

Amsterdam Exchange：阿姆斯特丹交易所

Amun：底比斯的阿蒙神

Amunemhet Ⅰ：阿蒙尼姆赫特一世，古埃及第十二王朝建立者。

Amunhotpe Ⅲ：阿蒙霍特普三世

Amunhotpe Ⅳ：阿蒙霍特普四世

Amun-Re：阿蒙神，古埃及底比斯的主神。太阳神拉可以说是全埃及地位最高的神灵，阿蒙神和拉神融为一体，成为阿蒙一拉，称为"众神之王"。

Anchises：安喀塞斯，在希腊神话中是一位特洛伊王室旁支成员，被女神阿佛洛狄忒迷恋，与她生下埃涅阿斯。在特洛伊城陷落后，其子背着他逃出了城，最后死于西西里。

Andreas Vesalius：安德烈·维萨里，比利时医生、伟大的生物学家、近代人体解剖学的创始人。

Angles and Saxons：盎格鲁人和撒克逊人，两个早期征服英国的民族。

Ankara：安卡拉，土耳其首都。

Anne Boleyn：安妮·博林，英格兰王后，英格兰国王亨利八世的第二任妻子，英格兰女王伊丽莎白一世的母亲。

Anti-Fascist Alliance：世界反法西斯联盟

Antoninus Pius：安东尼·庇护，罗马帝王，公元138～161年在位，"五圣主"中的第四位。

Antony：安东尼(前83～前30)是一位古罗马政治家和军事家。他是恺撒最重要的军队指挥官和管理人员之一。前33年后三头同盟分裂，前30年马克·安东尼与埃及女王克利奥帕特拉七世一同自杀身亡。

Aphrodite：阿佛洛狄忒，古希腊性爱与美貌之女神，相当于罗马的维纳斯。

Apollo：阿波罗，希腊神话中十二主神之一，是主神宙斯与暗夜女神勒托所生之子，阿尔忒弥斯的孪生哥哥，全名为福玻斯·阿波罗（Phoebus Apollo），意思是"光明"或"光辉灿烂"。阿波罗被视为司掌文艺之神，主管光明、青春、医药、畜牧、音乐等，是人类的保护神、光明之神、预言之神、迁徙和航海者的保护神、医神以及消灾弥难之神。

Apulia：阿普利亚，意大利城市。

Aquinas 阿奎那（1226～1274），中世纪经院哲学的哲学家和神学家。他把理性引进神学。

Arabian Desert：阿拉伯沙漠

Arabian Peninsula：阿拉伯半岛

Archimedes of Syracuse：锡拉库扎的阿基米德，古希腊最著名的数学家、工程师及物理学家。

Aristarchus of Samos：萨摩斯的阿里斯塔克斯，希腊天文学家。

Aristophanes：阿里斯托芬，雅典剧作家。

Aristotle：亚里士多德（前 384～前 322），古希腊斯吉塔拉人，世界古代史上最伟大的哲学家、科学家和教育家之一。柏拉图的学生，亚历山大的老师。亚里士多德是希腊哲学的集大成者，他将前人的辩证法、本体论与宇宙论等观念进行了综合，建立了希腊哲学中全面的体系。亚里士多德也是西方政治学的鼻祖和科学哲学的奠基者。

Ascanius：阿斯卡尼俄斯，古罗马诗人维吉尔所著拉丁史诗《伊尼特》中主人公 Aeneas 之子，意大利 Alba Longa 城的创建者。

Ashurbanipa：亚述巴尼拔，亚述帝国最后一位伟大的君主。

Ashur-uballit Ⅰ：阿舒尔乌巴利特一世，亚述帝国的一位国王，他的统治标志着亚述成为一个强大的帝国。

Ashurbanipal：亚述国王亚述巴尼拔

Asia Minor：小亚细亚

Assembly：国民议会

Assur：亚述神

Assyria：亚述帝国，the Assyrians 亚述人。

Aswan：阿斯旺，埃及南部城市，著名古城、旅游景点和贸易中心，是世界上最干燥的地方之一。

Aten：太阳神阿吞

Athens：雅典，希腊首都。

Attila：阿提拉，匈奴帝国国王（433～453），最成功入侵罗马帝国的野蛮入侵者。

Augustinian monastery：奥古斯丁修道院，位于德国的埃尔福特市。

Augustus：奥古斯都，即罗马帝国开国君主屋大维（前 63～14）。

Aurelian：奥勒良（214～275），罗马帝国皇帝，270～275 年间在位。他统治时收复了罗马帝国曾经失去的三分之二的疆域，初步解决了罗马帝国在第 3 世纪的危机。

Avignon：阿维尼翁，法国东南部城市。

Aztec Empire：阿兹特克帝国，古代墨西哥文化舞台上最后一个角色，创造了辉煌的阿兹特克文明，开创了阿兹特克族最兴盛的时期。

Babylon：巴比伦王国，位于美索不达米亚平原，大致在当今的伊拉克版图内，是西方文明的摇篮。

Baghdad：巴格达，伊拉克首都。

Bahamas：巴哈马群岛，西印度群岛的三个群岛之一，位于佛罗里达海峡口外的北大西洋上。这个群岛由700多个海岛和2400多个岛礁组成，总面积13939平方公里。

Balkan Peninsula：巴尔干半岛

Baltic Region：波罗的海地区

Baroque：巴洛克风格

Bartholomeu Dias：巴塞洛缪斯·迪亚斯，航海家，1487年被葡萄牙国王约翰二世选派去非洲南端探险，成为绕好望角航行的第一位欧洲人。

Bastille：巴士底狱，一座非常坚固的要塞。根据法国国王查理五世的命令，按照12世纪著名的军事城堡的样式而建造起来。到18世纪末期，成为控制巴黎的制高点和关押政治犯的监狱。

Benedict：本尼迪克特(姓氏，男子名)

Bernard of Clairvaux：克勒福的圣伯纳德，一位著名的中世纪敬虔追求主的圣徒，法国修道士改革者和政治人物，在第二次十字军东征的召集上起到重要作用。

Bismarck：俾斯麦(1815～1898)，普鲁士宰相兼外交大臣，是德国近代史上杰出的政治家和外交家，被称为"铁血首相"。

Black Sea：黑海

Bloody Mary：血腥玛丽，即玛丽一世，英格兰和爱尔兰女王。都铎王朝的第四任君主，其父为亨利八世。曾下令处决过三百个反对者，因此被称为"血腥玛丽"。

Boniface：卜尼法斯，英国天主教传教士，活跃于德国。

Boris Yeltsin：鲍里斯·叶利钦

Bosnia：波斯尼亚

Bourbon Dynasty：波旁王朝，一个在欧洲历史上曾断断续续地统治纳瓦拉(1555～1848)、法国(1589～1848)、西班牙(1700至今)、那不勒斯与西西里(1734～1816)、卢森堡(1964年至今)等国和意大利若干公国的跨国王朝。值得一提的是，波旁王室的近代成员都以保守著称，因此在美式英语中，波旁一词成为对极端保守主义者的称呼。

Bourges：(法国)布尔日

Brancacci chapel：佛罗伦萨卡尔米内教堂的布兰卡奇礼拜堂

Brandenburg-Prussia：勃兰登堡－普鲁士公国

British Isles：不列颠群岛，包括大不列颠和爱尔兰两个大岛以及附近的5500多个小岛；群岛上有英国和爱尔兰共和国两个国家。

Bruges：布鲁日，比利时西北部城市。

Bulgaria：保加利亚

Burgundian：(法国)勃艮第

Byzantine Empire：拜占庭帝国，位于欧洲东部。领土曾包括亚洲西部和非洲北部，是古代和中世纪欧洲历史最悠久的君主制国家。拜占庭帝国共历经 12 个朝代，93 位皇帝。帝国的首都为新罗马。

Cairo：开罗，埃及首都。

Cambyses：冈比西斯，居鲁士继任者。

Camille Pissarro：卡米耶·毕沙罗(1830～1903)，法国印象派艺术大师。

Canaan：迦南，巴勒斯坦一地区，位于约旦河与地中海之间。按旧约全书，这里被认为属于"应许之地"，是一块"流着奶和蜜"的土地，据传由上帝赐给 Abraham 及其后裔，见《圣经·创世记》。

Cape of Good Cape：好望角

Carl Jung：卡尔·荣格，瑞士心理学家和精神分析医师，分析心理学的创立者。早年曾与弗洛伊德合作，曾被弗洛伊德任命为第一届国际精神分析学会的主席。

Carloman：卡洛曼，查理·马特的一个儿子。其父去世后按照传统分得了一半的国土，与兄弟丕平共同管理国家。

Carolingian Empire：加洛林王朝的帝国

Carthage：迦太基，位于非洲北部，今突尼斯的奴隶制城邦，腓尼基人所建，公元 146 年被罗马帝国所灭。

Cathedral of Florence：佛罗伦萨大教堂，又名"圣母百花大教堂"，世界第四大教堂，建于 1296～1436 年。

Catholic Church：天主教会，当今基督宗教中最大的分支，占了一半的基督徒人口。天主教会的源头来自耶稣基督当初所创建的教会，并由其十二位门徒传播开去，当中以圣伯多禄宗徒为首，一般所称之"天主教"，并以教廷作为最高权力机构。

Chaeronea：克罗尼亚，希腊东部一古城，公元前 338 年马其顿的菲利普在此击败希腊联军。

Chaldea：迦勒底王国，即新巴比伦王国，位于古巴比伦王国南部。

Chaos:卡俄斯，希腊神话中的混沌之神。他是创造神，具备最初的生命繁衍力。

Charlemagne：查理曼大帝，法兰克国王(768～814)，是罗马灭亡后西欧第一个帝国的创始人。

Charles Darwin：查尔斯·达尔文，英国生物学家，进化论的奠基人。出版《物种起源》这一划时代的著作，提出了生物进化论学说，从而摧毁了各种唯心的神造论和物种不变论。

Charles de Gaulle：夏尔·戴高乐，法国将军、政治家，曾在第二次世界大战期间领导自由法国运动并在战后成立法兰西第五共和国并担任第一任总统。

Charles Martel:查理·马特(676～741)，法兰克王国墨洛温王朝末期的宫相。他平定内乱，抗击外敌，实行改革，因战功赫赫被称为"铁锤查理"。

Charles Ⅴ：查尔斯五世，神圣罗马帝国的皇帝。

Christianity：基督教

Christopher Columbus：克里斯托弗·哥伦布

Church of San Lorenzo：圣·洛伦佐教堂

Church of San Spirito：圣灵教堂，位于佛罗伦萨。

Church of Santa Maria del Carmine：佛罗伦萨卡尔米内教堂

Cicero：西塞罗，(前 106～前 43)，古罗马政治家、雄辩家、著作家。

Clairvaux：12 世纪中叶克莱尔沃修道院

Claude Debussy：克劳德·德彪西(1862～1918)，法国作曲家，音乐评论家。在三十余年的创作生涯中，德彪西形成了一种新的音乐风格——印象主义风格，对欧美各国音乐产生了深远影响。

Claude Monet：克洛德·莫奈，法国画家，印象派代表人物和创始人之一。莫奈是法国最重要的画家之一，印象派的理论和实践大部分都由他推广。他擅长光与影的实验与表现技法。

Cleopatra Ⅶ：克丽奥帕特拉七世(前 69～前 30)，埃及托勒密王朝最后一位女王。她才貌出众，聪颖机智，擅长手腕，心怀叵测，一生富有戏剧性。特别是卷入罗马共和末期的政治漩涡，同恺撒、安东尼关系密切，并伴以种种传闻逸事，使她成为文学和艺术作品中的著名人物。

Clovis：克洛维斯，5 世纪统一高卢的国王，在高卢语中作 Louis，即后来的路易斯国王。

Colosseum：罗马圆形大剧场，亦译作“罗马斗兽场”、“罗马大角斗场”、“罗马竞技场”、“罗马圆形竞技场”，建于公元 72 至 82 年间，由 4 万名战俘用 8 年时间建造而成。位于今天的意大利罗马市中心，是古罗马时期最大的圆形角斗场。现仅存遗迹。

Colossus of Memnon：门农，埃及底比斯附近阿蒙霍特普三世的巨大石像，每在日出时发出竖琴声，170 年经罗马皇帝修复后不再发声。

Concert of Europe：欧洲协同体

Concord：康科德

Concordat：宗教协定，作为罗马天主教领导人的教皇和世俗(国民)政府之间的协定。宗教协定通常规定在涉及两派的事件上宗教和民事的权限。1801 年，教皇庇护七世和拿破仑·波拿巴签订了一个协议，恢复法国革命之前罗马天主教在法国的地位。

Confederation of Independent States：独联体，全称为独立国家联合体，由前苏联大多数共和国组成的进行多边合作的独立国家联合体，简称“独联体”。

Constantine：君士坦丁，古罗马皇帝(306～337)，是世界历史上第一位信仰基督教的皇帝。他在 313 年颁布米兰赦令，承认基督教为合法自由的宗教，并于 330 年迁都拜占庭。此外，他的一系列改革措施为欧洲从奴隶社会向封建社会的过渡起到了重要作用。

Constantinople：君士坦丁堡

Continental Army：大陆军

Corinth：科林斯，希腊海港城市。

Cornwall：康沃尔郡，英格兰西南端一个地区。

Corsica：科西嘉岛，位于法国本土东南部，撒丁岛以北，法国最大的岛。

Cosimo de' Medici：科西莫·德·美第奇(1389～1464)，第一个佛罗伦萨僭主，梅第奇政治朝代的创建者。

Crassus：克拉苏，罗马政治家和将军，他与尤里乌斯恺撒和庞培组成了三人寡头政治。

Crete：克里特岛，希腊所属的地中海岛屿。

Crimean War：克里米亚战争，1853 年 10 月 20 日因争夺巴尔干半岛的控制权而在欧洲爆发的一场战争。土耳其、英国、法国、撒丁王国等先后向俄国宣战，战争一直持续到 1856 年，以俄国的失败而告终。

Cronus：克洛诺斯，地神该亚和天神乌拉诺斯所生的十二位提坦神中最年幼者，称为和平之神。他推翻了父亲乌拉诺斯的残暴统治并领导了希腊神话中的黄金时代，直到被自己的儿子宙斯推翻。

Ctesiphon：(伊拉克)泰西封

Cumberland：坎伯兰郡(英格兰一郡名)

Cyclopes：库克罗普斯，独眼巨人，只有一只眼睛长在前额正中的巨人族。他们群居住在库克罗普斯岛上，以岛上的野生物和他们豢养的羊群为食。他们是神祇的仆人，为各神祇工作。

Cyprus：塞浦路斯(地中海东部一岛)

Cyrus：居鲁士，波斯国王。

Dacia：达契亚，古罗马一省份。

Dada Movement：达达运动，1916 年至 1923 年间出现于法国、德国和瑞士的一种艺术流派。达达主义是一种无政府主义的艺术运动，它试图通过废除传统的文化和美学形式发现真正的现实。

Damascus：大马士革，叙利亚的首都和最大城市，位于叙利亚西南部。史前时代就有人居住，在罗马统治时成为繁华的商业中心，在十字军东征期间是穆斯林的大本营。

Dante Alighieri ：但丁(1265～1321)，意大利人，诗人。

Danube：多瑙河，在欧洲仅次于伏尔加河，是欧洲第二长河。它发源于德国西南部的黑林山的东坡，自西向东流经 9 个国家，是世界上干流流经国家最多的河流。

Darius Ⅰ "the Great"：大流士一世，波斯帝国国王，随冈比西斯二世出征埃及，被任命为万人不死军的总指挥，被认为是影响了世界历史进程的帝王。

David：大卫，扫罗继任者，定都耶路撒冷，开辟了以色列历史上的黄金时代。

Delta area：三角洲地区

Democritus：德谟克利特(约前 460～前 370)，古希腊属地阿布德拉人，古希腊伟大的唯物主义哲学家、原子唯物论学说的创始人之一。古希腊伟大哲学家留基伯是他的导师。

Denmark：丹麦，北欧国家，首都哥本哈根。

Desiderius Erasmus：德西德里乌斯·伊拉斯谟，中世纪尼德兰著名的人文主义思想家和神学家。

Diocletian：戴克里先，公元 286 年罗马皇帝。他结束了罗马帝国的第三世纪危机

(235～284)，建立了四帝共治制，使其成为罗马帝国后期的主要政体。为试图更有效地控制帝国，将其分为东、西两个罗马帝国。

Directory：督政府，法国大革命时期根据《共和三年宪法》建立的政府。1795 年热月党人于 10 月解散国民公会，成立新的政府机构督政府。

Dolly：多莉(克隆羊)。1996 年 7 月 5 日，英国科学家伊恩·维尔穆特博士用一个成年羊的体细胞成功地克隆出了一只小羊，因与其“父亲”一模一样，取名“多莉”。

Dominic：圣道明，创立道明托钵僧兄弟会的西班牙神父，以讲道、祈祷、守斋、善表劝化异端徒。

Domitian：图密善(14～96)，罗马帝国皇帝。他是弗拉维王朝的最后一位皇帝。他生性残暴，是一位暴君。

Donate di Donatello：多纳泰罗，意大利早期文艺复兴第一代美术家，15 世纪最杰出的雕塑家。

Duchy of Milan：米兰公国，1395～1797 年间意大利北部的一个国家。

East India Company：东印度公司，始建于 1600 年，是英国、法国、荷兰等继葡萄牙和西班牙殖民扩张后 17 世纪新兴的殖民国家为了处理在殖民地地区的一些事物而成立的机构。最初，英国人主要是利用东印度公司作生意，后来成了英国殖民者侵略印度的工具。

EC：欧洲共同体，西欧国家推行欧洲经济、政治一体化过程中形成的，并具有一定超国家机制和职能的国际组织。又称“欧洲共同市场”，简称“欧共体”。

ECSC：欧洲煤钢共同体。1950 年法国外长舒曼提出“欧洲煤钢联营计划”(即“舒曼计划”)，建议愿将本国经济中的煤钢部门管理权委托给某一独立机构的国家成立煤钢共同市场。此后，法、西德、意、比、荷、卢等 6 个西欧国家开始在此计划基础上进行谈判。1951 年 4 月 18 日，在美国的支持下，法国、联邦德国、意大利、比利时、荷兰、卢森堡六国根据“舒曼计划”在巴黎签订了为期 50 年的《欧洲煤钢共同体条约》。

Edward Ⅵ：爱德华六世，英国国王，亨利八世独子。

EEC：欧洲经济共同体，欧洲共同体中最重要的组成部分。

Eisenach：艾森纳赫，德国图林根州的一座城市。

Eleanor：埃莉诺，英王理查德的母亲。

Elijah：以利亚，公元前 9 世纪以色列的先知，见《圣经·列王记》。

ElizabethⅠ：伊丽莎白一世，于 1558 年至 1603 年任英格兰王国和爱尔兰女王，是都铎王朝的第五位也是最后一位君主。

Elizabethan Era：伊丽莎白时代。伊丽莎白是英格兰女王，在位时间是 1559 年 11 月 17 日至 1603 年 3 月 24 日。伊丽莎白一世的统治时期是英格兰趋向强盛和国家建立最重要的一个时期。

Encyclopedist：百科全书派，18 世纪法国启蒙思想家在编纂《百科全书》的过程中形成的派别，以狄德罗为主要代表。

Epicurus：埃皮克提图，公元前 1 世纪时斯多葛学派哲学家、教师。

Eratosthenes of Cyrene：昔兰尼的厄拉多塞，希腊科学作家、天文学家、数学家和诗人。

Estates General：三级会议，法国中世纪的等级代表会议。参加者有僧侣、贵族和市民三个等级的代表，通常是国家遇到困难时，国王为寻求援助而召集会议。

EU：欧洲联盟，简称欧盟，总部设在比利时首都布鲁塞尔，由欧洲共同体发展而来的，是一个集政治实体和经济实体于一身、在世界上具有重要影响的区域一体化组织。

Euclid：欧几里得，古希腊数学家，他把逻辑学中的演绎原理应用到几何学中，借以由定义明确的公理导出语句。

EURATOM：欧洲原子能共同体，由欧洲联盟成员国组成的国际组织。1957 年 3 月 25 日，《欧洲煤钢联营条约》成员国签订《罗马条约》，决定成立共同市场及原子能共同体。如今，欧洲原子能共同体已经在欧洲联盟架构内。

Euripides：欧里庇底斯，古希腊戏剧家。

Euro：欧元，是欧洲货币联盟(EMU)国家的单一货币。

Exodus：出埃及事，古代以色列人在摩西率领下离开埃及一事；《出埃及记》，《圣经·旧约》中的第 2 卷。

Ezekiel：以西结，公元前 6 世纪的以色列祭司、先知，相传《以西结书》为其所作。

Filippo Brunelleschi：布鲁涅内斯基，意大利初期文艺复兴时期建筑家、数学家、画家、雕刻家。

Florence：佛罗伦萨，意大利都市名。

Flying shuttle：飞梭，1733 年由钟表匠约翰·凯伊发明，大大提高了织布效率，也刺激了对棉纱的需求，是 18 世纪中期英国工业革命开始时，棉纺织业中的贡献之一。

Francesco Petrarch：弗朗西斯克·彼特拉克，意大利学者、诗人，早期的人文主义者，被称为“人文主义之父”。他与但丁、薄伽丘齐名，文学史上称他们为“三颗巨星”。

Franciscan：圣芳济修会

Franco-Prussian War：普法战争，在德法两国称为德法战争，是普鲁士为了统一德国，并与法国争夺欧洲大陆霸权而爆发的战争。由法国发动，最后以普鲁士大获全胜，建立德意志帝国告终。

Frederick Barbarossa：神圣罗马帝国皇帝腓特烈一世，1152～1190 年在位。

Frederick Ⅱ：弗雷德里克二世，即腓特烈二世，生活在 13 世纪上半叶的欧洲，既是西西里国王，也是德意志国王，并加冕为神圣罗马帝国的皇帝。他在西西里实行集权统治，组织并参加了第六次十字军东征。

Gabriel：《圣经》加百利，七大天使之一，上帝传送好消息给人类的使者。

Gaelic：苏格兰盖立语

Gaea：该亚，希腊神话中的大地之神，是众神之母，也是所有神灵中德高望重的显赫之神。

Galen：加伦，希腊解剖学家，内科医生和作家。

Galileo Galilei：伽利略·伽利雷，意大利物理学家、天文学家和哲学家，近代实验科学的先驱者。

Gaul：高卢，西欧的一古老地区，位于莱茵河南部和西部、阿尔卑斯山西部、比利牛斯山北部，基本相当于现代的法国和比利时。

Geneva：日内瓦，瑞士城市。

Genoa：热那亚，意大利西北的一座城市。

Georges Braque：乔治·布拉克(1882～1963)，法国画家，立体主义代表。他与毕加索同为立体主义运动的创始人。

George Stephenson：乔治·史蒂文森，蒸汽机车的发明人。

Gilgamesh：吉尔伽美什，传说中的苏美尔国王。

Giordano Bruno：乔尔丹诺·布鲁诺，文艺复兴时期意大利的哲学家、科学家。

Giotto：乔托，意大利画家、雕刻家、建筑师。

Giovanni Boccaccio：薄伽丘(1313～1375)，意大利人，作家。

Giovanni Pico della Mirandolà：乔万尼·皮科·德拉·米朗多拉(1463～1494)，意大利文艺复兴时期的著名思想家。他的《关于人的尊严的演说》被称为"人文主义宣言"。

Goshen：歌珊地，基督教《圣经》中以色列人出埃及以前居住的下埃及肥沃地区。

Great Plague：又称"Great Death"或"Black Death"，黑死病，人类历史上最严重的瘟疫之一。

Greece：希腊

Gregory：格雷戈里(男子名，古代罗马教皇之名)

Grendel：格伦德尔，英国史诗《贝奥武夫》中记述的一只凶猛的怪兽。

Guillaume de Lorris：基洛姆·德·洛利思，法国诗人，《玫瑰传奇》上卷的作者。

Guillaume Farel：纪尧姆·法雷尔，欧洲宗教改革运动领路人。

Hadrian：哈德良，公元117～138年在位的罗马皇帝。他下令建造哈德良长城。

Haggai：哈该，公元前6世纪希伯来先知，据传系《圣经·旧约》中的《哈该书》的作者。

Hammurabi：汉谟拉比，古巴比伦第六代国王。

Hannibal：汉尼拔(前247～前183)，迦太基著名统帅。第二次布匿战争中，迦太基为了弥补战败损失，派兵入侵西班牙，准备反击罗马，罗马得知其备战，准备兵分两路进攻迦太基和西班牙，但迦太基名将汉尼拔先发制人，于公元前218年率大军翻越阿尔卑斯山直捣意大利。同年11月，汉尼拔在波河南支流的特列比亚河击败前来拦截的罗马4万大军。

Hanging Gardens：空中花园，是古代世界七大奇迹之一，又称"悬园"。

Hatshepsut：哈特谢普苏特，埃及女王。她发展贸易，大兴土木，在底比斯附近建造了达尔巴赫里御庙。

Hattusas：哈图萨斯

Hebrew Bible：希伯来《圣经》，成为基督教的《旧约》。

Henry Ⅳ：亨利四世(1050～1106)，法兰克尼亚王朝/萨利安王朝第三位罗马人民的国王和神圣罗马帝国皇帝，也是巴伐利亚公爵。

Henry Ⅵ：亨利六世(1165～1197)，霍亨斯陶芬王朝的德意志国王(1190～1197年在位)和神圣罗马帝国皇帝(1191年加冕)。

Hera：赫拉，奥林匹斯山十二主神之一。古希腊神话中的天后，她是克罗诺斯和瑞娅的长女，宙斯的姐姐和第三位妻子，相对应于罗马神话的朱诺。赫拉是古希腊神话中奥林匹斯主神之一，被尊称为"神后"。

Herakleopolis：希拉克利欧波力斯，埃及第九和第十王朝首都。

Herbert Spencer：赫伯特·斯宾塞（1820～1903），英国社会学家，被称为"社会达尔文主义之父"。斯宾塞提出的学说把进化理论适者生存应用在社会学，尤其是教育和阶级斗争领域。

Herod：希律，犹太王（前40～4）。据《新约》讲，他命令杀死伯利恒所有两岁以下的儿童，借以杀死尚处于襁褓中的耶稣。

Hesiod：赫西奥德，古希腊诗人，生活在大约公元前8世纪，其作品《工作与时日》包括生产技术的指导和伦理道德的训诫；《神谱》把纷繁复杂的希腊诸神系统化为一个单一的世系，从而把希腊神话纳入了一个统一体，是希腊奥林巴斯教发展的重要里程碑。

Hiroshima：广岛，世界上第一个被原子弹严重破坏的城市，在原子弹爆发之处建造了平和纪念公园，以祈求永久的和平。

Hispaniola：伊斯帕尼奥拉岛（海地岛）

Hittite：赫梯

Hohenzollern：霍亨索伦家族，德意志的主要统治家族。其始祖布尔夏德一世约在1100年受封为索伦伯爵。16世纪中叶，该家族在索伦前冠以"霍亨"（意为"高贵的"）字样，称为"霍亨索伦家族"。该家族是勃兰登堡、普鲁士及德意志帝国的统治家族。

Holy Roman Empire：神圣罗马帝国，全称为"德意志民族神圣罗马帝国"或"日耳曼民族神圣罗马帝国"，是962年至1806年在西欧和中欧的封建帝国。早期为统一的国家，中世纪后演变为一些承认皇帝最高权威的公国、侯国、伯国、宗教贵族领地和自由市的政治联合体，其历史可追溯至罗马帝国。

Holy Synod：圣议会，神圣宗教会议。

Homer：古希腊盲诗人，通译为荷马。生平和生卒年月不可考。相传记述公元前12～前11世纪特洛伊战争及有关海上冒险故事的古希腊长篇叙事史诗《伊利亚特》和《奥德赛》，即是他根据民间流传的短歌综合编写而成。据此，他生活的年代，当在公元前10～前9、8世纪之间。荷马史诗是《伊利亚特》与《奥德赛》的合称。到公元前3世纪和前2世纪，又经亚里山大里亚学者编订，各部为24卷。

Horace：贺拉斯，古罗马诗人、批评家，奥古斯都时期的宫廷诗人。代表作《诗艺》集中体现了他的美学思想，诗歌作品有《讽刺诗集》、《歌集》等。

Horus：荷鲁斯，奥西里斯之子。

House of Commons：英国议会下院（平民院）

House of Hanover：汉诺威王朝，于1692～1866年间统治德国汉诺威地区，1714～1901年间统治英国的王朝。

House of Lords：英国议会上院（贵族院）

Houston Stewart Chamberlain：豪斯顿·斯蒂华·张伯伦（1855～1927），英籍德裔思想家。张伯伦把日耳曼人看成是主宰种族，他的著作对希特勒等人产生了深远影响，纳粹党人继承了他的种族理论,并把他奉为先知。

Huguenot:胡格诺,16～17 世纪法国新教徒形成的一个派别。

Hungary:匈牙利

Hyksos:西克索斯王朝

Iason:伊阿宋,古希腊神话人物。希腊神话中夺取金羊毛的主要英雄。他是埃宋的儿子、克瑞透斯的孙子,希腊神话中的忒萨莉亚王子。

Igor Stravinsky:伊戈尔·斯特拉文斯基(1882～1971),美籍俄裔作曲家、指挥家、西方现代派音乐的重要人物。其代表作品有《春之祭》(*The Rite of Spring*)等。

Inca:印加文明,在南美洲西部、中安第斯山区发展起来的著名的印第安古代文明。它的影响范围北起哥伦比亚南部的安卡斯马约河、南到智利中部的马乌莱河,全长 4800 公里,东西最宽处 500 公里,总面积达 90 多万平方公里,人口超过 1000 万。

Investiture Controversy:主教叙任权之争,指 11 世纪末至 12 世纪初,教皇与神圣罗马帝国皇帝之间的权力之争。始于教皇格列高利七世与皇帝亨利四世为主教及修道院长叙任权属于谁而产生的争议,终于 1122 年,亨利五世与教皇卡利克斯特二世签订沃尔姆斯宗教协定,双方达成妥协。

Iraklio:伊拉克利翁,希腊克里特岛中北部最大的城市和港口,北滨爱琴海。是古希腊米诺斯文化的发源地之一。

Iran:伊朗

Iron Lady:铁娘子,指英国首相玛格丽特·撒切尔。

Isaac:以撒,《圣经》中希伯来族长,亚伯拉罕和撒拉之子,雅各和以扫之父。

Isaac Newton:艾萨克·牛顿,英国著名物理学家、数学家、科学家和哲学家。其代表作《自然哲学的数学原理》中提出的万有引力定律以及牛顿行动定律是经典力学的基石。

Isabella d'Este:伊莎贝拉·黛丝贴,意大利文艺复兴时期曼图亚的女侯爵。

Isaiah:以赛亚,公元前 8 世纪希伯来预言家

Isis:伊西斯神,奥西里斯之妻

Islam:伊斯兰教(在中国旧称"回教","清真教")

Israel:以色列王国

Italian peninsula:意大利半岛

Jacob:雅各,《圣经·创世记》中 Isaac 之子,以色列人的祖先,又名 Israel。

Jean de Meung:让·德·梅恩,法国民间诗人,《玫瑰传奇》下卷的作者。

Jean-Paul Sartre:让·保罗·萨特,法国 20 世纪最重要的哲学家之一,法国无神论存在主义的主要代表人物,也是优秀的文学家、戏剧家、评论家和社会活动家。

Jeremiah:耶利米,公元前 7～前 6 世纪希伯来先知,《圣经》中的人物。

Jerome:圣哲罗姆,拉丁文学者,写成的拉丁语《圣经》,是第一本将圣经由希伯来文译成拉丁文的权威性著作。

Jerusalem:耶路撒冷,巴勒斯坦城市。

Jesus:耶稣,基督教信奉的救世主。

Johannes Gutenberg：约翰尼斯·古登堡，西方活字印刷术的发明人，被称为“德国印刷术之父”。

Johannes Kepler：开普勒，德国天体物理学家，提出了著名的行星运动三大定律。

John Calvin：约翰·加尔文，16 世纪法国著名的宗教改革家和神学家，基督教新教的重要派别加尔文教派（在法国称“胡格诺派”）创始人。

John Duns Scotus：司各托，13～14 世纪苏格兰罗马天主教著名神学家和哲学家。

John Locke：约翰·洛克，全面系统地阐述宪政民主基本思想的第一位作家，其思想深刻地影响了美国的开国元勋及法国启蒙运动中的许多主要哲学家。

Judaea：犹地亚，古巴勒斯坦南部地区，古代罗马统治的一个城市。

Judah：犹大王国

Jugurtha：朱古达，努米底亚（今属阿尔及利亚）国王。公元前 2 世纪，努米底亚已是罗马附庸，公元前 113 年，努米底亚发生王位之争，朱古达打败并杀死罗马人支持的政敌。公元前 111 年，罗马元老院向朱古达国王宣战，朱古达战争爆发。

Julius Caesar：恺撒（前 100～前 44），古罗马将军、政治家、历史学家。

Junker：德国的容克贵族，原指无骑士称号的贵族子弟，后泛指普鲁士贵族和大地主。起源于 16 世纪，第二次世界大战后基本消亡。

Jupiter：朱庇特，罗马神话中的神，是罗马统治希腊后将宙斯之名改变成为朱庇特。他是罗马神话中的主神，第三任神王；科洛诺斯和瑞亚之子，掌管天界；以贪花好色著称，奥林匹斯的许多神祇和许多希腊英雄都是他和不同女人生下的子女。他以雷电为武器，维持着天地间的秩序，公牛和鹰是他的标志。

Justinian：东罗马帝国皇帝

Kamose：卡摩斯，埃及第 17 王朝的末代国王。

Karnak：卡纳克（阿拉伯语）神庙，在卢克索城的北边，与卢克索神庙相比占地更大，建筑更加高大雄伟。

Khufu：胡夫法老

King Henry Ⅷ：亨利八世，英国都铎王朝第二任国王，也是爱尔兰领主，后来更成为爱尔兰国王。

King Philip Ⅱ：菲利普二世

Kingdom of Naples：那不勒斯王国，由中世纪到 1860 年意大利半岛南部的国家。

Knossos：克诺索斯，克里特岛上的一座米诺斯文明遗址。被认为是传说中米诺斯王的王宫。

Lagash：拉加什，底格里斯河—幼发拉底河流域的城邦国。

Laissez-faire：自由放任政策。自由放任主义反对政府对经济的干涉，并且反对政府征收除了足以维持和平、治安和财产权以外的税赋。

Latium：拉丁姆，古地区名。在今意大利中西部拉齐奥区，以居住拉丁人得名。公元前 2000 年初，拉丁人从东北移居于此，为古罗马国家的发源地。

Lebanon：黎巴嫩

Lepidus：雷必达（约前 89～前 12），古罗马政治家。自公元前 43 年起，与安东尼、屋大维共同统治罗马，史称罗马后三头同盟，曾任古罗马最高祭司长。

Legislative Assembly：立法会议

Leo：利奥（男子名）

Leonardo Bruni：莱昂纳多·布鲁尼，意大利文艺复兴时期著名的人文主义历史学家。

Leonardo da Vinci：莱昂纳多·达·芬奇，意大利文艺复兴时期伟大画家、雕刻家、建筑学家。

Leonid Brezhnev：列奥尼德·勃列日涅夫，前苏联政治家，曾任苏联共产党中央第一书记，苏联最高苏维埃主席团主席和军队最高领导人。

Leucippus：留基伯（约前 500 ～约前 440），古希腊唯物主义哲学家，原子论的奠基人之一。

Lexington：来克星顿，美国马萨诸塞州一小镇，因美国独立战争在此打响而著名。

Libya：利比亚，北非国家。

Livy：李维，古罗马历史学家，其代表作《罗马自建城以来的历史》（*History of Rome*）充满了爱国思想、道德说教和复古主张。

Lord Byron：拜伦，英国浪漫主义文学的杰出代表。

Louis XIV：路易十四

Louis-Napoleon Bonaparte：路易一拿破仑·波拿巴（1808～1873），法兰西第二共和国总统，法兰西第二帝国皇帝，为拿破仑一世之侄。

Low Countries：低地国家，指荷兰、比利时、卢森堡三个国家。

Lower Canada：下加拿大，加拿大地区名，魁北克省的前身。

Lower Egypt：下埃及，即北部尼罗河下游三角洲地区。

Lucretius：卢克莱修，罗马的哲学家和诗人。他继承古代原子学说，特别是阐述并发展了伊壁鸠鲁的哲学观点，认为物质的存在是永恒的，反对神创论；认为宇宙是无限的，有其自然发展的过程；承认世界的可知性，驳斥了怀疑论。著有哲学长诗《物性论》。

Luddite：卢德派，或卢德分子。

Luxor：卢克索神庙。卢克索位于埃及中部，古名底比斯，一直是古埃及法老建都最多的城市。

Lyons：里昂，法国中东部一城市，位于罗纳河与塞纳河交汇处玛亢的南部。

Macedonia：马其顿，位于古希腊北部，相当于今天的阿尔巴尼亚和南斯拉夫南部地区，当古希腊进入黄金时代时，马其顿才出现国家，腓力二世统治时期，马其顿开始强大，后来腓力于公元前 336 年死于宫廷阴谋，其子亚历山大继位，并开始了他的征服霸业。公元前 323 年，他制定了出征阿拉伯的计划，先头部队已经出发，但据说他本人在大军出发前一天暴病而死。他死后，部将立即展开争夺权利的斗争，大战的结果是帝国分裂为托勒密王国、塞琉古王国、马其顿王国。

Macedon：马其顿王国

Magdeburg：马格德堡，德国萨克森一安哈特州首府。

Malabar Coast：马拉巴海岸

Manetho：马涅托，古代埃及僧侣，第一位伟大的历史学家和“埃及史之父”。其《埃及史》提供了第一部有系统的、完整的埃及法老史，其王朝体系为现代埃及学研究奠定了相对年代学的基础。

Mansfeld：曼斯费尔德，德国一城市。

Mantua：曼图亚，意大利北部一城市。

Marcus Aurelius：马克斯·奥里留斯，古罗马皇帝，161～180年间在位。奥里留斯是一位具有哲学家风格的统治者，他把斯多葛学派的哲学主张用于政治统治。

Marduk：马杜克，古代巴比伦人的主神，原为巴比伦的太阳神。

Margaret Thatcher：玛格丽特·撒切尔，英国保守党第一位女领袖，历史上第一位女首相，蝉联三届，任期长达11年。

Marius：马略(约前157～前86)，古罗马将军和政治家，前107年任执政官，针对当时罗马军队兵源匮乏等问题，实行军事改革，取消兵役财产资格的规定，军队的给养和武器装备由国家供给，加强军队训练。前106年，偕部将苏拉进军努米比亚，翌年俘获朱古达，凯旋罗马，结束了朱古达战争。

Mars：古罗马战神、罗马的保护神，其重要性仅次于朱庇特。马尔斯在希腊神话中是阿瑞斯神。

Marsilio Ficino：费其诺(1433～1499)，人道主义者、哲学家，早期意大利人。

Martin Luther：马丁·路德，16世纪欧洲宗教改革倡导者，新教路德宗创始人。

Massaccio：马萨乔，15世纪意大利文艺复兴时期画家。他是第一位使用透视法的画家，其壁画是人文主义一个最早的里程碑。

Massachusetts：马萨诸塞，美国一个州，正式名称为“马萨诸塞联邦”，是新英格兰地区的一部分。在中文中，通常简称“麻州”或“麻省”。

Mecca：麦加，位于沙特阿拉伯西部，穆罕默德诞生地，伊斯兰教第一圣地。

Medina：麦地那，沙特阿拉伯西部城市，伊斯兰教创立人穆罕默德的陵墓所在地，伊斯兰教圣地之一。

Mediterranean：地中海，世界上最大的陆间海，被北面的欧洲大陆、南面的非洲大陆和东面的亚洲大陆包围着，东西共长约4000千米，南北最宽处大约为1800千米。

Memphis：孟菲斯，古代埃及城市。废墟位于开罗之南。

Menes：美尼斯，古埃及第一王朝建立者。

Menno Simons：门诺·西门，荷兰人，教士，基督教门诺宗主要发起人。

Mercia：麦西亚，中世纪早期七国时代的七国之一，位于今英格兰中部。

Mercury：墨丘利，在罗马神话中他是朱庇特与女神迈亚所生的儿子，担任诸神的使者和传译，又是司畜牧、商业、交通旅游和体育运动的神，还是小偷们所崇拜的神。他是朱庇特最忠实的信使，为朱庇特传送消息，并完成朱庇特交给他的各种任务。他行走敏捷，精力充沛，多才多艺。

Mesopotamia：美索不达米亚，西南亚地区，《圣经》中被称为“伊甸园”，是古希腊语，意思是两河之间的土地，原义“河间地区”，亦称“两河流域”。美索不达米亚为人类最古的文化摇篮之一，灌溉农业为其文化发展的主要基础。公元前4000年已有较发达文化，曾出现苏美尔、阿卡德、巴比伦、亚述等文明。此后又经过波斯、马其顿、罗马与奥斯曼等帝国的统治。第一次世界大战后，其主要部分成为独立的伊拉克。

Messiah：弥赛亚，犹太人期盼的复国救主。

Michelangelo：米开朗基罗，意大利雕刻家、画家、建筑家及诗人。

Mikhail S. Gorbachev：米卡黑尔·戈尔巴乔夫，末代苏联共产党中央总书记(1985～1991)。

Milan：米兰，意大利北部城市。

Miltiades：米太亚得，出身贵族，古希腊雅典统帅。约公元前524年任执政官。曾率领希腊人取得了马拉松战役的胜利。

Mitanni：米坦尼王国

Montenegro:黑山共和国(前南斯拉夫西南部)，亚德里沿海岸边的地区。

Moses：摩西，公元前13世纪的犹太人先知，《旧约圣经》前五本书的执笔者，带领希伯来人到达神所预备的"流着奶和蜜之地"——迦南。

Mughal Dynasty：莫卧儿王朝，1526～1858年统治南亚次大陆绝大部分地区的伊斯兰教封建王朝。

Muhammad：穆罕默德，伊斯兰教鼻祖。

Mycenae：迈锡尼，位于伯罗奔尼撒半岛，希腊神话里流传了两千年之城。迈锡尼文明由此得名。

Nagasaki：长崎，日本九州岛西岸著名港市，长崎县首府。1945年8月9日遭到美军原子弹袭击。

Nahum：那鸿，传为公元前6世纪的犹太先知。

Naples：那不勒斯，意大利港市。

National Convention：国民公会，法国大革命时期建立的最高立法机构。1792年8月10日巴黎人民起义推翻王权后，立法议会决定在普选基础上产生另一制宪议会，以美国1787年费城制宪会议的名称Convention命名。

Nazareth：拿撒勒，巴勒斯坦地区北部古城。

Nebhepetre Mentuhotpe：内布赫珀特拉·曼图霍特普，埃及第十一王朝法老。

Nebuchadnezzar Ⅱ：尼布甲尼撒二世，新巴比伦国王，攻陷耶路撒冷。在位期间修建了著名的伊什塔尔门和空中花园(古代世界奇迹之一)。

Neo-Babylonian Empire：新巴比伦帝国

Nero：尼禄，公元54～68年罗马皇帝。残酷与渎职引发了广泛的暴动致使他自杀身亡。

Neville Chamberlain：内维尔·张伯伦，英国政治家，1937～1940年任英国首相。

New England：新英格兰地区，位于美国大陆东北角、濒临大西洋、毗邻加拿大的区域。新英格兰地区包括美国的六个州，由北至南分别为：缅因州、新罕布什尔州、佛蒙特州、马萨诸塞州、罗德岛州、康乃狄格州。(麻省)首府波士顿是该地区的最大城市以及经济与文化中心。

Niccolo Machiavelli：尼克罗·马基雅维利，意大利的政治哲学家，文艺复兴中的重要人物。

Nicholas Ⅰ：沙皇尼古拉斯一世，于1825～1855年在位。他被认为是俄国最反动皇帝中的一位。

Nicolaus Copernicus：尼古拉·哥白尼，波兰天文学家，近代天文学的奠基人。

Nile：尼罗河

Nineveh：尼尼微，亚述首都。

Noah：诺亚，基督教《圣经》故事人物，洪水灭世后人类的新始祖。

Northumbria：诺森伯利亚，北英格兰一盎格鲁一撒克逊王国，公元7世纪由伯尼西亚和德伊勒联盟建立。诺森伯利亚的大部分在9世纪被入侵的丹麦人占领，954年被韦塞克斯吞并。

Nubia：努比亚，非洲东北部古国，是埃及尼罗河第一瀑布阿斯旺与苏丹第四瀑布库赖迈之间地区的称呼，从古至今一直被认为是地中海地区的埃及与黑色非洲之间的连接地。

Octavian：屋大维，罗马帝国的开国君主，元首政制的创始人，统治罗马长达43年。他是恺撒的甥孙，公元前44年被恺撒收为养子并指定为继承人。恺撒被刺后登上政治舞台。公元前1世纪，他平息了企图分裂罗马共和国的内战，被元老院赐封为“奥古斯都”，并改组罗马政府，给罗马世界带来了两个世纪的和平与繁荣。

Oliver Cromwell：奥利弗·克伦威尔

Orléans：奥尔良，法国城市，1429年法国女英雄贞德领导人民在此打败英国占领军。

Osiris：奥西里斯，埃及神话中的司阴府之神，大地之神的第一个儿子，死亡判官。

Otto von Bismark：奥托·冯·俾斯麦，普鲁士宰相兼外交大臣，是德国近代史上杰出的政治家和外交家，被称为“铁血首相”。

Ovid：奥维德，古罗马最伟大的诗人之一，其代表作为长诗《变形记》(*Metamorphoses*)和《爱的艺术》(*Art of Love*)。

Pablo Picasso：帕布罗·毕加索，西班牙画家、雕塑家，现代艺术的创始人，西方现代派绘画的主要代表。

Palestine：巴勒斯坦地区

Pantheon：罗马万神庙，古罗马城中心供奉众神的庙宇。它是古罗马建筑的代表作之一，建于公元120～124年间。

Papal States：教皇国，由许多昔日的独立或半独立城邦、小国和贵族领地构成的共同体。在文艺复兴时期，教皇国成为意大利最重要的政治力量之一。

Pazzi Chapel：帕奇小礼拜堂，位于佛罗伦萨。

Pearl Harbour：珍珠港，地处瓦胡岛南岸的科劳山脉和怀阿奈山脉之间平原的最低处，美国海军的基地和造船基地。

Peloponnesus War：伯罗奔尼撒战争，公元前431～前404年斯巴达和雅典之间的战争，古代希腊史上的一次大战。

Peloponnesus：伯罗奔尼撒半岛，位于希腊南部。

Peninsular War：半岛战争，拿破仑战争中最主要的其中一场战役，发生在伊比利亚半岛，交战方分别是西班牙、葡萄牙、英国和拿破仑统治下的法国。这场战役被称作“铁锤与铁砧战役”。“铁锤”代表的是数量为4～8万的英一葡联军，指挥官是第一任威灵顿公爵，阿瑟·韦莱斯利；同另一支“铁砧”力量，即西班牙军队和游击队，以及葡萄牙民兵相配合，痛击法国军队。战争从1808年由法国军队占领西班牙开始，至1814年第六次反法同盟打败了拿破仑的军队结束。

Pepin the Short：矮子丕平，查理·马特另一个儿子，也称丕平三世，公元751～768年在位的法兰克国王，查理曼大帝的父亲，加洛林王朝的创建者。

Percy Bysshe Shelly：帕西·碧西·雪莱，英国文学史上最有才华的抒情诗人之一，更被誉为诗人中的诗人。他创作的诗歌节奏明快，积极向上。

Pergamum：珀加蒙，古希腊国王。

Persia：波斯，西南亚国家，现在的伊朗。

Peter：彼得，也被称为西蒙彼得。西蒙是他的名，彼得是耶稣给他的绰号，是石头的意思。本名西门巴约拿。

Persian Empire：波斯帝国

Peter Abelard：阿伯拉尔，12世纪法国杰出的神学家和哲学家。他坚持理性和实验，著名的学说为三位一体论。

Peter the Great：彼得大帝，是后世对沙皇彼得一世的尊称。作为罗曼诺夫朝仅有的两位“大帝”之一，彼得大帝一般被认为是俄国最杰出的沙皇。他制定的西方化政策是使俄国变成一个强国的主要因素。

Philip Ⅱ “Augustus”：法王“奥古斯都”腓力二世

Philip Ⅱ of Spain：腓力二世，强大的神圣罗马帝国皇帝查理五世（西班牙的卡洛斯一世）之子，玛丽一世的丈夫。

Philistia：非利士，《圣经》中巴勒斯坦西南海岸古国。

Piankhy：匹安赫国王

Pisa：比萨，意大利中部一城市。

Plato：柏拉图（约前427年～前347年），古希腊伟大的哲学家，也是全部西方哲学乃至整个西方文化最伟大的哲学家和思想家之一。他和老师苏格拉底、学生亚里士多德并称“古希腊三大哲学家”。柏拉图一生著述颇丰，代表作品有《申辩篇》、《理想国》、《法律篇》等。

Pompey：庞培（前106～前48），古代罗马共和国末期著名的军事家和政治家，贵族出身。

Pontius Pilate：本丢·彼拉多，罗马帝国朱迪亚行省的执政官。根据新约圣经所述，彼拉多审判并处死了耶稣。

Pope Innocent Ⅲ：教皇英诺森三世，1198～1216年在位。他在位期间教廷势力达到顶峰，并曾发动第四次十字军东征，镇压异教徒。

Pope Leo Ⅹ：教皇利奥十世

Pope Paul Ⅲ：教皇保罗三世，1534～1549年在位。他将英格兰国王亨利八世逐出教会，推动反宗教改革运动，承认耶稣会，召开特伦特宗教会议。

Pope Paul Ⅳ：保罗四世，1555～1559 年在位。

Populares：古罗马平民派，是精英的领导人。在晚期的罗马共和国，他们倾向于去使用平民会议，努力去突破显贵与贵人派支压制自由的力量，获得政治上的权力。

Predynastic Egypt：（古埃及）前王朝时期

Proletariat：无产阶级

Promised Land：督教《圣经》中的应许之地——迦南，指上帝答应给阿伯拉罕及其后裔的土地。

Protestant：新教徒

Prussia：普鲁士，一般指 17～19 世纪间的普鲁士王国。由于普鲁士在短短 200 年内崛起并统一德国，建立了德意志第二帝国，所以普鲁士有时也是德国近代精神、文化的代名词。

Ptolemy：托勒密，古希腊地理学家、天文学家、数学家。

Punic War：布匿战争

Punt：古埃及的贸易伙伴，具体地理位置不详。

Pyramid Age：金字塔时代

Pyrenees：比利牛斯山，欧洲西南部最大的山脉，分隔欧洲大陆与伊比利亚半岛，也是法国与西班牙的天然国界。

Queen Catherine：凯瑟琳王后，亨利八世的第一任妻子。

Ramesside Period：新王国时期

Ramses Ⅱ：拉美西斯二世。他留给我们两个世界文明的东西，一是他本人的木乃伊，另一个就是阿布辛贝勒神庙。

Raphael：拉斐尔，意大利画家、建筑学家。

Re：太阳神，日神。

Red Sea：红海

Rhine：莱茵河，西欧第一大河，发源于瑞士境内的阿尔卑斯山，流经德国注入北海。

Rhode Island：罗德岛州，全名是罗德岛与普洛威顿斯庄园，也名"罗得岛与普罗维登斯种植园州"。

Robert Grosseteste：罗伯特·格莱斯泰斯特，中世纪数学家（1175～1253）、牛津主教。他于 1215～1221 年任牛津大学校长，1229～1235 年为神学讲师。

Robert Owen：罗伯特·欧文，英国空想社会主义者、企业家、慈善家。

Robespierre：罗伯斯庇尔，法国革命家。他是法国大革命时期重要的领袖人物，也是雅各宾派政府的实际首脑之一。

Rococo：洛可可艺术

Roman Empire：罗马帝国

Romania：罗马尼亚（欧洲巴尔干半岛东北部国家）

Romanov Dynasty：1613～1917 年统治俄罗斯的封建王朝。1613 年 1 月，米哈伊尔·费多罗维奇·罗曼诺夫被推举为沙皇，开始了其在俄国的统治。1917 年罗曼诺夫王朝在二月革命中被推翻。

Romulus Augustulus：罗慕路·奥古斯都路斯，西罗马帝国的最后一位皇帝。476年，被罗马军队统帅奥多亚克(Odoacer)废黜，成为西罗马帝国灭亡的标志。

Rubicon：卢比肯河，意大利北部河流。"跨越卢比肯"隐含不能再回头的意思。

Sabine：萨宾人，古意大利部落，以其特殊的宗教信仰和习俗著称。

Saint Ignatius Loyola：圣依纳爵·罗耀拉，耶稣会的创始人。

Saite Period：赛特时期

Saladin：萨拉丁(1137～1193)，埃及的最高统治者苏丹，创立了阿尤布王朝，曾指挥抗击十字军东征。

Samaria：撒马利亚，古巴勒斯坦中部城市，以色列王国首都。

Samuel Taylor Coleridge：塞缪尔·泰勒·柯勒律治，英国诗人和评论家。

Santa Maria delle Grazie in Milan：圣母感恩教堂，意大利城市米兰的一所教堂和修道院，以修道院食堂内列奥纳多·达·芬奇所作的壁画《最后的晚餐》而著称，1980年列为世界遗产。1943年8月15日，教堂和修道院遭到英美飞机轰炸，食堂大部分被毁，但是《最后的晚餐》所在的那面墙却得以幸存。

Sarajevo：萨拉热窝，波斯尼亚一黑塞哥维那的首都和经济、文化中心。原是塞尔维亚的首都。

Sardinia：撒丁岛，意大利半岛海岸以西岛屿和区。

Sargon：萨尔贡，阿尔德王朝国王。

Sargon Ⅱ：萨尔贡二世

Saul：扫罗，公元前1025年统一了以色列各支派。

Scandinavia：斯堪的纳维亚，北欧地名。

Scipio Africanus：大西庇阿，古罗马，古罗马统帅和政治家。

Second Republic：法兰西第二共和国。它是1848年11月4日到1852年12月2日间统治法国的共和政体。1848年法国二月革命爆发。二月革命成功后，七月王朝崩溃，资产阶级取得政权，建立了法兰西第二共和国，后被法兰西第二帝国取代。

Seljuk：塞尔柱王朝，在11～13世纪统治中亚和西亚的突厥王朝。

Seneca：塞内加(约前4～65)，古罗马时代著名的斯多葛学派哲学家，曾是尼禄皇帝的导师和顾问。

September Massacre：九月大屠杀

Septimius Severus：谢普提米乌斯·塞维鲁(146～211)，罗马皇帝，193～211年间在位。塞维鲁是军人出身，他的政权以部队为后盾，将罗马军队扩充到了前所未有的地步，实施暴君统治并建立军事独裁。

Sergei Diaghilev：佳吉列夫(1872～1929)，俄国艺术活动家。音乐、绘画、戏剧、舞蹈等各方面的艺术修养都很高。

Seth：赛特，奥西里斯之弟。

Shamash：沙玛什，巴比伦和亚述神话中的太阳神。

Shamshi-Adad：沙姆希一阿达德，亚述国王。

Sicily：西西里岛，地中海最大和人口最稠密的岛，属于意大利。

Sigmund Freud：西格蒙德·弗洛伊德，犹太人，奥地利精神病医生及精神分析学家，精神分析学派的创始人。其代表作为《梦的解析》(*The Interpretation of Dreams*)。

Silesia：西里西亚，中欧的一个历史地域名称。目前，该地域的绝大部分地区属于波兰，小部分则属于捷克和德国。西里西亚现在最大的城市是历史名城弗罗茨瓦夫和卡托维兹。

Sinai Peninsula：西奈半岛，埃及东北部。

Sirius：天狼星

Sistine Chapel：罗马梵蒂冈的西斯廷教堂

Socrates：苏格拉底(前469～前399)，著名的古希腊的思想家、哲学家，他和他的学生柏拉图及柏拉图的学生亚里士多德被并称为"古希腊三大哲学家"。

Solomon：所罗门，大卫之子。

Sophocles：萨大克里斯，古希腊剧作家。

Songs of heroic deeds：英雄史诗，又称为武功歌，例如《罗兰之歌》。随着封建制度的开始形成，人们逐渐产生了国家统一的愿望。频繁的战争鼓励了尚武精神，促使了英雄史诗的形成。

Sparta：斯巴达。古代希腊最强大的的城邦中，雅典第一，斯巴达第二。"斯巴达"原来的意思就是"可以耕种的平原"。约在公元前11世纪，一个叫作多利亚人的希腊部落，南下侵入拉哥尼亚，他们毁掉原有的城邦，在这里居住下来，这就是多利亚人的斯巴达城——不过它既没有城墙，也没有像样的街道。斯巴达人就是指来到这里的多利亚人。

Spartacus：斯巴达克斯，抵抗罗马的"角斗士战争"(前73年～前71年)的领袖。

St. Bede：圣比德(673～735)，英国历史学家及神学家。

St. Peter's Cathedral：圣彼得教堂

Stonehenge：巨石阵，英格兰史前文化神庙遗址。

Sudan：苏丹，非洲东北部国家，红海西岸，北邻埃及，是非洲面积最大的国家。

Sulla：苏拉(约前138～前78)，古罗马统帅、政治家、独裁者。早年在马略领导下参加朱古达战争和对日耳曼人作战。前93年任大法官。前88年任执政官，为争夺米特拉达梯战争指挥权与马略发生冲突，相互仇杀，争得兵权后率兵东征。前83年率军返回意大利，次年彻底肃清马略派，进占罗马城，残杀政敌，并自任终身独裁官。当政期间多次对古罗马宪法进行改革，性格既勇敢又狡猾，被人形容为"半狐半狮"。

Switzerland：瑞士

Syria：叙利亚，西南亚国家。

Tacitus：塔西佗，古罗马元老院议员、历史学家。他提出了客观主义的治史原则，其代表作为《编年史》、《历史》和《日耳曼尼亚志》。

The Apennines：亚平宁山脉

The Ark of the Covenant：约柜

The Enlightenment：启蒙运动

The First Continental Congress：第一次大陆会议。1774年9月5日，北美殖民地在费城召开了殖民地联合会议，史称"第一次大陆会议"。除佐治亚缺席外，其他12个殖民地的 55 名代表都参加了会议。大陆会议通过了《权利宣言》,要求英国政府取消对殖民地的各种经济限制和五项高压法令。

The First Intermediate Period:第一过渡期,第七王朝至第十一王朝初期。

The First Triumvirate:史称“前三头”。公元前 60 年,克拉苏、庞培和恺撒结成秘密的政治同盟,共同反对元老院。相对于屋大维、安东尼和雷必达组成的后三头同盟。

The Great Famine:爱尔兰大饥荒

The Late Dynasty Period:(古埃及)晚期

The Middle Assyrian Empire:中亚述时期

The Neo-Assyrian Empire:新亚述时期,即新亚述帝国。

The Old Assyrian:古亚述时期

The Orthodox Church:东正教,基督教其中的一个派别,主要是指依循由东罗马帝国所流传下来的基督教传统的教会。它是与天主教、基督新教并立的基督教三大派别之一。

The Persian Wars:希波战争是古代波斯帝国为了扩张版图而入侵希腊的战争,战争以希腊获胜,波斯战败而告结束。这次战争对东西方经济与文化的影响远大过于战争本身。

The Pope:教皇

The Punic War:布匿战争,是古罗马与迦太基之间的战争。两国冲突是因为争夺地中海沿岸地区的霸权,尤其是西西里岛的拥有权。战争 23 年后,罗马胜利,加了许多条件才和迦太基签订和约。

The Second Continental Congress:第二次大陆会议。1775 年 5 月 10 日,第二届大陆会议在费城召开。与会代表 66 人,新代表中有本杰明·富兰克林和托马斯·杰斐逊。波士顿富商约翰·汉考克被选为会议主席。在反英革命战争业已开始的情况下,大陆会议在性质上来说,已发展为国家政权组织,开始起着常设的中央政府的作用。

The Society of Jesus:耶稣会,为天主教的主要修会之一。

The Ten Commandments:《圣经》中的“十诫”

The United Provinces of the Netherlands:尼德兰联邦共和国

Theatre of the Absurd:荒诞派戏剧,第二次世界大战以后西方戏剧界最有影响的流派之一。荒诞派戏剧在 20 世纪 50 年代最早出现在法国,后来风行于法国、英国、美国。荒诞派戏剧在创作上吸取了表现主义、象征主义和超现实主义的表现手法并加以融汇,从思想内容和艺术表现方法上独辟蹊径,进行了大胆的试验和创新,创作出了一批离奇怪诞、迥异于传统戏剧的作品,因此被戏剧评论家们称为“先锋派”、“反戏剧派”。60 年代初,英国戏剧家埃斯林将其定名为“荒诞派戏剧”。

Thebes:底比斯,新王国时代首都,位于埃及南部的尼罗河畔,已有四千年的历史。卡纳克神庙和卢克索神庙是底比斯古城著名的古埃及文明遗迹和世界文化遗产。

Theodora:西奥多拉

Theodoric:西奥德利克,东哥特(474～526)国王,493 年在意大利建立了东哥特王国。

Theodosius：迪奥多西一世，罗马帝国皇帝，392 年统治整个罗马帝国，是最后一位统治统一罗马帝国的君主。395 年，他把帝国分为东、西两部分，分别交由其两个儿子统治。

The Tyrrhenian Sea：第勒尼安海，意大利以西地中海的一部分。

Thirty Years' War：三十年战争，由神圣罗马帝国的内战演变而成的全欧参与的一次大规模国际战争。这场战争是欧洲各国争夺利益、树立霸权以及宗教纠纷剧化的产物，战争以波希米亚人民反抗奥地利帝国哈布斯堡王朝统治为肇始，最后以哈布斯堡王朝战败并签订《威斯特伐利亚和约》而告结束。

Thrace：色雷斯（自爱琴海至多瑙河的巴尔干半岛南部地区）

Thutmose Ⅲ：图特摩斯三世

Thutmose Ⅳ：图特摩斯四世，古埃及第十八王朝的第八位法老，阿蒙霍特普二世之子

Tiberius Gracchus：提比略·格拉古，罗马社会改革家。

Tiberius：提比略，全名提比略·克劳狄乌斯·尼禄，罗马帝国第二位皇帝，公元 14～37 年在位。执政后期，由于党派之间的斗争的阴谋，使得他采用残暴的手段对付政敌。在罗马古典作家的笔下，他的形象被定位为暴虐、好色。

Tiglath-pileser Ⅲ：提格拉特帕拉沙尔三世，亚述帝国建立者。

Tigris River：底格里斯河，流经土耳其和伊拉克。

Tigris-Euphrates：底格里斯河一幼发拉底河。

Titan：提坦神，是地神该亚和天神乌拉诺斯生下的十二位神。他们是巨人，因此也被称为提坦巨人。

Torah：（犹太教）法律；《旧约》的首五卷，法律书。

Trajan：图拉真，罗马帝国皇帝（98～117），罗马帝国五贤帝之一。他在位时立下显赫的功劳，使罗马帝国的版图在他的统治下达到了极盛。

Treaty of Versailles：《凡尔赛和约》，全称《协约国和参战各国对德和约》，是第一次世界大战后，战胜国（协约国）对战败国（同盟国）的和约，主要目的是惩罚和削弱德国。

Triple Alliance：三国同盟，一战之前德国、奥匈帝国、意大利在维也纳结成的秘密同盟。

Triple Entente：三国协约，英、法和俄三国在 1907 年签订的互相谅解和互相支持的协议。

Trojan Aeneas：埃涅阿斯，阿佛洛狄忒之子。在古代希腊、罗马神话中，他是特洛伊战争中的战斗英雄。传说中，就是埃涅阿斯家族的后代子孙们，在稍后的时代中建立了罗马城。

Trojan War：特洛伊战争

Tsar：沙皇，俄罗斯帝国皇帝 1546～1917 年的称呼。第一位沙皇是伊凡四世，最后一位沙皇是尼古拉二世。

Turkey：土耳其

Tutankhamen：图坦卡蒙，古埃及第十八王朝国王。1922 年，英国埃及学家 H. Carter 发现其陵墓。

Tycho Brahe：第谷，丹麦人，天文学家。

Tyre：提尔古城，古代腓尼基著名城市，位于黎巴嫩首都贝鲁特以南。1984 年被列入《世界遗产目录》。

Ulrich Zwingli：茨温利，瑞士宗教改革运动领袖。

Umayyad：伍麦耶王朝，阿拉伯哈里发的第一个王朝(661～750)，首都位于大马士革。

Umma：乌姆马，底格里斯河一幼发拉底河流域的城邦国。

University of Erfurt：埃尔福特大学，位于德国的埃尔福特市，创建于 1392 年，在德国名列前茅。

Upper Canada：上加拿大，加拿大地区名，安大略省的前身。

Upper Egypt：上埃及，即南部地区。

Ur：乌尔，古代美索不达米亚南部苏美尔的重要城市，遗址在幼发拉底河西南约 16 公里处。

Uranus：乌拉诺斯，地神该亚之子。他从该亚的指端诞生，象征希望与未来，并代表了天空。乌拉诺斯既是该亚的儿子，也是该亚的丈夫和十二提坦神、独眼巨人与百臂巨人的父亲。

Urbino：意大利乌尔比诺

Ur Ⅲ：乌尔第三王朝，又称为“乌尔帝国”。

Ur-Nammu：乌尔纳母，乌尔第三王朝首位君主，在位期间统一美索不达米亚。

Uruk：乌鲁克，美索不达米亚西南部苏美尔人的古城城名，位于今伊拉克境内。

Utnapishtim：乌塔那匹兹姆

Valens：瓦林斯(约 328～378)，东罗马帝国皇帝，364～378 在位。

Valerian：瓦勒良，罗马帝国皇帝，在罗马 3 世纪危机中通过内战而成为皇帝。260 年，瓦勒良率军东征波斯萨桑王朝时被俘虏，最后卒于波斯。

Vanity Fair：《名利场》，英国 19 世纪小说家萨克雷的成名作品，是英国著名的讽刺性批判现实主义小说。故事取材于热闹的英国十九世纪中上层社会。

Vasco da Gama：瓦斯科・达・伽马，葡萄牙航海家，欧印航线的发现者。

Vastly Kandinsky：瓦西里・康定斯基(1866～1944)，俄裔法籍画家、艺术理论家、抽象主义创始人。其代表作为《白色的线》(*Painting with White Border*)。

Vatican：梵蒂冈，罗马教廷所在地、教皇政府。

Venice：威尼斯，意大利港市。

Venezia：威尼斯省

Venus：维纳斯，罗马神话中的司爱与美的女神。

Verdun：凡尔登，位于默兹河畔，地处丘陵环绕的谷地，西距巴黎 225 千米，东距梅斯 58 公里，有“巴黎钥匙”之称。

Vincent van Gogh：文森特・凡・高(1853～1890)，荷兰后印象派画家。凡・高是表现主义的先驱，对 20 世纪艺术影响深远，其代表作品为《星空》(*Starry Night*)和《向日葵》等。

Virgil：维吉尔，古罗马最伟大的诗人。其代表作有史诗《埃涅阿斯纪》和诗集《牧歌》。

Volscian：沃尔西人，古意大利民族。

W. B. Yeats：威廉·巴特勒·叶芝(1865～1939)，爱尔兰诗人、剧作家，20世纪最伟大的英语诗人之一。叶芝于1923年获得诺贝尔文学奖。

Wales：威尔士

War of Austrian Succession：奥地利王位继承战争，因奥地利王位继承权问题而引起，于1740～1748年以中欧为主要战场展开。

Waterloo：滑铁卢镇，距比利时首都布鲁塞尔以南大约20公里。1815年，在滑铁卢，拿破仑率领法军与英国、普鲁士联军展开激战，法军惨败。随后，拿破仑以退位结束了其政治生涯。后来滑铁卢被用来比喻惨痛的失败。

Weimar Germany：魏玛共和国，形容1919～1933年期间统治德国的共和政体之历史名词。由于共和国的宪法(一般称为《魏玛宪法》)是在魏玛召开的国民议会上通过的，因此这个共和政府被称为魏玛共和国。

Wessex：韦塞克斯，位于英国西南部。

Western Hemisphere：西半球

William Ⅰ：德皇威廉一世(1797～1888)，出生于普鲁士王家，少年从军参加反拿破仑战争，中年残酷镇压了护宪运动，号称"屠夫霰弹亲王"。继承普鲁士王位后，改革军制，任用三杰，三战而一统德国，建立德意志第二帝国。

William Ⅱ：德皇威廉二世，是德意志第二帝国皇帝和普鲁士国王，1888～1918年在位。

William Harvey：威廉·哈维，医生、生理学家、胚胎学家。哈维的贡献是划时代的，他的工作标志着新的生命科学的开始，属于发端于16世纪的科学革命的一个重要组成部分。

William Wordsworth：威廉·华兹华斯，英国浪漫主义诗人。

Witternberg：威登堡，德国一历史名城，在柏林与莱比锡之间，距柏林大约有100多千米，因马丁·路德而闻名。

Wolfgang von Goethe：约翰·沃尔夫冈·歌德，18世纪中叶到19世纪初德国和欧洲最重要的剧作家、诗人、思想家。歌德除了诗歌、戏剧、小说之外，在文艺理论、哲学、历史学、造型设计等方面，都取得了卓越的成就。

Yugoslavia：南斯拉夫，1929～2003年建立于南欧巴尔干半岛的国家，由原本从奥斯曼土耳其帝国争取独立的斯拉夫民族各族组成。1992～2003年间陆续解体，成为历史名词。

Yahweh：耶和华神

Yorktown：约克城，英国英格兰东北部城市，北约克郡首府，隶属于约克郡一亨伯，具有自治市地位。

Zama：扎马，北非古城。

Zemsky Sobor：全俄罗斯缙绅会议

Zemstvos：(俄)地方自治会

Zeno：芝诺，希腊哲学家，斯多葛派的创始人。

Zeus：宙斯，希腊神话中的主神，第三代神王，克洛诺斯和瑞亚之子，乌拉诺斯和该亚之孙。他是众神之神，奥林匹斯山的最高统治者。

Zoroaster：琐罗亚斯德，拜火教创始人。

Zurich：苏黎世

Key to Exercises

CHAPTER ONE

Ⅰ. 1. C 2. A 3. C 4. B 5. D

Ⅱ. 1. the beginnings; city-states

2. Upper and Lower; black land; red land
3. the Old Testament; record
4. terrorism; brutality; Persians
5. Neo-Babylonian Empire; the Hanging Gardens

Ⅲ. 1. Because the surviving monuments are pyramidal royal tombs with their associated funerary buildings. The pyramid is an ever-present reminder of the majesty and might of the absolute monarch. It symbolises a staircase to heaven for the king's spirit. It reflects the immense wealth of a society unified in exploiting the Nile and the great power of the rulers.

2. They were the kings who made the Hebrew nation the leading power in the area of Palestine and Syria.
3. Religious contribution, Judaism;
   It had tremendous impact on later civilisations, serving as the basis for major religious systems in the future, especially Christianity and Islam.
4. By 650 B. C. the whole civilised Near East accepted for the first time a single master, the great king of Assyria, "ruler of the four rims of the world". The Assyrians broke ground in trying to create a single state out of many different peoples. Their attempt to create a centralised monarchy was later imitated by others. They protected a beneficial peace on the Near East for nearly three centuries against barbarians who might have destroyed its civilisation had they succeeded in seizing control.
5. Their tolerant attitude toward the many different cultural elements in their empire is of great importance because it was from the Persians that the Greeks derived and transmitted westward knowledge of many ancient Near Eastern ideas.

Ⅳ. (only for reference)

1. Environment: Both valleys have similar physical characteristics. First, the two systems originate in areas that provide a fairly regular supply of water and then course through territory that has little natural rainfall. In the end each enters an area of fertile land, Mesopotamia for the Tigris-Euphrates and the Delta for the Nile. The Nile floods with even more predictable regularity than the Tigris-Euphrates. Another feather is that the annual floods were capricious, especially in the Tigris-Euphrates Valley. To assure a water supply for agriculture demanded a tremendous output of human labour and a level of large-scale planning, organisation and technology invested in cutting canals, building dikes and reservoirs, and regulating the flow of water to the fields at the proper time during the growing season. The successful meet of the challenge resulted in the first higher civilisations.

   In spite of the similarities, differences existed in the patterns of life. The flood season in the Tigris-Euphrates Valley was less regular and predictable than the Nile floods, and it was more difficult to construct and maintain an irrigation system in the broader plain area of Mesopotamia. As a result, an everlasting threat of flood, drought, and famine hung over the inhabitants of Mesopotamia, creating an attitude of uncertainty and fatalism that is reflected in the literature and art. Another difference lay in the role of geography. No natural barriers protected Mesopotamia. Therefore, those first mastering the Tigris-Euphrates Valley were constantly attacked by tough herders, formidable nomads and hardy farmers from the east, the west and the north respectively. These people had a significant effect on Mesopotamian society, but meanwhile they helped spread Mesopotamian influence outward into the more primitive areas. By contrast, the Nile Valley was protected from invaders by forbidding natural barriers, the deserts, the rapids, and the Mediterranean, with the only accessible entry into Egypt, a narrow easily defensible passage connecting the Delta to the Sinai Peninsula and Asia.

   Political, economic, social and cultural life: First, in the history of Mesopotamian civilisation, about 3000 B. C. large and complex city-states were established by outsiders rather than the local villagers, the first city builders being the Sumerians. Between 3000 B. C. and 2400 B. C., empires formed, the first being Akkad. While in Egypt, the villages did not unite into city-states, instead small kingdoms formed. Then about 3100 B. C. all Egypt was united under a single ruler, pharaoh.

   Second, in view of the political systems, differences outweigh similarities. In the period of city-states in Mesopotamia, effective system of government was grounded in religious belief that each city had been created by a god or goddess. In empire-building era, in order to use political power to create common bonds among peoples of different languages, ethnic origins, religious beliefs, and cultural traditions, new ideas and practices in government were instituted, typically in Hammurabi's reign. He called himself the "king of kings". The king was said to be the sole agent of the deities in determining the destiny of the huge community, and in his own right he was judge, lawgiver, military leader, and spokesman to the gods. His authority was based on a well-organised army. He also established a centralised bureaucracy with specialised departments. He tried to create a common religion in his empire. Furthermore, the most significant measure was his law code. At the same time, the aristocracy of priests, landowners, and royal servants performed a crucial function. Like Mesopotamia, Egypt was dominated by a relatively small aristocracy. At its top stood the pharaoh and his family, having control over all elements of society and the total wealth of the state. Though the central feature of the political system was also the absolute power of the king, pharaoh, he was a special kind of ruler, a god, the son of the sun god Re, and he was destined to eternal life along with the other gods and goddesses. Every person was his servant, subject to his unchallengeable law. The king's power was supported by a highly developed administrative system centred in the royal palace. The high official, including a chief minister, a treasurer, a chief of irrigation, high priests and priestesses, who were assisted by numerous state servants of lesser rank. Egypt was divided into forty-two nomes, which were further divided into villages. Each nome was controlled by royal officials. During the Middle Kingdom, the concept of maat was interpreted in a way that emphasised the pharaoh's responsibility for providing justice, protection, respect for the lower classes of society, which gave the governing a humane quality.

Third, in the aspect of economy, both civilisations share similar agricultural system, a carefully organised agricultural system based on irrigation. While in Mesopotamian society, this system was complemented by a flourishing trade and industry, in Egypt, artisans and merchants added to the wealth.

Fourth, as to social order, due to the attacks of outsiders and violent intercity rivalry for land and power, there was a lack of stability in Mesopotamia. However, the surviving evidence suggests that Egyptian society seemed stable, secure and lacking in deep social tensions.

Fifth, in terms of religious life, Mesopotamian religion was polytheistic. And a rich mythology represents an impressive attempt to describe the powers of the deities and to spell out their relationships to one another and to the human community. Life at all levels in Mesopotamia was lived as a ritual aimed at pleasing a multitude of unpredictable spirits to get safety and prosperity in return. As a result, predictive techniques involving dream interpretation, reading the stars (astrology) and so on were developed. Besides, a tone of pessimism and fatalism permeated the Mesopotamians' view of life, which may partly be due to a lack of any moral dimension in Mesopotamian religion. Similarly, the deities worshipped by the Egyptians numbered in the thousands. And Egyptian culture was rooted in powerful religious beliefs that inspired and shaped every aspect of thought and expression. Besides, the efforts to explain the role of the deities also resulted in a rich body of mythology. But in contrast to the Mesopotamians, the Egyptians did not live in constant fear of the gods and goddesses; rather, they shared the world comfortably and confidently with them. Another difference lies in a unique aspect of Egyptian religion, concern with immortality. Though the Egyptians also made effort to please the gods and win their favour for earthly benefits, like the Mesopotamians, during the Middle Kingdom, the new element of the moral worth attached to each person was added to the concept of immortality. This moral awareness was unknown in Mesopotamia.

Sixth, like cuneiform writing, Egyptian system of writing, hieroglyphic, began as pictographs. Gradually symbols representing sounds were developed and these were combined to form words.

Seventh, compared with Mesopotamian literature, on the whole, Egyptian literature is gay and confident in mood. It is more varied and versatile but less profound; the Mesopotamians never developed lyric poetry, romances, and tales of fancy, but the Egyptians produced nothing comparable to the *Epic of Gilgamesh*.

Eighth, the architects of both civilisations created impressive work, but they used different materials. A lack of stone in the Tigris-Euphrates Valley resulted in the use of clay bricks as the chief building material in architecture, while the Egyptian architects worked in many materials, including mud, reeds, brick and wood, but the most monumental work was in stone. And the Great Pyramid stands as one of the great construction feats of all time.

Ninth, Egypt's sculptors matched its architects in skill, whose work feathering massive, stiff, unemotional portrayals of human forms following fixed proportions. They tried to show feeling and purpose: the power of a god or goddess. However, Mesopotamian sculptors gave a distinctive character to the faces of their subjects. Their work was strongly influenced by ideal geometrical forms, and is solid, stiff, and motionless.

Last but not least, the Egyptians made advances in technology and practical science that rivaled the work of the Mesopotamians. Both of the civilisations developed a system of time reckoning, numbering system, medical knowledge and techniques, and their accurate information about the movements of the stars laid the basis for astronomy.

2. Hammurabi's most significant measure was the issuance of his famous law code as a practical way of unifying his subjects and maintaining a civilised order. It provides considerable insight into almost every aspect of everyday life there and provides valuable material for the understanding and study of Old Babylonian society.

   The code recognised three social classes in Babylonia (nobles, freemen, and slaves) and emphasised the principle of retaliation ("an eye for an eye, a tooth for a tooth") and punishments for crimes that were severe and varied according to the social status of the victim. It also included laws dealing with job performance, marriage and family affairs, and even sexual relations. It reveals a society with a system of strict justice.

CHAPTER TWO

Ⅰ. 1. C 2. D 3. B 4. D 5. A

Ⅱ. 1. Minos
2. Mycenae
3. courage; honour
4. Polis
5. the Macedonian king Philip Ⅱ

Ⅲ. 1. The *Iliad* and the *Odyssey* supposedly deal with the heroes of the Mycenaean age of the 13th century B. C. According to the Homeric view, Greece was a society based on agriculture in which a landed warrior-aristocracy controlled much wealth and exercised considerable power. Homer's world shows the values of aristocratic heroes. The Homeric poems give us our first glimpse of the Greek's view of divinity—vain, vengeful, and volatile. In Home's writing, which idealised the warrior spirit, excellence was interpreted as courage and skill in battle. Homer's masterpieces greatly contributed to the shaping of the Greek spirit. Homer's heroes who pursued honour and confronted hardship with bravery are always admired by the Greeks.

2. The Dark Age of Greek world(1100 — 750 B. C.), both implying the difficult conditions and our lack of knowledge about the period. Near the very end of this so-called Dark Age appeared the work of Homer who definitely wrote Greeks, who were known as Achaeans Ⅰ into one of the brightest page of western civilisation.

3. Sparta and Athens were the major Greek city-states. All the other states eventually sided with one of the two principal powers. After the defeat of Persians, the two rivals—Sparta and Athens differed from each other in a wide range from social structure to ideologies. The divergence at last evolved into radical conflict—the long and costly Peloponnesian War that broke out in 431 B. C.
4. All southern and western Europe and the new lands including Americas and Australia share a common cultural heritage originated in Greece. That culture in poetry, philosophy, music, architecture, sculpture, government, that humanity of outlook which has bound together the peoples of Europe had its roots in Greek civilisation which laid the foundation of western civilisation.
5. The word Hellenistic is derived from a Greek word meaning "to imitate Greeks". It is an appropriate way, then, to describe an age that saw the extension of the Greek language and ideas to the non-Greek world of the Near East. The Hellenistic era was a period of considerable cultural accomplishment in many areas—literature, art, science, and philosophy and the great Hellenistic cities of Alexandria and Pergamum stood out as two leading cultural centres. Rich Hellenistic kings had sufficient resources to patronise culture.

Ⅳ. (only for reference)

1. By far the most important form, at least with regard to later Western history, was the Athenian democracy, particularly as it appeared in the Age of Pericles during the 5th century B. C. The Greek polis was a politically autonomous community of people living in a defined territory comprising a civic centre with surrounding arable countryside. Its society included both agricultural and non-agricultural labourers who were organised by a centrally located authority to defend the state, contribute to material needs, share in unified worship of the gods, and decide matters of public policy and personal disputes. The polis was governed by the assembly consisting of all male citizens which had final authority in the passing of laws after free and open debate. This institution created the foundations for Athenian democracy. (The word democracy comes from the Greek words demos—people and kratia—power.) Every male citizen (over eighteen years of age) was a member of the Assembly, the sole legislative body of the city-state. From the Assembly a Council of Five Hundred was chosen annually to supervise the administrative affairs of the polis; from the Council, an executive committee of fifty was chosen to execute the daily business of administration for a term lasting one-tenth of a year; one member of this committee was chosen as chairman for one-day period. Since all these selections were made by lot, any citizen of the polis might have an opportunity to serve as

the chief administrative officer of Athens for one day and the capability to serve constituted the fully qualified citizen.

2. Sparta and Athens were different in ideologies. Sparta was an agrarian economy. The lands were cultivated by public serfs, the helots, who had to contribute a certain amount of their product to their Spartan masters. Since the Spartans did not have to earn a living, they devoted their whole life from the age of seven onwards to military training. Boys were taken from their mothers at the age of seven and put under control of the state for military training. The long and intensive training was to make the Spartans probably the best soldiers of the world and the state the most military dominated. The strategy and policy of Sparta accounted for the power of conquest. Consequently, the Spartans would all the more strengthen their power to surpass them. Spartan citizens were discouraged from studying philosophy, literature, or the arts—subjects that might encourage new thoughts. The art of war and ruling was the Spartan ideal. All other arts were frowned on. The contribution of Sparta to Western civilisation amounts to the heritage left by this sheer military state.

The Athens by 700 B. C. had established a unified polis on the peninsula of Attica, relatively poor soil of land. From the early 6th century B. C. reforms Athens became increasingly democratic. This period saw the flowering of democracy in Athens under the leadership of Pericles (495 — 429 B. C.) and witnessed the mighty confrontation at the end of the 5th century B. C. between Greek states and the mammoth Persian Empire—The Persian Wars. The bravery of Spartans and intelligence of Athenian and ever increasing army of the Greeks had at last defeated the Persian army.

After the defeat of Persians, the two rivals—Sparta and Athens different from each other in a wide range from social structure to ideologies. The divergence at last evolved into radical conflict—the long and costly Peloponnesian War that broke out in 431 B. C. At the beginning of the war, both sides were confident of their winning strategies. The Athens planned to shelter themselves behind the solid wars while the overseas empire and navy keep them supplied. The Spartans kept attacking Athens hoping to fight them beyond the walls. In the second year of the war, the crowded city of Athens was wiped out of possibly one-third of its population in the epidemic of a plague. Pericles died the following year (429 B. C.), to worsen the situation. Nevertheless, the Athenians fought on for another twenty-seven years before Athens was besieged in 404 B. C.

Charming and powerful as the Greek states were, they all the same dissolved themselves in between the two leagues headed respectively by Athens and Sparta. In the 4th century B. C. the great city-states fell easy prey to the invading

Macedonians from the north. King Philip Ⅱ (359—336 B. C.) turned Macedonia into the chief power of the Greek world. He was soon drawn into the interstate conflicts of the Greeks and the Macedonian army crushed the Greeks in 338 B. C. The independent Greek polis came to an end as Philip formed a league of the Greek states. Before Philip could invade the Persian Empire, however, he was assassinated in 336 B. C. , leaving the task to his son Alexander, who became the king in 334 B. C. at the age of twenty with the consensus of the courtiers. Young as he was, Alexander was in many ways prepared for kingship by his father, who had taken Alexander along on military campaigns and even had given him control of the cavalry at the important battle of Chaeronea. Alexander soon established his authority in securing the Macedonian frontiers and controlling the rebellious Greece.

CHAPTER THREE

Ⅰ. 1. A 2. B 3. D 4. C 5. A

Ⅱ. 1. Greeks
2. Praetor
3. Centuriate
4. Carthage
5. The First Triumvirate

Ⅲ. 1. Roman conquest consists of three stages: the conquest of Italy, the conquest of West Mediterranean through the destruction of Carthage and the conquest of the Eastern Mediterranean with the domination of the Hellenistic world in that area. The long road to Empire was engineered and paved by the Roman army who were highly trained, well equipped and strictly disciplined. Rome enjoyed the most sustained series of military triumphs the world had ever seen. The enormous wealth grabbed from the defeated opponents all the more stimulated the expansion of the Romans. The ever evolution of Roman political and legal institution had in some way provided elites for political or military offices. The strong and powerful Rome made her citizenship an appeal to many aliens.

2. Octavian was prompt to stabilise the military and administrative structures of the Roman Empire. In order to effectively control the enormous Empire, Augustus made an effort to get on good terms with the senate and started a new policy of governing the provinces. He inaugurated the new constitutional order of the Princeps and the aristocratic senate. Elites were constantly put into the senate and assigned important offices. The authority of Augustus made him able to overrule the senatorial governors and establish a uniform imperial policy.

3. The Gladiatorial shows were an integral part of Roman society. They took place in amphitheatres of a scale of capacities from a few thousand to tens of thousands.

The most famous one, the Colosseum was built in the 1st century and could seat fifty thousand spectators. In most cities and towns, the amphitheatres were the biggest buildings. Modern sports, such as boxing, show the heritage of the gladiatorial shows in ancient Rome.

4. Romans' contact with the Jews began in 63 B. C. , and Judaea had been made a province by 6 A. D. . In the midst of the confusion and conflict in Judaea, Jesus of Nazareth (6 B. C. —29 A. D.) began his public preaching.

   Jesus' disciple Peter, "second founder of Christianity" founded the Christian church at Rome, and was honoured to be the first Pope (the representative of Jesus on earth as concerning Catholic Church). Peter provided a universal foundation for the spread of Christ's ideas. Christian missionaries travelled on the Roman roads to spread spreading their "good news". A Latin translation of the Greek New Testament that appeared soon after 200 helped the spreading of Christianity in the Roman world. Christianity grew slowly in the 1st century, took root in the second, and had spread widely by the third. In the 4th century, Christianity flourished after Constantine became the first Christian emperor. Christianity had triumphed when it was made the official religion of the Roman Empire under Theodosius "the Great" (378—395).

5. Roman society was featured by the conflicts between the patricians and the plebeians. Despite the rise of power on the part of the plebeians, they still felt inferior because they really never knew exactly what the laws were since the past common law was handled by the upper class. The laws had never been put into writing and were only known by the patricians. The Plebeians insisted that the government write down the laws. Finally in 451 B. C. the patricians agreed to engrave the laws on 12 bronze tablets and to set them in the Forum for all to see. This is known as *The Twelve Tables of Law*. These 12 Tables became the basis for the future Roman law. The Plebeians had soon won the right to serve in some public offices and in 287 B. C. they won a great victory, and they were given the right to make laws for the republic in the Assembly of Tribes. The great progress in the study and codification of the law in the 2nd and 3rd century created the "classical age of Roman Law" and laid foundation for the development of law in the western world.

Ⅳ. (only for reference)

1. Roman conquest consists of three stages: the conquest of Italy, the conquest of West Mediterranean through the destruction of Carthage and the conquest of the Eastern Mediterranean with the domination of the Hellenistic world in that area. The long road to Empire was engineered and paved by the Roman army who were highly trained, well equipped and strictly disciplined. Rome enjoyed the most

sustained series of military triumphs the world had ever seen. The enormous wealth grabbed from the defeated opponents all the more stimulated the expansion of the Romans. The ever evolution of Roman political and legal institution had in some way provided elites for political or military offices. The strong and powerful Rome made her citizenship an appeal to many aliens.

The Romans knew how to govern people, establish legal structures, and construct the roads that took them to the ends of the known world. Throughout their empire, they carried their law, their political institutions, their engineering skills, and their Latin language. And ever after the Romans were gone, those same gifts continued to play an important role in the civilisations that came after them.

In order to effectively control the enormous Empire, Augustus made an effort to get on good terms with the senate and started a new policy of governing the provinces. He inaugurated the new constitutional order of the princeps and the aristocratic senate. Elites were constantly put into the senate and assigned important offices. Governors were selected from the senate to administer the provinces. Some provinces were under the name of the senate, for which the senate was responsible to designate the governors; other provinces were allotted to the princes, which the princeps assigned legates to govern as long as the princeps chose. The authority of Augustus made him able to overrule the senatorial governors and establish a uniform imperial policy.

2. The Romans were a practical people. Unlike the Greeks, who reserved their citizenship for small, select groups, the Romans often offered their citizenship to the peoples they conquered, thus laying the groundwork for a strong, integrated empire. The Romans also did not hesitate to borrow ideas and culture from the Greeks. Roman strength lay in government, law and engineering. The Romans knew how to govern people, establish legal structures, and construct the roads that took them to the ends of the known world. Throughout their empire, they carried their law, their political institutions, their engineering skills, and their Latin language. And ever after the Romans were gone, those same gifts continued to play an important role in the civilisations that came after them.

The Greeks had also considerable influence on Rome. The Greeks reached the southern Italy during the age of Greek colonisation (750—550 B. C.) and brought with them the alphabetic writing system and their advanced art and literature, etc. No wonder many historians consider Roman culture the continuation of Greek culture. Romans would be pleased to agree. Roman historians, proud of the rise of their city, recorded the traditional story that associated the founding of Rome with the Trojan mythology in which the wandering Trojan Aeneas was related to the founding of Rome.

Romans also traced their history to legendary stories that tell of the heroes who made Rome great. According to Roman legend, Rome was founded by the twin brothers Romulus and Remus. Whatever is the origin of Rome, humble or celebrated, Rome has written itself into history with its undoubted glory and grandeur.

CHAPTER FOUR

Ⅰ. 1. D 2. B 3. D 4. C 5. D

Ⅱ. 1. the Western Roman Empire
2. the 5th; 11th centuries
3. the Romanesque style and the Gothic style
4. the Imperial Coronation of 800
5. The manor; castles

Ⅲ. 1. After the Roman Empire lost its predominance, a great many Germanic kingdoms began to grow into the nations known as England, France, Spain, Italy, and Germany in its place. These nations of Western Europe were in the scene of frequent wars and invasions. The political unity had given way to widespread destruction and confusion. Hunger and disease killed many lives, and thousands of towns and villages fell into ruin and great areas of land lay waste. There was no central government to keep the order. The only organisation that seemed to be able to unite Europe was the Christian church. Christianity was almost the all and the one of Medieval lives in Western Europe and took lead in politics, law, art, and learning for hundreds of years.

2. The word "feudalism" was derived from the Latin "feudum", a grant of land. In Europe, Feudalism was mainly a system of holding land in exchange for military service and a form of local and decentralised government.

3. Above all the cultural characteristics of this period were mainly the heritage and achievement of Roman culture and the emergence of Hebrew and Gothic culture.

4. In the Middle Ages, some "national epics" were written in vernacular languages—the languages of various national states that came into being at that period, and some monks advocated translating the Bible in vernacular languages. Literary works were no longer all written in Latin. It was the starting point of a gradual transition of European literature from Latin culture to a culture that was the combination of a variety of national characteristics.

5. (1) Gothic was an outgrowth of the Romanesque. It was given directions by a different aesthetic and philosophical spirit and it reflected a much more ordered feudal society with full confidence. (2) Romanesque architectures characterised by massiveness, solidity, and monumentality with an overall blocky appearance.

Sculpture and painting, primarily in churches, developed a wonderful unity with architecture. Both arts are often imbued with symbolism and allegory. They are not based on natural forms but use deliberate distortions for expressive impact. (3) Gothic cathedrals soared high, their windows, arches and towers reaching heavenward, flinging their passion against the sky.

Ⅳ. (only for reference)

Cause: The crusading movement grew out of developments in both east and west. In the east, the balance of power between the Byzantine Empire and various Muslim Caliphates was upset by the 11th century arrival of a new power: the Seljuk Turks converted to the Islamic faith. In the west, the papacy, under the direction of Gregorian movement, regained its control over the emperors. The direct reason for the crusades was that the Islamic Seljuks defeated a Byzantine army and occupied Asia Minor. So when the desperate Byzantine emperor appealed to the west for help, he wrote to Pope Urban Ⅱ instead of the holy Roman Emperor or any other secular monarch. The pope decided to respond to this challenge.

Process: (1) Popular Crusade and the first Crusade: In 1095, Pope Urban Ⅱ summoned Christian warriors to take up the cross and reconquer the Holy Land. In the powerful address to the Frankish aristocracy, the pope called on the French warriors to avenge Seljuk atrocities and to drive the "the infidel" from Jerusalem. He also promised that they will obtain the remission of their sins and be sure of the incorruptible glory of the Kingdom of Heaven. Enthusiastically, the French warriors poured into crusading armies, so did the peasants, townspeople, women, children, even the infirm and the aged. This army was poor, ill-equipped, disorganised, lacking in military discipline, and encouraged by simply religious faith. It was not strange that they were quickly cut down by the Seljuk troops; the survivals continued their dream by joining a more professional force that arrived the following year. And this is later called the "Popular Crusade". In 1097, another force, composed mainly of knights from France, Normandy, and Norman Sicily, came with a better preparation. From the very beginning, the crusaders and their Byzantine allies differed in objective. The crusaders were focused on nothing but the conquest of the Holy Land, while the Byzantines wanted only the recapture of the provinces of Asia Minor. So the crusaders soon broke with the Byzantines and hurled themselves across Asia Minor into Syria. In the summer of 1099 they conquered Jerusalem. The goal of the First Crusade had been achieved and in the Holy Land the crusaders celebrated their victory by plundering the city and cruelly slaughtering its Muslim and Jewish inhabitants. The conquered lands were organised into four crusader states: the county of

Edessa, the principality of Antioch, the county of Tripoli, and the kingdom of Jerusalem. And this is called the First Crusade.

(2) The second and third Crusades: The Second Crusade (1147—1148) was inspired by the powerful preaching of Bernard of Clairvaux(1090—1153) and led by a king of France and a Holy Roman Emperor. The campaign began with high hopes but ended in defeat and disaster at the hands of Seljuk Turks in Asia Minor. In 1187 Jerusalem was recaptured by the Muslims under Saladin, Sultan of Egypt, causing Emperor Frederick Barbarossa and the kings of France and England, Philip Ⅱ "Augustus" and Richard "the Lion-Hearted", to embark on the Third Crusade (1187—1192). This was a strong start, but the crusade quickly faltered. Eventually, Richard negotiated a settlement whereby Saladin agreed to allow Christian pilgrims free access to Jerusalem. However, on his way home, Richard fell into hostile hands and became the prisoner of Frederick Barbarossa's son, the Emperor Henry Ⅵ (1165—1197), until his mother, Eleanor, could raise the ransom to buy his freedom.

(3) Later Crusades: The 13th century witnessed a sequence of failures of various other crusades. The Fourth Crusade initiated by Pope Innocent Ⅲ in 1193 ended with the fall of Latin Empire of Constantinople. In Germany in 1212, a visionary, ill-organised enterprise known as the "Children's Crusade" ended in tragedy. The Fifth Crusade (1217—1221) attempted to recover the Holy Land by way of the powerful Muslim state of Egypt. The crusade achieved some early successes, but its ultimate failure marked an end to papal leadership of the western crusaders. In the Sixth Crusade, the German emperor Frederick Ⅱ (1194—1250) led a largely peaceful expedition and obtained possession of Jerusalem by an agreement with the sultan of Egypt without papal support, which marked an important shift in crusading from papal to royal initiative. The last two major crusades, poorly organised by the pious king of France, Louis Ⅸ, were complete failures, especially after the fall of Acre, which marked an end of the crusader states in the Holy Land.

Effects: The Crusades left a complex and troubling legacy in world civilisation. On the one hand, the greed, violence, and religious militancy at the heart of the crusading movement also fostered the growth of a persecuting mentality within Europe. On the other hand, however, the Crusades gave Europeans a new awareness of the world beyond their own local realms of religion and small-town economies. The interaction of Christian Europe with the Muslim world was actually both more intense and more meaningful in Spain and Sicily than in the Holy Land. Economically they surely promoted the economic growth of the Italian port cities, especially Genoa, Pisa, and Venice. It was certainly not the crusades that caused the trade recovery. Even without the crusades, Italian merchants would have established new trade relations with the eastern world.

Long before the arrival of plague in the mid 14th century, Europe was in trouble. Signs of disintegration were everywhere: famine, economic depression, war, social upheaval, a rise in crime and violence, and a decline in the power of the universal Catholic Church.

Economic reason: Among all the economic reasons of the decline of the Medieval Age stands the Black Death (the Great Plague) overwhelmingly. By the end of the 13th century and beginning of the 14th century, Europe entered a period that was called a "little ice age". A small shift in overall temperature patterns resulted in shortened growing seasons and disastrous weather conditions, including heavy storms and constant rain. Between 1315 and 1317, northern Europe experienced heavy rains that destroyed harvests and caused serious food shortages, resulting in extreme hunger and starvation. Southern Europe seemed to have been struck by similar conditions, especially in the 1330s and 1340s. Hunger became widespread. Some historians have pointed out that famine could have led to chronic malnutrition, which in turn contributed to increased infant mortality, lower birth rates, and higher susceptibility to disease because malnourished people were less able to resist infection. It was the most terrible natural disaster in European history, ravaging Europe's population and causing economic, social, political, and cultural upheaval. The grief brought by the plague cannot be measured, but the more tangible effects can be observed clearly: innumerable deserted villages, unoccupied and dilapidated districts within city walls and a severe shortage of labour. At the same time, with grim efficiency, the disaster also provided a sudden, radical solution to the problem of rural overpopulation. With more than 30% of the whole population dead within two years, there was an abundance of land left for those who survived.

Social Crisis: The dramatically population decreasing of the 14th century had a disastrous influence on economy and society. Economic dislocation was accompanied by social upheaval. Both peasants and noble landlords were affected by the demographic crisis of the 14th century. Most noticeably, Europe experienced a serious labour shortage, which caused a dramatic rise in the price of labour. At the same time, the decline in population depressed the demand for agricultural produce, resulting in falling prices for output. Eventually the poor peasants began to seek their freedom through revolts. The first arose in 1358, when a series of protests by French peasants escalated into a widespread revolt in the region around Paris. Known as the Jacquerie, it was crushed within a few weeks. In 1381, English peasants had their turn in a rebellion that spread through much of England and then to London. Similar popular uprisings occurred in the Holy Roman Empire, Hungary, Norway, Finland, Sweden and the Netherlands. Although most of those revolts were ended in being put down quickly, the message they had brought up was not. The English rebels had explicitly sought to end the social inequalities that were at the heart of aristocratic privilege. In other words, these revolts provided the landed elite with a good incentive to develop less exploitative methods of manorial management. The countryside was not the one and only place to find revolts. The towns and cities of Western Europe lost relatively large numbers of people to the Great Plague. Commercial and industrial activity suffered almost immediately from the catastrophe. An oversupply of goods and an immediate drop in demand led to a decline in trade after 1350. Some industries suffered greatly. Bourgeois merchants and manufacturers responded to a decline in trade and production by attempts to restrict competition and resist the demands of the lower classes. Tensions between "haves" and "have-nots" were especially high. Quickly the uprisings of workers began to terrorise those commercially important big cities. Although the peasant and urban revolts sometimes resulted in short-term gains for the participants, the uprisings were relatively easily crushed and their gains quickly lost. Geographically dispersed, rural and urban rebels were not united and had no long-range goals. Immediate gains were uppermost in their minds. Accustomed to ruling, the established classes easily combined and crushed dissent when faced with social uprising. Nevertheless, the rural and urban revolts of the 14th century ushered in an age of social conflict that characterised much of later European history.

Religious crisis: It is certainly true that the Great Plague had affected the religious practices in Europe severely. Many religious responses to the plague were beyond the church's control, such as the hysterical attacks that Christians launched against Jews. And, many times, the panicked people cast angry eyes at the Church. Why had the Church not warned the faithful of God's anger? Why were clergy dying in even greater numbers than the laity? In the 14th and 15th centuries, the church faced serious threats to its credibility and power. The death of Gregory XI (1370—1378) in the spring of 1378 brought the beginning of the Great Schism. When the College of Cardinals met in conclave to elect a new pope, the citizens of Rome, fearful that the French majority would choose another Frenchman who would return the papacy to Avignon, threatened that the cardinals would not leave Rome alive unless a Roman or Italian were elected pope. Wisely the terrified cardinals duly elected the Italian archbishop of Bari as Pope Urban VI (1378—1389). Five months later, a group of dissenting cardinals, the

French ones, declared Urban's election null and void and chose one of their members, a Frenchman, who took the title of Clement Ⅶ and promptly returned to Avignon. Because Urban remained in Rome, there were now two popes, initiating what was called the Great Schism of the church. Europe's loyalties became divided: France, Spain, Scotland, and southern Italy supported Clement, while England, Germany, Scandinavia, and most of Italy supported Urban. These divisions generally followed political lines. The French supported the Avignonese, so did their allies; their enemies, particularly England and its allies, supported the Roman pope. The need for political support caused both popes to subordinate their policies to the policies of these states. The Great Schism badly damaged the faith of Christian believers. The pope was widely believed to be the leader of Christendom and held the keys to the kingdom of heaven. Since both lines of popes denounced the other as the Antichrist, such a spectacle could only undermine the institution that had become the very foundation of the church. The Great Schism introduced uncertainty into the daily lives of ordinary Christians.

CHAPTER FIVE

Ⅰ. 1. D 2. C 3. C 4. B 5. A

Ⅱ. 1. humanism

2. Purgatory

3. heliocentric (sun-centred) system

4. *On the Fabric of the Human Body*

5. civic humanism

Ⅲ. 1. The Renaissance is the rise of new culture of the rising bourgeoisie from the early 14th century to 17th century in Europe. The word Renaissance is derived from French, meaning "rebirth". The "Dark Age" had passed, and the thinkers and artists believed they were experiencing a rebirth of cultural forms of Greece and Rome. Their contributions were not only the recovery and application of antiquity or Greco-Roman civilisation, but innovation and novelty to a large extent, which marked a new age.

2. Francesco Petrarch was one of the early humanists and was regarded as the father of humanism because of his unparalleled devotion to the spread of humanism in the 14th century. He contributed greatly to the collection and spread of the Latin manuscripts. However, he encouraged his pupils to study Greek so as to enhance humanist learning. He followed Cicero's example and suggested that education should stress rhetoric and moral philosophy—wisdom with eloquence. Education should not only be the study of knowledge but also the proper use of it for public good and communication. He was also a scholar, poet, who combined interest in classical culture and Christianity and left deep influence on literature throughout

Western Europe. He was known as a devoted student of antiquity who had a passion for finding and commenting on the works of the ancients. In 1341 he was crowned as a poet laureate in Rome. He was famous for the poems (*Song Book*) inspired by the Lady whom he named Laura (some scholars believed she was a fancied character).

3. The three giants in the High Renaissance were Alighieri Dante, Francesco Petrarch and Giovanni Boccaccio.

   Dante was the greatest Italian poet and one of the most important writers of European literature. During his exile, he started to write *The Divine Comedy*, a long story-poem in 100 cantos (14,233 lines) through the three worlds of the afterlife. It is the tale of the poet's journey through Hell and Purgatory and through Heaven. Dante's idea was to make the world of his poem a mirror of the world of the Christian God of his era.

   Petrarch was an Italian scholar, poet, and was regarded as the founder of humanism, who combined interest in classical culture and Christianity and left deep influence on literature throughout Western Europe. In 1341 he was crowned as a poet laureate in Rome. He was famous for the poems (*Song Book*) inspired by the Lady whom he named Laura (some scholars believed she was a fancied character).

   Giovanni Boccaccio was an Italian poet. In 1358 he completed his great work, the *Decameron*. His excellent narrative skill and the abounding poetical sentiments encouraged his readers to sigh with admiration. The classical and the romantic traditions, which were both prominent characteristics in European literature, could be seen in *Decameron*.

4. Niccolo Machiavelli, once involved in overthrowing the Medici family's domination, was active in the Italian political activities after the family had been out of power. In 1513, he produced the famous political book *The Prince*, which discussed how to keep and expand the state's power as a successful ruler. He completely renounced the theory of divine right of monarch that was overwhelming in the Medieval Ages, and expounded a new political theory that ascribed no divine origin to the state. In his point of view, the overriding purpose of a monarch was to keep the survival of his state by hook or by crook. Moral and religious considerations should take no place in a prince's thinking of rule. His approach to political power was different from previous political theorists and far more realistic than that of the medieval forebears.

5. The art of printing made a profound impact on the life and study of the European intellectuals. It gave the scholars and scientists of that age more sufficient and more convenient access to the ancient literatures. It not only helped to widen the

outlook and the knowledge of the intellectuals, but also made realistic the cultural and scientific communication among different countries. The new printing system contributed a lot to the publication and spread of many religious books, Latin and Greek classics, medieval grammars, legal handbooks, philosophy books and popular romances.

Ⅳ. (only for reference)

1. Humanism in the Renaissance played an important role in the development of natural science. People were divorced from the bondage of Medieval theology and were expected to pursue ideological emancipation. People took more emphasis on reality and scientific experiments and exploration. Meanwhile, human's creativity was brought into full play and human's curiosity was perpetually expanded and constantly satisfied. Furthermore, the development of manufacture also quickened the steps of the natural science. Finally, the scientific and technical accomplishments of the ancient Greece, Rome, Arab and China provided enlightenment of the European scientific development.

   The upheavals occurring in the arts and humanities were mirrored by a dynamic period of change in the sciences. Some had seen this flurry of activity as a "scientific revolution", heralding the beginning of the modern age. Others had seen it merely as an acceleration of a continuous process stretching from the ancient world to the present day. Renaissance saw significant changes in the way the universe was viewed and the methods with which philosophers sought to explain natural phenomena.

   Science and art were very much intermingled in the early Renaissance. Yet the most significant development of the era was not a specific discovery, but rather a process for discovery, the scientific method. This revolutionary new way of learning about the world focused on empirical evidence, the importance of mathematics, and discarding the Aristotelian "final cause" in favour of a mechanical philosophy. Early and influential proponents of these ideas included Copernicus and Galileo.

   The new scientific method led to great contributions in the fields of astronomy, physics, biology, and anatomy. With the publication of Vesalius's *On the Fabric of the Human Body*, a new confidence was placed in the role of dissection, observation, and a mechanistic view of anatomy.

2. Humanism is the most significant hallmark of the Renaissance, which is an educational and cultural programme based on the ancient Greek and Roman classics. But the Renaissance humanists did not subordinate the classics to the requirements of Christian doctrines. Rather, they valued ancient literature for its own sakek—for its clear and graceful style and for its insights into human

nature.

First, in art: The Renaissance art stressed proportion, balance and harmony. The pursuit for nature and the focus of human beings became the primary goals of the Renaissance artists. So the Renaissance art is a significant symbol of humanism. From the artistic work at that time, people can taste the lively world and the active and worldly life.

For example, Giotto applied the natural landscape settings in place of the simple golden or blue background in the Medieval Ages. He was best at the emotional expression and what was important in human nature. He opened up a new road for the modern European painting and he was called the "founder of the modern figure painting".

Second, in literature: Francesco Petrarch (1304 — 1374) was one of the early humanists and was regarded as the father of humanism because of his unparalleled devotion to the spread of humanism in the 14th century. The Florentine intellectuals also took Cicero as a model. Leonardo Bruni (1370 — 1444), the distinguished humanistic historian, wrote a biography of Cicero entitled the *New Cicero*. In the book, he enthusiastically eulogised Cicero's contribution on politics and literature in his whole life. Bruni also wrote the biography of Dante and that of Petrarch in order to publicise their humanistic thinking. At the beginning of the 15th century, the fusion of Florentine civic spirit and pride cut a new way for the humanist movement in Florence, which was later called "civic humanism" by the modern scholars. Civic humanism reflected the values of the urban society of the Italian Renaissance. Many humanists involved in social and political events.

In 1434, Cosimo de' Medici began to rule Florence. A dramatic conversion from active city life to Platonism occurred in the second half of the 15th century. A large number of scholars had committed themselves to philosophy, especially to the study of Plato thinking. Ficino and Mirandola were two predominant representatives. Ficino dedicated his life to the translation of Plato and the exposition of the Platonic philosophy known as Neoplatonism. He integrated Christianity and Platonism to prove the consistency of humanism, Christianity and Platonism. Mirandola's most well-known work was entitled *Oration on the Dignity of Man*. The significance of the book lies in its eloquent summation of the Renaissance interest in humans and the belief in the dignity of human life.

Third, in science: Humanism contributed a lot to the development of natural science. People were divorced from the bondage of Medieval theology and were expected to pursue ideological emancipation. People took more emphasis on reality and scientific experiments and exploration. Meanwhile, human's creativity was brought into full play and human's curiosity was perpetually expanded and constantly satisfied. Furthermore, the development of manufacture also quickened the steps of the natural science. Finally, the scientific and technical accomplishments of the ancient Greece, Rome, Arab and China provided enlightenment of the European scientific development.

CHAPTER SIX

Ⅰ. 1. B 2. C 3. D 4. B 5. A

Ⅱ. 1. indulgences

2. *Institutes of the Christian Religion*

3. preaching

4. Anabaptist

5. King Henry Ⅷ; *Supremacy*

Ⅲ. 1. In Luther's eyes, the masses were just common beings. They were so weak and powerless that they could not promise sufficient good works to achieve salvation. Consequently, faith in the promises of God but not good works could help human beings ensure salvation. Luther obtained his thinking by elaborately digging into the Bible. Justification by faith became the most important doctrine of the Protestant Reformation and the Bible always served as the beacon light on their path to explore religious truth and ethics.

2. Calvin believed in the absolute sovereignty of God, in other words, the salvation or the damnation of human beings was predestined by God, which must not be changed by all means. He called it the "eternal decree". Predestination, which was one of the most important aspects of Calvin's doctrine of salvation, stood on a prominent position in the process of the development of Calvinism.

3. Calvin believed it was the church that was responsible for supervising and disciplining its members. The church was a divine institution in which the words of God could be preached and the sacraments could be carried out. This thinking was implemented when he later had the opportunity to set up his church in Geneva.

With the help of Farel, Calvin began to carry out his plan of reforming the city of Geneva. He established the Consistory for enforcing moral disciplines by admonishing and correcting deviants. The moral life, the daily behaviour and the doctrinal orthodoxy of Genevans were all under the control of this court. However, the Consistory went to an extreme with the expansion of its power. In order to practice his doctrine of the separation of church and state, Calvin kept the two institutions apart in Geneva and enabled the church, which he thought a divine institution, to work independently. Under the leadership of Calvin, the Eucharist was forbidden in Geneva.

The State was not supposed to interfere with the use of fonts, the unleavened bread in the Lord's Supper, and with the celebration of the church festivals. Step by step, Genevan citizens could not tolerate Calvin with his firm and tough control, so he felt it hard to carry out his dramatic reform there. Consequently, Calvin, together with his faithful ally—Farel, was forced to leave Geneva in 1538.

4. The most important doctrinal issue they disagreed on was the nature of the Eucharist. Luther, like the Catholics, believed that the bread and wine of the Eucharist was spiritually transformed into the body and blood of Christ, while Zwingli believed that the Eucharist only symbolised the body and blood of Christ. At the heart of the dispute was the nature of Jesus Christ himself. For Luther, what made the spiritual transformation of the Eucharist into the physical body and blood of Christ was the dual nature of Christ: as both God and human, Christ was both spiritual and physical, God and human being. Zwinglian Protestantism overwhelmingly stressed the divine nature of Christ. Jesus Christ was divine. Therefore, any implicit suggestion in the practice of the Eucharist that Christ was human must be rejected.

5. First, The divorce of the King Henry Ⅷ provided a chance for the reformation in England, so that the English Reformation was initiated by the king, not the church.

   The king's request for annulment got no response from Pope Clement Ⅶ. Dissatisfied with the Pope's neglect and motivated by the strong desire to have a male heir, Henry Ⅷ decided to grant himself a divorce in their own England's ecclesiastical courts. Thomas Cranmer, the head of the court, declared the annulment in 1533.

   In England, all appeals to Rome were banned and penalties of praemunire against those who brought papal bulls into England were demanded by the House of Commons. The paramount power of the king was largely promoted. In addition, the Church was not allowed to make any regulations without being assented to by the King. All the compulsory measures by the Commons against the Church infuriated Pope Clement, so that he announced that the King Henry and Thomas Cranmer were excommunicated from the Church, declared the annulment in 1533 to be invalid, and he refused to acknowledge Henry's marriage with Anne Boleyn.

   Moreover, the papal nuncio was forced to leave England and diplomatic relations with Rome were cut off. The Church of England was controlled by the King Henry, not by Rome.

   Second, After Henry's death in 1547, he was succeeded by his son, Edward Ⅵ

(1547 — 1553), who was a Protestant. As a result, the Church of England became rich in the colour of Protestantism via the efforts of Cranmer.

Third, Mary came into power in 1553. As soon as she rose to power, she did her utmost to carry forward the Roman Catholic faith in England again. She took decisive measures to fulfil her ambition, including abolishing the religious proclamations of Edward Ⅵ and putting down heresy with ruthless force. During her reign, she did not capture the confidence or the support of her subjects, because she constantly catered to the papacy and the Roman Catholic Church.

Fourth, Queen Elizabeth Ⅰ became the next ruler of England. During her reign, Elizabeth made the Church of England (a Protestant denomination) the state religion. *The Thirty-Nine Articles of Religion* was established in 1567, which became the guiding principles of the Anglican doctrine of the English Church. The Church of England became the state religion. Standing up to great outside pressures, she also unified a Protestant England and defeated the Spanish armada in 1588. Under her reign, the national power of England was increasing day by day in every respect.

Ⅳ. (only for reference)

1. The great German religious reformer, Martin Luther marked the beginning of the reformation for the total disappointment with the church and the abuse of the church power.

Justification by faith is the core of Luther's teachings. According to him, the masses were just common beings. They were so weak and powerless that they could not promise sufficient good works to achieve salvation. Consequently, faith in the promises of God, but not good works, could help human beings ensure salvation. Justification is the act by which a person is made to deserve salvation. Luther redefined his thinking by carefully studying the Bible. Justification by faith became the most important doctrine of the Protestant Reformation with the Bible serving as a guide to explore religious truth and ethics.

Luther challenged the church officials openly and posted his *Ninety-Five Theses* on the door of the Castle Church. The Reformation began formally. An essential thinking of Martin began to emerge in the *Ninety-Five Theses* and ran through his other works afterwards, in other words, he believed the Christian salvation should be achieved by contrition for sins and trust in God's mercy. Faith was undoubtedly a prerequisite to gain salvation, which was a gift by God.

In *On the Freedom of a Christian Man*, he expounded his main doctrine, justification by faith. In the *Address to the Nobility of the German Nation*, he appealed for the remove of the papacy in the country and advocated the princes to set up a reformed German church. In *The Babylonian Captivity of the Church*, he fought against the sacramental system which the pope of the church insisted upon. He further suggested reforming monasticism and assenting to clergies' marriages.

His doctrines got approval throughout Germany and even spread over some other European countries during the early 16th century. The whole of Germany was permeated by the preaching of evangelical sermons around 1520s.

However, in June 1524, peasants in Germany rose in revolt against their lords and turned to Luther for support. But Luther supported the rulers. To Luther, the state and its rulers were ordained by God and given the authority to maintain the peace and order necessary for the spread of the Gospel.

Luther's reform was based on the support of the princes and magistrates in the country. As a result, the Lutheran churches, advanced as state churches both in Germany and Scandinavia, were ruled by the state. The church members were all supervised and disciplined by the state. Luther also established new religious services to replace the Mass. Consequently, Luther did not live up to the peasants' expectation for supporting them against their lords in the peasants' war in June 1524.

2. While the spread of the reformation gradually put great pressure on the Church, the church power was activated to seek a new religious order and to appeal for a counter reformation. Consequently, the revival of Roman Catholicism was called the Catholic Reformation, also termed Counter Reformation.

   The Society of Jesus is a religious order founded by Saint Ignatius Loyola in 1534. He wrote *The Spiritual Exercises*, and made it a useful tool by which people would be taught to follow the glory of God through the Catholic Church. The Society was organised in the form of a military command with strict rules and disciplines to control the members. All members swore that they would show their allegiance and obedience to the papacy.

   They earnestly asked the papacy to raise an international movement for the revival of Christian universalism and they carefully avoided local corruption. Countermeasures were taken to raise people's hope for life.

   The Jesuit Constitutions written by Ignatius contributed to a centralised organisation, took emphasis of absolute self-abnegation and advocated the obedience to Pope and superiors. Expanding in strength, they espoused three doctrines which enabled their origination to gain popularity. (1) They founded schools in many countries in Europe. (2) The teachers recruited were required to have a good knowledge of classical studies and theology in order to educate their students in the struggle against the progress of Protestantism. (3) They made contribution to the revival of Catholicism in Germany and Eastern Europe.

Confronted with the Protestant Reformation and the corruptions of popes and cardinals, papal reform came in the 1540s under the influence of the hardliners. They viewed any compromise with Protestant theologies as heresy. When Cardinal Caraffa came into power, he successfully encouraged Pope Paul Ⅲ to establish a Roman Inquisition in 1542.

The Roman Inquisition was a system of tribunals held in the Roman Catholic Church in the second half of the 16th century, directed to suppress heresy. People who were thought to commit a large number of crimes, such as sorcery, blasphemy and witchcraft were prosecuted by the Inquisition. Also, the Roman Inquisition censored printed literature.

The Council of Trent was promoted by Pope Paul Ⅲ in 1545 in the city of Trent. The Council's purpose was to oppose the reformation and eliminate the severe abuses. It declared that the Scripture in Latin by the Catholic Church was the only legal work which could only be interpreted by the Church. People should abide by tradition as well as by Scripture in religious matters. Not only faith but also good works were responsible for salvation. The Council stressed the importance of education in religion and advocated the construction of mission schools. The traditional Catholic teachings were reaffirmed in the council. The seven sacraments (baptism, Eucharist, Reconciliation, Confirmation, Marriage, Holy Orders and Anointing of the Sick), the Catholic doctrine of transubstantiation, and clerical celibacy were all upheld. The efficacy of indulgences and the belief in purgatory were both strengthened. The Council of Trent affirmed the supremacy of the popes and the unification of the church. It was the most impressive embodiment of the ideals of the Counter-Reformation.

CHAPTER SEVEN

Ⅰ. 1. A 2. B 3. B 4. D 5. B

Ⅱ. 1. Cromwell; Charles Ⅰ
  2. Victorian Age
  3. circulation of the blood; pump
  4. philosophes
  5. textile; "cottage industry"

Ⅲ. 1. Economic profit, religious zeal and glory led to the European expansion. Firstly, the Europeans have long been attracted to lands outside of Europe. Secondly, Europeans were driven by the desire to popularise Christianity to other parts of the world. Thirdly, overseas voyage and expansion were seen as a manifestation of power and glory of the country.

  2. Scepticism, travel literature and the ideas of Isaac Newton and John Locke led to

the arrival of the Enlightenment. With the arrival of the Scientific Revolution, widespread scepticism was felt in the 18th century. Many Europeans began to call into question the traditional religious truths and values. They started to become sceptical about what they used to consider right. Besides, travel literature led many Europeans to re-evaluate their own civilisation. The ideas of Newton and Locke seemed to offer the hope of a "brand new world" built on reason.

3. Popular culture refers to the often unwritten and unofficial culture committed to the lives of artisans, peasants and the urban poor. In these sectors of the society, culture primarily meant recreation and was essentially public and collective. Group activity often occurs in a variety of celebrations: family festivals, such as weddings; community festivals in Catholic Europe that celebrated the feast day of the local patron saint; annual festivals, such as Christmas and Easter that go back to medieval Christianity; and Carnival, the most spectacular form of festival, which was celebrated in the Mediterranean states of Spain, Italy, and France as well as in Germany and Austria. Characterised by great indulgence, all of these festivals were celebrated in a secular fashion: chatting, drinking, singings, etc., even though they were supposed to fulfil religious functions. It should be noted that popular culture was not entirely based on an oral tradition; there was a popular literature as well. So-called chapbooks, printed on cheap paper, were short brochures sold by itinerant peddlers to the lower classes. They contained both spiritual and secular material as well as lives of saints and inspirational stories.
4. Joseph II was not a practical reformer but a doctrinaire idealist. He alienated the nobility and the church by freeing the serfs and attacking the monastic establishment respectively. His attempt to rationalise the administration of the empire by imposing German as the official bureaucratic language alienated the non-German nationalities.
5. Glorious Revolution refers to the revolution in British history, the events of 1688—1689. In 1688, a group of prominent English noblemen invited the Dutch chief executive, William of Orange, husband of James' daughter Mary, to invade England. With almost no bloodshed, England had undergone its "Glorious Revolution". In January 1689, Parliament offered the throne to William and Mary, who accepted it along with the provisions of a *Bill of Rights*. The *Bill of Rights* affirmed Parliament's right to make laws and levy taxes and helped establish a system of government based on the rule of law and a freely elected Parliament, thus laying the foundation for a constitutional monarchy.

Ⅳ. (only for reference)

1. European expansion had great impact on both the conquerors and the conquered. The native peoples of the New World, with their own qualities and traits, were brutally conquered and their civilisations inevitably destroyed. In addition to a drastic decrease in population due to European diseases, their established social and political structures were replaced by European institutions, religions, languages, and cultures. In Africa, European involvement in slave trade had devastating effects, especially in coastal areas. Portuguese trading posts in the East had little impact on native Asian civilisations, although Dutch control of the Indonesian archipelago was more invasive. China and Japan remained intact during this age while India was subject to ever-growing British encroachment.

   European expansion to the Central and South America brought about great changes in the population structure of the natives. By 1501, Spanish rulers had authorised marriage between Europeans and Native American Indians. Another group of people brought to Spanish and Portugal America were the Africans who were forced to work the plantations. Africans also contributed to Latin America's multiracial character. Mulattoes—the offspring of Africans and whites—joined mestizos and descendants of whites, Africans and native Indians to produce a unique society in Latin America.

   The ecological condition of the conquered areas was also affected by the European expansion. Europeans brought horses and cattle to the Americas. Horses fundamentally changed the life of the natives. Europeans also brought new crops like wheat and cane sugar, which were to be cultivated by native or imported African slaves. The Europeans also contributed to the exchange of world agriculture by spreading New World plants to other parts of the world. In the 16th century, for instance, the Europeans introduced sweet potatoes and maize to Africa.

   The course of European expansion was undoubtedly a process of religious conquest. It was noted in the preceding section that one of the most important motives of the European Expansion was the religious zeal. Actually, since the beginning of their conquest of the New World, Spanish and Portuguese rulers were intending to Christianise the native peoples. Under the guidance of this policy, the Catholic Church played an important role in the New World. Catholic missionaries—especially the Dominicans, Franciscans, and Jesuits—spread to different parts of the Spanish Empire.

   Christianity was not the only thing the missionaries brought to the New World, even though they were driven by a strong religious zeal. In addition to Christianisation, the Catholic Church also constructed hospitals, orphanages, and schools. Monastic schools instructed Indian students in the elementary skills of reading, writing, and arithmetic. The Catholic Church also provided nunneries, places of prayer and quiet contemplation, but women in religious orders, many of them of aristocratic background, often lived well and worked outside their establishments by running schools and hospitals.

Overseas expansion of European nations also changed the life of Europeans themselves. For some Europeans, expansion aboard brought them hopes for land, riches, and social advancement. One Spaniard commented in 1572 that many "poor young men" left Spain for Mexico, where they hoped to get landed estates by which they could be called "gentlemen". Many ordinary European women found new opportunities for marriage in the New World because of the lack of white women.

European expansion satisfied their strong desire for gold and silver as well as other precious metals. One Aztec commented that the Spanish conquerors "longed and lusted for gold. Their bodies swelled with greed, and their hunger was ravenous; they hungered like pigs for that gold". But gold and silver were only two of the products that became part of the exchange between the New World and the Old. While bringing to the New World horses, cattle and wheat, Europeans were taking new agricultural products such as potatoes, chocolate, corn, tomatoes, and tobacco back to Europe. With the arrival of these products, new foods and new drinks appeared in Europe. Chocolate, which had been brought to Spain from Aztec Mexico, became popular by 1700. The first coffee and tea houses opened in London in the 1650s and spread rapidly to other parts of Europe.

European expansion led to fierce competition and bitter conflicts, which were further intensified later. The Anglo-Dutch trade wars and the British-French rivalry over India and North America became part of a new pattern of worldwide warfare in the 18th century. Bitter competitions also resulted in state-supported piracy in which governments authorised private captains to attack shipping from other countries and keep part of the proceeds for themselves.

Expansion also dramatically altered the Europeans' view of the world. At the beginning of the travels in the 15th century, Europeans depended on maps that were sometimes fanciful and inaccurate. Their voyages and expansions helped them to create more accurate maps showing a realistic portrayal of the world. Map projection, a new technique to represent the round surface of a sphere on a flat piece of paper, was devised to further help the voyagers.

In the course of European expansion, the New World natives experienced unexpected psychological buffet, which, to a certain extent, helped determine the direction in which world history was to develop. The relatively easy European success in conquering and dominating native peoples reinforced Christian Europe's belief in the inherent superiority of European civilisation and religion, which was incessantly bolstered in the following stages of history and pervaded Western civilisation's relationship with the rest of the world.

2. The Enlightenment seeks to liberate human beings from the darkness of the medieval ages by attacking traditional religion, advocating religious toleration, denouncing slavery, and basing human thoughts on reason.

   The Enlightenment blossomed forth in its fullest glory in France during the 18th century under the leadership of Voltaire (1694—1778) and other like-minded critics of the established order. Voltaire epitomised the Enlightenment in somewhat the same way as Luther did the Reformation or Leonardo da Vinci the Italian Renaissance. Voltaire was especially well known for his criticism of traditional religion and his strong attachment to the ideal of religious toleration. In 1763, he penned his *Treatise on Toleration* in which he argued that religious toleration had created no problems for England and Holland and reminded governments that "all men are brothers under God". As he grew older, Voltaire became even more strident in his denunciations of religious fanaticism, intolerance, and superstition. Throughout his life, Voltaire championed not only religious tolerance, but also deism, a religious outlook shared by most other philosophes. Deism was built on the Newtonian world-machine, which implied the existence of a mechanic (God) who had created the universe. To Voltaire and most other philosophes, God had no direct involvement in the world he had created and allowed it to run according to its own natural laws.

CHAPTER EIGHT

Ⅰ. 1. A 2. B 3. C 4. D 5. C

Ⅱ. 1. Appalachians; Mississippi River
   2. Bill of Rights
   3. James Watt
   4. bourgeoisie
   5. Rhode Island

Ⅲ. 1. Behind the American Revolution as a complex movement was one fundamental fact: significant differences had arisen between the American and British political worlds. Whereas representation in Britain was indirect in that the members of Parliament did not speak for local interests but their entire kingdom, in the colonies representation was direct and representatives were not only expected to reside in and own property in the communities electing them, but also to represent the interests of their local districts.

The rapidly growing population had created a booming economy in the American wilderness. Despite formidable obstacles, colonial merchants, especially in New England and the Middle Atlantic colonies, slowly developed commercial exchanges within America and then extended their transactions to Great Britain, the West Indies, and continental Europe. American entrepreneurs were increasingly intent on expanding their economic interests and minimizing external constraints.

Of great importance to the outbreak of the Revolution was the growing awareness of independence of the Americans. By the 1760s, the American colonists had developed a sense of a common national identity. British society was seen by American colonists as old and decadent in sharp contrast to the youthfulness and vitality of their own.

Another source of hostility toward established authority among the American colonists was their religious traditions, particularly Puritanism, which viewed the Bible as the law of the state. Puritans acquired two habits that were crucial to the development of political liberty: dissent and resistance. When transferred to the realm of politics, these Puritan tendencies led Americans to resist authority that they considered unjust.

2. By the eve of the Revolution, a strong aspiration for national independence had been ubiquitous throughout the 13 colonies. Pioneering, courageous and with a strong sense of solidarity, the colonists in North America were eager and willing to achieve freedom and independence at any price. Therefore, they were passionately involved in the campaign that was to put into practice the ideals of liberty, equality and democracy.

   Other factors also helped ensure the ultimate victory of the colonists. The two Continental Congresses held in Philadelphia provided consistent and firm leadership for the colonists. George Washington's military capability enabled his Continental Army to win the eventual victory over the British. The *Declaration of Independence* drafted by Thomas Jefferson greatly inspired all the colonists and considerably uplifted their morale.

   Of great importance to the Revolution was the assistance provided by other European countries that tried to gain revenge for their defeats in earlier wars by the British. The French were particularly generous enough to supply arms and money to the American colonies from the beginning of the war.

3. Industrialisation on the Continent followed a path that was somewhat different from that in Britain. Lacking technological knowledge, European ministers and entrepreneurs went to visit British factories and mines in hope of borrowing the key industrial secrets that would unlock the prosperity of a new age. A second

difference between the British and continental industrialisation lies in the role that the government plays in the Industrial Revolution. Governments in most of the continental countries were accustomed to playing a significant role in economic affairs. A third difference is that European industrialisation was not the thunderclap it was in Britain. In France, for instance, it was a slow and gradual development that took advantage of traditional skills and occupation and gradually modernised the marketplace. In Germany, the process of industrialisation was faced with the political divisions of the empire, and the economic isolation of the petty states, and the wide dispersion of vital resources.

4. Despite the sharp increase of towns and cities in size and number, living condition was miserable for many of the inhabitants. Already overcrowded, devoid of mass transportation facilities, and equipped at best with vastly inadequate sanitation facilities, the cities became more densely packed and unhealthy each year. Rich and poor alike suffered in this environment of diseases, crimes, and ugliness, although the poor obviously bore the brunt of these evils.

5. Ruthless exploitation and wretched working conditions led workers to seek means of change and improvement. Despite government opposition, new associations known as trade unions were organised by skilled workers in a number of new industries, including the cotton spinners, ironworkers, coal miners, and shipwrights. The purpose of these unions was mainly to preserve their own workers' positions by limiting entry into their trade and to gain benefits from the employers.

   On the other hand, workers also resorted to violence in their attempts to improve their living and working conditions. The Luddite Riots was such an example in case.

   The industrial workers' efforts to change the current situation and improve their working and living conditions were better shown in the movement known as the Chartism. Organised by the London Working Men's Association, the movement sought to achieve political democracy.

Ⅳ. (only for reference)

1. Napoleon was one of the greatest military commanders in history. Apart from that, Napoleon did well in governing France. As the ruler of France, most of his domestic reforms proved progressive. On the other hand, Napoleon was a sheer dictator and an aggressive conqueror. A firm defender of France as he was at the beginning, Napoleon later turned into a ruthless invader and brought disasters to the peoples and nations he conquered.

   Napoleon's religious policies promoted tranquillity at home and a good image abroad. After arduous negotiations, Napoleon and the pope signed the Concordat of 1801, according to which the Catholic Church was no longer an enemy of the French government. Moreover, the agreement also reassured those who had acquired church lands during the Revolution that they would not be stripped of the lands, which obviously made them become supporters of the Napoleonic regime. The balance of church-state relations tilted firmly in the state's favour, for Napoleon intended to use the clergy as the major supporter of his regime.

Napoleon's greatest achievement was the codification of law, a task begun during the Revolution. Napoleon completed seven codes of law, of which the most important was the *Civil Code* (or *Code Napoleon*). The *Civil Code*, along with other codes of criminal and commercial law, covered all aspects of civil life from birth to death, all civic aspects related to family and property, contractual responsibilities, and civil liberties. It clearly reflected the revolutionary aspirations for a uniform legal system, legal equality, and protection of property and individuals.

Napoleon was well aware of the significance of science. To assure French predominance, he supported important work in the areas of physics and chemistry, and made science a pillar in the new structure of higher education.

Napoleon also worked on optimising the bureaucratic structure of France by developing a powerful, centralised administrative machine. Administrative centralisation required a bureaucracy made up of capable officials, and Napoleon worked hard to develop one. Promotion in civil and military offices was to be based not on birth but only on demonstrated abilities.

Napoleon was a dictator. The ideal of republican liberty and democracy had been destroyed by Napoleon's thinly disguised autocracy. His France was a police state with a vast network of secret police and spies. The police shut down plays containing any hint of disagreement or criticism of the government. The press was controlled by the state. It was impossible to express an opinion without Napoleon's approval.

A defender of France at the very beginning, Napoleon turned himself later into an invader. In defending the country, Napoleon's Grand Army defeated the continental members of the coalition against him. Later, however, Napoleon's efforts to conquer other countries and peoples transformed him from a defender of France into an avid invader. His enslavement of other peoples resulted in increased national identity which finally led to the collapse of the Empire.

2. A large variety of far-reaching social changes were related to the Industrialisation. Although much of Europe remained bound by its traditional ways, already in the first half of the 19th century, the social impact of the Industrial Revolution was being felt.

With the advent of new inventions and technologies, the appearance and development of factory system during the Industrial Revolution changed the life style of most Europeans. Industrial capitalists realised that it was much more efficient to bring workers to the machines and organise their labour collectively in factories than to leave the workers dispersed in their cottages, hence the advent of the factory system. The rise of the factory system resulted in a tremendous growth of productivity in manufacturing and a seemingly fantastic increase of manufactured goods. This factory system was the origin of the modern mill town and industrial city, which played an important role in the urbanisation process in Europe.

The Industrial Revolution led to a dramatic growth in population and the shift of population from rural to urban areas and the growth in size and number of cities. Cities had traditionally been centres for princely courts, government and military offices, churches, and commerce. By 1850, especially in Great Britain and Belgium, they had become places for manufacturing and industry, growing in number, size and population.

One of the most important impacts of the Industrial Revolution on the social structure is that it pushed the industrial and commercial middle class to the dominant position in the society. The Industrial Revolution destroyed forever the old division of society into clergy, nobility, and commoners. The development of industry and commerce caused a corresponding development of a bourgeoisie, a middle class comprising people of common birth who engaged in trade and other capitalist ventures. From the 18th century on, as industry and commerce developed, the middle class grew in size, first in England and throughout Europe. The new industrial entrepreneurs—the bankers and owners of factories and mines—came to amass much wealth and play an important role alongside the traditional landed aristocracy of their societies. As the new bourgeoisie bought great estates and acquired social respectability, they also sought political power, and in the course of the 19th century, their wealthiest members would hold high offices in much of European countries and merge with those old elites.

The Industrial Revolution simplified the class structure of the society by reducing it into a sharpened distinction between the middle class and the labouring class, or the industrial proletariat. Ruthlessly exploited by factory owners, workers in the new industrial factories faced wretched working conditions. Therefore, class struggle between the bourgeoisie and the industrial workers became irreconcilable.

CHAPTER NINE

I. 1. D 2. A 3. C 4. C 5. D

Ⅱ. 1. the Concert of Europe
2. Gothic
3. prose; novel
4. relativity
5. Japanese

Ⅲ. 1. Politically, liberals came to hold a common set of beliefs. Liberal political thought was rooted in the writings of John Locke and of his philosophes. Liberals in the 19th century believed that their progress would contribute to the perfection of individuals and progress of the society. Liberals believed that individuals were entitled to equality before the law to engage in careers they chose, and should be ensured freedoms such as freedom of the press, of speech, and of assembly, while government's powers should be limited. Moreover, most liberals advocated religious toleration for all, an extension of the jury system, and separation of church and state.

2. The early socialists were romantics, for they dreamed of a new social order, a future utopia, where each individual could find happiness and self-fulfilment. They preferred cooperation to competition. Their being impractical in political ideals led them to be labelled as Utopian Socialists by later Marxists.

3. Although Darwin's ideas were eventually accepted, they were initially objected by some people for its debasement of humans. Some of Darwin's claims even provoked the most profound opposition. Some were disillusioned by Darwin's view of human beings as offspring of apes rather than unique beings of nature while others upset by his claim of life as a struggle for survival.

4. Naturalism applied scientific reasoning to the realistic world. In literature, it extended the tradition of realism, aiming at an even more faithful, unselective representation of reality without moral judgment. Naturalism differed from realism in its assumption of scientific determinism, which led naturalistic authors to emphasise man's accidental, physiological nature rather than his moral or rational qualities. Individual characters were described as helpless victims of heredity and environment, motivated by strong instinctual drives from within and distressed by social and economic pressures from without. Naturalism is a type of "realism" usually characterised by a pessimistic world view.

5. According to Social Darwinism, persons, groups, and races are subject to the same laws of natural selection as Charles Darwin had perceived in plants and animals in nature. According to the theory, the weak were diminished and their cultures delimited, while the strong grew in power and in cultural influence over the weak. Social Darwinists held that the life of humans in society was a struggle

for existence ruled by "survival of the fittest", a phrase proposed by the British philosopher and scientist Herbert Spencer.

The emergence of development of social Darwinism revived racism. Perhaps nowhere was the combination of extreme nationalism and racism more evident than in Germany where racist nationalism was expressed in volkish thought. The concept of the Volk (nation, people, or race) had been an underlying idea in German history since the beginning of the 19th century. According to racism, modern-day Germans were the only pure successors of the Aryans, who, under German leadership, must be prepared to fight for Western civilisation and save it from the destructive assaults of inferior races. The racist theory had a great impact on pan-German and German nationalist thought, particularly Adolf Hitler's National Socialist movement.

Ⅳ. (only for reference)

1. One of the major features that distinguished the Second Industrial Revolution from the first was the rise of steel as the basic industrial material. With the development of new method of rolling and shaping, steel almost entirely supplanted iron for railroad rails, for the framework of large buildings, for bridges, and for other purposes where a cheap metal with a high degree of tensile strength was desired.

The Second Industrial Revolution was characterised by the wide use of electricity and a range of new products that came with it. The electricity was produced by a generator and then converted by electric motors into mechanical energy which was in turn put into use in industrial production. New inventions followed the wide use of electricity. The telephone was invented in 1876 by Alexander Graham Bell and the wireless telegraph by Guglielmo Marconi in 1895. The invention of wireless telegraph paved the way for the emergence of radio, the wireless telephone, and television. The first commercially practical generators of electrical current were developed in the 1870s.

The Second Industrial Revolution was also marked by the partial replacement of coal by gas and oil as principal sources of power as well as the invention of the internal combustion engine. The processing of oil and gasoline made possible its widespread use as a source of power in transportation. An oil-fired engine was made in 1897, and by 1902, the Hamburg-Amerika Line had switched from coal to oil on its new ocean liners.

The value of the internal combustion engine was more evident in the development of automobile and the airplane. In 1900, the whole world produced only 9,000 cars; by 1906, Americans had surpassed the initial lead of the French. The car industry was revolutionised by an American, Henry Ford, when he introduced the mass production of the Model T. by 1916, Ford's factories were producing 735,000 cars a year. In the meantime, air transportation was also transformed when the Wright Brothers, Orville and Wilbur, made the first flight in 1903 at Kitty Hawk, North Carolina.

Another typical feature of the Second Industrial Revolution was the introduction of automatic machinery, an enormous increase in mass production, and a division of tasks of labour into minute segments of the manufacturing process. Machines were invented to direct and operate other machines and to complete whole series of manufacturing processes which formerly required much human labour. The development of precision tools led to the creation of assembly line for production. First used in the United States for small arms and clocks, the assembly line had moved to Europe by 1850.

2. Between 1880 and 1914, Western powers started imperial expansion, "new imperialism", to satisfy their demand for control over new territories in Asia, Africa, and the Pacific. They gained increasing dominance over much of the rest of the world, taking with them Western culture and institutions to the indigenous societies.

   The economic motivation for the new imperialism was clearly seen. Due to the rapid expansion of industry in Europe and the United States, the West was engaged in imperial expansion hoping that they could find new markets, new sources of raw materials, and new investment outlets for surplus capital.

   Nationalism was probably a greater drive behind the new imperialism. As European affairs grew tense, ambitious European states competed to establish colonies abroad that served as ports and fuelling stations for their navies. These new ports also served to demonstrate international power.

   Then, too, imperialism was tied to Social Darwinism and racism. Social Darwinists proposed that nations that were strong and successful at expanding industry and empire would survive while others would not; they maintained that superior races should control inferior ones by military force indicating national strength and power.

   Religious zeal also played an important role in the shaping of New Imperialism. Most Europeans considered it their duty to "civilise""ignorant" peoples. This notion of the "white man's burden" helped at least the more idealistic individuals to rationalise imperialism in their own minds. Nevertheless, the belief that the superiority of their civilisation obligated them to impose modern industry, cities, and new medicines on supposedly primitive nonwhites, even if they had to be killed to do so, was yet another form of racism.

CHAPTER TEN

Ⅰ. 1. C 2. A 3. D 4. B 5. C

Ⅱ. 1. lightning war
2. stream of consciousness
3. heroic age of physics
4. consumer society
5. European Atomic Energy Community

Ⅲ. 1. The Cold War adequately embodied the incompatible political ambitions of two nations—the United States and the Soviet Union based on their divergent historical experiences. It was not only the outcome of the ideological conflicts between the two powers, but also a product of their increasing desires for hegemony in the world. During the war years, both the capitalist and socialist countries worked together to fight against the Fascist forces. When the war was ended, however, the conflicts came to the fore.

2. Spurred on by the Vietnam War and out of a growing political consciousness, the youth rebellion became a youth protest movement by the second half of the 1960s. After World War Ⅱ, European states began to create greater equality of opportunity in higher education by eliminating fees, and universities experienced an influx of students from the middle and lower classes. But it also brought problems. Classrooms with too many students, irresponsibility of professors to their courses, lack of democracy in university administration, and too many outdated courses led to an outburst of student revolts in the late 1960s. For many students, the calls for democracy within the universities were a reflection of their deeper concerns about the direction in which Western society was heading.

3. Most Eastern European countries had little or virtually no experience with democratic systems. Ethnic divisions made political unity almost impossible and the rapid conversion to market economies also proved unsuccessful. As a result, unemployment climbed. Wages remained low while prices skyrocketed. States in Eastern Europe faced dangerous and uncertain futures.

4. Despite variety in styles, abstract expressionist paintings share several broad characteristics. They are basically abstract—i. e., they depict forms not drawn from the visible world. They emphasise free, spontaneous, and personal emotional expression and they exercise considerable freedom of technique and execution to attain this goal, with a particular emphasis laid on the exploitation of the variable physical character of paint to evoke expressive qualities (e. g., sensuousness, dynamism, violence, mystery, and lyricism). They show similar emphasis on the unstudied and intuitive application of paint in a form of psychic

improvisation akin to the automatism of the surrealists, with a similar intent of expressing the force of the unconscious in art. They display the abandonment of conventionally structured composition built up out of discrete elements and their replacement with a single unified, undifferentiated field, network, or other image that exists in unstructured space.

5. Despite the advances that were produced by the alliance of science and technology, they also brought problems. The optimistic assumption that scientific knowledge enables human beings to manipulate the environment for their benefit was questioned by some in the 1960s and 1970s who believed that some technological advances had far-reaching side effects on the environment. The threat of global warming and the widespread proliferation of dying forests and lakes made environmental protection one of the important issues of the 1990s.

Ⅳ. (only for reference)

1. The sense of meaninglessness that inspired the Theatre of the Absurd also underscored the philosophy of existentialism which was rooted in the disillusionment of the late 19th century, the atmosphere of anxiety in the early 20th century brought about by the two world wars, the Great Depression, and the tensions of the Cold War. Two of the most celebrated exponents of existentialism were Albert Camus (1913—1960) and Jean-Paul Sartre (1905—1980). According to Camus, the world was absurd and without meaning; humans, too, are without meaning and purpose. The theme he touched on was the anguish of individuals struck by awareness of God's nonexistence and of an impending engagement with nothingness which would exist through eternity. However, in terms of the responses to this absurdity of existence, Camus stood firm against suicide and nihilism. Life may be absurd, but this is not justification for resignation. The other leading light of existentialism, Sartre, described himself as an atheist who viewed existentialism as an approach to the consequences of the world without God. He argued that there is no meaning in existence; consequently, there are no final rights and wrongs in life. Individuals are just born, simply exist, and are free. Therefore, they themselves are responsible for making decisions, taking actions, laying down their own standards and rules by which they abide in their life. Ultimately, death comes to all.

   Another response to the despair came from religious revival, one expression of which was the attempt by such theologians as the Protestant Karl Barth (1886—1968) and the Catholic Karl Rahner (1904—1984) to adapt traditional Christian teachings to the contemporary life. Karl Barth appealed for reaffirmation of the

Christ who is the inspiration of faith. He also affirmed the uniqueness of Christianity and reasserted the spiritual power of divine revelation. History is, as Barth saw it, an arena where the individual's faith is always being tested. Karl Rahner attempted to revitalise traditional Catholic theology by incorporating aspects of modern thought. He is best known for his work in Christology and for his integration of an existential philosophy of personalism with Thomistic realism, by which human self-consciousness and self-transcendence are placed within a sphere in which the ultimate determinant is God.

In the Catholic Church, attempts at religious renewal also came from two charismatic popes—John XXIII and John Paul II. Pope John XXIII (1881—1963) called the Second Vatican Council (1962—1965) in the spirit of Christian tolerance and unity. The Council liberalised a number of Catholic practices. The Mass was henceforth to be celebrated in the vernacular languages rather than Latin. John Paul II (b. 1920), a Pole, was the first non-Italian to be elected pope since the 16th century. His numerous travels around the world helped strengthen the Catholic Church throughout the non-Western world. He projected an updated image of the Catholic Church, which embodied dynamism and activism. However, he held a conservative attitude towards faith and morals by turning down the liberalisation of church policy on theological doctrines, the priesthood, the family and sex.

2. Despite the pluralism after World War II spawned by an age of instant communication and ever-growing technology, the United States has been the most influential force in shaping popular culture in the West and, to a lesser degree, the entire world. Many people, not always admiringly, spoke of the "coca-colonisation" of the world. Through its music, movies, and television, the powerful country has spread its culture, way of living, particular values and the American Dream to millions of people around the world.

   Movies and televisions were the primary means by which the United States spread its popular culture throughout the world after World War II. Movies of the United States took the lead and thus dominated both European and American markets. In 2000, movies in the United States attained a box office of $ 7.7 billion, a record high in history. American television productions have also demonstrated remarkable wide appeal. The television series *Dallas* was as popular and well-known in Europe as in the United States.

   The United States also dominated popular music since the end of World War II. Popular music is rooted in the tribulation of urban blacks, the traditionalism of rural whites, the protest of activists, and the hopes and aspirations of the common people. All the forms, folk music, R&B, country and western, and the various shades of rock, soon spread to the rest of the world, where local artists transformed them in their own ways.

The leading role the United States played in popular culture after World War Ⅱ was also evident in the development of sports. Support from the government and craze of the American people made sports boom in the country. Most people are engaged in sports activities or simply watch the games. Basketball, baseball, American Football, and rugby are among the most popular games in the country. Due to the development of satellite television and various electronic breakthroughs as well as the United States' efforts to extend its overseas market, sports as part of the popular culture has also spread to the rest of the world. Basketball players like Michael Jordan (b. 1963) and Kobe Bryant (b. 1978) enjoy the same popularity in other countries of the world as in the United States. More and more foreign players entering NBA also means that the league has had an increasingly important impact on the whole world.

Bibliography

Badian, E. *Roman Imperialism in the Late Republic*. New York: Cornell University Press, 1971.

Beatty, John & Johnson, Oliver. *Heritage of Western Civilisations Selected Readings* (2nd Ed.). Vol. Ⅰ. Englewood Cliffs, New Jersey: Prentice-Hall, Inc., 1958.

Beatty, John L., et al. *Heritage of Western Civilisation: Ancient Civilisation and the Emergence of the West* (9th Ed.). Beijing: Peking University Press, 2004.

Bennett, Judith M., et al. *Medieval Europe: A Short History* (10th Ed.). Beijing: Peking University Press, 2007.

Burckhardt, Jacob. *The Civilisation of the Renaissance in Italy*. London: Penguin Books, 1995.

Burns, Edward McNall. *Western Civilizations*, Vol. Ⅰ (7th Ed.). New York: W. W. Norton & Company, Inc., 1968.

Cambers, Mortimer. *The Western Experience*, Vol. Ⅱ: *Since the 16th Century*. Boston: McGraw-Hill College, 1998.

Clogg, Richard. *A Concise History of Greece*. Shanghai: Shanghai Foreign Language Education Press, 2006.

Cunningham, Lawrence S. & Reich, John J. *Culture & Values*, Vol. Ⅱ: *A Study of the Humanities with Readings*. Boston: Wadsworth Cengage Learning, 2009.

Dickens, Charles. *Oliver Twist*. Beijing: Beijing Foreign Language Teaching and Research Press, 1991.

Gibbon, Edward. *The History of the Decline and Fall of the Roman Empire*. Haikou: Hainan Publishing House, 2001.

Greaves, Richard L., et al. *Civilisations of the West: The Human Adventure*. New York: Harper Collins College Publishers, 1994.

Hallo, William H. & Simpson, William Kelly. *The Ancient Near East A History* (2nd Ed.). Orlando: Harcourt Brace & Company, 1998.

Harrison, John B., et al. *A Short History of Western Civilisation* (6th Ed.). N. Y.: Alfred A. Knopf, Inc., 1960.

Hause, Steven & Maltby, William. *Western Civilisation: A History of European Society*, Vol. Ⅰ: *From Antiquity to the Old Regime*. Wadsworth Publishing Company, A Division of International Thomson Publish Inc., 1999.

Hollister, C. Warren. *Medieval Europe: A Short History* (2nd Ed.). New York: John Wiley & Sons, Inc., 1968.

Homer. *Odyssey*. trans. E. V. Rieu. Harmondsworth, 1946.

Jacobs, C. M. trans. "An Open Letter to the Christian Nobility of the German Nation Concerning the Reform of the Christian Estate," in *Works of Martin Luther*, Vol. Ⅱ. Philadelphia: Muhlenberg Press, *1915*.

Jaeger, Werner. *Paideia: The Ideals of Greece*, Vol. Ⅰ. trans. Gilbert Highet. Oxford University Press, 1939.

Joycc, James. *Ulysses*. Nanjing: Yilin Press, 1996.

Kishlansky, Mark. *Civilisation in the West*, Vol. C: Since *1789*. London: Longmans, 2001.

Kishlansky, Mark. *A Brief History of Western Civilisation*. Beijing: China Renmin University Press, 2008.

Kishlansky, Mark., et al. *Civilisation in the West*, Vol. B: *From 1350 to 1850* (4th Ed.). New York: Priscilla McGeehon, 2001.

Kishlansky, Mark., et al. *A Brief History of Western Civilization: The Unfinished Legacy* (5th Ed). Beijing: China Renmin University Press, 2008.

Kitto, H. D. F. *The Greeks*. Baltimore: Penguin Books, 1957.

Locke, Louis G., et al. *Literature of Western Civilisation*. Vol. Ⅰ. New York: The Ronald Press Company, 1952.

Perry, Marvin. *Western Civilisation: A Brief History*. Boston: Houghton Mifflin Company, 2001.

Perry, Marvin., et al. *Western Civilisation, Ideas, Politics, and Society*. Boston: Houghton Mifflin Company, 2000.

Plato. *The Republic*. trans. F. M. Cornford. New York: Oxford University Press, 1945.

Sasson, Jack M. *Civilisations of the Ancient Near East*. New York: Scribner, 1995.

Scarre, Christopher & Fagan, Brian M. *Ancient Civilisations*. US: Christopher Scarre and the Lindbriar Corp., 1997.

Spielvogel, Jackson J. *Western Civilisation: A Brief History*, Vol Ⅰ: *To 1715*. Belmont: Wadsworth, 1999.

Spielvogel, Jackson J. *Western Civilization* (4th Ed.). Vol. Ⅰ: *To 1715*. Wadsworth: Wadsworth, 2000.

Spielvogel, Jackson J. *Western Civilisation: A Brief History*. Beijing: Peking

University Press, 2006.

Stavrianos, L. S. *The World Since 1500: A Global History*. New Jersey: Prentice Hall, 1966.

Sullivan, Richard E., et al. *A Short History of Western Civilisation, Since 1600*. New York: McGraw-Hill, Inc., 1994.

Tatlock, Jessie M. *Greek and Roman Mythology*. Beijing: Central Compilation & Translation Press, 2008.

The Episcopal Church. *Book of Common Prayer*. Oxford: Oxford University Press, 1979.

Wordsworth, William. "The Tables Turned," in Andrew J. George (Ed.), *The Complete Works of Wordsworth*. Boston: Houghton Mifflin, 1904.

(美)爱德华·麦克诺尔·伯恩斯、菲利普·李·拉尔夫著,罗经国、陈筠等译:《世界文明史》第1卷,商务印书馆1987年版。

(意)贝纳多·罗格拉著,宋杰、宋纬译:《古罗马的兴衰》,明天出版社2001年版。

马万利:《世界历史与文化(上)》,合肥工业大学出版社2004年版。

李占频、张书珩:《世界文明史快读(下)》,远方出版社2004年版。

刘明翰、海恩忠:《世界史简编》,山东教育出版社1982年版。

刘文龙、袁传伟:《世界文化史(近代卷)》,浙江人民出版社1999年版。

王立新:《西方文化简史》,河南人民出版社2005年版。

王佐良、祝玉等:《欧洲文化入门》,外语教学与研究出版社1992年版。

赵立行:《世界文明史讲稿》,复旦大学出版社2007年版。

周一良、吴于廑:《世界通史上古部分》,人民出版社1962年版。

庄锡昌:《西方文化史》,高等教育出版社1999年版。

http://eyeofthefish.org/national-architecture/

http://image.baidu.com/i?tn

http://images.google.com.hk/imgcat/imghp?hl=zh-CN

http://en.wikipedia.org/wiki/Phoneician_alphabet

http://www.usu.edu/markdamen/1320hist&civ/chapters/05spaces.htm

http://www.hf.uib.no/i/religion/popularikonografi/exhib02.html

http://www.erfurtweb.de/

http://www.brainyquote.com/

http://www.lifecoachingforchristianwomen.com/tag/the-crucifixion/

http://www.wikipaintings.org/en/paolo-veronese/the-resurrection-of-christ/

http://www.whycatholicsdothat.com/ascension/